Eurasianism

Russian, Eurasian, and Eastern European Politics

Series Editor: Michael O. Slobodchikoff, Troy University

Mission Statement

Following the collapse of the Soviet Union, little attention was paid to Russia, Eastern Europe, and the former Soviet Union. The United States and many Western governments reassigned their analysts to address different threats. Scholars began to focus much less on Russia, Eastern Europe and the former Soviet Union, instead turning their attention to East Asia among other regions. With the descent of Ukraine into civil war, scholars and governments have lamented the fact that there are not enough scholars studying Russia, Eurasia, and Eastern Europe. This series focuses on the Russian, Eurasian, and Eastern European region. We invite contributions addressing problems related to the politics and relations in this region. This series is open to contributions from scholars representing comparative politics, international relations, history, literature, linguistics, religious studies, and other disciplines whose work involves this important region. Successful proposals will be accessible to a multidisciplinary audience, and advance our understanding of Russia, Eurasia, and Eastern Europe.

Advisory Board

Michael E. Aleprete, Jr

Gregory Gleason

Dmitry Gorenburg

Nicole Jackson

Matthew Rojansky

Richard Sakwa

Andrei Tsygankov

Stephen K. Wegren

Christopher Ward

Books in the Series

Understanding International Relations: Russia and the World, edited by Natalia Tsvetkova

Geopolitical Prospects of the Russian Project of Eurasian Integration, by Natalya A. Vasilyeva and Maria L. Lagutina

Eurasia 2.0: Russian Geopolitics in the Age of New Media, edited by Mark Bassin and Mikhail Suslov

Executive Politics in Semi-Presidential Regimes: Power Distribution and Conflicts between Presidents and Prime Ministers, by Martin Carrier

Post-Soviet Legacies and Conflicting Values in Europe: Generation Why, by Lena M. Surzhko-Harned and Ekaterina Turkina

Eurasianism

An Ideology for the Multipolar World

Paolo Pizzolo

LEXINGTON BOOKS
Lanham • Boulder • New York • London

Published by Lexington Books
An imprint of The Rowman & Littlefield Publishing Group, Inc.
4501 Forbes Boulevard, Suite 200, Lanham, Maryland 20706
www.rowman.com

6 Tinworth Street, London SE11 5AL

British Library Cataloguing in Publication Information Available

Library of Congress Cataloging-in-Publication Data

Names:
Title:
Description:
Identifiers:
Subjects:
Classification:
LC record available at

Contents

Foreword

Geopolitics and Eurasianism

Michael O. Slobodchikoff

[B02.0]   Following the collapse of the Soviet Union, little attention was paid to Russia, Eastern Europe, and the former Soviet Union. The United States and many Western governments reassigned their analysts to address different threats. Scholars began to focus much less on Russia, Eastern Europe and the former Soviet Union, instead turning their attention to East Asia among other regions. With the descent of Ukraine into civil war, scholars and governments have lamented the fact that there are not enough scholars studying Russia, Eurasia, and Eastern Europe. Scholars must again turn their focus on this extremely important geographic area. There remains much misunderstanding about the politics of the region. With tensions between governments at heightened levels unprecedented since the Cold War, scholarship addressing the politics of the region is extremely vital. The Russian, Eurasian, and Eastern European Politics Book Series aims at remedying the deficiency in the study and understanding of the politics of Eurasia.

[B02.1]   One of the first major scholars to study and understand the importance of Eurasia was Halford Makinder. He argued that whoever controlled the heartland (Central Asia), would rule the world.[1] Since Makinder's work, many scholars have continued to argue over the actual geographical boundaries of Eurasia. Some define it as Russia and what is now the former Soviet Union. Other scholars have broadened those boundaries to include Western Europe and Asia as well. More importantly, Makinder's work really created a new philosophical orientation. One that focused on the importance of a Eurasian identity.

[B02.2]   Since Makinder's important work, many scholars have focused on both the geopolitics of Eurasia as well as the Eurasian identity, with some arguing that Eurasianist identity forms in the heart of Eurasia, while others argue that it is formed in the periphery. However, in recent years, Russian philosophers and politicians have increasingly focused on Eurasianism to provide an alternative to the liberal global order.

Ultimately, it became apparent that scholars and policy makers alike would need to return their focus on Eurasia and Eurasianism. This book carefully examines Eurasianism and its growth in popularity as an identity that rivals that of the West. This book should be read by all specialists in Eurasia as it shows the growth of this identity and its importance in the geopolitical conflict to come between those defending the current global order and those trying to develop an alternative to that order. [B02.3]

Michael O. Slobodchikoff [B02.4]
Series Editor [B02.5]
Lexington Russian, Eurasian and Eastern European Politics Book Series [B02.6]

NOTE [B02.7]

1. Makinder, H.J. 1904. "The Geographical Pivot of History." *The Geographical Journal.* 23(4). Pp. 421–437. [B02n1]

Introduction

[B03.0]   This research is focused on the study of Eurasianism, a political—and geopolitical—doctrine that is still rather mysterious and cryptic for the Western
audience but that nonetheless has been present in the intellectual and political
debate of Eurasian countries—above all in Russia, in former Soviet states
like Kazakhstan, and in Turkey—for almost one century. The initial idea that
stimulated the wish to investigate the topic of Eurasianism originated from
the study of Mackinder's geopolitical thought. Sir Halford J. Mackinder was
a British geographer, explorer, and scholar who introduced the idea of "geographical pivot of history" and "Heartland" to describe what he believed to
represent relevant geopolitical concepts. In his studies, he argued that the
international power that gained control over the Eurasian landmass would
become the world hegemon. From a British perspective, the risk of a pan-
continental Eurasian state, be it under German or Russian rule—or under a
German-Russian condominium, for that matter—, would embody a mortal
threat to maritime powers like Great Britain and the United States and would
put at stake trade, international law, and sovereignty. Specifically, according
to Mackinder, who controlled Eastern Europe would control the Heartland—
i.e. the Eurasian core—, who controlled the Heartland would control the
World Island—i.e. Eurasia—and, finally, who controlled Eurasia would ultimately control the World. Although Mackinder's studies date back to the
early and first half of the 20th century, what triggered my interest was that
from a diachronic perspective, at least throughout modern history, the strategic interest in ruling Eurasia does not seem to have changed. In fact, I noticed
that the control of the Eurasian landmass has been somehow a constant
objective that different powers have shared. Since the outbreak of the French
Revolution, at least four major events almost reached the objective of unifying Eurasia under a single rule: Napoleon's invasion of Central Europe and

the Russian Empire, Wilhelmine Germany's intervention in the First World War against France and Russia, Hitlerite Germany's eastward expansion and invasion of the Soviet Union, and the Soviet enlargement and dominion in Eastern Europe after the Second World War. Curiously—or perhaps not surprisingly—, all these attempts were averted or contrasted by the direct and indirect intervention of the sea powers of Great Britain and, later, the United States. In this perspective, can we affirm that the effort to rule the key strategic zones of Eurasia represents a continual goal that powers in search of global hegemony constantly pursue? In other words, is it just a random occurrence that different powers struggle for controlling the same regions in Eastern Europe or in the Russian-Eurasian space or is there a precise strategic intention? This research led me to believe that the latter argument—as Mackinder noted—offers a better explanation of the phenomenon.

The second element that raised my interest in Eurasianism was Spykman's corollary to Mackinder's theory. Nicholas J. Spykman, a well-known geo-strategist, introduced the theory of the Rimland, which represents a reformulation of Mackinder's Heartland theory from the opposite perspective. Whereas Mackinder believed that the power who controlled the Heartland would control Eurasia, Spykman argued that who controlled the Eurasian peripheral zones—which form a crescent spreading from Western Europe to the Korean Peninsula through the Middle East, the Indian Subcontinent, and Indochina—would rule Eurasia. Apparently, this theory encounters some empirical evidence if we consider the containment strategy that the United States promoted against the Soviet Union during the Cold War to avoid a deeper penetration of the USSR in the Eurasian rims—e.g. in Germany, Greece, Turkey, the Middle East, Indochina, and so on. [B03.1]

Finally, the third author who contributed in raising my attention towards Eurasianist studies has been Haushofer. Karl Haushofer, a geopolitician, historian and soldier that contributed to frame Nazi Germany's foreign policy, had thoroughly studied Mackinder's theories in the attempt of using them against Britain itself. Following Mackinder's postulates on Eurasia's strategic relevance, one of his main theorizations was the idea of creating a Eurasian *Kontinentalblock* between Germany, Russia, and Japan in opposition to the British Empire. This project was probably one of the main vectors that led Germany to sign the Molotov-Ribbentrop nonaggression pact with Russia and that promoted the idea of making the USSR a member of the Tripartite Pact.[1] [B03.2]

Besides classical geopolitical theories, I soon discovered that the term Eurasia bore a specific importance as a strategic and even philosophical concept for the political doctrine known as Eurasianism. While examining Eurasianism and geopolitics, I discovered a controversial and charismatic Russian character that represents one of the major exponents of contemporary Eurasianism: Aleksandr Dugin, a person often linked to the Russian far- [B03.3] right that would have played a significant role in directing Vladimir Putin's political choices. Dugin's thought—albeit extremely eclectic, dogmatic, and cryptic—offers today the most significant contributions for the understanding of the Eurasianist ideology.

[B03.4]   The aim of this research is to investigate what kind of ideology Eurasianism is and to clarify its goals and objectives. As we will see, Eurasianism possesses many characteristics that are typical of ideologies, including a normative, dogmatic and subjective narrative, not necessarily supported by empirical evidence. Specifically, the research wishes to examine Aleksandr Dugin's neo-Eurasianist ideology, since it represents probably one of the most organic and structured theories on the topic of Eurasianism. The research wishes also to explore geopolitical schemes that highlight the strategic relevance of the Eurasian continent, paying specific attention to Mackinder's Heartland theory. From a point of view of international relations, the research will try to depict the kind of international order Eurasianism would wish to establish, based on the principles of multipolarity, civilization, and alter-globalism.

[B03.5]   The main hypotheses that the research assesses are the following. First, whether the Eurasianist ideology—and specifically Aleksandr Dugin's neo-Eurasianism—would represent a theoretical contribution for the description of the advent of a multipolar international order or would embody an inefficient, normatively biased, and often naïve hermeneutic instrument. Second, whether geopolitical theories could still offer a valid tool for interpreting international relations and global power. Third, whether Eurasia could be considered a truly strategic continent for global hegemony.

[B03.6]   Russian Eurasianism may be considered a conservative political ideology grounded in the philosophy of traditionalism, on geopolitical narrative, and on the idea of Russia's special historical mission. One of its basic assumptions claims that Russia is neither European nor Asian, but rather a unique country that blends characteristics of both Europe and Asia. It also claims that Russia possesses two imperial heritages: the heritage of the nomadic empires of the Eurasian steppes—specifically of Genghis Khan's Mongol Empire—and the heritage of the Byzantine Empire—expressed in the myth of Moscow as the "Third Rome".

[B03.7]   As a philosophical movement, Eurasianism was conceived by Russian intellectual émigrés who had fled the country after the advent of the Bolshevik rule and later reappeared, in its contemporary guise, after the demise of the Soviet Union. The Slavophile movement is sometimes considered to be the predecessor of Eurasianism, since it rejected Russian westernization and believed in Russia's specific cultural identity. However, several differences separate Eurasianists from Slavophiles, like the idea that the Slavic element would not be the distinguishing feature of Russian identity, which would result instead in the synthesis between the Slavic and the Turanian components. Eurasianists believed that the cultures of the Turanian peoples were closer to Russian culture compared with the cultures of western Slavs (Poles, Czechs, Slovaks, etc.). The Eurasianists also rejected pan-Slavism and its political project aimed at integrating in a single country all Slavic nations. Instead, they proposed the creation of a Eurasan empire that included different nations and ethnic groups that shared a common civilizational model (eastern Slavs, Finno-Ugrics, Turkic peoples, Caucasians, Mongols, etc.). The idea of creating a Eurasian empire is closely linked to the ideology of Turanism.[2] The word Turanism comes from Turan, a historical region in Central Asia. Turanism—or pan-Turanism—is a nineteenth century ideology produced by some Turkish, Hungarian, German and Ottoman intellectuals to promote the union, collaboration and "renaissance" of all Turanian peoples, including the Finns, Japanese, Koreans, Turks, Mongols, Manchus, Sami, Samoyeds, Hungarians, and so on.

Prince Nikolai S. Trubetzkoy was the first Eurasianist to proclaim, in [B03.8] 1925, that Russia was not the successor of Kievan Rus' but rather of Genghis Khan's Mongol Empire. Russians and Turanic nomads would share a common cultural background based on personal devotion, political obedience, heroism, and spiritual hierarchy. These values would be incompatible with European liberalism and commercialism, and therefore Eurasianism would represent an antithesis of Westernism.

As for the Bolshevik Revolution, though condemning its atheistic and [B03.9] Marxist connotation, Eurasianists still viewed it as a Eurasan project of resistance against the West: deprived of its ideology, the Soviet Union would represent for Eurasianists the perfect example of Turanian empire.

Generally, at least four broad interpretations of Eurasianism are in use [B03.10] today. The first is the far-right interpretation—advocated by Dugin—that perceives Eurasianism as both a global campaign against Western liberal-democratic values and a tool for neo-imperial regional integration centered on Russia. A more moderated view conceives Eurasianism as a Russian instrument to reassert its international role, pivoting on the analysis of institutional processes of Eurasian integration such as the one espoused by the Eurasian Economic Union (EAEU). Instead, the liberal strand of Eurasianism rejects the nationalist and chauvinist rhetoric in favor of a pragmatic understanding of the relations that may connect the Eurasian continent with the rest of the world. Lastly, there is a non-Russian Eurasianist approach promoted by some countries—primarily Kazakhstan, Turkey, and Iran—, which adopts a unique interpretation of the phenomenon. In this research, we will investigate the far-right Eurasianist interpretation as conceived by Aleksandr Dugin.

The research is divided into seven chapters. The first chapter analyses the [B03.11] concept of ideology. The study of ideologies represents a useful methodological tool for analyzing Eurasianism. Since Eurasianism is essentially an ideology, it appears useful to understand how and why ideologies develop and what their main characteristics are. However, defining the concept of ideology is often an arbitrary and disagreeing procedure, since it is difficult to demonstrate the superiority of one definition to another. The word ideology appeared for the first time in France at the end of the 18th century and was used to describe a new science aimed at studying the origins of ideas. At that time, ideology as a science therefore studied the faculties of thinking, judging, remembering, and wishing in relation to the formation, origin, character, meaning, and significance of ideas. However, the word "ideology" was soon accused of depicting a doctrinal and abstract set of ideas detached from reality. As we will see in detail, Karl Marx assumed that an ideology represented a set of philosophical, ethical, political, and religious doctrines that would justify the relations of productions imposed by the dominant class. During the 19th and 20th centuries, ideology became one of the essential subjects that both sociology and political science attempted to scrutinize, although its intrinsic scientific validity was often questioned. While being assimilated by sociology, the concept of ideology gradually turned into a generic term applicable to any political doctrine, to social movements supported by a theoretical frame, and to specific cultural, political, economic, and social inclinations. Authors like Giovanni Sartori and Karl Popper have accused ideology of contrasting with the scientific method and its empiricism. In the last decades, many scholars of political theory and political science have attempted to offer a definition of the concept of ideology, which still remains a rather ambiguous notion. As a minimal definition, we may affirm that an ideology represents a set of beliefs, opinions, values, and norms that guide a specific social group. Ideologies can be analyzed in relation to several variables, like for instance the location of their action, their role, the subject that created them, their position in society, their functions, their goals, their structure, and so on. Ideologies can be classified in many ways, however, following a minimal classification, we can divide them into seven main groups: liberalism, conservatism, socialism, anarchism, communism, nationalism, and fascism. Liberalism hinges on the autonomous and self-sufficient value of the individual, promoting a society in which state interventionism is minimal. Conservatism is an ideology that opposes revolutionary projects and radical changes and upholds the need to maintain the sociopolitical status quo. Socialism focuses on the necessity to suppress social privileges and to promote total equality among social members. Anarchism promotes the abolition of any kind of government that imposes its rule over individuals and supports the idea of the abolition of the state. Communism endorses a social system in which private property is abolished, means of productions are collectivized and managed by the entire society, and all economic policies are rigidly planned. Nationalism promotes the exaltation and defense of the nation, which is considered the chief social value. Fascism is a political movement that combines some elements of the socialist doctrine with ultra-nationalist ideology.

From a methodological perspective, Eurasianism can be considered a full-fledged ideology—since it presents many of the elements that typically characterize ideologies—that epitomizes a strand of conservatism. The term conservatism designates any political philosophy that supports tradition in its various representations—religion, culture, identity, beliefs, and customs—and that contrasts all thrusts that encourage radical social change. Some expressions of conservatism tend to preserve the status quo or to slowly reform society, while others seek to return to the principles of earlier times. Commonly, conservatism contrasts the ideas of liberalism, socialism, and fascism—because perceived as too progressive or revolutionary—and usually belongs to the right-wing political spectrum. The main adversary of conservatism is represented by all forms of radicalism that demand a process of change and that question traditional institutions. Radicalism, in all its aspects, implies a radical change, which is incompatible with the principles of conservatism. Historically, the political use of the term conservatism appeared after the French Revolution, developing a full-fledged semantic connotation during the 1820s, also thanks to the philosopher Edmund Burke, who is considered its intellectual father. Conservatism may be divided into several strands in relation to the scope of its action: cultural conservatism, social conservatism, religious conservatism, fiscal conservatism, bio-conservatism, neo-conservatism, paleo-conservatism, and so on. [B03.12]

Eurasianism can be considered a conservative ideology that includes cultural, social, religious and biological aspects of conservatism. However, it does not revolve around the need to maintain the contemporary status quo against progressivism but wishes to replace current societies—especially Western post-liberal ones—with a social order based on traditionalism. In fact, Eurasianism sponsors a worldwide revolution—albeit conservative—to accomplish its goals: given the revolutionary action it endorses, it is thus unclear whether Eurasianism may be considered a pure conservative ideology or a hybrid one. It could be affirmed that Eurasianism represents a typical strand of post-Soviet conservatism that underscores alter-globalism, civilizational identitarism, religious heritage, anti-liberalism, anti-communism, anti-racism, traditional order, geopolitical analysis, and historical discourse. [B03.13]

Dugin's neo-Eurasianism represents one of the last manifestations of Russian political thought of the 20th century. During the 20th century, Russian society had been hit by many traumatic events that contributed to shape Russia's philosophical mindset. The first was the fall of the czarist regime and the Bolshevik advent to power, which represented a total shift in Russia's ideological paradigm. The second was the witness of Stalin's horrible persecutions and purges, which spread terror and hopelessness in the minds of the people. The third was the invasion of the Soviet Union by Nazi Germa- [B03.14] ny in 1941 and the barbarization of the Second World War, which turned into an ideological total struggle for the survival of fascism or communism. Finally, the last was the sudden demise of the Soviet state and the introduction in Russia of alien liberal reforms. The collapse of the Soviet Union generated for the first time the awareness of a downsizing of the importance of Russia and its declassing from international superpower to second rank state. After 1991, Russia was confronted with two alternatives. The first was to embrace the idea of the "end of history" as theorized by Francis Fukuyama, adopting the values and principles of the liberal-democratic West. The second was to look back to Russian history and culture, and to search in this framework for elements that could offer a characteristic Russian identity, erasing the memory of the Soviet era experience and looking back to the czarist imperial epoch. In this context, intellectual currents appeared that pivoted on the theme of Russia's historical uniqueness as a state bridging Europe and Asia with a tradition of solid centralized power and imperial mission: among these currents was neo-Eurasianism. Under Putin's leadership, Russian political thought witnessed a renewal of the ideological component, with a strong focus on nationalism, patriotism, neo-imperialism, prestige, and the pursuit of national interest. Specifically, since 2008, Russia developed a markedly neo-imperialist character based on the values of conservatism, statism, and alter-globalism. Conservatism is often used as an ideological justification to support Russian interests in the post-Soviet area or to challenge the existing unipolar world order. The Eurasianist component of contemporary Russian conservatism is clearly expressed in the importance given to political geography. Refusing both Western liberalism and Slavic nationalism, Putin's regime—probably due to Dugin's influence and advise—strengthened its orientation towards neo-Eurasianism. The neo-Eurasianist aspects of Putin's rule can be found in the will to rediscover Russia's imperial identity, in the interest for integrating Eurasian regions, in the support for the advent of a multipolar world, in the consolidation among society of traditional values that contrast with Western cosmopolitism and globalism. It is true that Putin's policy does not follow explicitly the ideology of Eurasianism, however some of his choices are characterized by a Eurasianist thrust, like for instance the creation of the Eurasian Economic Union. Despite the differences between a normative construct like Eurasianism and an empirical economic institution like the EAEU, there is a veiled connection between the two.

[B03.15]   The second chapter represents a historical and philosophical account describing the evolution of the Eurasianist doctrine, from early—or classic—Eurasianism to neo-Eurasianism, and the main theoretical contributions given by its advocates. Originally, as seen, Eurasianism appeared as a sociopolitical ideology founded by the Russian émigrés who escaped from the motherland after the Bolshevik October Revolution. At that time, it mainly represented an intellectual movement with small political impact, based on a nostalgic and romantic vision of the Russian Empire. The foundational beliefs that edified the Eurasianist doctrine included the idea that the Russian culture was neither European nor Asian, but rather an exclusive blend that combined Western and Eastern traits and that belonged both to Europe and to Asia, without however reducing itself to one or the other. According to this construal, Russia's nature is specifically Eurasian, sharing features both with Europe and Asia. Russia's Eurasian aspect has characterized the country's historical evolution, shaping it with a spontaneously autocratic mentality and an inclination towards imperialism, in contrast with the Western-European and Atlanticist liberal tradition and its universal claims. Since the beginning, the Eurasianist doctrine has been very critical towards the Western cultural model shaped on the so-called "Romano-Germanic civilization," which— according to Eurasianists—in the long term forged a social paradigm founded on individualism, egoism, competition, materialism, atheism, unrestricted technological progress, consumerism, and economic exploitation. Among the main founding fathers of early Eurasianism that will be examined in the research are intellectuals like N. S. Trubetskoy (1890–1938), P. N. Savitsky (1895–1965), G.V. Florovsky (1839–1979), G.V. Vernadsky (1877–1973), and I. A. Il'in (1883–1954).

Classic Eurasianism and neo-Eurasianism are interconnected through L. [B03.16] N. Gumilëv's (1912–1992) thought. Gumilëv founded his Eurasianist idealism on the so-called "passionarity theory" based on the notion that each ethnos—which is considered a biological spontaneous formation—is influenced by cosmic energetic impulses that produce a special vital activity that gives birth to particularly talented individuals capable of building new civilizations. Moreover, Gumilëv focused his Eurasianist philosophy on the theory of "ethnogenesis," which affirms that an ethnos consists of a group of individuals, peoples, nations, tribes, or clans kept together by a common historical destiny, each of them with specific, immutable, cultural and biological features. Finally, Gumilëv paid close attention to the study of the proto-history and history of the nomadic Eurasian empires founded by Turkic-Mongol peoples—e.g. Huns, Tatars, Bulgars, Mongols—, showing a continuity between these empires of the steppes and Russia.

Classic Eurasianist thought and Gumilëv's legacy contributed to the birth [B03.17] of neo-Eurasianism, which arose at the end of the 1980s due to the reforms introduced by perestroika, which would have ultimately led to the demise of the USSR and to the introduction of the Western liberal model in Russia during Yeltsin's presidency. Neo-Eurasianism extended the range of early Eurasianism by combining it with new ideologies and methodologies such as traditionalism, geopolitics, the concepts of "New Right," "New Left," and "Third Way," the theory of the right of peoples above human rights, ecology, eschatological messianism, the idea of conservative revolution, and the rebirth of spirituality. Neo-Eurasianism espouses the idea of "rejection of the

West," perceiving it as a deviant cultural model. Specifically, this repudiation refers to Western Atlanticism, embodied by the United States, Great Britain and other Anglo-Saxon countries, but not necessarily to continental Europe, which may be integrated under certain conditions in the Eurasianist mindset. In terms of philosophical history, neo-Eurasianism wishes to interpret history in the light of geographical determinism and civilizational relativism, referring to authors like Danilevsky, Spengler, Toynbee, Gumilёv, and Huntington. In terms of its political platform, neo-Eurasianism is strongly influenced by Vilfredo Pareto's school, highlighting the relevance of elitist political doctrines. Key elements of the neo-Eurasianist ideology are the rehabilitation of hierarchy, the Orthodox conception of power as "*kat'echon*," the replacement of the idea of representative democracy with that of "organic"—i.e. direct—democracy ("*demotia*") meant as the full participation of a people in forging its destiny, the fundamental call for a conservative revolution and for a "third way" in economics beyond capitalism and socialism.

[B03.18]   The most influential neo-Eurasianists that will be scrutinized in this research are Aleksandr Panarin and—above all—Aleksandr Dugin. Originally a follower of National-Bolshevism, Dugin believes in the political combination of the far-right with the far-left, in the geopolitical dychotomy between tellurocracy (expressed by Eurasianism) and thalassocracy (expressed by Atlanticism), and in the foundation of a new "conservative" post-Soviet empire.

[B03.19]   In chapter three, we will try to describe the liaison that connects Eurasianism with geopolitics. Eurasianism, especially neo-Eurasianism, bases much of its ideological narrative on geopolitical analysis. The core subject of Eurasianism, as the name suggests, bears a geographical connotation: Eurasianists attribute to the geographical concept of Eurasia a strategic and geopolitical meaning.

[B03.20]   Dugin represents one of the main Eurasianist authors analyzing the strategic weight of the Eurasian landmass following the scheme of the contraposition between sea powers and land powers, that is a typical hermeneutical tool that geopolitics makes use of.

[B03.21]   However, geopolitics may be considered a controversial tool to interpret international relations since its validity is rather debatable and its narrative is characterized by normativity and dogmatism. Indeed, geopolitics is just one among many tools for understanding the dynamics of international relations, and its truthfulness and empirical nature can be significantly questioned. Nonetheless, the Eurasianist ideology considers geopolitical norms as valid to disclose the essence of global power.

[B03.22]   Geopolitics studies the relations between political power and geographical landscape. It can be considered the analysis of international relations from a spatial and geographic perspective aimed at underlining the strategic relevance of political and physical geography for the pursuit of international power. Geopolitical theories privilege the analysis of the geographical factor in the international system, believing that geography represents one of the most stable elements of international relations, given the fact that it incarnates a concrete and fixed reality.

Historically, geopolitics started to appear as an organic subject in the late 19th century. Between 1890 and 1920, the discipline orbited around the works of Alfred T. Mahan, who focused his attention on sea-power, Friedrich Ratzel, who focused on the idea of living biological organism to describe the existence of states, Halford J. Mackinder, who focused on the threats originating from land-power, and Rudolf Kjellén, who presented the world subdivision in pan-regional blocs. Authors who contributed to the development of geopolitics have also been Nicholas J. Spykman, one of the greatest theorists of Atlanticism and of the strategy of containment against Soviet Russia (expressed in the Rimland theory), and Karl Haushofer, who promoted the idea of creating a continental Eurasian block to marginalize sea power. [B03.23]

Geopolitics has been subject to great criticism. One criticism refers to its overestimation of the geographical factor in interpreting the reality of international relations. Geopolitics has been critically asked whether geographic determinism could bear consistency in the context of globalization and of the abolition of rigid state borders. The idea of pursuing the national interests in the frame of strict geographical borders has often been labeled as outdated and overcome by the rise of global governance and meta-state institutions that dilute the sovereignty of national states. Moreover, the proliferation of transnational institutions and organizations like the United Nations or the European Union, international regimes, and global networks, as well as the increased role of civil society would have resized the role of the state as exclusive international actor. Some critics believe that international relations cannot be explained only referring to geopolitics, omitting variables like domestic politics, economics, trade, political ideologies, constructivist worldviews, religion, psychology, and so on. The underestimation of the role of domestic factors and individuals has been perceived as a major weakness of geopolitics. Finally, ideologically speaking, geopolitics has been criticized for its alleged propensity towards the promotion of expansionism, militarism and imperialism. [B03.24]

Notwithstanding, Dugin builds his neo-Eurasianist political doctrine upon geopolitical analysis, which would consist of three main elements: geography, culture and history, and national interest. Dugin's geopolitical narrative is aimed at creating a powerful unified polity under the hegemony of Russia in Euro-Asia and a German-French axis in Europe, claiming that the "Eurasian Empire" will be fabricated on the rejection of Atlanticism and Western liberal values. Considering geopolitics as a dogmatic ideology, Dugin uses the classical geopolitical schemes of Heartland, Rimland, and World-Island to explain contemporary international events. In this sense, he views the [B03.25] eastern NATO enlargement as an Atlanticist plan to expand in the Rimland for the benefit of thalassocracy. At the same time, he considers a possible agreement between Germany and France for the creation of an independent European army as a step forward for the creation of a continental power that would advantage tellurocracy. Dugin reckons that the geopolitical ideology is based on a Hegelian dialectic struggle between tellurocracy and thalassocracy, whose synthesis would be the advent of the global empire. The dichotomy between land power and sea power would have reached its full maturation during the Cold War, where the two cultural-political forms of Marxism and liberalism controlled the Heartland and the Outer Crescent of the World-Island respectively. Following Mackinder's scheme, Dugin portrays the geopolitical map of the world in three zones: the inner continental Eurasian space, the continental crescent, and the insular crescent.

[B03.26]   Dugin believes that Russia would bear a geopolitical "manifest destiny" aimed at the unification of the Eurasian landmass and the replacement of Western liberal principles with more conservative values. Through the lenses of geopolitical analysis, Dugin affirms that all events concerning politics, culture, and religion would symbolize parts of the gigantic conflict between land power and sea power, which would eventually lead to the formation of a great empire and the fall of another. The four possible outcomes of the geopolitical struggle between sea power and land power would be four: that the victory of thalassocracy would annihilate the civilization of tellurocracy; that the victory of thalassocracy would end the cycle of conflict between the two civilizations but would not spread its liberal-democratic model upon the rest of the world, though ending geopolitical history; that the defeat of global tellurocracy that occurred after the demise of the Soviet empire is only momentary since Eurasia will return to its pan-continental mission in a new form; that the victory of tellurocracy would found the international system on a civilizational model and enclose the cycle of history.

[B03.27]   Chapter four will present some classic geopolitical theories that focus on the Eurasian continent. Specifically, it will investigate Halford Mackinder's geopolitical thought and expose his chief contribution to geopolitics, namely the Heartland theory. The purpose is to try to show how this theory has deeply influenced neo-Eurasianist thought by emphasizing the strategic importance of the Eurasian continent for global hegemony. Geopolitically, Eurasia represents a strategic continental bloc created around Russia or its enlarged base—that is the former Soviet countries and satellites—in active or passive antagonism with the strategic initiatives of the contrasting Atlanticist bloc headed since 1945 by the United States of America with its NATO allies plus Japan. The relevance of the Eurasian landmass for strategic and geopolitical purposes follows the ideas developed in the 20th century by the exponents of classical geopolitics.

Mackinder was among the first authors to adopt a methodical scientific [B03.28] approach to the study of geography, as exposed in his article *On the Scopes and Methods of Geography*. He highlighted in quite deterministic terms the relevance of geography for the interpretation of the historical evolution of nations and described the interconnections between physical and political geography. He also contributed to analyzing the core features of British maritime power and the connections with its natural rival, namely continental power.

Mackinder's major geopolitical contribution, namely the Heartland theo- [B03.29] ry, was first formulated in 1904 in the famous article *The Geographical Pivot of History*. The theory was further implemented in 1919, at the end of the First World War, and in 1943, during the Second World War. Mackinder believed that within Eurasia laid a vast pivotal region whose possession would have allowed the rule over the rest of the Eurasian continental land-mass. Specifically, he claimed that a country dominating Eastern Europe would dominate the Heartland, a country dominating the Heartland would dominate Eurasia, and a country dominating Eurasia would dominate the world. The holder of Eurasia could create a hegemonic global empire capable of combining tellurocratic and thalassocratic power, transforming the other peripheral continents into secondary actors, economically and strategically reliant on it. Mackinder believed that the world's pivotal region was repre-sented by the Eurasian inner continental vast landlocked area inaccessible to sea power. Mackinder's main concern was a potential combination of land and sea power that would attach the core Eurasian region with its marginal rims, perceiving it as a serious threat to the international balance of power.

In 1919, after the end of the First World War, Mackinder readapted the [B03.30] concept of the Heartland to the new international context, confirming the idea that it represented a geographical landlocked region inaccessible to mar-itime power located in the core of Eurasia, surrounded by semi-circular cres-cents, whose political and strategic control would lead to the dominion of the Eurasian continent, whose control, in turn, would lead to the dominion of the entire world. After the war, Mackinder supported the idea of creating a tier of buffer states between Germany and Russia to prevent them from gaining hegemony on Eastern Europe.

At the same time, the geopolitician Karl Haushofer made use of Mackind- [B03.31] er's Heartland theory for supporting German expansionism. Haushofer be-lieved that the Heartland theory could encourage the creation of an alliance between Germany and Russia. The plan for a continental alliance—also known as *Kontinentalblock*—consisted in the creation of common borders between Germany, Russia, and Japanese bridgeheads in continental Asia. Haushofer believed that the continental block formed by Mitteleuropa, Eur-asia and Greater Japan would avert future conflicts and grant the isolation and marginalization of sea powers, namely Great Britain and the United

States. Moreover, Haushofer supported the idea that the international order should have been expressed by big spaces known as pan-regions. The pan-regions were described as macro-areas that included a dominant power in the role of hegemonic actor and other minor actors revolving around it. The dominant power would consider the pan-region as its own sphere of influence.

[B03.32]   Finally, Nicholas Spykman—the theorizer of the notion of Rimland—reformulated Mackinder's theory giving opposite strategic values to Eurasia: whereas Mackinder focused his strategic analysis on the core of the Eurasian continent, Spykman considered its surrounding rims more decisive for Eurasian rule, stating that who controlled the Rimland controlled Eurasia. In relation to the control of the Rimland, Spykman believed that the sea power's interest consisted in avoiding the unification of Heartland and Rimland by constituting bridgeheads in the latter, while the land power's interest involved the need to break the encirclement carried out by the sea power through controlling parts of the Rimland.

[B03.33]   Chapter five will describe the fain features of Dugin's neo-Eurasianist ideology, including the core concepts that characterize its doctrinal corpus and its main programmatic goals. Neo-Eurasianism is conceived as a dogmatic and normative philosophy that believes to represent a hermeneutic tool to unfold and interpret the world from an idiosyncratic perspective. As an ideology, it is based on a constructivist analysis that somewhat reechoes Huntington's theoretical paradigm based on civilizational struggle. One of the assumptions of Eurasianism is that different civilizations exist, each possessing some unique characteristics. In this sense, the Eurasianist narrative interprets civilizations as organic wholes with their own identity and way to understand history, religion, politics, culture, and strategy. Neo-Eurasianism is essentially a conservative philosophical-political doctrine, strongly influenced by National-Bolshevism and closely linked to traditionalism. Eurasianist conservatism is based on civilizational pluralism and aims at preserving the cultural traditions and uniqueness of peoples. Unlike the modern world, the traditional world—i.e. the pre-modern world—is considered genuine and untainted. Eurasianism refuses all forms of cultural leveling and of civilizational racism; it vigorously opposes the suppression of cultural differences and upholds the project to develop a diverse multipolar world order that would preserve the essential traditions of nations. In this sense, the Russian Federation's model, in which a myriad of ethnicities and peoples live together conserving their own cultural, religious, and traditional identity, is considered as an example for the creation of an identitarian multipolar international order.

[B03.34]   In this broader context, Dugin's thought represents a specific branch of neo-Eurasianism based on the relevance of classic geopolitical theories for explaining international relations, on the need for introducing a worldwide cultural revolution grounded on the principles of nationalism, cultural diversity, spirituality and traditionalism against the materialistic, consumerist and standardized globalized world, and on the search for a "third way" alternative to capitalism and socialism both in politics and economics. Dugin's Eurasianism aims at promoting an alternative doctrine that would challenge and eventually replace globalism, Atlanticism, and the Western US-led world order. However, rather than anti-globalist, Eurasianism appears as an alterglobalist philosophy, offering an alternative form of globalization based on the principles of multipolarity. Being essentially an "eastern" ideology, Eurasianism describes its post-modernism as the post-modernism of pluralism opposed to Western post-modernism, which is believed to be cosmopolitan and universalistic.

Eurasianist culturology contrasts what it considers the veiled cultural racism of Atlanticism, based on the alleged Western civilizational superiority. [B03.35] Dugin describes Eurasianism as the philosophy of multipolar mundialization, which appeals to the union of all societies and peoples of the world to build an organic and authentic environment, in which each component would be the result of its historical traditions and local cultures. Some of the main features of Dugin's neo-Eurasianism include the allure for traditionalism, a hermeneutical approach to international relations based on geopolitics, an ideological closeness to philosophers like Carl Schmitt and Martin Heidegger, the project of implementing a worldwide conservative revolution, and a civilizational *Weltanschauung* based on structural and cultural anthropology. Dugin's doctrine is normatively anchored to the idea of an eternal struggle between the civilization of Land and the civilization of the Sea, dogmatically believing in the philosophical and strategic superiority of the former. Dugin promotes the idea of the integration of Eurasia, marginalization of thalassic powers, and construction of a peaceful multipolar world order. The five core pillars that Dugin considers as the founding principles of neo-Eurasianism are the differentiation of civilizations, traditionalism, the rights of nations above individual human rights, ethnocentrism, and distributive justice.

In the years 2007–2008, Dugin introduced a new interpretation of his neo- [B03.36] Eurasianist philosophy, announcing the birth of the so-called "Fourth Political Theory" based on the overcome of the three classical theories of liberalism, Marxism, and fascism. The Fourth Political Theory represents an attempt to contrast liberalism through the assimilation of some elements of Marxism with some of fascism, though rejecting others. For instance, it discards all the ideas of evolution, growth, modernization, progress, and development typical both of Marxism and fascism, replacing them with the idea of conservation, which finds its philosophical manifestation in conservatism. The aspects that the Fourth Political Theory accepts both from Marxism and fascism are anti-capitalism, anti-liberalism, and anti-individualism. However, what it rejects is materialism, atheism, and progressivism from

Marxism, and racism and chauvinism from fascism. Unlike previous political theories, the Fourth Political Theory believes that time can be reversible, and that history is not a linear progression that follows a straight path. The Fourth Political Theory is highly influenced by Carl Schmitt's philosophy, from which assimilates the concepts of "Large space," "Empire," the rights of nations, geopolitical sovereignty, and the struggle between thalassocracies and tellurocracies.

[B03.37]   The full program of Dugin's political project is comprised of the so-called "Manifesto of the Global Revolutionary Alliance." The Manifesto is grounded on the idea that the modern world has come to its existential end and that the current historical cycle represents the final one, since all processes that constitute the flow of history have come to a stalemate. The evolution of capitalism would have led to the end of capitalism itself due to the over-stretching of its natural limits. The self-destruction of capitalism would be caused by the progressive growth of financial institutions and practices totally disconnected with real economy, from the balance of aggregated supply and demand, from the production and consumption ratio, and from sustainable development. The world's wealth is believed to be concentrated in the hands of a few financial oligarchies that would manipulate the global economy for their own profits. The Manifesto also views global demographic expansion as a reason for unsustainable exploitation of resources, augmentation of pollution, and destruction of natural habitats. Moreover, it opposes the globalist attempts to interfere in the domestic affairs of sovereign states and the spread of a materialistic and consumerist logic of free market and ultra-capitalism. Instead, what the Manifesto suggests is the introduction of an economic model alternative to speculative financial capitalism, the fair and equal distribution of natural resources, the preservation of social collective structures that preserve the identities of nations, and the creation of an international order based on national sovereignty, multipolarity, civilizational big zones, and non-interference in the affairs of other states. Finally, the Manifesto promotes a global revolution against the current world order that would gather all political and social forces dissatisfied with the status quo.

[B03.38]   Chapter six describes the main ideological and political antagonists of neo-Eurasianism, namely post-liberalism, Atlanticism, and unipolar globalism. After the demise of the Soviet Union, Western liberalism represented the only ideology left, since it managed to contrast and defeat the rival ideologies of conservatism, monarchism, traditionalism, fascism, socialism, and communism. The triumph of liberalism implied the affirmation of the model of the free market; its bourgeois-capitalist identity contributed in spreading the principles of technological development, individualism, materialism, economic reductionism, selfishness, and the fetish for money. After its global establishment, liberalism exported a lifestyle based on consumerism and hedonism and changed into an anti-political ideocracy that become the symbol of Western civilization. Moreover, the triumph of liberalism and its spread would have coincided with its own evolution into post-liberalism, i.e. an individualist anti-political doctrine that would have replaced *homo politicus* with *homo oeconomicus*. The post-modern man living in a post-liberal environment was unhooked by all forms of socio-political collective identity and drawn towards universality, cosmopolitism, and globalism. The replacement of the social collectivity with the individual introduced the need to build a new international order no longer based on sovereign and national states but on world government and global governance. The corrosion of traditional collective polities became the starting point for the birth and development of the phenomenon of globalization. Postmodernity would represent the expression of the worldwide diffusion of post-liberalism and post-modernism would indicate a specific civilizational term strictly linked to the theory of progress, based on the belief that human development bears a progressive and unidirectional character and that men represent a universal self-centered phenomenon.

Postmodern men, thoroughly influenced over the last two centuries by European philosophy—specifically by Descartes and Kant—, would have replaced objective reality with subjectivism, leading to the annihilation of social bonds and collective identity. [B03.39]

The transition from a bipolar international order to a unipolar represented the historical condition from which the idea of globalism could rise. This idea was built on the principles of the universalization of free market economics, political democracy, and the ideology of human rights, with the idea of spreading these values to the entire world. Dugin claims that globalism would represent a challenge to Eurasian civilizations, as well as to African and American ones: being a Western phenomenon, it would negatively influence all peoples and cultures that bear different values and norms. Thus, in its pure essence, globalism would represent the worldwide imposition of the Western-Atlanticist paradigm. [B03.40]

Along with post-liberalism and globalism, Atlanticism represents the other major antagonist of Eurasianism. The term Atlanticism denotes a geopolitical expression that encompasses several concepts: it describes the Western sector of world civilization, both from a historical and geographical point of view; it represents the member states of the North Atlantic Treaty Organization; it includes the unified information network created by Western medias; and it incarnates the free market system, which coincides with the spread of liberal democracy and the implementation of the process of globalization. Atlanticism would aim at placing the entire world under NATO control and at imposing the social, economic, and cultural features of Western civilization upon it. [B03.41]

Chapter seven will examine Dugin's neo-Eurasianist project for the construction of a new multipolar global order. According to Dugin, the future [B03.42] international order should be based on multipolarity, the rediscover of Russian geopolitical mission, and the establishment of integrated geo-economic zones and big spaces divided into civilizational blocs. The multipolar world order should be founded on the cooperation between different peoples and civilizations for promoting peace and mutual prosperity, on a close partnership between European and Asiatic countries, on the integration of the post-Soviet space into a united Eurasian polity, on the improvement of multilateral dialogue between religions and ethnic groups, on the conservation of the cultural, religious, and ethnic identities of nations, and on the safeguard of international peace.

[B03.43]   Dugin's Eurasianism advocates the demise of traditional states in favor of integrated civilizational structures ("Great Spaces") united into geo-economic belts ("Geo-economic zones"). Accordingly, the map of the multipolar world would be divided into four zones, or poles; in turn, each pole would be divided into several great spaces. The four zones would be the Anglo-American zone, the Euro-African zone, the Pan-Eurasian zone, and the Pacific-Far East zone. The Anglo-American zone is formed by three great spaces: the North American Large Space, the Central American Large Space, and the South American Large Space; the Euro-African zone is divided in three great spaces: the European Large Space, the Arab-Islamic Large Space, and the Trans-Saharan Large Space; the Pan-Eurasian zone includes four great spaces: the Russian-Eurasian Large Space, the Islamic continental Large Space, and the Hindu Large Space; finally, the Pacific-Far East zone is formed by three great spaces: the Chinese Large Space, the Japanese Large Space, and the New Pacific Large Space.

[B03.44]   Neo-Eurasianism questions both the existing order of nation-states based on the principle of national sovereignty and the supranational globalist project. Eurasianists beleive that the Westphalian state system based on the principles of sovereignty and territorial integrity no longer corresponds to the current global balance of powers, since the appearance of trans-national and sub-national actors would require the need to create a new paradigm in international relations. According to Eurasianists, one of the chief features that will characterize the future of international relations is the dichotomy between globalism and regionalism: in this sense, the future world order will be characterized either by a single global government or by regional geo-economic and geopolitical blocs.

[B03.45]   According to Eurasianism, Russia should give absolute priority to geopolitics and base its foreign policy on geopolitical calculations. The ultimate Russian geopolitical mission would be to integrate the Eurasian post-Soviet space and to forge a global alternative to the Atlanticist world order.

[B03.46]   The Eurasianist project could only be accomplished by preserving Russia's nuclear potential and the Russian veto in the UN Security Council. In the future multipolar world, the nuclear potential of NATO and Russia (and its military allies) should remain in substantial equilibrium, since the mutually assured destruction threat could avoid the potential outbreak of total war.

At the domestic level, the Eurasianist project seeks to introduce the so-called "system of the Autonomies," conceived as local subdivisions of the Great Spaces and based on political self-determination and direct democracy. The relations between local authority and Great Spaces' strategic center would be disciplined by a federal system of norms.   [B03.47]

NOTES   [B03.48]

1. The Tripartite Pact was an agreement between Germany, Italy and Japan signed in Berlin on 27 September 1940 that forged a defensive military alliance eventually joined by most German satellites or allies including Hungary, Romania, Bulgaria, Croatia, and Slovakia. Vyacheslav Molotov was sent to Berlin to discuss the pact and the possibility of the Soviet Union joining it. On 25 November 1940 the Soviet Union sent a revised version of the pact to Germany, who was left unanswered. The invasion of the Soviet Union in June 1941 made all chances of a German-Soviet agreement vanish.   [B03n1]

2. The word Turanism comes from Turan, a historical region in Central Asia.   [B03n2]

Chapter One

Ideology as a Methodological Tool for Interpreting Eurasianism

[1.0]

INTRODUCTION

[1.1]   Defining Eurasianism is primarily a methodological problem. Given its ec-lectic and multifaceted nature, it may be unclear whether Eurasianism may be considered a full-fledged political theory or rather an assimilation of dif-ferent sets of theories based on traditionalism, conservatism, and geopolitics. From a methodological point of view, Eurasianism may be analyzed through the lenses of an ideological belief with its intrinsic normative narrative and its dogmatic rigidity. Like all ideologies, Eurasianism is not a valid frame-work to explain the world from an empirical and scientific point of view, but it is considered a valid hermeneutical and epistemological tool for those who firmly believe in its set of doctrines: in this sense, exactly like communism or fascism, it bears a merely subjective validity whose scope is limited to its supporters. During our research, we will assume that Eurasianism may be considered as an ideology that is closely linked to conservatism and alter-globalism.

[1.2]   Indeed, Eurasianism—especially neo-Eurasianism—represents a political doctrine that bases much of its theoretical framework on the norms of geo-politics. As the name "Eurasianism" suggests, the core subject for the study of this doctrine has a geographical connotation: Eurasia is firstly a geograph-ical concept, which unfolds a strategic and political meaning.

[1.3]   This chapter will investigate whether Eurasianism possesses all the char-acteristics to be considered a full-fledged ideology. It will also try to describe to which ideological branch it belongs, despite its rather unique nature. Final-ly, it will analyze what would be its collocation within the spectrum of contemporary Russian political thought.

THE DEFINITIONAL ANALYSIS OF IDEOLOGIES [1.4]

The concept of ideology is rather problematic to define since it remains a [1.5] highly flexible theoretical notion. Indeed, the process of definitional analysis is often arbitrary and conflicting, since it is complex—if not impossible—to demonstrate the superiority of one definition to another. Nonetheless, while some believe that ideology represents a dogmatic, unchangeable paradigm, for others it may refer to dominant modes of thought or to a tool that revolutionary movements use to challenge the status quo; some affirm that it is based on the concrete interests of a social class, while others claim it is characterized by an absence of self-interest. Indeed, "few concepts in the social science lexicon have occasioned so much discussion, so much disagreement, and so much self-conscious discussion of the disagreement, as 'ideology'."[1]

Despite the numerous attempts by scholars to offer a conclusive and [1.6] unambiguous definition of the concept, the term ideology is still a controversial and unclear notion in academic debates. According to a part of the literature,[2] political ideologies represent comprehensive systems of belief and shared normative mental maps; they may be considered as "[. . .] patterned ideas believed to be 'true' by significant social groups, [which] are codified by political elites who contend over control of political meanings and offer competing plans for public policy."[3] Given their simultaneous sociological, political, philosophical, and psychological nature, some scholars have stressed the relevance of a comparative and transdisciplinary study of ideologies.[4] Often, political ideologies translate the largely unconscious social imaginary into a concrete political agenda.

The word ideology appeared for the first time in France at the end of the [1.7] 18th century thanks to Antoine-Louis-Claude Destutt de Tracy, who used it to denominate the new science aimed at studying the origins of ideas.[5] Specifically, the French philosopher used the term to indicate a kind of science that studied ideas as facts of consciousness. Ideology thus studied the faculties of thinking, judging, remembering, and wishing in relation to the formation, origin, character, meaning, and significance of ideas. Soon, this project led to the appearance of a current of thought known as "*idéologie*," which represented one of the final outcomes of the Enlightenment; those who adhered to this philosophical movement were renamed "*ideologues*" (e.g. P. Cabanis, J. D. Garat, C. F. Volney e P. C. F. Daunou). During the years of the Directory regime (1795–1799) and of the Consulate (1799–1804), the *idéologues* played a relevant cultural role in promoting the revolutionary ideals.

Following É. Bonnot de Condillac's sensualist and psychologic epistemo- [1.8] logical approach, the *idéologues* attempted to apply the methodology of positivistic science to the study of society and men. Some (P. Cabanis) focused their researches on the relations between body and mind, some (C. F. Volney) on linguistics, some others on economics (J. B. Say).

[1.9]   The *idéologues'* manifest opposition towards Napoleon's rule—expressed both through the press and in political institutions—contributed to shaping a negative connotation of the word "ideology," which turned into a synonym to depict a doctrinal and abstract intellectual, wholly detached from reality. Since then, the adverse interpretation of the word ideology became predominant and constant.

[1.10]   Nonetheless, the term "ideology" assumed its complete significance in the context of Karl Marx's philosophical and economic investigations. According to Marx, an ideology represented the set of philosophical, ethical, political, and religious doctrines that expressed and justified the relations of productions imposed by the dominant, exploitative class. Marx and Engels criticized the exponents of the Hegelian Left accusing them of being "ideologists" that fought their philosophical battles against phantoms of reality—i.e. ideas—believing to succeed in provoking effective revolutions.[6] Notwithstanding, Marx's elaboration of the concept is significantly more complex than a generic accusation of metaphysical vagueness. Marxism perceives ideologies as overturned representations of reality. This overturning follows the typical Hegelian conception of history. According to Marx, Hegel instituted a dominion of ideas or historical illusions based on the self-determination of concepts expressed by self-consciousness, which erased from history all material elements. Marx opposes the Hegelian "ideologic" conception of history with his own "anti-ideologic" and materialistic one. Per Marx, the materialistic production—and the socio-economic relations that it creates—represents the core element of history. Materialistic production creates all kinds of social relations, primarily relations of ownership (juridical) and relations between classes (political). Therefore, ideology is the elaboration of juridical and political doctrines that justify social relations, supported by metaphysical paradigms—religious and philosophical—aimed at perpetrating the status quo.

[1.11]   The Marxist conception of ideology assumed different connotations in the 20th century. Lenin continued to believe in the negative connotation of the term when referred to the bourgeois ideology, considering it as "false consciousness," but viewed it in a positive sense when it exemplified the "science of revolutionary action" applied to scientific socialism. In a benign perspective, Leninism claims that the socialist ideology coincides with the revolutionary consciousness that the vanguard of the proletariat should instill in the proletarian masses. On the contrary, Antonio Gramsci manifested a more skeptical position, believing that ideologies were systems of ideas capable of acting as a bonding agent for social groups, which however pivoted on an oversimplification of reality and expressed a propensity towards dogmatism.

Although ideology became one of the essential elements of study both by sociology and politics, its intrinsic scientific validity was often questioned. In this sense, it is worth noting Vilfredo Pareto's division between science—linked to observation and reasoning—and ideology—associated with feeling and faith.[7] According to Pareto, ideology is a non-scientific theory that may be evaluated by its persuasive strength and its social utility. Similarly, the sociologist Karl Mannheim attributes two interpretations to the term: a "particular" ideology represents a counterfeit of a real situation aimed at preventing its knowledge, whereas a "total" ideology embodies a full-fledged *Weltanschauung* through which certain groups hide the real state of society in a conservative function. Unlike utopias—that may lead to their realization—, for Mannheim an ideology is based on transcendental ideas that contrast with reality and that cannot be implemented.[8]

[1.12]

During the 20th century, while being assimilated by sociology, the concept of ideology turned progressively into a neutral categorization, indicating whatever sufficiently coherent system of ideas and values aimed at directing social, economic, and political behaviors of individuals. Consequently, ideology became a generic term applicable to any political doctrine, to social movements supported by a theoretical frame, and to specific cultural, political, economic, and social inclinations. For instance, Jean Meynaud broadly defines ideology as a conceptual organization of a certain amount of collective goals acknowledged as desirable. Some intellectuals like Karl Jaspers persist in depicting ideology in a derogatory manner, indicating it as a corpus of abstract, useless or mystifying ideas and as a self-deception for the sake of justification, concealment, and evasion.[9]

[1.13]

Besides these generic connotations, the term has also preserved, however, a more specific and finite meaning that is used to indicate determinate political doctrines and movements like communism, Nazism, and fascism. These major "totalitarian" ideologies indeed share some common features: a somewhat articulated theoretical background that intends to explain social and political processes in an exhaustive manner; the attempt to totally transmute and renovate society and men according to a precise schema; the intensive participation of militants, which often resembles religious fervor; the leading role of a single, well organized political party.

[1.14]

In the last decades, several contemporary scholars of political theory and political science have attempted to offer a definition of the concept of ideology. For instance, it has been defined as "an organization of opinions, attitudes, and values—a way of thinking about man and society."[10] For others, it is "a consistent integrated pattern of thoughts and beliefs explaining man's attitude towards life and his existence in society and advocating a conduct and action pattern responsive and commensurate with such thoughts and beliefs."[11] Moreover, ideologies are "systems of belief that are elaborate, integrated, and coherent, that justify the exercise of power, explain and judge

[1.15]

historical events, identify political right and wrong, set forth the interconnections (causal and moral) between politics and other spheres of activity."[12] While some consider ideology as "a typically dogmatic, i.e. rigid and impermeable approach to politics,"[13] others view it as "a logically coherent system of symbols which, within a more or less sophisticated conception of history, links the cognitive and evaluative perception of one's social condition—especially its prospects for the future—to a program of collective action for the maintenance, alteration, or transformation of society."[14] Finally, more recent definitions described ideologies as "sets of ideas by which men posit, explain and justify ends and means of organized social action, and specifically political action, irrespective of whether such action aims to preserve, amend, uproot or rebuild a given social order,"[15] or as "a system of collectively held normative and reputedly factual ideas and beliefs and attitudes advocating a particular pattern of social relationships and arrangements, and/or aimed at justifying a particular pattern of conduct, which its proponents seek to promote, realize, pursue, or maintain."[16] Samuel Huntington defines ideology as "a system of ideas concerned with the distribution of political and social values and acquiesced in by a significant social group."[17]

[1.16] It has been stated that "all expressions of political thought, irrespective of the various readings to which they may be subject, [. . .] adopt the form of ideologies."[18] Though often distorting and harmful, ideologies are still human and social products that bind together different worldviews, enabling collective action in furthering or impeding the aims of a society: "On the whole they are outgrowths of understandings and perceptions that permeate societies and that emanate from them, albeit often in a mutually competitive mode and usually articulated and refined by intellectual and political elites."[19] Therefore, "the study of ideologies is unquestionably the study of substantive, concrete configurations of political ideas that matter to, and in, societies."[20]

[1.17] A detailed comprehensive framework for a definitional analysis of the concept of ideology has been explored through a recent scholarly publication, in which the author collects all attributes associated with the term ideology in contemporary social science discourse and analyzes it in relation to different variables.[21] First, the concept is related to the location of its action, which can either be the thought, the behavior, or the language. If ideology represents a kind of thought, then it may be represented as a set of beliefs, values, principles, attitudes, and ideals that shape a type of political thinking. On the other hand, ideologies may not only incarnate purely ideational and philosophical schemas, since they direct or at least influence political and social behavior and therefore can be considered as behavioral patterns. Or, another basic approach to the definition of the concept could refer to a set of linguistic symbols and discourse; in this sense, the paradigm of an ideology would not derive from the values and beliefs of the ideologists, but rather from the linguistic norms in which they are embedded.

The second attribute for analyzing ideology can be the subject matter. In this sense, ideology can either pertain to politics, power, or the world at-large. Ideology and politics are deeply intertwined and it may be affirmed that an ideology is formed to adapt to a political reality—or, rather, that a political reality is shaped on an ideology—; thus, ideology is inseparable from politics, otherwise it would represent a mere theoretical speculation. Another interpretation can relate ideology to power, linking the notion to relationships based on coercion or domination and to the distribution of power within societies. Finally, ideologies can refer to the world at-large, expressing the total structure of the mind of an epoch or class, a worldview, a cultural system, a symbol-system, or a belief-system. [1.18]

A third attribute is given by the subject, i.e. who creates and bears ideologies. The first category includes a social class by and large: for instance, from the Marxist perspective, ideology refers primarily to the views of a specific social class and it always expresses—allegedly—class positions. The second category refers to any social group since ideology could incarnate the claims of any socially significant group and class and most people acquire an ideology by identifying with a social group. The final category links ideology to the individual: an ideology could express the ideas of a single individual and be distinguishable from all others. [1.19]

The fourth attribute is position. In relation to its position in society, an ideology can be either dominant or subordinate. If it is dominant, it expresses the tool that the ruling class utilizes for justifying its rule, since it helps to support elites while exercising their power. If it is subordinate, it symbolizes an instrument used by groups or individuals who protest against the existing sociopolitical order: in this sense, an ideologist can also be defined as a revolutionary, that is somebody who wishes to overcome the status quo and found a new social order. [1.20]

A fifth attribute describes the functions of ideologies, which can be various: an ideology can explain society and social life, it can allow repression, it can promote social integration by binding individuals to a community through the establishment of an authoritative set of norms and values, it can trigger motivation and enthusiasm connecting ideals with social action, and, finally, it can legitimize political societies. [1.21]

The sixth attribute refers to motivation: an ideology can either be rooted in interests, can be an end in itself, or may be characterized by the absence of short-term interests (or expediencies). When an ideology is interest-based, the interests may refer not only to the ideologue's material interests of his class but to broader interests of the whole social group and community. [1.22]

Finally, the seventh attribute of ideology is its cognitive and affective structure. An ideology presents the following structural features: a coherent [1.23] narrative, a degree of contrast vis-à-vis other ideologies, a degree of abstract idealism, a concrete and specific program, a hierarchical model of ideological reasoning, a stability in the choice of its set of values and beliefs, an understandable political agenda, a degree of sophistication, a degree of facticity, a clear and simple explanation of its nature and purposes, a degree of distortion of reality, a deep, passionate, and emotional commitment, a degree of insincerity and rhetoric expressed by propaganda, a dogmatic, immutable nature, and both a conscious (rational) and unconscious (instinctive) stimulus.

[1.24]   Despite numerous diversities and nuances, it is possible to frame a general taxonomy of ideological ideal types, dividing them into the following categories: liberalism, conservatism, socialism, anarchism, communism, nationalism, and fascism.[22]

[1.25]   Liberalism is a philosophical and political movement that pivots on the autonomous and self-sufficient value of the individual. It constantly tends to limit state interference in social life, rigidly delimitating the public sphere from the private. The intellectual premises of the liberal movement in European history date back to the Renaissance, the Protestant Reformation, and the Enlightenment. Liberal thought evolved gradually, absorbing in its doctrinal corpus different concepts: the idea of religious freedom; political and civic liberties vis-à-vis monarchic absolutism; the doctrine of division and balance of powers inspired by the English institutional model and theorized by Montesquieu; the concept of natural law as theorized by Grotius; Smithian economic individualism focused on free competition, trade, and market; Lockean justification of private property; freedom of consciousness and thought as promoted by Spinoza; safeguard of civic rights; equality before the law; democratic political participation; and so on. During the 19th century, liberalism's major antagonists were both dynastic absolutism—be it traditional-monarchic or Bonapartist—and Jacobean democratic radicalism—as expressed in the republican phase of the French Revolution and, later, in European socialist uprisings. Then, in the succeeding century, the antagonists became the "totalitarian" regimes expressed on one hand by nationalistic fascisms and by communist rule on the other.

[1.26]   Conservatism—as we will consider more in details in the next section—is a political and cultural movement that emerged in the late 18th century in contraposition with the French Revolution, specifically thanks to Edmund Burke. Generally, it opposes utopian projects of creating perfect societies and radical changes. Its core attributes are a strong confidence in the rule of law and an inclination towards traditional social values such as family and religion. Conservatism highlights the value of continuity vis-à-vis social change, safeguarding the traditional sociopolitical order against innovative and progressist impulses. Historically, it supported the post-revolutionary and post-Napoleonic Restoration and contrasted liberal uprisings against the status quo that occurred throughout Europe in the first half of the 19th century. Philosophically, conservatism contributed to the theorization of movements like idealism, positivism, romanticism, and somewhat nationalism.

Socialism is an ideology that focuses on the necessity to suppress social [1.27] privileges—juridical, social, and economic—and wishes to promote total equality among social members. The final goal of socialism is the deletion of social classes. Social and economic equality would be pursued through the collectivization of the means of production (land, capital, labor, technology) and through the fair redistribution of produced goods and services among society. Philosophically, socialism finds precursors in some theories stemming from the Judeo-Christian tradition promoting social equality and communion of goods. Since the 19th century, chiefly due to the Industrial Revolution, socialism became the core movement of working classes. The socialist doctrine has been gradually enriched, from the French Revolution onwards, by the philosophical systems promoted by Saint-Simon, Owen, Fourier, Proudhon, Marx, and Engels.

Anarchism promotes the abolition of any kind of government that im- [1.28] poses its rule over individuals and, consequently, supports the idea of the abolition of the state. Generally, it comprises a set of doctrines and trends developed throughout three centuries, from the English Revolution (17th century) to the end of the 20th century. The key assumption that unites all anarchic strands is the idea that governments are useless and harmful, and that people should get rid of them (literally, "anarchism" means "absence of rule"). The most significant philosophical contributions to the development of modern anarchism were offered by Proudhon, Bakunin, and Kropotkin.

Communism is an ideology that derives from the doctrinal corpus elab- [1.29] orated by Marx and Engels. It promotes a social system in which private property is abolished, means of productions are collectivized and managed by the entire society, and all economic policies are rigidly planned. Communism, which appeared in the second half of the 19th century, can be considered an outcome of Marx's scientific socialism. Some precursors of the communist ideology have been More, Campanella, Fourier, Cabet, Owen, Blanqui, Saint-Simon, and Babeuf. In the *Manifesto of the Communist Party* (1848), Marx and Engels expressed the idea that history has been the result of a constant class struggle between exploiting rulers and exploited subjects and that its development had followed the dialectics between development of productive forces and corresponding social relations. Accordingly, communism is conceived as the answer to the intrinsic contradictions of the capitalist society, which promotes progress in production but distributes the profits unequally, polarizing society between a ruling class that owns the means of production and an increasing mass of underpaid or exploited workers. Communism believes in the necessity to endorse a revolution that would replace the "dictatorship of the bourgeoisie" with the "dictatorship of the proletariat," that is with the dominion of the majority. The communist society would need to pass through a "socialist" transition phase before implementing its agenda. Communist ideology has been characterized by different strands, including Leninism, Trotskyism, Stalinism, Maoism, etc.

[1.30]   Nationalism is a political and ideological movement that promotes the exaltation and defense of the nation. Historically, it emerged in Europe after the French Revolution and during the19th century as a result of the birth of national states. Its core assumption is the exaltation of the idea of nation, which is considered to be an entity that exists before the state, characterized by a group of people that shares the same culture, language, race, heritage, and history. Most nationalistic movements aim at transforming the state into a "national power" either through colonialist and imperial expansionism or through territorial irredentism. In France, some of the main exponents of nationalist ideology have been M. Barrès, C. Maurras, and L. Daudet.

[1.31]   Finally, fascism is a political movement originally founded in Italy by Benito Mussolini (1919) that combines some elements of the socialist doctrine with the nationalist ideology. The core assumptions of fascist ideology are extreme nationalism and chauvinism, revolutionary unionism, the exaltation of the Nietzschean myth of the "will to power" (*"Wille zur Macht"*), the opposition to egalitarianism, a disdain for parliamentarism, the exaltation of the military, an antagonism towards liberalism and communism, the integration of all social classes into the paradigm of the state, the nationalization of the masses, and so on. Besides Italian fascism, many strands of fascist movements and ideologies appeared throughout Europe during the 1920s and 1930s, most notably German Nazism, which was characterized by a racialist model built upon the belief in the superiority of the Aryan race.

[1.32]   From the point of view of International Relations (IR), ideological analysis involves the study of the content, nature, and effects of international ideologies. International ideologies involve inter-subjective systems of thought consisting of basic claims concerning the nature of the international order and international actors, which embody divergent conceptions of key concepts including sovereignty, anarchy, power, community, interest, institutions, and the state.[23] The most well-known international ideologies include realism, liberalism, constructivism, internationalism, globalism, cosmopolitanism, communitarianism, feminism, nationalism, idealism, and militarism. Some authors argue that the fractious nature of International Relations as a discipline has contributed to the creation of five distinct paradigms of ideological analysis: analytical, historical, philosophical, critical, and reflexive.[24] A recent study[25] attempted to show that the doctrinal approach that IR scholars adopt is often connected to their personal political beliefs. The research—conducted through cross-national surveys—showed that realists tend to be the most conservative and right-leaning IR scholars, while liberals tend to be more left-leaning; at the same time, constructivists appeared as less conservative than rationalists, while post-positivists showed a deep connection with the political left; instead, Marxists and feminists manifested the most pronouncedly left-leaning inclination, while neoliberal institutionalists located themselves in-between liberals and realists. [26]

In recent years, especially after the fall of communism and the end of the bipolar world, some scholars noted that the notion of ideology suffered a conceptual crisis. Francis Fukuyama, for instance, announced the triumph of liberal democracy and the arrival of a post-ideological world. As Ernesto Laclau puts it, "the crisis of the notion of 'ideology' was linked to two interconnected processes: the decline of social objectivism and the denial of the possibility of a metalinguistic vantage point which allows the unmasking of ideological distortion."[27] The concept of ideology has been subjected both to definitional inflation and linguistic exploitation and misinterpretation. [1.33]

Some authors have endeavored to contrast ideology with the empiricism of science. Sartori, for instance, located ideology on a truth-error dichotomy, questioning its scientific validity and its applicability to reality, since it did not fall under the domain of logic and verification and it appeared too dogmatic and closed to argumentation.[28] Likewise, Popper considered ideologies as a system of prejudices and follies that could be contrasted only through the scientific method and its objectivity, obtained through public critique, testing and replicability.[29] Skepticism, which believes in empirical reason, pragmatism and scientific positivism, powerfully rejects the epistemic value of ideologies,[30] although it may be argued that skepticism could be itself an ideology. [1.34]

From a methodological perspective, if we accept the definition of ideology as a set of beliefs, opinions, values, and norms that guide a specific social group, it can be affirmed that Eurasianism may be considered a full-fledged ideology. As we will see, Eurasianism presents many of the characteristics that we have attempted to underline in this section. For instance, if we follow the above-mentioned schema, we may apply to Eurasianism the attributes that have been associated with ideologies. In terms of location, Eurasianism can be considered as a type of political thinking based on beliefs, values, principles, and ideals, as well as a kind of linguistic discourse that emphasizes key words like geopolitics, civilization, empire, traditionalism, conservatism, and so on. In terms of the subject matter, Eurasianism refers primarily to politics, since it is a political doctrine with a political program, as well to the world at-large since it wishes to promote a specific global order based on multipolarity and civilizational spaces. As for the subject entitled to promote the Eurasianist ideology, it is both groups of people—which include exponents of far-right associations, far-left associations, anti-Western/Atlanticist movements, anti-globalist movements, ecologist movements, identitarian movements, religious organizations, etc.—and single individuals that bear their proper vision of Eurasianism (e.g. Aleksandr Dugin and Aleksandr [1.35]

Panarin). In terms of its position, Eurasianism is clearly a subordinate ideology that protests the existing socio-political international and domestic order and heavily criticizes the world's dominant ideology, i.e. Western-led post-liberalism and globalism. When considering functionality, Eurasianism as an ideology appears as explanatory—in the sense that it wishes to explain what it believes to be wrong with contemporary society and to construe a normative narrative illustrating how the world should be—, motivational—because it is action-oriented, programmatic, and prescriptive—, and legitimizing—since it believes to be supported by a just cause that defends its theoretical paradigm and practical action. Furthermore, it may be considered as non-interest based, since it appears as devoid of material self-interest. As for its cognitive structure, Eurasianism is internally coherent, for it is characterized by a consistent, integrated, organized, and logical structure, it bears a high level of external contrast vis-à-vis other ideologies—primarily post-liberalism and globalism—, it is characterized by a degree of abstraction, it presents the features of concreteness—since it proposes a concrete political program—, of stability—since its core arguments endure without changes—, of facticity—since its program is conceived for a factual realization—, of simplicity—because it is meant to state unambiguous, clear, and simple concepts—, of conviction—because it involves a high level of emotional, passionate, and deep commitment—, of dogmatism—since the values it believes in are considered immutable and unchangeable—, and of distortion of reality given by its dogmatic narrative. Finally, it is characterized by an ambivalent conscious and unconscious nature, intertwining rational thinking with quasi-supernatural elements.

[1.36]   CONSERVATISM AS AN IDEOLOGICAL NARRATIVE

[1.37]   The term conservatism indicates any political philosophy that favors tradition in its various representations—religion, culture, identity, belief, custom—and opposes all forces that promote radical social change. While some expressions of conservatism tend to preserve the status quo or to slowly reform society, others seek to return to the values of earlier times. The former kind of conservatism does not reject change per se but believes that changes should be organic and spontaneous rather than revolutionary and sudden since any unnatural alteration of society would lead to unintended consequences and unpredictable hazards.

[1.38]   Generally, conservatism is opposed both to the ideas of liberalism and socialism, since the former entails a progressivist inclination and the latter a revolutionary action. Likewise, conservatives oppose fascist ideologies, which are also perceived as revolutionary and radical. However, conservatives usually belong to the right-wing political spectrum.

Conservatism has influenced—and has been influenced by—different [1.39] ideologies and philosophies. For instance, nationalism and conservatism share many values, although the former may assume more rigid and exaggerated forms. Moreover, conservatives tend to disbelieve the xenophobic or racist sentiments that are prominent in some far-right wing movements.

From a historical point of view, the political usage of the term conserva- [1.40] tism began to appear only after the French Revolution and took its full-fledged semantic connotation during the 1820s. The beginnings of conservatism as an ideology can be traced to the reaction to the events carried out by the French Revolution. In this sense, conservatives were those who challenged the progressivism and radicalism of the French Revolution and wished to turn back to the pre-revolutionary sociopolitical order. Thus, conservatism expressed all reactionary forces that upheld the system of the *Ancien Régime* and backed the European Restoration after the Napoleonic saga.

In Anglo-Saxon countries and beyond, the Anglo-Irish philosopher Ed- [1.41] mund Burke is considered the intellectual father of conservatism. In his famous *Reflections on the Revolution in France* (1790), Burke argued vehemently against the French Revolution and the radical rationalist aspects espoused by the Enlightenment. He supported instead the value of inherited institutions and traditions, including the historical development of the state, which he believed was the result of the wisdom of previous generations. He also sponsored the continuation of other important social institutions such as the family and the Church.

Conservatism may be divided into several strands in relation to the scope [1.42] of its action. The first is cultural conservatism, which is an ideology that supports the preservation of the heritage of a nation or culture, usually by the adaption of norms and systems handed down from tradition. The second is social conservatism, which claims that societies should be grounded on moral and traditional models, with specific reference to family, behavior, lifestyle, and so on. The third is religious conservatism, which either seeks to promote the role of religion in society or to preserve a belief in its original or pristine form (integralism). Another is fiscal conservatism, which is an economic philosophy of prudence in government spending and debt. One more is bio-conservatism, which represents a position of hesitancy vis-à-vis technological development and skepticism towards biotechnological transformations (e.g. cloning, genetic engineering, etc.). Finally, there are also specific expressions of conservatism that pertain to the United States' social mindset: the first is neo-conservatism, which is a movement that developed in the US in opposition to the perceived liberalism of the 1960s and that pivots on an interventionist foreign policy, free trade and free market economics, and a general condemnation of countercultures; the second is paleo-conservatism, which emphasizes religious heritage, national and Western identity, tradition, civil society, anti-interventionist policies, and classical federalism and opposes illegal immigration, authoritarianism, and social democracy.

[1.43]   According to Huntington, conservatism bears three kinds of contrasting definitions: aristocratic, autonomous, and situational.[31] According to the aristocratic definition, conservatism is an ideology historically linked to the "reaction of the feudal-aristocratic agrarian classes to the French Revolution, liberalism, and the rise of the bourgeoisie at the end of the eighteenth century and during the first half of the nineteenth century."[32] In this perspective, while liberalism embodies the ideology of the bourgeoisie and socialism the ideology of the proletariat, conservatism incarnates the ideology of aristocracy, supporting the notions of feudalism, status, *Ancien Régime*, landed interests, medievalism, and nobility against those of middle class, labor, commercialism, industrialism, democratism, liberalism, and individualism. Secondly, in relation to its autonomous definition, conservatism would not necessarily relate to the specific interests of a social group or class, but it would rather express an autonomous system of ideas that bear universal values such as justice, order, balance, and moderation. Thus, conservatism could be embraced by all classes and social groups, as far as they accept the worldview it promotes. Finally, according to the situational definition, conservatism is a recurring kind of historical situation in which a direct challenge is directed against the institutional status quo to replace the current social paradigm with another founded on the conservative mindset. Debatably, Huntington's thesis assumes that conservatism is not the monopoly of the aristocratic class in history (aristocratic definition), nor is it appropriate in every age and place (autonomous definition), but it is rather the expression of a specific historical situation (situational definition).[33]

[1.44]   Following Burkeian political theory, Huntington highlights the existence of at least six major assumptions of the conservative creed.[34] First, the assumption that human beings are basically religious animals and that religion represents the foundation of civil society, since the threat of divine sanctions and punishment legitimizes the existing social order. Second, the assumption that society is the natural, organic product of slow historical growth and the state and its political institutions derive from the wisdom of the ancestors. The third assumption is that humans are both irrational and rational creatures, therefore they are naturally inclined towards prudence, experience, custom, and habit rather than just logic and abstractions. The fourth assumption is that the community is superior to the individual: the state is not an expression of a random set of anonymous individuals, but it is rather the manifestation of a historical community that shares the same nationality, culture, tradition, religion, or ethnicity. The fifth assumption claims that humans are essentially unequal since no equality exists in nature; in fact, societies are complex organizations that include a variety of classes, orders, and groups structured according to differentiation, hierarchy, and leadership. Finally, the sixth assumption states that—given the wickedness of human nature—all revolutionary efforts to remedy the existing evils will eventually result in even greater ones.

Huntington underlines seven characteristic features of conservative thought that serve the purpose of justifying the established order: "the 'divine tactic' in history; prescription and tradition; the dislike of abstraction and metaphysics; the distrust of individual human reason; the organic conception of society; the stress on the evil in man; the acceptance of social differentiation."[35] He also adds that "the essence of conservatism is the rationalization of existing institutions in terms of history, God, nature, and man."[36]   [1.45]

Typically, whereas non-conservative ideologies tend to be ideational and transcendental, conservatism shows an inclination to be institutional and immanent, since it rejects ideals and utopias that could endanger the traditional status quo.   [1.46]

The main antagonist of conservatism is represented by all forms of radicalism that entail a process of change and by all forces that criticize traditional institutions. Conservatism does not only represent the absence of change, but the systematic and methodical resistance to change. Arguably, Huntington tends to distinguish between a conservative and a reactionary by affirming that, unlike the former—who simply desires to maintain the existing status quo—, a reactionary is a critic of existing society who wishes to recreate in the future an idea that he assumes to have existed in the past and therefore is a radical. The argument in support to the alleged radicalism of a reactionary is that, similarly to progressivists—who seek for a change forward—, reactionaries also look for change, but for a change backward; conservatives, instead, oppose all kinds of changes.[37] Hence, conservatism is essentially a repetitive and static ideology that challenges all forms of evolution and revolution.   [1.47]

Other authors like Michael Oakeshott claim that conservatism does not represent an ideology, but only a personal predisposition towards the maintenance of the status quo, since conservatism opposes per se the notion of ideology.[38] Per Oakeshott, conservatism is merely a disposition in manners of thought and behavior that does not automatically imply the subscription to a certain set of beliefs and principles that constitute an ideology. Oakeshott also believes that unlike conservatism, which is essentially anti-rationalist, all ideologies belong to the rationalist approach of politics.   [1.48]

Furthermore, Friedrich von Hayek believes that conservatism is characterized by a legitimate and widespread attitude of opposition against radical change. However, Hayek blames this kind of conservatism by stating that it cannot properly avert progressivist development since it does not offer a consistent alternative to it.[39] Hayek adds that since it opposes everything except for what is represented by the status quo, conservatism deprives itself of the weapons needed in the struggle of ideas.   [1.49]

[1.50]   After this premise, it may be stated that Eurasianism can be considered as a conservative ideology that includes cultural, social, religious and biological aspects of conservatism. However, it does not only focus on maintaining the contemporary status quo against progressivism, but rather to replace the current societies—especially the Western post-liberal ones—with a social order based on traditionalism: in this sense, Huntington would consider Eurasianism a reactionary ideology rather than a conservative. This idea may find consistency if we consider that Eurasianism sponsors a worldwide revolution—albeit conservative—to pursue its programmatic goals: as we have seen, part of the literature considers conservatism devoid of, and even hostile to, revolutionary action. Generally, it is consistent to include Eurasianism—at least its neo-Eurasianist version—in one of the strands of post-Soviet conservatism,[40] noting that the core elements it emphasizes are alter-globalism, civilizational identitarism, religious heritage, anti-liberalism, anti-communism, anti-racism, traditional order, geopolitical analysis, and historical development.

[1.51]
THE NATURE OF CONTEMPORARY RUSSIAN CONSERVATISM AND ITS EURASIANIST COMPONENT

[1.52]   During the 20th century, Russian society had been hit by numerous traumatic events that raised profound doubts about the philosophical existence and essence of Russia and its people. First, the czarist rule had experienced a bloody revolutionary collapse and the advent to power of a completely different regime whose ideological legitimation represented the opposite of the previous. The shock of the October Revolution of 1917 resulted in five years of gruesome civil war that was leading Russia on the brink of dismemberment and dissolution. The final victory of the Bolsheviks and the consolidation of the Soviet state under Stalin helped to radically change Russia's social, economic, and cultural character. The collectivization of the 1930s, the horrors of Stalin's persecutions and purges, the invasion and near defeat at the hands of Nazi Germany in 1941 were all traumatic events that shaped Russian philosophical mentality and worldview.

[1.53]   Later, the demise of the Soviet Union represented a turning point for Russian political thought. The sudden collapse of the Soviet geopolitical titan deeply affected the Russian mindset and contributed in a significant way to spread the awareness of a downsizing of the importance of Russia and to declass it from international superpower to second rank state. The citizens' emotions and feelings that followed this traumatic event reflected on their philosophical and social perceptions and on the need to rediscover their own proper identity. In 1991, the old beliefs that had been instilled in three generations of Soviet citizens had collapsed. The result of it was that Russian society in its entirety underwent a political and cultural crisis that did not spare the rulers, the ordinary people, and the intellectuals.

During the Soviet era, Russian philosophy of state was committed to a massive program of indoctrination in the official ideology of Marxism-Leninism and scientific communism. Apart from the belief in the economic and political principles of Marxism, there was no space for other free lines of thought. In this sense, the history of the Russian state was reinterpreted in the light of the secular class struggle between exploiters—boyars, czars, bourgeoisie, landowners, clergymen—and exploited—proletariat, peasants, serfs. Accordingly, nationalism was deterred in favor of internationalism and the idea of universal friendship: the ethnic and cultural differences between peoples were overcome by the Marxist slogan "Workers of the world unite; you have nothing to lose but your chains!" During the Second World War, the philosophy of nationalism was highly criticized and closely linked to the ideology of fascism, which had been contrasted and ultimately defeated. At the same time, no theological discourse was tolerated and the philosophers whose thought was closely combined to religion were persecuted, deported, and murdered. Moreover, Western political concepts and publications were forbidden from circulation and non-aligned political thought was censored and suppressed. Pre-Soviet Russian thinkers were forced to emigrate, repressed, or skewed to fit into the official Soviet version of Russian historical evolution and philosophical thought. [1.54]

In the Soviet state, philosophy became a supreme juridical and political institution at the service of the Leninist—and later Stalinist—version of Marxism: as state philosophy, it ruthlessly victimized individual thinkers and annihilated all possible conceptual alternatives. Whereas in other countries the superlative value and the highest level of authority was assigned to societal pacts, to religious beliefs, or to economic profits, in communist Russia it was philosophy that served as the ultimate criterion of truth and the source of political legitimation. Devotion to the teachings of dialectical and historical materialism was the prerequisite of civil allegiance and professional success. No working classes or social categories could succeed in their respective fields without a basic Marxist philosophical training and a materialistic-atheistic cultural approach. [1.55]

Russian philosophy elaborated in detail the utopian project of Marxist thought, systematizing it in the form of dialectical and historical materialism, and shaping society according to the principles of real socialism.[41] In other words, whereas Marxism remained a speculative, though influential, theory in Western social sciences, in Russia it was tested in practice in the shape of Soviet bolshevism. For the first time in human history, philosophy became the guiding principle of all economic, political, social, and cultural activities of a country. The theory of dialectical and historical materialism played the role that in traditional societies belonged to mythology and theology. The [1.56]

Soviet ideocratic state turned into a unique experience for conceptualizing the entirety of reality and a laboratory for the testing of general concepts. The cherished union of state and philosophy that since Plato had inspired chief Western thinkers, including Hobbes and Hegel, was implemented in Russia, though manifesting itself as one of the most liberticidal forces in history: never in the history of mankind did a Hobbesian Leviathan appear as blatantly as in the USSR.

[1.57] Comprehensibly, during the Soviet epoch, all intellectuals and dissidents who opposed the official Marxist-Leninist doctrine were persecuted, exterminated, or silenced through exile, death sentences, labor camps, bans on publications, and so on. From the perspective of free-thinking, this persecution represented a complete misery: the persecuted—both religious and laic thinkers—testified with their courage the horrors of communism. The Soviet repression of free thought and speech created a swarm of martyrs never seen before in the history of political thought, giving a more profound meaning to the very vocation of the philosopher.

[1.58] Two main kinds of dissident intellectuals existed: those who adhered to Western liberal-democratic values like Andrey A. Amal'rik (1938–1980) and Andrey D. Sakharov (1921–1989), and those who related to the traditional values of Russian culture like Aleksandr I. Solzhenitsyn (1918–2008). This cleavage between dissidents reechoed the late 19th century debate among Russian intellectuals, divided into Westernizers who promoted a rapid assimilation of Western values—individual freedom, rule of law, limited government, constitutional monarchy—, and Slavophiles, who strived for the acknowledgement of the uniqueness of Russian civilization and for the need to construct a distinctive structure for Russia's evolution.

[1.59] When Mikhail S. Gorbachëv came to power in 1985, the Communist Party made a serious effort aimed at reforming the structure of the Soviet state. Gorbachëv's program of perestroika ("reconstruction") included different features such as economic reforms, a new attitude towards political thinking, and a new foreign policy oriented towards the promotion of reconciliation with the West and the acknowledgement of the universality of human values and rights. Where domestic policy was concerned, Gorbachëv encouraged the Soviet people to complain against state officials through a new policy of openness in the media known as *glasnost'*. The practical result of Gorbachëv's reforms was to destabilize the solidity and unity of Soviet ideology and to enhance a process of political and economic unraveling that would leave the USSR towards its end.

[1.60] After the August 1991 coup organized by Soviet reactionaries at the head of a coalition of liberal-democrats and moderate nationalists, Gorbachëv's successor in the Kremlin, President Boris Yeltsin embraced a policy of "shock therapy" aimed at reshaping most aspects of Soviet society.

The formal dissolution of the Soviet Union in December 1991 and the [1.61] consequent radical economic reforms launched in 1992 represented the ultimate traumas that Russia had to face in the short span of a single century. At that time, most nationalists and many liberals blamed Yeltsin's reforms for the economic chaos the Russian Federation experienced in 1992. The anti-Yeltsin opposition forces controlled the Duma until October 1993, when Yeltsin dissolved the legislature by force. Yeltsin's decision to attack the separatist region of Chechnya in December 1994 alienated many of the remaining liberals, and the questionable way the war was fought further enraged both communists and nationalists. Much of the political groups that supported Yeltsin were composed by mere pragmatists and careerists who wished to align with whomever had won the struggle for state power but lacked any political and philosophical values to believe in. Therefore, in terms of political philosophy, the transition from the Soviet Union to the Russian Federation represented a shift from the Marxist ideology to mere pragmatism oriented at introducing a comprehensive modernization of Russian society.

At the time of Yeltsin's political direction, Gennady A. Zyuganov's Communist Party represented the main opposition force. However, this political [1.62] faction did not bear a clear alternative program that could realistically counter the government. During the 1990s, the Communist Party turned into a chief defender of parliamentarism as far as the Duma gave to its representatives the opportunity to criticize Yeltsin, without conceiving concrete policies of their own. The philosophy of the Communist Party did not radically redefine Marxist ideology and did not shift towards forms of socialism or social democracy but did introduce some nationalist and patriotic symbolism in its rhetoric.

The other political force that opposed Yeltsin and his clique were the [1.63] nationalists, who believed they had the potential to fill the ideological vacuum of post-communism. The nationalist forces revolved around the figure of Vladimir V. Zhirinovsky. After Zhirinovsky's electoral success in the December 1993 parliamentary elections, both liberal-democrats and communists swung in the nationalist direction.

During the 1990s, Russian intellectuals had to come up with some expla- [1.64] nations for why their society kept experiencing such shocks, why the Soviet system had collapsed so suddenly, and what part should Russia play in the context of the new post-Cold War world order. The political discourse was harshly polarized between "reformers" and "reactionaries," liberal-democrats and national-communists, traitors who sold Russia to the West and patriots who were striving for the motherland's territorial integrity, prestige, and heritage.

At that time, Russian political thinkers confronted with two alternatives, [1.65] neither particularly attractive. The first was to declare the advent of the "end of history" as theorized by Francis Fukuyama, and to embrace the values and principles of the liberal-democratic West. In this sense, their task would be to try to adapt the liberal ideological paradigm to the post-Soviet context, and successively to acknowledge either its success or failure in Russia. If the model would have succeeded, there would not be such a thing as a truly Russian political thought, resulting in a mere variant of Western liberal and rationalist tradition.

[1.66]   The second alternative was to look back to Russian history and culture, and to search in this framework for elements that could offer a distinctively Russian identity. This implied to erase the Soviet era—which represented an application of Western philosophical models, from Marxism to Fordism— and to look back to the czarist epoch. Notwithstanding, the main issue to face was how to re-apply the czarist autocratic tradition in the context of a continuously globalized and open-minded international environment and to hold on to religious orthodox customs in a secularized age. Not surprisingly, Western observers and lobbies were hoping in that time that Russia would adopt the liberal and globalist model.

[1.67]   Generally, few Western academics have published on Russian political thought since 1991, with some significant exceptions.[42]

[1.68]   Some of the most serious post-1991 intellectual currents of Russian political thought pivot on the theme of Russia's historical uniqueness and of its role of cultural bridge between Europe and Asia with a tradition of solid centralized power. According to these currents, which are somewhat influenced by Eurasianism, Russian thought is markedly dichotomous, structured around bipolar opposites: East vs. West, Europe vs. Asia, weak society vs. strong state. The mainstream of such analysis is well represented by academics like Yuri Pivovarov and Alexander Akhiezer. Pivovarov traces the evolution of what he calls the "Russian System" of a single power center from the Mongols through the czarist empire. The actual exercise of power takes place through personal networks, hidden from view and not captured by strict constitutional norms: this outline would reproduce itself in all three 20th century regimes—Soviet communism, Yeltsin democracy and Putin electoral authoritarianism.[43] On the other hand, Akhiezer sees the core of the matter in the specific features of Russian society—still rooted in quasi-mystical concepts of tradition and community (*sobornost'*): Russian society oscillates between angry rejection and hopeful worship of the state and Russian thinkers believe that social differentiation that comes with modernization is a challenge and a threat.[44]

[1.69]   Once Vladimir V. Putin became president in 2000, Russian political thought witnessed a renewal of the ideological component compared to the previous Yeltsin era. The Russian state somewhat seemed to turn to an ideocratic orthodoxy based on nationalism, patriotism, neo-imperialism, prestige, and national interest. At the same time, the regime marginalized other political forces that opposed governmental policies.

As a ruler, Putin's political doctrine presents itself as an eclectic mixture [1.70] of elements from the three prevailing political philosophies that represent the Russian society of the years 2000s: liberalism, communism, and nationalism. The liberal aspects of the leader's policies showed his commitment to the market economy and rule of law, as well as a smart ability to forge close personal ties with leaders of Western liberal democracies, at least until the outbreak of the Ukrainian crisis in 2014. At the same time, the leader rejuvenated the communists' nostalgia for the Soviet past, though underlining that it could not be recuperated. Finally, from the nationalistic point of view, he reasserted with vigor Russian national interests by fighting inner secessionism—for instance in Chechnya—, by reaffirming Russian influence in former Soviet countries like Georgia and Ukraine, and by interweaving stronger relations with countries of the Commonwealth of Independent States in the frame of the realization of a future Eurasian bloc.

Under Putin's rule, Russian intellectuals have highlighted the theme of [1.71] the uniqueness of Russia's history and civilization, considering the country as a natural connector of Europe with Asia. The vastness of the Russian Federation also implies—according to Russian political thinkers—the need for the establishment of a strong centralized power, which is the only kind of power that Russia experimented with throughout its historical development, from the age of the so called "Mongol yoke" to the age of the czars and the Soviets.

In philosophical terms, Russia was the first non-Western nation to challenge [1.72] the Euro-centric historical model and cultural standard, offering an alternative civilizational model that replaced rationalism, legalism, and individualism with spiritualism, traditionalism, and collectivism. At the same time, Russian thought never denied multiculturalism, which represented one of the salient traits of the Russian Empire and the Soviet Union. However, Russian multiculturalism differs from the Western variety, since it safeguards all different identities without imposing a dominant standard and maintains a clear separation between them.

Russian thought is also characterized by a unique synthesis of philosophy [1.73] and religion. This kind of "religious philosophy" displays an outstanding inclination towards spirituality—in harmony with the theological doctrine of the Orthodox Church—, which has no analogies in the history of human thought. Uncorrupted by the philosophical tradition of the Enlightenment, the Russian thought ignores and rejects the typically Westerner dichotomy between revelation and rationalization, faith and reason, religion and science: in this sense, Russians conceive all the above-mentioned aspects as single parts of an overarching knowledge that does not contradict itself. Thus, the Russian theory of epistemology rests upon the concept of the integrity, totality, and indivisibility of knowledge; this principle also extends to the ontological dimension, as the axiomatic unity of being and essence. Furthermore, Russian metaphysics investigates as far as possible the features of the meta-terrestrial world, attempting to grasp the nature of the invisible and subtle elements of the meta-human intelligence and superior realities.

[1.74]   Russian philosophy is not an end in itself or a mere speculative exertion, but on the contrary, it bears specific goals for pursuing practical transformations of life and society. The role of this transformation is entrusted to the "intelligentsia"—a typically Russian phenomenon—, which embodies a powerful social stratum whose specific task is the implementation of general ideas into reality. The focus of the "intelligentsia" is to live and act in accordance with philosophical ideas and impose them on the society in general.

[1.75]   Since Russian thought suffered most harshly from totalitarian manipulations, it also elaborated philosophical strategy of resistance to despotism. Such trends and schools of thought produced the Russian variants of existentialism, dialogism, culturology, Christian liberalism and ecumenism, structuralism, and conceptualism, which arose in opposition to Soviet totalitarianism and demonstrated the variety of intellectual methods challenging state ideocracy. Most of these intellectual challenges to the official Marxist-Leninist doctrine ended up in the elaboration of concepts like "self-constructing personality," "ethics of creativity" (Berdyaev), "dialogue," "polyphony" (Bakhtin), "semiosphere," "typology of cultures," "national image of the world," and "national repentance and self-limitation" (Solzhenitsyn), which all provided an eclectic choice of strategies for countering totalitarian thinking.

[1.76]   Particularly, since the beginning of the 20th century, existentialism played a special role in Russian thought. It was the great writer Dostoyevsky's merit to initially embrace existentialism as a coherent set of new philosophical ideas. Through existentialism, Russian philosophy laid a foundation for the criticism of rationalism, objectification, and "essentialism"—i.e. the metaphysics of general laws which was indifferent to individuality. Rozanov, Berdyaev and Shestov anticipated many aspects of European thought: they expressed existentialist views twenty or thirty years before existentialism became a leading movement in Western philosophy.

[1.77]   Russian culturology and structuralism represent important contributions to the philosophy of culture, anthropology, and semiology. In Russia, these schools of thought stressed the integrity and interrelatedness of all cultural activities and languages and the necessity of dialogue among various cultures and systems of ideas. Unlike Anglo-Saxon multiculturalism, which stresses plurality and self-identity of cultures, Russian thought is more prone to a trans-cultural approach whereby each culture can achieve its identity only confronting with another, dissimilar culture.

Furthermore, Russian conceptualism manifests a pioneering contribution   [1.78]
to post-modernist and post-structuralist thought. By demonstrating the relativity and self-referentiality of all sign-systems, conceptualism criticizes the
basic notion of "reality" as proposed by ideological outlines. Conceptualism
depicts the breakthrough of Russian thought into the post-ideological and
post-utopian dimension, the demystification of all authoritative and objectiv-
istic discourses, including those of Marxism and structuralism.

From a practical point of view, the philosophical thought of the post-   [1.79]
Stalin era, including such movements like structuralism, personalism, culturology, and religious philosophy, has anticipated and stimulated to a large
extent the post-Soviet transition of Russia from totalitarianism to democracy,
introducing elements like the demystification of ideology, the freedom of
personality, the plurality of cultural languages, and the acceptance and interaction of different cultures and religions.

In conclusion, there are two opposing tendencies that are peculiar to   [1.80]
Russian philosophy: one proclaims the prevalence of generalization and unification as tools for the religious and historical transformation of reality and
leads to ideocracy and totalitarianism; another preserves the unsurpassable
value of individuality and discloses the relativity and futility of all general
ideological constructs.

Even from the point of view of International Relations, Russian theory   [1.81]
divides into the three distinct ideological traditions of Westernism, statism,
and civilizationalism, each one highlighting the relevance of, respectively,
the concepts of West, independent state, and Russian civilization in and of
itself.[45] This division into three distinct ideologies about the representation of
Russia's IR theories follows roughly the triple conceptualization exposed by
Martin Wight.[46]

According to Westernism, Russia is essentially similar to Western na-   [1.82]
tions, sharing with them the same philosophical, cultural, and historical paradigm. Scholars who endorse the Westernist narrative believe in the superiority of the Western liberal paradigm and on its universal scope based on
"democratic unipolarity."[47] Some liberal scholars, following Fukuyama's
theory of the "end of history," claim that no alternatives may exist to Western
liberalism.[48] As a consequence, some believe that Russia ought to adopt
standards of Western pluralistic democracy to be peaceful and progressivist
and eventually accept America's supremacy.[49] According to another liberal
view, today non-state actors, movements, networks, civil society, etc. are at
least as powerful as states and therefore Russia should abandon its excessive-
ly state-oriented attitude.[50] Interestingly, Dmitri Trenin claims that the age of
Russia as the pivotal region of the former Soviet Union is over and that the
concept of a Russia-centered Eurasia no longer exists, arguing in favor of
Russia's gradual geopolitical retreat from the former Soviet space.[51] Moreover, some authors have assumed a radical reorientation of Russian foreign

policy toward the West and Atlanticism, gaining a full-fledged status—or even joining—transatlantic economic and security institutions like the European Union and NATO. [52]

[1.83]   On the other hand, according to statism, Russia is typically represented by a strong independent state whose chief priority is to contrast external threats that may put at stake its national security. Statism is a clear expression of Russian realist theory and is generally based on the idea that the post-cold war international system is characterized by "pluralistic unipolarity" in which the unipolar center is represented by a group of leading countries—among which is Russia—rather than just the United States. [53] In this narrative, some countries bear a leading role as regional powers and maintain an independence vis-à-vis Western globalism. For instance, Primakov argues that Russia should still act in all geopolitical directions in order to secure and organize the post-Soviet space and resist unilateral hegemonic ambitions in the world. [54]

[1.84]   Finally, according to civilizationalism, Russia's nature is conceived as principally different from that of Western countries. The civilizationalist ideological vision has given birth to Russian essentialist and constructivist IR theories. Some essentialists follow Huntington's frame and claim that the international system is characterized by incompatible multipolar civilizational struggles. [55] Instead, constructivists acknowledge that the world is divided into civilizational poles which are not necessarily doomed to conflict. For instance, according to the Euro-East constructivist approach, Russia ought to absorb the West, rather than being absorbed by it. [56] Indeed, Eurasianism belongs to the civilizationist branch of Russian IR theories. For Eurasianism, Russia is an organic unity distinctive from both European and Asian cultures that bears the geopolitical mission of unifying the Russian-Eurasian civilizational zone. [57] Eurasianists uphold the idea of restoring Russia's geopolitical status as Eurasian Heartland and as imperial self-sufficient power. [58] Adhering to the geopolitical schema of contraposition between land powers and sea powers, Eurasianism believes that Russia incarnates Mackinder's Eurasian Heartland, that NATO embodies a hostile alien in Eurasia, and that a self-sufficient empire represents the natural state of Russian political order. [59]

[1.85]   Currently, Russian society is still rooted in concepts soaked with traditionalist, mystical, and conservative elements, and pays special attention to communitarian solidarity and sense of identity. The Russians wish to appear as an inseparable societal block motivated by a common purpose and a shared love for the motherland. In this sense, Russian thinkers perceive postmodernist social diversity and multiculturalism more as a threat and challenge rather than an opportunity and a resource. Today, Russian internal factors strongly support the Eurasianist direction as the dominant political doctrine, which eventually defines Russian foreign policy. Since 2008, Russia has become significantly influenced by a neo-imperialist vision of itself based on the values of conservatism, statism, and alter-globalism. Conservatism is used as an ideological justification to support Russian interests in the post-Soviet area or to challenge the existing unipolar world order. The Eurasianist component of Russian conservative thought is expressed very clearly in the importance given to political geography. Political geographic theory would still have a role to play and a strong relation would exist between landscape and political expressions that figure upon it.[60] Rejecting Western liberalism and Slavic nationalism, Putin's regime strengthened its orientation towards neo-Eurasianism, emphasizing the special path of Russian-Eurasian civilization. Russian conservatism and Russian Eurasianism are therefore somewhat synonyms and pivot on the basic following elements: authority of central power, Russian imperial identity, Russia's interest in Eurasian regions, support for the multipolar world, and consolidation of traditional values in opposition to Western cosmopolitism.

NOTES   [1.86]

1. John Gerring, "Ideology: A Definitional Analysis." *Political Research Quarterly* 50, no. 4 (1997): 957–59, doi:10.2307/448995. [1n1]

2. See Michael Freeden, *Ideologies and Political Theory: A Conceptual Approach* (Oxford: Clarendon Press, 2008); John J. Schwarzmantel, *Ideology and Politics* (Los Angeles: SAGE, 2008); Lyman T. Sargent, *Contemporary Political Ideologies: A Comparative Analysis* (Belmont, CA: Wadsworth, 2009); Manfred B. Steger, *Globalisms: The Great Ideological Struggle of the Twenty-first Century* (Lanham, MD: Rowman & Littlefield, 2009). [1n2]

3. Manfred B. Steger and Erin K. Wilson, "Anti-Globalization or Alter-Globalization? Mapping the Political Ideology of the Global Justice Movement," *International Studies Quarterly* 56, no. 3 (2012): 440, doi:10.1111/j.1468-2478.2012.00740.x. [1n3]

4. See Slavoj Žižek, *Mapping Ideology* (London: Verso, 1994); Terence Ball, Richard Dagger, and Daniel I. O'Neill, *Political Ideologies and the Democratic Ideal* (New York: Routledge, 2019). [1n4]

5. Antoine Louis Claude Destutt De Tracy, *Mémoire Sur La Faculté De Penser. De La Métaphysique De Kant Et Autres Textes* (Paris: Fayard, 1993); Antoine Louis Claude Destutt De Tracy, *Projet D'éléments D'idéologie* (Paris: L'Harmattan, 2005). [1n5]

6. Harald Bluhm, *Karl Marx, Friedrich Engels: Die Deutsche Ideologie* (Berlin: Akademie Verl., 2010). [1n6]

7. Vilfredo Pareto and Georges Henri Bousquet, *Les Systèmes Socialistes* (Paris: Giard, 1926); Vilfredo Pareto, *Trattato Di Sociologia Generale* (Torino: Unione Tipografico-Editrice Torinese, 1988). [1n7]

8. Karl Mannheim and Gernot Kaube, *Ideologie Und Utopie* (Frankfurt Am Main: Klostermann, 2015). [1n8]

9. Karl Jaspers, *Die Geistige Situation Der Zeit* (Berlin: De Gruyter, 1933). [1n9]

10. Theodor W. Adorno et al., *The Authoritarian Personality* (New York: Harper, 1950), 2. [1n10]

11. Karl Loewenstein, "The role of ideologies in political change." *International Social Science Bulletin* 5, no. 1 (1953): 52. [1n11]

12. Herbert Mcclosky, "Consensus and Ideology in American Politics," *American Political Science Review* 58, no. 2 (1964): 362, doi:10.2307/1952868. [1n12]

13. Giovanni Sartori, "Politics, Ideology, and Belief Systems," *American Political Science Review* 63, no. 2 (1969): 402, doi:10.2307/1954696. [1n13]

14. Willard A. Mullins, "Sartori's Concept of Ideology: A Dissent and an Alternative," in *Public Opinion and Political Attitudes*, ed. Allen R. Wilcox (New York: Wiley, 1974), 235. [1n14]

[1n15]   15. Martin Seliger, *Ideology and Politics* (London: Allen & Unwin, 1976), 11.
[1n16]   16. Malcolm B. Hamilton, "The Elements of the Concept of Ideology," *Political Studies* 35, no. 1 (1987): 39, doi:10.1111/j.1467-9248.1987.tb00186.x.
[1n17]   17. Samuel P. Huntington, "Conservatism as an Ideology," *American Political Science Review* 51, no. 2 (1957): 454, doi:10.2307/1952202.
[1n18]   18. Michael Freeden, "Ideology and Political Theory," *Journal of Political Ideologies* 11, no. 1 (2006): 13–14, doi:10.1080/13569310500395834.
[1n19]   19. Ibid, 14.
[1n20]   20. Ibid.
[1n21]   21. Gerring, "Ideology," 966–79.
[1n22]   22. Steger and Wilson, "Anti-Globalization or Alter-Globalization?," 440.
[1n23]   23. Benjamin Martill, "International Ideologies: Paradigms of Ideological Analysis and World Politics," *Journal of Political Ideologies* 22, no. 3 (2017): 236, doi:10.1080/13569317.2017.1345139.
[1n24]   24. Ibid.
[1n25]   25. Brian Rathbun, "Politics and Paradigm Preferences: The Implicit Ideology of International Relations Scholars," *International Studies Quarterly* 56, no. 3 (2012): 607–22, doi:10.1111/j.1468-2478.2012.00749.x.
[1n26]   26. Ibid, 610–14.
[1n27]   27. Ernesto Laclau, "The Death and Resurrection of the Theory of Ideology," *Mln* 112, no. 3 (1997): 319–20, doi:10.1353/mln.1997.0038.
[1n28]   28. Sartori, "Politics, Ideology, and Belief Systems," 398–99
[1n29]   29. Karl Popper, *The Open Society and Its Enemies* (London: Routledge, 1966), 216–23.
[1n30]   30. Patrick Corbett, *Ideologies* (London: Hutchinson, 1963), 139–40.
[1n31]   31. Huntington, "Conservatism as an Ideology," 454–55.
[1n32]   32. Ibid, 454.
[1n33]   33. Ibid, 473.
[1n34]   34. Ibid, 456–57.
[1n35]   35. Ibid, 457.
[1n36]   36. Ibid.
[1n37]   37. bid, 460.
[1n38]   38. Michael Oakeshott, *Rationalism in Politics and Other Essays* (Carmel, IN: Liberty Fund, 1991).
[1n39]   39. Friedrich Hayek, "Why I Am Not a Conservative," in *The Essence of Hayek*, eds. Chiaki Nishiyama, Kurt R. Leube, and W. Glenn Campbell (Stanford: Hoover Institution Press, 1984), 281–98.
[1n40]   40. Although Eurasianism is not an ideology merely spread in Russian and former Soviet countries, since subcurrents of it exist in Turkey, Iran, Serbia, Eastern Europe, and even estern Europe.
[1n41]   41. Real socialism refers to socialism as was de facto implemented in the Eastern bloc and to distinguish it from the traditional notion of ideal socialism.
[1n42]   42. Axel Kaehne, *Political and Social Thought in Post-communist Russia* (London: Routledge, 2009).
[1n43]   43. Yuri Pivovarov and Andrei Fursov, "'The Russian System:' An Attempt to Understand Russian History," *Social Sciences* 33, no. 4 (2002).
[1n44]   44. Aleksandr S. Akhiezer and Viktor V. Il'in, *Rossiiskaya Gosudarstvennost': Istoki, Traditsii, Perspektivy.* (Moscow: Moskovskii gosudartvennyi universitet, 1997).
[1n45]   45. Andrei P. Tsygankov and Pavel A. Tsygankov, "National Ideology and IR Theory: Three Incarnations of the 'Russian Idea'." *European Journal of International Relations* 16, no. 4 (2010).
[1n46]   46. Ibid, 26.
[1n47]   47. Vladimir M. Kulagin, "Mir v XXI veke: Mnogopolyusnyi Balans Sil ili Global'nyi Pax Democratica?," in *Vneshnyaya Politika i Bezopasnost' Sovremennoi Rossiyi, 1991–2002*, ed. Tatyana A. Shakleyina (Moscow: Rosspen, 2002); Vladimir M. Kulagin, "Netlennost' Avtoritarnosti?," *Mezhdunarodnyye Protsessy* 6, no. 1 (January–April 2008).

48. Lilia F. Shevtsova, "Presentation," in *Rossiya i Zapad* (Foundation "Liberl'naya mis- [1n48]
siya," 2003).
49. Victor Kremenyuk, "Rossiya Vne Mirovogo Soobschestva," *Mezhdunarodnyye Prot-* [1n49]
sessy 4, no. 3 (June 2007).
50. Oleg N. Barabanov, "Global'noye Upravleniye i Global'noye Sotrudnichestvok," in [1n50]
Globalizatsiya: Chelovecheskoye Izmereniye, eds. Anatoly V. Torkunov, Andrey Yu. Melville,
and Mikhail M. Narinsky (Moscow: MGIMO, Rosspen, 2002); Oleg N. Barabanov, "Suverennyye Gosudarstva i Global'noye Upravleniye," in *"Privatizatsiya" Mirovoi Politiki: Lok-*
al'nyye Deystviya—Global'nyye Rezul'taty, ed. Marina M. Lebedeva (Moscow: MGIMO,
2008); Marina M. Lebedeva, "Politicheskaya Sistema Mira: Proyavleniya 'Vnesistemnosti'," in
"Privatizatsiya" Mirovoi Politiki: Lokal'nyye Deystviya—Global'nyye Rezul'taty, ed. Marina
M. Lebedeva (Moscow: MGIMO, 2008).
51. Dmitry V. Trenin, *The End of Eurasia: Russia on the Border between Geopolitics and* [1n51]
Globalization (Washington: Carnegie Endowment for International Peace, 2003).
52. Andrei V. Kozyrev, *Preobrazheniye* (Moscow: Mezhdunarodnyye Otsosheniya, [1n52]
1995).se
53. Aleksei D. Bogaturov, "Pluralisticheskaya Odnopolyarnost' i Interesy Rossiyi," *Svobod-* [1n53]
naya Mysl' 2 (1996); Aleksei D. Bogaturov, "Amerika i Rossiya: Ot Izbiratel'nogo Partnerstva
k Izbiratel'nomu Soprotivleniyu," *Mezhdunarodnaya Zhizn'* 6 (1998); Aleksei D. Bogaturov,
"Sovremennyi Mezhdunarodnyi Poryadok," *Mezhdunarodnyye Protsessy* 1 (June 2007).
54. Yevgeny M. Primakov, "Mezhdunarodniye Otnosheniya Nakanune XXI Veka: Proble- [1n54]
my, Perspektivy," *Mezhdunarodnaya Zhizn'* 10 (1996); Yevgeny M. Primakov, "Rossiya v
Mirovoi Politike," *Mezhdunarodnaya Zhizn'* 5 (1998).
55. Nikolai A. Nartov, *Geopolitika* (Moscow: UNITI, 1999); Gennady A. Zyuganov, *Geo-* [1n55]
grafiya Pobedy (Moscow: Mir, 1997); Gennady A. Zyuganov, *Globalizatsiya i Sud'ba Chelov-*
echestva (Moscow: Molodaya Gvardiya, 2002).
56. Gleb Pavlovski, "Rossiya Vsye Yeschye Ischet Svoyi Rol' v Mire," *Nezavisimaya Gaze-* [1n56]
ta (May 2004).
57. Tsygankov and Tsygankov, "National Ideology and IR theory," 8. [1n57]
58. Mark Bassin and Konstantin E. Aksenov, "Mackinder and the Heartland Theory in Post- [1n58]
Soviet Geopolitical Discourse," *Geopolitics* 11, no. 1 (2006).
59. Tsygankov and Tsygankov, "National Ideology and IR theory," 17. [1n59]
60. Andrew Kirby, "Pseudo-random Thoughts on Space, Scale and Ideology in Political [1n60]
Geography," *Political Geography Quarterly* 4, no. 1 (1985): 15, doi:10.1016/0260-
9827(85)90024-2.

Chapter Two

From Early Eurasianism to Neo-Eurasianism

A Historical and Philosophical Overlook

[2.0]   INTRODUCTION

[2.1]   Research aiming at examining the Eurasianist political theory should benefit from the main available sources concerning what has been developed over time—both theoretically and empirically—on the topic. These sources can be divided into two main groups: literature related to classical Eurasianism, with the works of the early founding fathers of Eurasianism and literature concerning the birth and development of the so-called neo-Eurasianist thought. Moreover, since Eurasianism embodies the result of disciplines altogether miscellaneous, it also requires the analysis of several sources belonging to different fields, specifically philosophy, anthropology, economics, history, and geopolitics. Therefore, a literature review on Eurasianism follows a specific historical excursus and chronological evolution that begins with the Bolshevik October Revolution of 1917 and culminates in today's expressions of an awakened Russian geopolitical consciousness, which somewhat leans towards Eurasianism.

[2.2]   Eurasiansim as a philosophical movement and political program possesses a worldwide scope. It is not just a mere Russian phenomenon, but different variants of it can be found in other countries of the Eurasian continent, chiefly in Kazakhstan and Turkey, as well as in Europe. Nonetheless, the following overview will focus primarily on the Russian strand of Eurasianism, leaving out its other general interpretations and expressions. Its purpose is to define and limit the theoretical framework implied in the study of

Russian Eurasianism, to place its analysis in a specific historical perspective—the demise of the czarist empire before and the collapse of the Soviet Union and birth of the contemporary Russian Federation later—, and to describe the main impulses and contexts that made the movement arise and develop.

EARLY EURASIANISM (1920–1930)   [2.3]

The Eurasianist movement (*Yevraziskoye dvizheniye*) first appeared in the   [2.4]
European intellectual context as an ideological and philosophical theory in the early 1920s. This movement was shaped by a group of intellectuals who belonged to the community of Russian émigrés that fled the Russian Empire after the advent of the Bolshevik October Revolution, the execution of the Romanov imperial family, and the outbreak of the Civil War (1917–1922). In this respect, Eurasianism represents a philosophy of exile that emerged among nostalgic members of the intelligentsia who found it difficult to abandon their homeland and dwell in foreign countries. At the same time, Eurasianism has been conceived and nourished in a specifically European context, following the methodological patterns of European political philosophy: thus, it is not surprising if Eurasianism—conceived as a philosophical current—repeats the same hermeneutical patterns of other European philosophical doctrines.

Since the very beginning, Eurasianist thought has been strongly influ-   [2.5]
enced by several cultural and political movements that appeared in Europe in the 19th century, including Slavophilism, pan-Slavism, and Orientalism. The Slavophiles, including Aleksey S. Khomyakov (1804–1860), Konstantin S. Aksakov (1817–1860), and Ivan V. Kireyevsky (1806–1856), believed in the uniqueness and originality of Russian civilization, which comprised two fundamental elements: the Slavic race and the Christian Orthodox faith. They believed that Russian culture should stay pure and strived for defending and preserving its typical traits against Westernization—which in the Russian Empire began after Peter the Great's "enlightened" reforms—and liberal modernism. They proclaimed the value of tradition, praised the greatness of the Russian imperial experience and alleged that the introduction of Western models could lead Russian society to a rapid decay.[1] Pan-Slavism was a political movement and ideology that, similarly to pan-Germanism, advocated for the political union of all Slavic peoples into a single country.[2] Finally, Orientalism appeared as an academic discipline that included the study of the art, history, linguistics, geography, and ethnography of the Eastern cultures of the Middle East, North Africa, Southern Asia, and Eastern Asia from a European methodological perspective.

[2.6]   One of the distinguishing traits of early Eurasianism was the idea that the Russian culture represented a peculiar civilizational combination, with elements deriving both from Western and Eastern traditions. Still, though belonging at the same time to the West and to the East, it did not reduce itself entirely to one or to the other: instead, Russia had developed through history an original synthesis of both. The Russian people were to be considered neither European nor Asiatic, but rather as belonging to an original Eurasian ethnic community, which had inevitably defined the specific historical evolution of the Russian state as well as its national interest and geopolitical constants.[3]

[2.7]   Eurasianists bore a millenarist and eschatological worldview that led them to give a mystical understanding of the revolutionary events of 1917. The Russian Revolution was conceived as an event of religious nature, which—thanks to the awakening and upheaval of the Asian masses of the Russian people—succeeded in destroying the old bourgeois world imported by Western civilization, unleashing the pursuit of new forms of social, cultural, and political organization. Interestingly, Eurasianists bore a twofold view of the Revolution: on the one hand, they condemned Bolshevik materialistic progressivism and the set of Marxist doctrines, but on the other, they were pleased to see the collapse of the "Westerner" Romanov rule.

[2.8]   Deeply influenced by idealism, Eurasianists held a romantic vision of the history of Eurasia. The Eurasian continental landmass was perceived as the cradle from which the glorious empires of humankind had appeared: the Macedonian Empire, the Roman Empire, the Mongol Empire, and so on. From this perspective, they perceived Russia both as the continuer of the Roman-Byzantine empire thanks to the legacy of Moscow as Third Rome after the demise of Constantinople (1453), and as the heir to Genghis Khan's Mongol empire, from which the Khanate of the Golden Horde had emerged.

[2.9]   The Russian cultured exile community was represented by intellectuals who belonged to diverse political spectrums—except for communism—that included exponents of monarchism, conservatism, liberalism, socialism, and even anarchism. This was just one of the several paradoxes that early Eurasianism featured. The Eurasianist doctrine officially presented itself as a "third-way" ideology that strongly rejected both communism and Western liberalism, but that showed likewise some hesitancy in adhering to fascism, monarchism or socialism, often combining some elements that were common to all.

[2.10]   Early Eurasianism was strongly influenced by the Russian idea of "otherness" in relation to the West. In this respect, the Romanov era was interpreted by Eurasianists as a period of forced Westernization of the Russian civilization especially due to the liberal reforms of Peter I the Great and Catherine II the Great. Eurasianists upheld the geographic ideology that considered Russia as a "third continent"[4] between Europe and Asia, neither

European nor Asian, but rather as a specific and complex reality with its own specificities. Millenarism, Asianism, pan-Mongolism, Scythism, as well as the brutal violence of the October Revolution and of the following five-year Civil War between Whites and Bolsheviks, contributed to creating the typical early Eurasianist *Weltanschauung*, often based on reductivist and Manichaen paradigms, upholding the idea of a deadly fight between the forces of Good and that of Evil.

The classic Eurasianist movement brought together elevated intellectuals [2.11] with different cultural backgrounds: there were geographers, linguists, philologists, historians, theologians, economists, ethnographers, orientalists, and so on. The disciplines these literati focused on were used as tools for the formation of a Eurasian comprehensive knowledge that included the description of languages, peoples, history, and religions of this vast area. Geographers, ethnographers, historians and anthropologists described the Eurasian big spaces, the variety of the ethnicities, the historical evolution of the continent, the habits and traditions of the rich ethnic mosaic. At the same time, linguists, philologists, and Orientalists began to study and classify the various Eurasian languages and their palaeogenesis, whereas theologians focused on the study of the religions of Eurasia, from Shamanism and Tengrism through to Buddhism and Islam.

The founding fathers of the Eurasianist movement were all dissidents [2.12] who opposed the demise of the Russian Empire and the advent of communist rule. Overall, their philosophical inclinations led them to sympathize during the Civil War for the White faction and for its generals: Aleksandr V. Kolchak, Nikolai N. Yudenich, Lavr G. Kornilov, Anton I. Denikin, Baron Pyotr N. Wrangel, Grigory M. Semyonov, and Baron Roman F. von Ungern-Sternberg.

The most influential intellectuals who contributed to developing the complex and variegated Eurasianist theory were the philologist and linguist Nikolai S. Trubetskoy (1890–1938), the geographer and economist Pëtr N. Savitsky (1895–1965), the music composer Pëtr P. Suvchinsky (1882–1985), the historian and theologian Georges V. Florovsky (1893–1979), the philosopher Lev P. Karsavin (1882–1952), the historian and geopolitician George V. Vernadsky (1877–1973), the jurist and philosopher Nikolai N. Alekseyev (1879–1964), the historian and theologian Ivan A. Il'in (1883–1954), the linguist Roman Jacobson (1896–1982), the jurist Mstislav V. Shakhmatov (1888–1943), the essayist and historian of literature Dmitry P. Sviatopolk-Mirsky (1890–1939), the orientalist and diplomat Vassily P. Nikitin (1885–1960), the Jewish philosopher Yakov A. Bromberg (1898–1948), and the Kalmyk historian Ėrenzhen Khara-Davan (1883–1941).

The first Eurasianist collection of articles was published in Bulgaria (Sofia) in 1921 under the name *Iskhod k Vostoku* ("Exodus to the East") and it was envisioned as a manifesto for the beginning of a new era of thought that could reshape the nature of Russian identity and discuss the future of Soviet Russia. At that time, Eurasianism appeared as a modernist and avant-gardist movement: the Eurasianists were considered as a new generation of Slavophiles who had embraced the era of futurism.

[2.15]   During the 1920s, the movement held seminars, lectures and conferences in various European capitals including Paris, Brussels, Prague, and Belgrade. It also managed to publish the weekly newspaper "Chronicle" and the literary journal *Versty*. Many Eurasianist intellectuals also contributed to writing the pamphlet *Put'* ("Path"), a literary organ of Russian religious Orthodox thought.

[2.16]   The literary scholar Sviatopolk-Mirsky played a large part in spreading the knowledge of Eurasianist thought among exponents of Russian émigré literature groups. After his expatriation to Great Britain (1921) and the beginning of his lectures on Russian literature at the University of London, Sviatopolk-Mirsky helped the Eurasianist movement to publish its works in journals and periodicals.

[2.17]   The 1920s can be considered the years of major development of classic Eurasianist thought. In these years, several publications appeared among which the first series of collected articles under the name *Yevraziyskiy Vremennik* ("Eurasianist Annals"), several pamphlets gathered in the *Yevraziyskaya Khronika* ("Eurasianist Chronicle")—distributed from 1925 to 1937—and the single essays written by the leaders of the Eurasianist movement concerning various topics on Eurasia. All publications focused on issues related to politics, history, religion, ethnography and Oriental studies.

[2.18]   Prince Trubetskoy was amongst the main contributors to the formation of the Eurasianist movement. A highly cultured linguist and historian, his teachings formed the nucleus of the Prague School of structural linguistics. He began his academic career delivering lectures at the Moscow University. When the Revolution broke out, he moved first to the University of Rostov-on-Don, then to the University of Sofia, and finally took the chair of Professor of Slavic Philology at the University of Vienna. Among his main works are *Yevraziystvo i Beloye Dvizheniye* ("Eurasianism and the White Movement") (1919), *Yevropa i Chelovechestvo* ("Europe and Humankind") (1920), *Russkaya Problema* ("The Russian Question") (1922), *Naslediye Chingiskhana. Vzglyad na Russkuyu Istoriyu ne s Zapada, a s Vostoka* ("The Legacy of Genghis Khan. A look at Russian History not from the West, but from the East") (1925), *K Probleme Russkogo Samopoznaniya* ("On the problem of Russian self-consciousness") (1927), and *Istoriya, Kul'tura, Yazyk* ("History, Culture, Language") (1995). He also contributed in publishing several articles in the aforementioned collection *Iskhod k Vostoku*.

[2.19]   Trubetskoy considered the Slavs as an independent component of the Western world, differing from both the Romance and the Germanic folks. Within the Slavic group, he asserted that the Russians belonged both to

Slavdom and to the realm of the steppes, being culturally and historically linked to the Turanian world despite their Slavic language and Orthodox religion. In the vast extensions of the Russian Empire, the Slavic and the Turanian elements were equally represented and enjoyed equivalent importance. Trubetskoy considered genetic or racial kinship less relevant for national identity building than language, and this would be one of the reasons why he would be persecuted by the Nazi regime in Austria. By affirming that cultural and linguistic affiliation could shape a group more distinctively than other variables, he believed that Russia's topogenesis was entirely attributable to a Eurasian identity.

Trubetskoy thoroughly analyzed the Turanian civilization in the attempt of demonstrating the intimate historical correlation with the Russian-Slavic one.[5] He believed to have found some solid interrelations between the languages, cultures, and sociopolitical behavior of Eurasian peoples. The Turanian languages—i.e. the languages spoken by the five ethno-linguistic groups of the Ugrics, Samoyeds, Turkics, Mongols, and Manchus—explain the essence of Turko-Mongolic societies and their intimate identity, or what he referred to as the Turanian "subconscious philosophical system."[6]   [2.20]

Trubetskoy believed that the substantial qualities of the Turanians justified a natural inclination for an ideocratic and autocratic regime. As the natural continuer of the Mongol Empire, Russia had inherited this inclination and the Europeanization of Russian society under the Romanov dynasty—particularly under the rule of Peter I and Catherine II—had weakened this natural predisposition. Trubetskoy also stated the relevance of the unity of Eurasia, resulting from a vertical relationship of each component to the whole.[7] The borders between the Russian-Eurasian civilization and the Asian cultures were imperceptible since a geographical continuity characterized the vast lands of the Eurasian supercontinent.[8]   [2.21]

In "Europe and Mankind," Trubetskoy denied the universality of the Western European model, denouncing European colonialism and its imperialistic socio-economic paradigm. The realization of Russia's Easterness was a logical consequence of the rejection of the Western liberal-democratic model. Trubetskoy committed himself to rehabilitating the Turanic element of Russian history, refuting the Eurocentric historiographical vision of Russia's history as the result of the sole Kievan, Muscovite and Romanov eras. Accordingly, Trubetskoy exalted those historical epochs of Russian history dominated by the Turanian element, like the period of the Mongol domination over a great portion of Russian lands (13th–16th centuries). Unlike the Western Slavic nations, he believed that the Russian national type was essentially Slavic-Turanian rather than simply Slavic.[9]   [2.22]

The Eurasian history was the result of a composition of two elements: the Russian-Slavic one and the Turanian-Mongolic. The cohabitation and common sharing of historical destiny between Slavs and Turanians constituted   [2.23] the pivot component of Russian history.[10] Trubetskoy also highlighted the relevance of the Mongol Empire forged by Genghis Khan and his successors, which offered Russia its hidden identity, a Eurasian common geographical distinctiveness, and a common rule over Eurasian lands. Through the imperial ideology inherited by the Mongols, Russia received its justification for empire-building and its geopolitical vocation as a telluric power.

[2.24]   Trubetskoy deepened the issue of the relevance of spirituality for the Eurasianist movement and its relations with the Eurasian religions.[11] The Orthodox variety of Christianity was viewed by Eurasianists as the main spiritual reference point. At the same time, other Asian religions were seen with skepticism: Confucianism was considered too pragmatic and rational; Islam professed by Central Asian Turkic peoples was blamed for having disfigured the ancient religions of the Turans, which focused on the cults of Shamanism and Tengrism; Buddhism was perceived as too passive because of its implicit opposition to reality and renunciation of the world; and Hinduism was criticized because of its justification for the creation of a fixed, unchanging, and static society based on the caste system.

[2.25]   Pëtr N. Savitsky was a geographer, economist, philosopher, and poet. He expressed his contributions to the Eurasianist movement in the works *Rossiya i Latinstvo* ("Russia and Latindom") (1923), *O Zadachakh Kochevnikoveden'ya: Pochemu Skify i Gunny Dolzhny Byt' Interesny dlya Russkogo?* ("On the Problems of Nomadism: Why Scythians and Huns should be of interest to a Russian?") (1928), *V Bor'be za Yevraziystvo* ("In Struggle for Eurasianism") (1931), *Kontinent Yevraziya* ("Continent Eurasia") (1997).

[2.26]   Savitsky's involvement in the Eurasian movement is specifically linked to the development of the so-called theory of topogenesis.[12] This theory—heavily influenced by geographical determinism—conjectures the existence of a mystical link between territories and cultures. The geographical environment is one of the chief factors for the rise of specific civilizations, significantly influencing their cultural and historical developmental path. History and territory are interconnected and the historical outcome of populations rests on the geographical variables of the land they inhabit: climate, soil, orography, flora, fauna, weather, waterways, etc. Geography is thus a living organism that interacts entirely with the peoples that it hosts, determining their specific characteristics. A stout interaction exists between natural and socio-historical environment: the two spheres are not separated but interact and communicate with each other.

[2.27]   Savitsky contributed to the development of the discipline of geosophy, namely that branch of geography that analyzes territory not only as an ordinary object related to natural sciences but as a valuable part of human history, culture, and national identity. According to geosophy, territories possess a metaphysical and philosophical value, and soils can explain the hidden meanings of civilizational events. Under this perspective, Savitsky believed that the territory of the Eurasian landmass justified its natural unification. Eurasia possessed a geometric and systemic nature from one area to another and this natural homogeneity implied its political unification. In other words, Eurasia could benefit from "natural borders," which supposedly extended from the Atlantic Ocean to the Pacific shores. Savitsky alleged to have discovered some structural geographical criteria that revealed the fleshly existence of Eurasia and that implied the need for the political unification of the continent, which appeared as a logical and natural point of arrival of a long-term historical process. Savitsky's thesis therefore opposed the conventional delimitation of the borders between Europe and Asia given by the Ural Mountains.

In Savitsky's analysis, four horizontal strips divided Eurasia from North to South, offering a clear definition of it: the tundra, the taiga, the steppe, and the desert. Three major plains transversely intersected these strips: the plain between the White Sea and the Caucasus; the Siberian plain; and the plain of Turkistan. The steppe strip can be considered as Russia's geopolitical core; throughout history, it served the purpose of permitting the Russian penetration and colonization of Eurasia, playing a similar role to the one the ocean-ways had for the Western-Eureopan thalassocratic powers in pursuing the conquest of the Indies and the Americas. Sir Halford J. Mackinder gave a similar interpretation to Russian eastward penetration, comparing it with the European geographic discoveries of the 15th–16th centuries.[13] Thanks primarily to the role of the Cossacks as Siberian pioneers and settlers, the Russian rule over the vast landmass that extends from the Baltic Sea to the Pacific Ocean made the project of the potential unification of Eurasia realistic. The steppes granted to Russia many aspects of its specific identity: a continentalist inclination (tellurocratic mind), the idea of an extensive space to subdue, the predisposition towards economic autarky, a stark mentality projected towards political isolationism, and geographical control of the pivotal Heartland. History and geography explained to Russia that who controls the steppes can potentially become the political unifier of Eurasia. Russia's territorial expansion is thus the natural expression of its identity and of its intrinsic imperial structure. Savitsky claimed that the Russian-Eurasian system represented a closed circle, a perfect continent, and a world unto itself. This unique continent could not accept any form of separatism, being per se unnatural. Moreover, he believed that Eurasianism and geopolitics were inherently and self-evidently associated, and that geography should serve the purposes of justifying political power and legitimizing the forge of empires. Due to its Eurasian oriental connections, Russia possessed natural claims towards Asia: the Eurasian culture justified Russian expansion in the Far East and towards the Pacific Ocean.

Savitsky also stressed the cultural and geographical closeness of Eurasian peoples, highlighting how the Russian ethnographic character was a mix of

[2.28]

[2.29]

Slavic, Ugro-Finnic, and Tatar-Mongolic phenotypes. He also noticed that the peoples of Eurasia shared some common tendencies, not just in the sphere of linguistics.[14] Furthermore, he stated that "all Slavic, Romance, Hindu, Finno-Ugric, Turkic, Mongolian and North Caucasian languages that are found inside Eurasia [. . .] are languages with common tendencies, despite their different origins."[15]

[2.30]   Like other Eurasianists, Savitsky admired the Mongol period of Russian history, considering it as the founding moment of the expression of the uniqueness of Russian cultural identity. He also believed that under the rule of the Tatars, Russian spiritual life could shape its real identity and framework.[16] Since the time of the Mongol dominion, the Russian state gained legitimacy through religion and absorbed Mongolic principles of statehood, combining them with its own Byzantine theological and political traditions. Apparently, the Orthodox church did not suffer under the Mongol yoke, since the Mongol leadership appeared to be tolerant and enlightened.

[2.31]   Roman Jakobson, a friend and colleague of Prince Trubetskoy, was a structural linguist too. In his works related to Eurasianism such as *K Charakteristike Yevraziyskogo Yazykovogo Soyuza* ("For the Characteristics of the Eurasian Union of Languages") (1930) he aimed at demonstrating the unity of Eurasian languages. When considering a linguistic family, Jakobson measured the important variables of tone, correlation of palatalization, and territorial continuity. Though belonging to different linguistic families (Indo-European, Ural-Altaic, Caucasian, etc.), he believed that Eurasian languages shared a common way of interpreting the surrounding geographical environment. Jakobson claimed that in the study of linguistic families the principle of place-development prevailed over the principle of filogenetic closeness. His teleological methodological approach to linguistics focused on the common goal languages aimed at rather than on the analysis of their paleogenesis: in this sense, Eurasian languages all headed towards a common direction, despite their diverse affiliation.

[2.32]   George V. Vernadsky was a Russian-born American historian who wrote numerous books on Russian history. Amongst his main historical publications are *Nachertaniye Russkoy Istorii* ("Inscription of Russian History") (1927), *Opyt Istorii Yevrazii* ("Experience of the History of Eurasia") (1934), *Drevnyaya Rus'* ("Ancient Russia") (1997), *Mongoly i Rus'* ("The Mongols and Russia") (1997), *Rossiya v Sredniye Veka* ("Russia in the Middle Ages") (1997), *Russkaya Istoriografiya* ("Russian Historiography") (1998). His views highlighted the importance of Eurasian nomadic cultures for the cultural and economic progress of Russia, thus anticipating some of the ideas advanced later by Lev Gumilëv. He also introduced the significant concept of "noosphere," which depicts the interaction between humanity and the biosphere. Vernadsky's definition of noosphere would have been borrowed by Gumilëv, who considered the biosphere an interaction between animate and inanimate matter. Gumilëv would later accept the idea implicitly exposed in Vernadsky's theses that the biosphere was currently entering the new geological era of the noosphere, which was characterized by the power of human intellect.

Paying great attention to Eurasian historical evolution, Vernadsky believed that the demise of the Turko-Mongol world soon after Tamerlane's death led to Russia's appropriation of the leadership in the Eurasian continent.[17]   [2.33]

Vernadsky also believed that geographical features had deeply influenced Russia's historical evolution: in Russia, history rested on geography. Russian awareness of time followed the immensities of its territory, and therefore chronological phases passed in a much slower way than in the West. Articulated by the slow rhythms of the seasons and by the harshness of climate, the perception of time in Eurasia followed a typically Oriental circular pattern rather than a linear one. Since in Eurasia time and space are so deeply interrelated that events take a longer time to unfold than in other continents, Vernadsky perceived Eurasia as a self-existing universe with proper distances, spaces, and units of measure.   [2.34]

Ėrenzhen Khara-Davan was a publicist and historian of Kalmyk nationality who broke drastically with Eurocentrism and addressed great importance to the cultures of the peoples of the Orient and especially to the nomadic cultures. His main work, a stunning report on Genghis Khan and the Mongol Empire, was published in Serbian under the name *Čingis-kan kak Polkovodec i Ego Nasledne* ("Genghis Khan as Commander and His Legacy") (1929). Khara-Davan stressed the importance of a nomadic way of life against a sedentary one. In his cult of nomadism, he condemned the sedentary and urban way of life, considering it as corrupted and insalubrious.[18] At the same time, he exalted the nomadic life, praising its healthy standards and vigorous values, as well as its strong relation with nature and its interaction with the surrounding environment.[19] Khara-Davan stressed that the Mongol Empire bore a universal character, later inherited by Russia, of both Western and Eastern nature, being the arbiter and mediator between the Indo-Chinese and the Mediterranean worlds, therefore giving unity to the Eurasian landmass. Finally, Khara-Davan saw in the birth of Muscovy the direct descendant of the Mongol Empire.[20]   [2.35]

The consolidation of the communist power in Russia and the birth of the Soviet Union in 1922 promoted the division of the Eurasianist movement into two parts: a faction based in Prague was hostile to the USSR, whereas another in Paris—the so-called "Clamart current"—was closer to the Soviet regime and published the Marxist weekly *Yevraziya* ("Eurasia"). This magazine condemned the founding fathers of Eurasianism, who were perceived as nationalistic, right-winged, and idealizers of Muscovy and Orthodoxy, claiming that Eurasianism should have perceived positively the Russian Revolu-   [2.36] tion—whose universal aim was to forge more equal societies and to recreate a natural order—and thus wished to institutionalize a Eurasianist political party modeled on the principles of Bolshevism.

[2.37]   Between 1934 and 1936, the *Yevraziyskiye Tetrad'* ("Eurasianist Notebooks") were published, although the editorial board by this time included only Savitsky and Alexseev as big names of the Eurasianist movement. Nevertheless, the Eurasianist movement was now on the defensive: the alternative ideology of fascism started to become predominant at that time in European countries. Consequently, during the 1930s Eurasianism started to decline as an intellectual and political movement, fading from the European scenario: by 1935 the movement had almost disappeared, continuing to survive only in Prague.

[2.38]   The outbreak of the Second World War symbolized the end of early Eurasianism: Marxist Eurasianists returned to the Soviet Union, Jakobson and Florovsky left Europe for the United States, Trubetskoy had died few months before the outbreak of the conflict, and Savitsky remained isolated in Central Europe. The consolidation in Europe and Russia of the two mainstream ideologies of fascism and communism resulted in a complete marginalization of the Eurasianist doctrine, ultimately overwhelmed and forgotten.

[2.39]   LEV NIKOLAYEVICH GUMILËV

[2.40]   Lev Nikolayevich Gumilëv (1912–1992) was an ethnographer, historian, and philosopher who personified a link between early Eurasianist thought and neo-Eurasianism. Son of the Russian poet Nikolay Gumilëv and of the poetess Anna Akhmatova, his main contributions to the Eurasianist philosophy resulted in the theory of ethnogenesis, in the theory of "passionarity," in the development of a Turkophile attitude, in the theory of "ethnic complementarity," and in the detailed study of proto-history and history of nomadic empires founded by Turkic-Mongol peoples in Eurasia. His main works on the history of the Turanian peoples and of the pre-Mongolic Turkic world formed the trilogy *Khunny: Sredinnaya Aziya v Drevniye Vremena* ("The Huns: Central Asia in Ancient Times") (1960), *Drevniye Tyurki* ("Ancient Turks") (1967) and *Khunny v Kitaye: Tri Veka Voyny Kitaya so Stepnymi Narodami* ("The Huns in China: Three Centuries of War between China and the People of the Steppes") (1974). He also issued *Otkrytiye Khazarii* ("The Discovery of Khazaria") (1966), which represents an interesting report on the Jewish Khazar khaganate (7th–11th centuries). Another notable essay is *Tysyacheletiye vokrug Kaspiya* ("One Thousand Years around the Caspian") (1990), in which the author, retracing the history of the various populations who crossed the Russian steppes, illustrates how climate fluctuations influenced nomadic migrations around the Caspian Sea's basin. In *Poiski Vy-*

myshlennogo Tsarstva: Legenda o "Gosudarstve 'Presvitera Ioanna'" ("Searching for an Imaginary Kingdom: The Legend of the Kingdom of 'Prester John'") (1970), the author investigated the chronicle of the legendary Prester John, a mythical Christian patriarch and king who was imagined residing either in India, Central Asia, or Ethiopia. In *Drevnyaya Rus' i Velikaya step'* ("Ancient Rus' and the Great Steppe") (1989), Gumilëv reported the account of the positive and closed relations between the Russian principalities and the peoples of the steppe during the Middle Ages. In 1989, he issued a series of articles entitled *Chërnaya Legenda: Druz'ya i Nedrugi Velikoy Stepi* ("Black Legend: Friends and Enemies in the Great Steppe") in which he denounced Western histography and its critical approach towards the period of the Mongol rule over Russia. Moreover, *Ot Rusi do Rossii* ("From Rus' to Russia") (1992) represents another remarkable work in which the author depicts the interactions between Slavs and Turko-Mongols as one of the factors of major development for Russia's history and for the forging of its empire. In 1992, he published the essay *Konets i Vnov' Nachalo* ("An End and a New Beginning") and in 1993 a collection of articles under the name *Ritmy Yevrazii: Epokhi i Tsivilizatsii* ("Rhythms of Eurasia: Eras and Civilizations").

Gumilëv devoted special scientific attention to the protohistory of the "nomad empires" of the East and to the discovery of the colossal ethnic and cultural heritage of the autochthone ancient Asian peoples, developing a Turkophile attitude based on the idea of "ethnic complementarity" between Slavs and Turanians. [2.41]

The chief work in which Gumilëv expressed his theories of ethnogenesis and passionarity has been the fundamental essay *Etnogenez i Biosfera Zemli* ("Ethnogenesis and the Biosphere of the Earth") (1978), which focuses on the understanding of the birth and features of ethnic groups. [21] [2.42]

The systematic elaboration of specific models to illustrate his ethnogenetic theory made Gumilëv the founder of the new science known as ethnology. From a methodological point of view, Gumilëv's study of ethnology diverged from the Western approach, applying elements borrowed from the sphere of natural sciences—specifically biology—rather than from human sciences. According to the author, ethnology is "a science that processes the subject matter of the humanities using the methods of the natural sciences." [22] Since peoples biologically belonged to the universe and followed the same natural laws of other living beings, ethnology should have been considered through the same methodology used for natural sciences. Thus, ethnology studied the science of the behavioral impulses of ethnic groups, just like ethology focused on the behavior of animal groups. [23] [2.43]

Gumilëv conceived history and ethnography as natural sciences, being disciplined by similar rules to those that define biology and chemistry. History was conceived as auxiliary to natural sciences: the author made extensive [2.44] use of the biological lexicon to describe the history of nations. Gumilëv's principle of ethnic essences—deeply influenced by bio-chemical considerations—represented a scientific methodology that overcame the traditional classic Eurasianist geographical ideology. Whereas for classic Eurasianists territory offered meaning to national identity, Gumilëv believed instead that biological determinism was the key factor for building a local distinctiveness. Spatial proximity was in fact insufficient for symbiosis since ethnic groups represented some bio-chemically closed entities. The genetic and chemical configuration of nations was much more relevant than territory for illustrating the original relations of kinship among nations.

[2.45]   In his subdivision of reality, Gumilëv described three main realms: the geographical realm based on landscape, the ethnic realm based on peoples, and the social-political realm based on the state. The first two realms were studied by natural sciences, while the latter was linked to human sciences. Within this schema, historiography appeared as an auxiliary discipline of geography and ethnology, and human history was explainable through the evolution of the ethnosphere. Gumilëv's theory of ethnicity defined "ethnos" a general set of individuals or collectivity based on a common historical destiny: thus, an ethnos could be a population, a nation, a tribe, or a family clan. The ethnos represents a bio-social organism, with a proper existing identity and uniqueness. The distinguishing features of an ethnos are based not in the nature of the soil where it had formed, but rather in its physical, chemical, biological, and genetic characteristics. Territory is an insufficient condition for determining the emergence of an ethnos, since ethnic groups owe their characteristics to the entire cosmic system and terrestrial environment of which territory is but a minor part. Due to physical rather than geographical determinism, anthropology could be understood not in relation to its spatial environment but rather to a general planetary-cosmic whole. Thus, the "ethnoi" derive from natural phenomena and from an energetic stream stemming from chemical elements: an ethnos is not just a biological element but also a physical and chemical parcel of the planetary essence. [24] Ethnogenesis—i.e. the appearance of an ethnos—arises from an original chemical energy that transfers an uncommon strength to men, taking about sixty generations to form and express itself. Each ethnos enjoys an approximate lifespan of 1500 years. "Once it emerges, an ethnos goes through a series of predetermined stages that may be likened to the ages of human being." [25] An ethnos is to be considered as similar to any other biological entity: it comes to life, grows, mellows, declines, and finally expires. Gumilëv called these progressive stages of the phenomenology of the ethnoi as the stage of ascent, stage of acme, pivotal phase, stage of inertia, stage of eclipse, and stage of homeostasis. In the end, an ethnos either disappeared or survived as a relic. Darwinist laws were the theoretical basis of Gumilëv's theory: he believed in the idea of the struggle for the survival of the fittest ethnos. He also believed that natural collectivity was intrinsically superior to individuality and claimed that Western decline was linkable to the liberal idea of individualism that had weakened Western nations.

The ethnos is not a sum of people but rather a complex systemic totality, indivisible and above individuality.[26] In Gumilëv's theoretical framework, each ethnos is a bio-social organism that presents a hierarchical structure that divides it into several sub- and supra-entities. The smallest ethnic entity is that of the sub-ethnos, then comes the ethnos, followed by the greater super-ethnos, and finally the biggest entity is that of the meta-ethnos.   [2.46]

The key element of the theory of ethnogenesis is the concept of passionarity. The theory of passionarity (*passionarnost'*) is considered to be one of the chief expressions of Gumilëv's thought. According to this theory, each ethnos—being a natural geo-chemical foundation—is subject to the influence of some "energetic drives" born out of the cosmos which cause the so-called "passionarity effect," which represents an amplified activity and intensity of life. In such conditions, the ethnos undergoes a kind of "genetic mutation," which leads to the birth of the "passionaries," who are individuals of a special temper and talent capable of forging empires and modifying the course of history. The theory of passionarity links the existence of ethnoi as collectives of peoples with the capability of men as organisms to absorb the bio-chemical energy of the biosphere's living substance.[27] Passionarity represents the opposite of mere survival: it leads nations to their greatest achievements, glories, and actions. The beginning of ethnogenesis manifests with an eruption of passionarity, a dissipation of the energy of the living substance of the biosphere.[28] Thus, passionarity represents a physical phenomenon capable of awakening the chemical and cosmic energies which drive nations to the pursuit of glory, happiness, and victory. Historical examples of passionaries have been Alexander the Great, Joan of Arc, and Napoleon. The passionarity theory considers both passionary and sub-passionary individuals, the idea of the biological age of nations, and the notion that the biosphere is a living substance that closely interacts with historical and anthropological events. Passionarity is a genetic attribute, hereditary and irrational that appears in an unexpected manner.   [2.47]

In his pessimistic view, Gumilëv believed that mankind was hampered by two disadvantages: on one hand, the weight of responsibility given by free choice—which could bring about either the survival or the extinction of the planet—and on the other a total lack of freedom since the struggle for survival annihilated many possible alternatives. Human history knows no variants: an event leads to a direct consequence, regardless of men's minds. History is a natural process driven by forces that exist despite the people's will that objectively shapes their fates.[29]   [2.48]

Gumilëv upheld a deeply deterministic vision: for him, territory was one of the chief elements of a complex determinism which entailed climate   [2.49] change, humidity, soil fertility, and so on. In his studies concerning the ancient nomadic nations of Eurasia, he described how landscape had deeply influenced their mentality and identity. Gumilëv's historical determinism led him to consider humanity as incapable of mastering the occurring events: it was causalism that brought about history, and not chance and casuality. Gumilëv's entire historical-philosophical system was based on mechanism, determinism, rationalism, realism, and on the explicit superiority of natural-ism over humanism. Nonetheless, there was still a little space left in historiography for the existence of what may be considered as an "x factor," or an undeterminable variable, which acted like chance: this idea, however, seems to contradict the essentially deterministic statements of Gumilëv's thought.

[2.50]   Gumilëv believed that humanity was subject to the same laws of develop-ment and competitiveness as the rest of nature. Natural laws were hidden and were to be discovered in order to gain complete access to the understanding of things. Therefore, it was vital to condemn those human actions that broke the natural order of things.

[2.51]   As for the Eurasian continent, Gumilëv considered it as a continuous Great Steppe that extended from the Yellow River to the banks of the Arctic Ocean.[30] This vast Eurasian zone included the territory of the Soviet Union, Tibet, and Mongolia. Gumilëv supported the idea of unity and irreducible distinctiveness and universality of Eurasia: according to him, Russia's east-ward expansion was not a conquest but a natural phenomenon,[31] and Eur-asian secessionism appeared as fundamentally against nature.

[2.52]   For Gumilëv, eight different super-ethnoi existed in Russia: the Russian, the steppic, the circumpolar, the Tatar-Muslim, the European, the Buddhist, the Byzantine (or Caucasian Christian), and the Jewish. Russia had managed through history to unify under its imperial rule these heterogeneous nations. The history of the Russian Empire incarnated the history of the convergence of the super-ethnoi of the Russians and of the steppic nomads in the steppic territories of Eurasia. Following the patterns of early Eurasianists, Gumilëv believed that the origins of the Russian Empire were to be found in Genghis Khan's autocratic principles of statehood. In a long-term perspective, the history of Russia could not be understood without the framework of the ethnic contacts between Russians and Tatars and the general history of the Eurasian continent. Russia's historical ethnogenesis followed three important stages: that of the Kievan Rus', of the Tatar domination, and of the rise of Muscovy. Under the Romanov rule (17th–19th centuries), Russia had be-trayed its Eurasian nature, opting for a Europeization of its society due to the "Frenchization" and "Germanization" of its customs.

[2.53]   Gumilëv strongly opposed ethnic assimilation and miscegenation. His mixophobic beliefs made him state that intermixing would lead ethnoi to their destruction: the mix of genes would result in the destruction of the ethnic collectivity. On the contrary, he was an apologist of endogamy and of the preservation of the nations' original gene pools. Instead of mixing together, nations should live together in a kind of natural symbiosis, cooperating while preserving their own peculiar features.[32] An example of advantageous "ethnic complementarity" between ethnoi was that of the Slavic Russians with the Turanians. Gumilëv's strict ethnocentric mentality made him condemn in harsh terms cosmopolitanism, which he considered an expression of the Western mentality.

Despite his intellectual prominence, many criticisms have been expressed towards Gumilëv. Communists considered him an anti-Marxist, Russian nationalists claimed he was a Turkophile and a Russophobic, and Western constructivists criticized his general methodological approach. He also received critics by monarchists (czarists), pan-Slavists, and race supremacists. He was accused of geographical determinism, Darwinism, biologism, and Turkophilism. However, both anti-Atlanticist Europeans and Russian nationalists accepted Gumilëv's position concerning the rejection of Western influence in Eurasia and the idea of ethnic preservation against miscegenation.   [2.54]

Gumilëv's theories served the ideological goal of promoting the Soviet mode of ethnic coexistence and stressing the special complementarity of the Russian and Turkic super-ethnoi, in contrast with the intrinsic and ceaselessly irreconcilable opposition between Russia and the Western model.[33]   [2.55]

NEO-EURASIANISM (1990S)   [2.56]

Neo-Eurasianism can be situated in the context of the disappearance of the Soviet Union, which many believe occurred for two main reasons: treason of its inner elites and machinations of the international forces of Atlanticism. The demise of the USSR represented the negation of Russia's imperial nature and its derating into a second-grade international power. The fall of the Berlin Wall, the end of the Warsaw Pact, and the dissolution of the Soviet Union introduced the unipolar world with the United States as the only superpower left. The humiliation perceived by Russian citizens led to a renewal of those philosophical currents that auspicated a return to the past glory. In this sense, neo-Eurasianism appeared as an ideology oriented towards an imperial reconstruction with a strong anti-Western and anti-Atlanticist component. Neo-Eurasianism cannot be considered as an anti-globalization theory, but rather as an alter-globalization philosophy that wishes to offer a new paradigm based upon cultural diversity, ethnic identity and multipolarity against the globalized unilateral American-led model. Thus, neo-Eurasianism is essentially a theory of the multipolar world: according to it, the globe is divided into different civilizational big spaces and each of them is conceived as unique and worthy of being preserved and safeguarded on   [2.57] equal footing. Neo-Eurasianism borrowed the idea of the civilizational model as the key factor for interpreting the world through the assimilation of the thought of Max Weber, Arnold J. Toynbee, Oswald Spengler, and Fernand Braudel and other exponents of the French "*Annales*" school of historiography.

[2.58]   In the mid-1980s, the Soviet society began to lose a satisfactory interaction with the external environment and with itself. The Soviet model of closed self-sustainable society was starting to fall apart. Different strata of society felt a need for change, though without fully understanding how and where this change should occur. In this context, different political and philosophical forces began to appear, splitting society into several parts: the "forces of progress" faced the "forces of reaction," the "reformers" faced the "conservators of the past," and the "partisans of reforms" faced the "enemies of reforms."[34] The idea of introducing reforms was actually based on the will to import in the Soviet Union the main aspects of liberal-democratic countries. The promoters of the reformation of society implicitly admitted the superiority of the Western model and the necessity to imitate it. Therefore, those who strived for introducing reforms became the unconditional supporters of the West, capitalism, and NATO, whereas the opponents of reforms embodied those who wished to endorse the continuation of the existence of the USSR, the Warsaw Pact, and real socialism. The pro-Western elites who wished to introduce liberal reforms had on their side a potential novelty and will of modernization that the anti-Westerners did not possess: this allowed liberal-democratic policies to prevail at the time of perestroika and in the 1990s.

[2.59]   The restructuring of the Soviet political and economic system resulted ultimately in the collapse of the Soviet state unity and in the formation of post-Soviet national entities, highly influenced by nationalism. However, soon after the adoption of Western economic and social models during Boris Yeltsin's presidency, Russian society began to understand that the liberal-democratic paradigm was something alien to Russia's historical development and far from the true Russian mentality. In other words, Russians had to choose between two variants: either turning into a Westernized state forgetting their own past or rejecting a model that could not satisfy their real spiritual and cultural needs. In this context, an anti-Western and anti-liberal opposition began to form, taking the shape of a variegated "national-patriotic opposition" that included part of the "Soviet conservatives," groups of "reformers" disappointed with "reforms" or "having become conscious of their anti-state direction," and groups of representatives of the patriotic movements, who wished to shape the sentiment of "state power" not in a communist sense, but rather in an Orthodox-monarchic or nationalist one. Thus, within the context of post-Soviet patriotism, neo-Eurasianism arose as an ideological and political phenomenon, gradually turning into one of the main directions of the newly re-born Russian patriotic self-consciousness.[35]

From a theoretical point of view, neo-Eurasianism renews the classic principles of the early Eurasianist movement transforming them into the foundations of an ideological and political program that wishes to challenge the current unipolar globalized world. The heritage of the classic Eurasianists was adopted as the fundamental *Weltanschauung* for the political and ideological struggle against the forces of post-liberalism, mondialism and Atlanticism.　　　　　　　　　　　　　　　　　　　　　　　　　　　　[2.60]

Neo-Eurasianism founds its conceptual framework on two criticisms. First, its "rejection of the West" rests on the criticism of the Western bourgeois capitalist and individualist society both from a social left-wing perspective and from a civilizational right-wing one. Secondly, it criticizes the so-called Roman-German civilization—of which it believes the Anglo-Saxon world to be the continuer—that claims to possess the right to universally impose its civilizational paradigm, considering itself intrinsically superior to others.[36]　　　　　　　　　　　　　　　　　　　　　　　　　　　[2.61]

For neo-Eurasianists, the spatial factor is extremely relevant for interpreting history and understanding civilizations. History is interpreted through cyclical models, following the long-term schemas of the history of civilizations. This geographical-anthropological approach, which directly links people to soil and hinges on ethnographic-cultural frames, was assimilated from the works of prestigious historians of civilization including Nikolay Y. Danilevsky, Oswald Spengler, Arnold J. Toynbee, and Lev N. Gumilëv.　　[2.62]

Traditionalism is one of the core aspects of neo-Eurasianist doctrine. In terms of historical dynamism, traditionalist philosophy denies the ideas of evolution and linear progress, replacing them with the theories of "cosmic cycles," of the "multiple states of Being," of "sacred geography," and so on. The elementary principles of the theory of cycles were postulated by the French esotericist René Guénon and other traditionalist intellectuals like Gaston Georgel, Titus Burckhardt, Mircea Eliade, and Henry Corbin. In the context of the theory of cycles, the history of Russia is conceived as the incarnation of a spatial-cyclical system opposed to the temporal-unilinear Western one.　　　　　　　　　　　　　　　　　　　　　　　　　　　[2.63]

Neo-Eurasianists follow a historiographic pattern that unveils the continuity of Russian historical evolution, divided into several stages. Russian history is construed following the hermeneutical tools of Nikolay V. Ustryalov's National-Bolshevik ideology and its conceptual development by Mikhail S. Agursky. The first stage is that of Kievan Rus' (9th–13th centuries), which is perceived as the appearance of Russian future national identity thanks to its closeness with the Byzantine Orthodox civilization. The successive phase is that of the Mongolian-Tatar domination (13th–15th centuries), which contributed to separating the Russian evolution to that of other European coun-　[2.64] tries. During the Mongol rule, the division between Western and Eastern Russians occurred, and the latter became the cradle from which the so-called Great Russians would emerge under the control of the Golden Horde.[37] The third stage is the formation of the Muscovite principality and its unification of Russian states under a single political entity (15th–17th centuries). During the Muscovite rise, three main historical events occurred: Moscow acquired a religious mission as defender of the Christian Orthodox faith, gaining the title of "Third Rome" after the conquer of Constantinople by the Ottomans in 1453; the rulers annexed other Russian principalities unifying Russia (Rus'); and the country expanded eastwards through Siberia conquering the Tatar and Siberian khanates, ultimately reaching the Pacific shores and Alaska.[38] The fourth period was that of the so-called "Roman-German yoke," embodied by the Romanov dynasty (late 17th–early 20th centuries). The Romanov rulers are perceived by neo-Eurasianists as guilty of having forcedly "Westernized" Russian society, importing cultural, civilizational, and behavioral models from Western European countries, thus betraying Russian true national and historical identity. The successive phase is that of the Bolshevik Revolution and the establishment of the Soviet rule (1917–1991). This peculiar phase of Russian history is perceived somewhat positively by neo-Eurasianists, who reject the Marxist general ideological and socio-economic schema, but still believe that the Soviet era resulted in a revenge of the Russian popular masses against the Western dominant elite and in a rediscovery of the genuine Eurasian geopolitical tradition of Russia (as the shift of the capital city once again in Moscow rather than in Saint Petersburg/Leningrad had shown). The final phase is that of contemporary post-Soviet Russia, which according to neo-Eurasianists should eventually end with the overcoming of the unipolar Atlanticist-globalist model, the spread of a worldwide conservative revolution, and the final establishment of the multipolar civilizational world.

[2.65]   In terms of its political platform, neo-Eurasianism appears on one hand as a conservative and traditionalist movement and on the other as an egalitarian, collectivist, and social experiment: indeed, it borrows ideological features that belong both to the far-right and to the far-left political spectrum, combining them in the attempt to oppose Western post-liberalism characterized by the logics of individualism, consumerism, egoism, cultural imperialism, and unilinear globalism. As an ideology, neo-Eurasianisim "utilizes the methodology of Vilfredo Pareto's school, moves within the logic of the rehabilitation of organic hierarchy, picks up some Nietzschean motifs, and develops the doctrine of the 'ontology of power', or of the Christian Orthodox concept of power as '*kat'echon*'."[39] The elitist doctrine is widely accepted by neo-Eurasianists: according to it, the individuals who form an elite are those whose influence, capacities, qualities or authority in society is greater than that of others and this condition would make them fit to govern. Therefore, the neo-Eurasianist doctrine sympathizes with the general theorizations of the elitists Gaetano Mosca, Vilfredo Pareto, and Robert Michels. Moreover, it wholly adheres to the foundations of traditionalist philosophy, assimilating the thought and works of René Guénon, Julius Evola, Henry Corbin, Titus Burckhardt, Oswald Spengler, Georges Dumézil, and Louis Dumont. One of the main theoretical postulates borrowed from traditionalist philosophy is the idea of the radical decay of the "modern world." The global concept of "modern world" is perceived as a negative category and as the antithesis of the positive category of the "world of Tradition": this dialectic interpretation justifies from a metaphysical point of view the criticism of the Western/Atlanticist civilization, defining the eschatological, critical, and fatal content of the fundamentally destructive processes originating from the West.[40] The perception of a Western moral decay is continual in Dugin's thought.[41]

Anthropological studies—specifically those carried out by Carl G. Jung and Claude Lévi-Strauss—are likewise of utter interest for neo-Eurasianist doctrine. Neo-Eurasianism pays attention to the origins of sacredness, religiosity, archaic initiation rites, myths, and customary habits of different ethnic groups. Semiology and symbolism are considered important tools for interpreting the hidden mysteries of human civilizations. The expeditions and discoveries made by the German *Ahnenerbe*,[42] specifically Hermann Wirth's paleo-epigraphic findings in Sweden, are regarded with extreme attentiveness. Linguistic, epigraphic, runologic, mythological, and folkloric studies are utilized for demonstrating the existence of common Eurasian ancestral roots. Dear to neo-Eurasianists are the studies concerning the history, language, and religion of Indo-Europeans, as well as the themes related to Eurasian sacred geography, ethnography, and mythology. Esotericism and occultism too play a key role in neo-Eurasianist interests, specifically Madame Blavatsky's theosophy, the Tibetan myth of Shambala/Shangri-La, the legend of the "King of the World," the myth of Agarthi, the chronicles of the Hyperboreans, and so on. [2.66]

Generally, neo-Eurasianists reject the principle of representative democracy in favor of that of organic or functional democracy as theorized by Jean-Jacques Rousseau, Carl Schmitt, Julien Freund, Arthur Moeller van den Bruck, and Alain de Benoist. The term used to represent the idea of organic democracy is that of "*demotia*," which replaces the ordinary term "democracy," indicating precisely a direct participation of the people in their own destiny.[43] [2.67]

Furthermore, specific attention is given to the revaluation of the role of ideologies through the theory of "ideocracy," which indicates the foundational socio-political power of ideologies against the post-ideological economic and market-oriented globalist framework. The elements that neo-Eurasianists count in order to mold the new *homo politicus*—who will eventually overcome the *homo oeconomicus*—are essentially borrowed from the ideologies [2.68] of conservatism, traditionalism, collectivism, corporativism, and national-bolshevism.

[2.69]   Neo-Eurasianist thought comprises a fundamental geopolitical component. Indeed, neo-Eurasianists reconsider the main classic geopolitical theories of the 20th century concerning Eurasia. These include Halford J. Mackinder's Heartland theory, Karl Haushofer's *Kontinentalblock* strategy and pan-regional worldview, Nicholas J. Spykman's Rimland theory, Carl Schmitt's dialectic model of sea power against continental power, Jean Thiriart's pan-Eurasian project, and so on. Thanks to Mackinder's geopolitical analysis, which contributed to defining the strategic roles of the Heartland, the World-Island, and the Inner and Outer Crescents, the term "Eurasia" acquired a fundamental geopolitical meaning. In this sense, Eurasianism began to indicate the continental configuration of a strategic—either existing or potential—bloc, created around Russia or its enlarged base, and antagonistic—either actively or passively—to the strategic initiatives of the opposed geopolitical pole of Atlanticism, headed since the mid-20th century by the United States, which outplaced Great Britain.[44] Many classic geopolitical theories seek to explain the strategic relevance of Eurasia and the historical antagonism between the thalassocratic West and the tellurocratic East. During the 19th century the two major Eurasian empires of that time, Great Britain and Russia, that is a sea power and a continental power respectively, struggled for imperial hegemony over Eurasia in what was then called "Great Game."[45] The "Great Game" may be considered a veiled challenge chiefly between Britain and Russia that implied a watchful use of diplomacy, intelligence and counterintelligence to win over the rival. During the Second World War, the relevance of controlling Eurasia to gain pan-regional hegemony led Germany to the invasion of the Russian core land. After the war, through the birth of the bipolar world, with the United States—a predominantly sea power—confronting the Soviet Union—a predominantly continental power—, the quest for global hegemony was still concentrated on the need to contain the Soviet influence and expansion over Eurasia on one hand, and to break the American and NATO encirclement on the other. Even today, as the Crimean and Ukrainian crises have shown, the United States and the European Union conceive strategies aimed at containing Russia's influence—avoiding it to reach, for instance, a strategic position in the Mediterranean Sea—whereas Russia tends to project its authority more intensively over the Balkans, Eastern Europe and the Caucasus, clashing against NATO's and EU's interests. Russian mentality has always suffered from the disease of considering its country as encircled, or even besieged. President Truman's post-Second World War "Containment Strategy"—elaborated in February 1946 by the diplomat George F. Kennan—and the deployment of NATO or US troops across the Soviet borders further nourished the Russian "phobia of encirclement." Historically, the czarist empire had continuously expanded into both the Heartland and the Rimland: this thrust was justified by the Russian need to obtain an outlet to the "warm seas" that would allow the continuation of trade during the winter, despite the glaciation of the Arctic Sea. The result was Russia's territorial expansion towards the Black Sea, the Mediterranean Sea, the Caspian Sea and the Yellow Sea. During the 19th century, the British Empire considered Russia's enlargement as threatening, mainly because it could interpose or shatter the British communication lines with the Indian Raj. Thus, Great Britain began to contain Russian power, often leading to the outbreak of conflicts (e.g. the Crimean War, 1853–1856). When this Russo-British antagonism shifted towards Central Asia, challenging British India with Russian Turkistan, a struggle for Eurasian hegemony became evident. During the Cold War, the United States replaced imperial Britain in containing the Soviet Union throughout several areas of the Rimland. At the same time, the USSR attempted to break the US-NATO encirclement in Europe, the Middle East, and the Far East. Today, old international actors reappear under different names but still confront each other for the same geopolitical purpose of gaining the hegemony over Eurasia, in what may be considered a "New Great Game." This confrontation implies issues related to NATO and EU enlargement, energetic supplies, the rise of the BRICS countries, and China's potential alignment with Russia. The appearance of a multipolar global order would pass through the struggle between the declining unipolar status quo and the upsurge of new power centers that question the Atlanticist hegemonic role in international relations. Within this frame, the Eurasian continent—specifically its European, Balkan, Caucasian, and Middle Eastern rims—embodies one of the main battlefields in which the 21st century balance of power will be forged, and the ultimate ordeal that will establish whether the future hegemony will shift towards the Eurasian and Asian powers in the frame of a multipolar project or if it will stay in the hands of Atlanticist and Western forces.

Another fundamental aim of neo-Eurasianist theory is that of striving to assimilate the social criticism of the so-called "New Left" into a conservative right-wing interpretation. This entails an utter reconsideration of the philosophical heritage of Michel Foucault and Gilles Deleuze. Criticisms towards the bourgeois Western model connects neo-Eurasianism to some positions typical of anarchism, neo-Marxism, and of the left-wing interpretation of anti-globalism.   [2.70]

Finally, neo-Eurasianism adheres to a peculiar third-way vision in economics, alternative to the liberal and communist models, based on a mix of public intervention and private initiative and on a heterodox set of economic principles including the idea of an economic autarchy of the Great Spaces, the adoption of Friedrich List's theory of the *Zollverein* (custom union), on the actualization of the theories of Silvio Gesell, Joseph Schumpeter, and   [2.71]

François Perroux, and on a specific Eurasianist reading of John M. Keynes's theories on macroeconomic intervention.[46]

[2.72]   Aleksandr S. Panarin (1940–2003) can be considered one of the main ideologues of the neo-Eurasianist movement. Among his major works are *Filosofiya Politiki* ("Philosphy of Politics") (1996), *Revansh Istorii: Rossiyskaya Strategicheskaya Initsiativa v XXI Veke* ("The Revenge of History: Russia's Strategic Initiative in the XXI Century") (1998), *Global'noye Politicheskoye Prognozirovaniye v Usloviyakh Strategicheskoy Nestabil'nosti* ("Global Political Forecasting in the Conditions of Strategic Instability") (2000), *Politologiya. O Mire Politiki na Vostoke i na Zapade* ("Political Science. On World's Politics in the East and the West") (2000), *Global'noye Politicheskoye Prognozirovaniye* ("Global Political Forecast") (2001), *Iskusheniye Globalizmom* ("The Temptation of Globalism") (2002), and *Pravoslavnaya Tsivilizatsiya v Global'nom Mire* ("Orthodox Civilization in a Global World") (2002).

[2.73]   In considering Russia's history, Panarin believed that the geographical-historical inclinations of the country led it towards the adoption of an imperial regime. Russia represented the world's leading driving force for the consolidation of an alternative model to US-led globalization. In adherence with the idea of Russia's messianic mission, Panarin believed that thanks to Russia's alter-globalization forces humanity would manage to overcome the Western model. Following the frame of classical Eurasianism, the intellectual matrix of Panarin's neo-Eurasianist thought is founded on the rejection of the West, which is perceived as responsible for all of Russia's illnesses and as the main factor that leads humanity towards destruction. In his *Pravoslavnaya Tsivilizatsiya*—which represents a spiritual response to the unrestrained forms of technological development and to the secularization of Western societies—he depicted the Western European model as hinging on the principles of capitalism, hedonism, consumerism, rationalism, and on what he called "democratic racism."[47] Panarin opposed the Western self-imputed universality and claimed that Eurocentrism represented a new form of colonization of other civilizations through the logic of unilateral development and cultural hierarchy.[48]

[2.74]   Panarin made a distinction between "Occidentalism" (*Zapadnichestvo*) and "Westernization" (*Vesternizatsiya*). Occidentalism indicated the constitutive elements of the European philosophical heritage: liberalism, rule of law, democratic regime, legalism, and constitutionalism. On the contrary, Westernization held a strongly negative connotation, being characterized by savage capitalism and financialism, social decline, moral decay, and a blind imitation of the Western lifestyle. Westernization did not affect all European countries, but some of them featured both phenomena, especially in Northern and Western Europe. Panarin perceived an opposition between two idiosyncratic Europes: on one hand was Atlanticist-universalistic Europe that upheld the Roman idea, and on the other a national-continental one, perpetuating the German idea.

In his geopolitical analyses, Panarin made use of Nicholas Spykman's   [2.75] model of the Rimland to explain the rivalry between continental and maritime powers. He portrayed the Rimland as a contended European zone between the continental and the Atlantic spaces: historically, the hegemons of both spaces have attempted to control it and to colonize it from a strategical and cultural point of view.

Panarin believed that whereas other civilizations developed in a cyclical   [2.76] fashion, the Western followed a linear conception of time and a narrow perception of historical development. He argued that civilizations could not be reduced one to another, each constituting a solid and closed structure based on different values that could not be traced back to the Western model. As bearer of unchangeable forms of social construction, each civilization would possess unique features and their disappearance would impoverish all humankind. Panarin's thought was highly influenced by cultural relativism, claiming that nations could not judge others on qualitative terms, that not one single universal valid model existed, and that every civilization should have autonomously pursued its way to modernity.

Echoing Oswald Spengler, Panarin often presented in his works the theme   [2.77] of the decline of the West and of the need for a radical refusal of the decaying Western system. In his *Revansh Istorii*, Panarin exposed his theses against Francis Fukuyama's idea of the end of history. He believed that the liberal-democratic paradigm had shown its intrinsic limits and, above all, its impossibility to be adopted on a universal scale.

One of Panarin's main theoretical goals was to renovate civilizational   [2.78] consciousness amongst the peoples of the world. Civilizational consciousness meant the awareness and acceptance of world's inherent diversity, which would ultimately provide the spread of a conceptual paradigm alternative to the Western globalist one.

Panarin theorized the new discipline of the so-called "global political   [2.79] prognostication," which deals with two specific topics: on one hand, it studies globalization in its historical dynamics, and, on the other, it analyzes the conditions for prognosticating a qualitatively different future.[49] Globalization is guilty of having created a democracy that is limited to a small group of privileged and extraterritorial people, while relegating the rest of human kind to low-intensity conflicts and permanent ecocide.[50] Panarin's conception of civilization is based on the idea of "plurality of history,"[51] which attempts to theorize possible alternatives to Western-led globalization, responsible for "privatizing" the world's future.[52] Panarin's framework is somewhat closely related to Samuel Huntington's pattern of the clash of civilizations: both espoused the idea of dividing the world into civilizational areas. Panarin's beliefs made him oppose the principles of European cosmopolitanism, humanism, and egalitarianism. The fatherland was conceived as the only entity that could provide access to universal certainties. However, instead of local-ethnic regional homelands or of Western-type national states, Panarin emphasized the need for swearing obedience to a "greater" fatherland capable of creating a civilizational area, i.e. an empire. He postulated the existence of a third way, a *juste milieu*, between Western egalitarian universalism and ethnic particularism of the non-European world.

[2.80] Oftentimes, Panarin highlighted what he considered to be the mistakes of the industrial society and the failure of Western society. He unwaveringly upheld the ecological argument in favor of anti-industrial societies. He also advocated the "revenge of the natural against the artificial," striving for replacing the logic of economics with cultural and religious-oriented values. [53]

[2.81] Russia is presented by Panarin as a global safeguard of polycentrism, showing to all that the West does not represent the sole driving force of development: "If Russia becomes the Third Rome once again, postindustrial society will have better chances of becoming alternative to the industrial ghetto." [54] The adoption of the Western model represents a geopolitical and cultural death that contrasts with the true national interests and civilizational values of countries. According to Panarin, it would be valuable to reestablish the Eurasian dichotomy between West and East rather than the false dilemma of globalization versus ethnicity, or of the North versus the South.

[2.82] Generally, Panarin opposed ethnic nationalism, national chauvinism, and the model of nation-state as emerged out of the French Revolution, and—unlike Gumilëv—he believed that the authenticity of Eurasia was based not on ethnic complementarity, but rather on the shared past of its peoples, on a common statehood, and on a united political imperial will. Eurasian pluralism was to be conceived as civilizational: while Westernized Europe gave primacy to individual rights—i.e. pluralism for individuals—, Eurasia upheld the idea of collective rights—regional, ethnic, religious—, recognizing the right of autonomy for all regions, nations, groups, and respecting the diversity of ways of life. The principle of civilizational pluralism replaces that of cultural individualism.

[2.83] Panarin supported the imperialistic idea. He believed that empires could be the only political systems capable of responding to the challenges of postmodern societies, because they promoted a civilizational awareness, dividing the world along distinct regional and ethnic lines, and provided an ideology of order to utilize as a bulwark against the chaos of modern liberal societies. They also represented the political personification of the geographical extensions of Eurasia, legitimizing its natural unification as a pan-continent. In other words, the imperial model was the natural response to Eurasia's national, linguistic, and religious diversities. The Eurasianist ideology would overcome all national and social differences, inspired by a fundamental imperial idea based on spiritual foundations. Eurasia would symbolize a great civilization that—although living in postmodernity—would renew asceticism and reject the industrial world. Asceticism would be the new value of the postindustrial world: consumerism would be wiped out from the human way of life for the sake of higher moral goals.

Panarin auspicated the birth of a hybrid political regime that combined market economy, a strong presidential administration, a modernizing economic nationalism and conservative values, an official ideology, a bureaucracy, nationally minded intellectuals, and a strategic international partnership with China and India.   [2.84]

In his radical views of the Jews, Panarin claimed that the Jewish people manifested a clear tendency to destroy a hosting culture and that the very phenomenon of globalization represented a kind of "Judaization" of the world.[55] He compared what he considered the Jew's despicable contributions to the historical development of Russia with the honorable heritage Indo-Europeans had left in the country.[56]   [2.85]

Finally, Panarin described the Russian civilizational model as based both on multi-ethnicity and on an organic coexistence of different peoples, cultures, traditions, and confessions. Following this peaceful and inclusive civilizational model, the alter-globalist countries of the world—specifically China—could coalize with Russia against Western hegemonic ambitions and the threat of radical Islamic expansionism.   [2.86]

Aleksandr G. Dugin (1962) represents the maximum exponent of contemporary neo-Eurasianist thought. Having written a conspicuous number of books concerning Eurasianist issues and themes, he may be considered the intellectual founder of the neo-Eurasianist movement.   [2.87]

Dugin's publications began in the early 1990s, just after the demise of the Soviet Union and the birth of the new Russian Federation. He edited various journals like *Elementy* ("Elements") (1992–1998), *Milyy Angel* ("Sweet Angel") (1991–1999), *Yevraziyskoye Vtorzheniye* ("Eurasian Imposition") and *Yevraziyskoye Obozreniye* ("Eurasian Review").   [2.88]

Dugin's thought is notably influenced by traditionalism, occultism and geopolitical theories that claim the strategic supremacy of the Eurasian continent.   [2.89]

Between 1985 and 1990, Dugin adhered to the right-winged version of neo-Eurasianism, closely linked to ultranationalist and conservative-monarchist circles. His ideas showed a clear inclination towards historical traditionalism, with orthodox-monarchic and "ethnic-*pochevennik*"[57] elements. At that time, Dugin held seminars and lectures to various groups belonging to the conservative-patriotic social and political spectrum. He criticized the Soviet paradigm accusing it of lacking the Russian genuine spiritual and nationalistic qualitative element.   [2.90]

[2.91]   In the early 1990s, Dugin's books began to spread outside the Russian borders into Western countries: in 1989 *Continente Russia* ("Russian Continent") appeared in Italy and in 1990 *Rusia Misterio de Eurasia* ("Russia Mystery of Eurasia") in Spain. In 1990, Dugin also commented on René Guénon's *La Crise du Monde Moderne* ("The Crisis of the Modern World") and published *Puti Absolyuta* ("The Paths of the Absolute"), exposing the theoretical foundations of traditionalist philosophy. He also founded institutions like the "Arctogaia Association," a publishing house and the Center for Meta-Strategic Studies.

[2.92]   Between 1991 and 1992, Dugin came closer to left-winged positions, connecting to Gennady A. Zyuganov's Communist Party. This coincided with a nostalgic revaluation of the Soviet period and with a tighter relation with left-winged neo-Eurasianists. He also became a fruitful publisher in the patriotic newspaper *Den'* ("Day"), later renamed *Zavtra* ("Tomorrow").

[2.93]   From 1993 to 1994, Dugin moved away from the Communist spectrum and became the main ideologist for the new National-Bolshevik Party (NBP) led by Eduard Limonov. Dugin started developing strong relations with the chief representatives of the European New Right including Alain de Benoist, Robert Steuckers, Carlo Terracciano, Marco Battarra, and Claudio Mutti.

[2.94]   At the same time, some intellectuals with more "democratic" views like G. Popov, S. Stankevic, and L. Ponomarev attempted to initiate a democratizing process of Eurasianism. Moreover, other variants of neo-Eurasianism appeared like those theorized by O. Lobov, O. Soskovets, and S. Baburin. The intellectual activity of Neo-Eurasianists increased thanks to various lectures and seminars on geopolitical issues and on Eurasian history held in schools and universities, as well as through the publication of articles and translation of relevant essays.

[2.95]   The time span that covers the years 1991–1999 can be considered the period of maximum development of the neo-Eurasianist political theory thanks to the publications of Dugin's main works: *Misterii Yevrazii* ("Mysteries of Eurasia") (1991), *Giperboreyskaya Teoriya: Opyt Ariosofskogo Issledovaniya* ("Hyperborean Theory: Essay on Ariosophical Research") (1993), *Konspirologiya* ("Conspirology") (1993), *Metafizika Blagoy Vesti: Pravoslavnyy Ezoterizm* ("Metaphysics of the good news: Orthodox esotericism") (1996), *Osnovy Geopolitiki: Geopoliticheskoye Budushcheye Rossii* ("Foundations of geopolitics: Russia's geopolitical future") (1997), *Konservativnaya Revolyutsiya* ("The Conservative Revolution") (1994), *Tampliyery Proletariat: Natsional-Bol'shevizm i Initsiatsiya* ("Templars Knights of the Proletariat: National-Bolshevism and Initiation") (1997). Specifically, the "Foundations of geopolitics" is considered a major study of International Relations and appears as the founding work of the Russian contemporary school of geopolitics.[58]

At the same time, the "Agraf" publishing house issued the main works of   [2.96]
the founding fathers of Eurasianism (Trubetskoy, Vernadsky, Alekseev and
Savitsky).

Unlike weaker versions of neo-Eurasianism—like the ones upheld by A.   [2.97]
Panarin, V. Paschenko, E. Bagramov,[59] T. Pulatov,[60] and F. Girenok—, Dugin managed to build what can be considered the "orthodox" neo-Eurasianist
doctrine, based on more radically anti-Western, anti-liberal and anti-globalist
positions.

In the 1990s, some direct and indirect references to Eurasianism started to   [2.98]
appear in the programs of the Communist Party (KPFR), the Liberal-democratic Party (LDPR) and the New Democratic Russia (NDR), which embodied respectively the left, center and right of Russia's political party spectrum.

Between 1998 and 2000, Dugin began to strengthen his ties with the   [2.99]
Russian Parliament. He managed to become adviser to the Duma speaker
Gennady N. Seleznëv of the Communist Party. In 1999, he also became
chairman of the geopolitical section of the Duma's Advisory Council on
National Security dominated by Vladimir V. Zhirinovsky's Liberal-Demo-
cratic Party.

Between 1999 and 2004, Dugin published *Nash Put': Strategicheskiye*   [2.100]
Perspektivy Razvitiya Rossii v XXI Veke ("Our Path: Strategic Development
Prospects of Russia in the XXI Century") (1999), *Absolyutnaya Rodina*
("Absolute Fatherland") (1999), *Russkaya Veshch': Ocherki Natsional'nyy*
Filosofii ("The Russian Thing: Essays on National Philosophy") (2001), *Yev-*
raziystvo: Teoriya i Praktika ("Eurasianism: Theory and Practice") (2001),
Filosofiya Traditsionalizma ("Philosophy of Traditionalism") (2002), *Osno-*
vy Yevraziystva ("Foundations of Eurasianism") (2002), *Filosofiya Voyny*
("Philosophy of War") (2004), and *Yevraziyskaya Missiya Nursultana Na-*
zarbayeva ("The Eurasian Mission of Nursultan Nazarbayev") (2004). Along
with numerous publications on newspapers like *Nezavisimaya Gazeta* ("Independent Newspaper") and *Moskovskiy Novosti* ("Moscow News"), Dugin
held continuous radio broadcasts on geopolitical issues and on neo-Eurasi-
sianism (1998–2000).

On the 21st of April 2001, the "Pan-Russian Political Social Movement   [2.101]
Eurasia" was founded, with a declaration of full support to the President of
the Russian Federation Vladimir V. Putin. Meanwhile, exponents of the
Muslim and Jewish world started to engage with the Eurasian movement: the
leader of the Center of Spiritual Management of the Russian Muslims,
Shaykh al-Islām Talgat Tadzhuddin, decided to adhere to the Eurasianist
ideology and at the same time a Jewish variant of neo-Eurasianism appeared
thanks to Avigdor Eskin, Avraam Shmulevich, and Vladimir Bukarsky.

In 2002, the constituent congress of the Eurasia Political Party was con-   [2.102]
vened in Moscow. The foundation of a Eurasianist party represented the apex

of the movement's fate. Dugin became its leader, its programmatic charter was adopted, and the members of its political council elected.

[2.103]   In November 2003, the International Eurasian Movement Congress was held. In that occasion, the delegates decided to abolish the Eurasia Political Party since the need for having a mere Russian political party was considered no longer sustainable for an international movement like the Eurasianist one. The party was abolished in favor of its transformation into a broader, international phenomenon.[61] In December, the government of the Russian Federation officially recognized the International Eurasian Movement and its organizational cells, which started to emerge in Kazakhstan, Belarus, Tajikistan, Kyrgyzstan, Ukraine, Azerbaijan, Armenia, Georgia, Bulgaria, Turkey, Lebanon, Italy, Germany, Belgium, Great Britain, Spain, Serbia, Poland, Slovakia, Hungary, Canada, and the United States. In December 2001, the Eurasia party was officially disbanded and, from then on, the International Eurasian Movement became the organizational structure of neo-Eurasianism.

[2.104]   Meanwhile, "Foundations of Geopolitics" was translated into Arabic and Serbian, and the "Conservative Revolution in Russia" was published in Italy.

[2.105]   Recently, the publishing house "Arktos" translated some of Dugin's latest works into English, including *The Fourth Political Theory* (2012), *Putin vs. Putin: Vladimir Putin Viewed from the Right* (2014), *Eurasian Mission: An Introduction to Neo-Eurasianism* (2014), *Last War of the World-Island: The Geopolitics of Contemporary Russia* (2015), *The Rise of the Fourth Political Theory* (2017), and *Ethnos and Society* (2018).

[2.106]   NOTES

[2n1]   1. Aleksandr Dugin, *Eurasian Mission: An Introduction to Neo-Eurasianism* (London: Arktos, 2014), 19–20.

[2n2]   2. Specifically, it concerned the Slavic peoples that belonged to non-Slavic empires like Austria-Hungary, the Ottoman Empire, and the German Empire.

[2n3]   3. Aleksandr Dugin, *Eurasia: La Rivoluzione Conservatrice in Russia* (Rome: Nuove Idee, 2004), 17–18.

[2n4]   4. The idea of the existence of a third Eurasian continent between Europe and Asia implies the idea of an economic and social third way which is neither West nor East, neither capitalism nor communism, and neither parliamentary democracy nor totalitarianism.

[2n5]   5. Nikolai S. Trubetskoy, "O Turasnkom Elemente v Russkoi Kul'ture," in *Rossiya mezhdu Yevropoi i Aziei: Yevrasiyskiy Soblazn* (Moscow: Nauka, 1993), 62.

[2n6]   6. Ibid, 142.

[2n7]   7. Nikolai S. Trubetskoy, "Vavilonskaya Bashnia i Smeshenie Yazikov," *Yevrasiyskiy Vremennik* 3 (1923): 334.

[2n8]   8. Nikolai S. Trubetskoy, "Verkhi i Nizy Russkoi Kul'tury," in *K Probleme Russkogo Samopoznaniya* (Paris: Yevraziyskoye Knigoizdatel'stvo, 1927), 135.

[2n9]   9. Nikolai S. Trubetskoy, "Naslediye Chingiskhana. Vzglyad na Russkuyu Istoriyu ne s Zapada, a s Vostoka," *Istoriya, Kul'tura, Yazik* (Moscow: Progress, 1995), 248.

[2n10]   10. Trubetskoy, "O Turasnkom Elemente v Russkoi Kul'ture," 59.

[2n11]   11. Nikolai S. Trubetskoy, "Religiy Indiy i Khristianstvo," in *Na Putiakh: Utverzhdenie Yevraziitsev* (Berlin, 1922), 178, 223.

12. In Russian, the theory is known with the name of *Meztorazvitie*, which indicates the development of the geographic and spatial area.   [2n12]

13. Halford J. Mackinder, "The Geographical Pivot of History," *The Geographical Journal* 23, no. 4 (1904), doi:10.2307/1775498.   [2n13]

14. Marlène Laruelle, *Russian Eurasianism: An Ideology of Empire* (Washington, DC: Woodrow Wilson Center Press, 2008), 36.   [2n14]

15. Ibid.   [2n15]

16. Pëtr N. Savitsky, *Šestina Sveta: Rusko jako Zemepisní a Historickí Celek* (Prague: Melantrich, 1933), 139.   [2n16]

17. George V. Vernadsky, *Opyt Istorii Yevrazii* (Berlin: Izdaniye Yevraziytsev, 1934), 15.   [2n17]

18. Èrenzhen Khara-Davan, *Čingis-kan kak Polkovodec i Ego Nasledne* (Belgrade: Feniks, 1929), 55.   [2n18]

19. Èrenzhen Khara-Davan, "O Kochevnom Byte," in *Tridtsatye Gody* (Paris, 1931), 83–86.   [2n19]

20. Khara-Davan, *Čingis-kan kak polkovodec i ego nasledne*, 3.   [2n20]

21. The theory of ethnogenesis was developed during the 1960s and 1970s and its outcome was presented in the 1978's essay *Etnogenez i Biosfera Zemli*.   [2n21]

22. Lev N. Gumilëv, *Etnogenez i Biosfera Zemli* (Leningrad: Gidrometeoizdat, 1990), 276.   [2n22]

23. Ibid, 19.   [2n23]

24. Lev N. Gumilëv, "Pis'mo v Redaktsiyu 'Voprosov Filosofii'," *Voprosy Filosofii* 5 (1989): 161.   [2n24]

25. Lev N. Gumilëv, *Ot Rusi do Rossii* (Saint Petersburg: Iuna, 1992), 20.   [2n25]

26. Gumilëv, "Pis'mo v Redaktsiyu 'Voprosov Filosofii'," 160.   [2n26]

27. Lev N. Gumilëv and Vladimir Iu. Yermolaev, "Gore ot Illiuzii," in *Osnovy Yevraziistva*, ed. Aleksandr Dugin, (Moscow: Arktogaya Tsentr, 2002), 467.   [2n27]

28. Lev N. Gumilëv, "Zametki Poslednego Yevraziitsa," in *Ritmy Yevrazii: Epokhi i Tsivilizatsii* (Moscow: Progress, 1993), 36.   [2n28]

29. Lev N. Gumilëv, *Chë r naya Legenda: Druz'ya i Nedrugi Velikoy Stepi* (Moscow: Progress, 1994), 322–23.   [2n29]

30. Gumilëv, "Zametki Poslednego Yevraziitsa," 77.   [2n30]

31. Ibid, 65.   [2n31]

32. Gumilëv, *Chërnaya legenda*, 130.   [2n32]

33. Laruelle, *Russian Eurasianism*, 78.   [2n33]

34. Dugin, *Eurasian Mission*, 22.   [2n34]

35. Ibid, 23–24.   [2n35]

36. In the spirit of the German Conservative Revolution and of the European "New Right," Dugin believes that the so-called "Western world" is differentiated into parts: an Atlantic component with the United States and Great Britain and a continental European component, which is the Roman-German proper. Whereas continental Europe is liable to be integrated in the pan-Eurasianist project, the Atlantic section should create its own geo-economic and civilizational space, gravitating around the United States.   [2n36]

37. The word Great Russians indicates the Russians who live in Russia proper, whereas the term Little Russians is used to describe the Ukrainians and White Russians the Byelorussians.   [2n37]

38. Yuri N. Semënov, *Die Eroberung Sibiriens* (Berlin: Ullstein, 1937).   [2n38]

39. Dugin, *Eurasian Mission*, 32.   [2n39]

40. Ibid, 33.   [2n40]

41. See Aleksandr Dugin, *Continente Russia* (Parma: All'Insegna del Veltro, 1991), 53.   [2n41]

42. The *Ahnenerbe* was an institute in Nazi Germany purposed to research the archaeological and cultural history of the Aryan race. Founded in 1935 by Heinrich Himmler, Herman Wirth, and Richard Walther Darré, the *Ahnenerbe* organized and launched expeditions in an attempt to prove that Nordic populations had once ruled the world.   [2n42]

43. Dugin, *Eurasian Mission*, 33.   [2n43]

44. Ibid, 34–35.   [2n44]

45. The theme of the "Great Game" has been thoroughly scrutinized through its historical development by Peter Hopkirk in several valuable essays: *The Great Game: On Secret Service in High Asia* (1990); *Foreign Devils on the Silk Road: The Search for the Lost Treasures of*   [2n45]

Central Asia (1980); *Trespassers on the Roof of the World: The Secret Exploration of Tibet* (1982); *Quest for Kim: in Search of Kipling's Great Game* (1996).

[2n46]   46. Dugin, *Eurasian Mission*, 36.

[2n47]   47. Aleksandr S. Panarin, *Pravoslavnaya Tsivilizatsiya v Global'nom Mire* (Moscow: Algoritm, 2002), 16.

[2n48]   48. Aleksandr S. Panarin, "Slavyano-Tyurkskoye Yedinstvo: Konstruktsiya Rossiyskoy Gosudarstvennosti," *Rossiya i Musul'manskiy Mir* 1 (1996): 59.

[2n49]   49. Aleksandr S. Panarin, *Global'noye Politicheskoye Prognozirovaniye* (Moscow: Algoritm, 2002), 8.

[2n50]   50. Panarin, *Pravoslavnaya Tsivilizatsiya v Global'nom Mire*, 148.

[2n51]   51. Aleksandr S. Panarin, "Predely Faustovskoy Kul'tury i Puti Rossiyskoy Tsivilizatsii," in *Rossiya i Vostok*, eds. Aleksandr S. Panarin and Boris S. Yerasov (1994), 40.

[2n52]   52. Aleksandr. S. Panarin, *Rossiya v Tsiklakh Mirovoy Istorii* (Moscow: Izdatelstvo Moskovskogo Universiteta, 1999), 66.

[2n53]   53. Ibid, 19.

[2n54]   54. Aleksandr S. Panarin, *Rossiya v Tsivilizatsionnom Protsesse. Mezhdu Atlantizmom i Yevraziistvom* (Moscow: Institut Filosofii RAN, 1995), 72.

[2n55]   55. Aleksandr S. Panarin, *Iskusheniye Globalizmom* (Moscow: Algoritm, 2000).

[2n56]   56. Panarin, *Global'noye Politicheskoye Prognozirovaniye*, 346.

[2n57]   57. The term "*pochevennik*" refers to the ideas of soil and land.

[2n58]   58. Laruelle, *Russian Eurasianism*, 110.

[2n59]   59. Ibid, 84–86.

[2n60]   60. Ibid.

[2n61]   61. Dugin, *Eurasian Mission*, 28.

Chapter Three

The Liaison between Geopolitics and Eurasianism

[3.0]
INTRODUCTION

[3.1] In this chapter we will try to describe the geopolitical aspects that characterize the Eurasianist ideology. Eurasianism—especially neo-Eurasianism—bases much of its doctrinal beliefs on geopolitical analysis. As the name "Eurasianism" suggests, the core subject for the study of this doctrine has a geographical connotation: Eurasia is chiefly a geographical concept, which unfolds a strategic and political meaning.

[3.2] Geopolitics is a controversial and debatable tool to interpret international relations. Generally, it is more closely linked to the realist and constructivist traditions, rather than to the liberal or Marxist ones. It is relevant to note that relying on geopolitical theories for justifying an ideological narrative—like Eurasianism does—is a highly normative procedure often characterized by bias and dogmatism. Indeed, geopolitics is just one among many other tools for understanding the dynamics of international relations, and its truthfulness and empirical validity can be significantly questioned; nonetheless, given its ideological and partisan nature, Eurasianism believes in the validity of geopolitics, whose norms, Eurasianists believe, unveil the spirit of global power.

[3.3] Aleksandr Dugin is perhaps the main Eurasianist author who—following the theories by Halford Mackinder and Karl Haushofer—thoroughly investigated the meaningfulness of the Eurasian landmass for strategic interests in the frame the contraposition between sea powers and land powers. Though fascinating, Dugin's analysis is strongly dogmatic and ideologic, since it represents part of his political project; indeed, many of his claims and suggestions lack empirical evidence or result in a reductivist study.

In the first section, we will give a quick historical overview of the birth [3.4]
and development of geopolitics, concentrating briefly on some key authors
and contributions; in the second, we will expose the main criticisms that have
been addressed to the theory of geopolitics; finally, in the last, we will
describe Dugin's interpretation of geopolitics and how he connects the subject to Eurasianism.

WHAT IS GEOPOLITICS? A QUICK OVERVIEW [3.5]

Geopolitical theories tend to privilege the geographical factor in analyzing [3.6]
the international system, considering that geography is per se the most stable
element of international relations, given the fact that all states are located
within a fixed geographical space. The geographical element—which can be
defined as the physical setting of human activity, whether political, economic, or strategic—can be considered as the most important factor influencing
on policy-making since it represents a concrete and fixed reality: "Geography
is the most fundamental factor in foreign policy because it is the most permanent."[1] Though omitting other important factors like the process of globalization, the international economic dependence, the domestic distribution of
power, the role of international networks, the role of civil society and mass
media, the relevance of financial markets, and so on, this definition still bears
to some extent a significant validity, since geographical factors define the
players in international relations, the stakes for which they contend, and the
terms by which they quantify their security in relation to others.[2] According
to Saul B. Cohen, geography—which represents the descriptive science of
the Earth—boasts three definitions: the science of area differentiation, the
science of spatial relations and interaction, and the science of distributions:[3]
therefore, a geographer examines such physical factors as space, topography,
and climate, relating them together. As for the geographical subject, it divides into the two main branches of physical and human geography, the latter
being of great interest for strategists and policymakers. Human geography
studies the ways in which physical factors interact with population, political
institutions, culture, communications, industry, technology, and civilization
of a country, and is in turn divided into sub-branches that include political
geography, economic geography, cultural geography, military geography,
and strategic geography. Within this context, geopolitics is a form of geographic reasoning that encompasses all these branches and puts in relation
international political power to the geographical setting.[4]

    Since the term "geopolitics" tends to bear ambiguous meanings, it is [3.7]
fruitful to clarify the definition of the word itself. Firstly, it is important to
distinguish between the words "political geography" and "geopolitics." Political geography analyzes the influence of political factors on geography,

whereas geopolitics investigates the relevance of geographical factors on the foreign policy of states with a predominant focus on strategic elements—including the political, military, economic, scientific and industrial interests of states.

[3.8]   Geopolitics may be defined as the study of international relations from a spatial and geographic perspective.[5] Its main aim is to outline the political and strategic relevance of geography for the pursuit of international power. Indeed, it can also be described as the study of the influence of geographical factors on the foreign policy of states.[6] Per Yvés Lacoste, geopolitics represents the study of the rivalries of power on territories contended by two or more states, or between different political groups or armed movements.[7] As a subject, it studies the various expressions of the projection of political power on the geographical landscape. It also questions how the factors of territory, population, strategic location, and natural resources affect the relations between different states and their struggle for world supremacy.

[3.9]   Historically, geopolitics began its affirmation as an organic subject in the late 19th century. Between 1890 and 1920—years that saw the appearance of what we may call "classic geopolitics"—it revolved around the works of four main thinkers: the naval strategist from the United States Alfred Mahan, who focused his attention on sea-power; the German geographer Friedrich Ratzel, who focused on the idea of a living biological organism to describe the existence of states; the British geographer Halford Mackinder, who focused on the perils deriving from land power; and the Swedish political scientist Rudolf Kjellén, who introduced the idea of a world division in pan-regional blocs. The four thinkers were all passionately interested in the territorial struggles between states and in the rise and fall of empires.[8]

[3.10]   The German geographer Friedrich Ratzel[9] is considered the founder of political geography, whose features he exposed in his main work *Politische Geographie* (1897). Highly influenced by a Darwinian vision of space, Ratzel believed that states represented living biological organisms that struggled for their existence. In his view, a nation guided by its state, winning the struggle for survival, grabbed and kept the territory that it deserved. The state's will—that had to coincide with that of its folk—ensured the true unity between territory and nation.

[3.11]   Ratzel believed in the existence of three main components that constituted political geography: the space (quantitative element), the position (qualitative element), and the perception of space (*Raumsinn*), which derived from the culture and history of each people. The conflict between peoples and the natural tendency towards territorial expansion originated from the need for space and from the perception of space. Usually, a commercial increase preceded a territorial expansion: historically, political borders always followed economic boundaries.

Ratzel coined the idea of "living space" (*Lebensraum*), a concept already predicted by Friedrich List (1789–1846), a German political scientist and founder of the historical school of economics who had migrated to America. Influenced by Darwinism, Ratzel developed an organic biological geography in which borders evolved constantly in relation to the demographic size of human populations: "While we regard borders as static, as the very representation of permanence, legality, and stability, Ratzel saw only gradual expansion, contraction, and impermanence in the affairs of nations. For him the map *breathed* [emphasis added] as though a living being, and from this came the idea of the organic-biological state whose expansion was written into natural law."[10] [3.12]

Political geography had to benefit from the analysis of the terrestrial space as a methodology to understand statecraft and national power: although a human creation, the state adhered perfectly to the territory where it was located. The birth, the growth, and the development of states did not depend on the will of the peoples that form them, but rather on the natural conditions of the environment. The state represented a dynamic rather than static entity; like a biological organism, it was born, it grew, developed, reached its apex, got older, declined and finally died. The case of the British Empire revealed the example of an insular state that used oceanic ways to gradually expand. Ultimately, this expansion enabled it to acquire the status of world power, but soon after its gradual decline began due to the rise of new world powers (e.g. the German Empire). It was only thanks to the result of World War One that the British Empire could reaffirm its predominance, enlarging even more its colonial possessions. [3.13]

Per Ratzel, the state represented a manifestation of life on the terrestrial surface. The general laws that determine the distribution and development of organisms on the earth likewise determined the distribution and development of states. The natural evolution of states followed the same rules of any other vital organism, changing from time to time. All polities, be they nation-states or empires, represented dynamic and ever-fluctuating realities. Being a fragment of organized land, the state was naturally inclined to expand and annex new territories. The paramount factors that thrust states to expand may be of social, economic, and religious nature. More areas to settle meant better qualities for the existence of a given population. According to natural laws, greater states tend to annex the smaller bordering polities: they are likely to begin their expansion by annexing the richer and closer, and then to proceed with the poorer and farther. [3.14]

Ratzel believed that the necessity for states' spatial expansion was a consequence of the inevitable quest for "vital space" (*Lebensraum*). According to the German thinker, the real impulse for state expansion relied on demographic growth rather than economic or nationalistic issues: whilst the population grew in number, the territory of the state underwent an increasing [3.15] contraction. Following a Malthusian principle, Ratzel exposed an inversed relation between growth of population and availability of land: the increase of the former led to a diminution of the latter and thus to the natural need for expansion.

[3.16]   Ratzel's vision of the world implies a condition of permanent warfare. Since the growth of a state is the expression of a continuous vital tension, not only war is inevitable, but it represents the natural condition of states. This condition of conflict does not necessarily mean armed warfare, but rather commercial competitiveness and partition of territories.

[3.17]   Another founding father of geopolitics was the Swedish political scientist Rudolf Kjellén.[11] In his famous work *Der Staat als Lebensform* ("The State as Life Form") (1917), this brilliant intellectual coined the term "geopolitics."

[3.18]   According to Kjellén, the term geopolitics represents one of the five terms that indicates the categories used for analyzing the forms of states, the other four being demopolitics (referred to culture and population), ecopolitics (referred to economics), sociopolitics (referred to society), and cratopolitics (referred to political institutions). Geopolitics is also divided into three branches: topopolitics—that refers to the relative position of the state in relation to other states—, morfopolitics—that analyzes the shape of the territory of the state—, and physiopolitics—that describes the physical features of the state's territory and its dimension.

[3.19]   The major part of Kjellén's geopolitical theory was conceived as an ideological tool against the thalassocratic hegemony of the British Empire. The Swedish thinker also feared Russian expansionism towards the relatively warm waters of the Baltic Sea and therefore suggested an interventionist role for Sweden that would counter Russian expansionist ambitions, taking as a model the Russo-Swedish conflict during the Great Northern War that opposed Charles XII to Peter I in the early 18th century.

[3.20]   Being a pan-Germanist and an imperialist, Kjellén was in favor of the rise of a German continental geopolitical power. He hoped that ultimately all German stocks—from the Netherlands, to Scandinavia, to Central Europe—would unite into a single polity that could counter the Slavic and the Latin peoples of Europe.

[3.21]   Recalling Ratzel, Kjellén categorized human societies in biological-racial terms, conceiving the state as the representation of the nation that dwelled in it. A stout, virile, and dynamic folk would produce a strong state with a greater need for a broader living space.[12]

[3.22]   Kjellén was one of the first promoters of a new international system based on multipolarity. His multipolar geopolitical scheme was built upon the subdivision of the world into pan-regional big spaces. He believed in the need for creating four pan-regions: the American pan-region hegemonized by the United States; the Mitteleuropean pan-region, controlled by a greater German Empire that would include Austria-Hungary and the Ottoman Empire, expanding till the Persian Gulf; and the eastern-Asian pan-region dominated by Japan. This pan-regional scheme made Kjellén one of the first theorizers of regional blocs.

Upholding the need for the Germanization of the Eurasian landmass, [3.23] Kjellén supported the plan for the creation of a pan-German Eurasian empire. His hopes for the birth of a Greater Germany were expressed by the necessity to build a Eurasian empire under German rule: "Kjellén transferred all his hopes to a Greater Germany—to stand forth against Russia and England, both of which he especially detested. Kjellén's German empire-of-the-future, as he cataloged it, included all of Central and Eastern Europe as well as the Channel ports along the French coast, and the Baltic provinces of Russia, Ukraine, Asia Minor, and Mesopotamia (to be connected to Berlin by a great railway)."[13]

Kjellén aimed at elaborating a theory of the state as a spatialized organ- [3.24] ism, compelled to expand in order to survive in a globally "closed" political system. According to him, geopolitics was a theory based on a link between international political action and world geography.[14] One of his famous quotes affirmed that the individuality of the state is a natural unity that unveils itself economically through autarchy, socially as collective solidarity, and demographically as nationality merging with the state.[15]

The intellectual efforts of Friedrich Ratzel and Rudolf Kjellén contributed [3.25] to the diffusion of the study of geopolitics and to the birth of further theoreti- cal models that would develop in other contexts.

Besides the Germanic environment in which geopolitics originated, one [3.26] of the most influential geopolitical schools to appear at the beginning of the 20th century was the French school of possibilism headed by Paul Vidal de la Blanche and Camille Vallaux. Geographical possibilism believed that the main geopolitical objective was to analyze the relationships between types of life and landscape on one hand, and state organization on the other.

Possibilists assumed that geographers should discover the laws that made [3.27] civilizational development possible and describe how states evolved during history. They also rejected the idea of living space, preferring to pay specific attention to the kind of life and environment that could help to evaluate the historical evolution of states.

Vidal de la Blanche believed in the importance of the study of the "kinds [3.28] of life" that derived from a human activity in a specific geographical context. The kinds—or genres—of life produced the cells of the single societies and their harmonic combination gave birth to great civilizations. Vallaux rejected Ratzel's theory on living space, focusing instead on the relevance of the geographical position: the evolution of the states did not rely on the influence of the physical characteristics—climate, soil, natural resources—but rather on regional differentiation. In other words, differentiated regions were the ones in which political and social vital organisms would form more easily, whereas regions with a low level of differentiation were inclined towards political instability and exposed to partial conquest or unification by external political forces.

[3.29]   Another chief geopolitical school has been the Anglo-Saxon one, headed by Alfred T. Mahan and Halford J. Mackinder.

[3.30]   The US Navy Captain Alfred Thayer Mahan[16] outlined the relevance of sea power for the purposes of world power. Mahan believed that sea power bore a greater strategic weight than land power and that throughout history thalassocratic powers showed to be superior to tellurocratic ones. Sea power was perceived as less threatening for international stability since navies possessed a limited capacity to extend coercive force inland.

[3.31]   According to Mahan, inner Eurasia did not represent the geopolitical pivot of empires—as per Mackinder—, but rather the Indian and Pacific Oceans, "for these oceans would allow for a maritime nation to project power around the Eurasian Rimland, affecting political developments inland—thanks to the same rail and road feeder networks—deep into Central Asia."[17]

[3.32]   Mahan exposed his ocean-centric view in the essay *The Influence of Sea Power Upon History, 1660–1783* (1890), which offered the theoretical background for world powers to engage in naval buildup plans prior to World War One.

[3.33]   Indeed, one of the main flaws of Mahan's sea power theory was the underestimation of the possibility that a telluric power would suddenly expand through land, gaining control in turn of thalassic power, adjoining it with its continental base.

[3.34]   Mahan's thought is closely linked to the American idea of "Manifest Destiny." The Manifest Destiny offered an ideological and geopolitical justification for the conquering of the American West and for the expansion of the US borders from the Atlantic Ocean to the Pacific Ocean. The idea of a Manifest Destiny originated from the original US ties that linked the country to the United Kingdom and from the belief in a special Anglo-Saxon civilizational mission. Moreover, the geographical features of the North American continent implied its natural unification, from one shore to another. By reaching the Pacific Ocean, the United States would become a continental super-island in the center of the two main global oceans, projecting an irresistible sea power that would outflank Eurasia from two sides. The hegemony over the Caribbean Basin, the control of the Hawaiian Islands and the Philippines, the realization of the Panama Canal, and Theodore Roosevelt's Corollary to the Monroe Doctrine were all pieces of a mosaic that would have granted American supremacy over the two wide oceans.[18]

[3.35]   Mahan also proposed the idea that the global hegemony of maritime powers could be kept through the control of a series of strategic beachheads around the Eurasian continent. He believed that this control would allow sea power to imprison terrestrial powers, blockading them from the access to the seas.

The study of the contraposition between land powers and sea powers—   [3.36]
which is one of the chief geopolitical leitmotivs—would later be developed
by the philosopher Carl Schmitt.[19]

Unlike Mahan, Sir Halford J. Mackinder focused his strategic thought and   [3.37]
concerns on the potential risks emerging from a continental power controlling the inner landmass of Eurasia, which he called the "Heartland." As we
will see in the next chapter, Mackinder feared the rise of a Eurasian empire
led by Germany or Russia that would rejoin land power with sea power,
therefore putting at stake the existence and prosperity of maritime nations
like Great Britain.

The Anglo-Saxon school would then find in Nicholas J. Spykman another   [3.38]
major exponent. This Dutch-American geopolitical thinker would be one of
the greatest theorists of Atlanticism and of the strategy of containment
against Soviet Russia. Spykman's most relevant geopolitical contribution
would be the formulation of the Rimland theory. This theory, although based
on Mackinder's studies on the Heartland and on the inner and outer crescents, would affirm the strategic superiority of the bordering strip of the
Eurasian continent rather than that of its inner land core.

As for Germany, the science of geopolitics—known in German as *Geo-*   [3.39]
politik—would be heavily influenced by the idea of politically and militarily
dominated space.[20] The theoretical fathers of the German school of *Geopoli-*
tik were Ratzel, with his important theories on the state as a living organism
and with the concept of *Lebensraum*, and Kjellén, with his pan-Germanist
views and his pan-regional international order. The German school of geopolitics found its major pillar in Karl Haushofer, who upheld the idea of
creating a continental Eurasian block capable of marginalizing sea power. In
the 1930s, German geopolitical science had reached its apex thanks to the
special contributions of the Munich School and its official journal *Die Zeits-*
chrift für Geopolitik ("Journal for Geopolitics"). The alignment of German
geopolitics with the Nazi regime and its quest for expansion cast a shame on
it: the geopolitical considerations of the German school were considered
responsible for the outbreak of World War Two because of their deep influence on Nazi foreign policy. Accordingly, after World War Two geopolitical
studies were totally neglected in the divided Germany and underwent a real
damnatio memoriae.

In other countries like Italy, geopolitical studies would be headed in the   [3.40]
late 1930s by Ernesto Massi through the creation of the magazine *Geopoliti-*
ca ("Geopolitics") (1939). Like in Germany, also in Italy geopolitics would
be considered a tool in the hands of the fascist regime, especially when it
justified the Italian imperialistic plans aimed at territorial expansion in the
Mediterranean, the Balkans, and Africa.

[3.41]   Finally, in Japan geopolitics was developed by the so-called Kyoto School and focused on supporting the Japanese rise as an imperial power, vindicating its rights to expand in continental East Asia and in the Pacific Ocean.

[3.42]   During the Cold War, geopolitics suffered a significant decline. The discipline was heavily criticized in the academic environment, which linked it to the material and moral disasters of World War Two, highlighting its intrinsic connections with imperialism. During these years, the geopolitical analysis was carried out only in military and strategic environments.

[3.43]   Nonetheless, during the 1980s the academic world and the experts of international relations showed a new and growing interest in classical geopolitics. Leading scholars in strategic studies such as Colin S. Gray and Geoffrey Sloan in Britain, Mackubin T. Owen and Francis Sempa in the United States promoted a rediscovery of classical geopolitical authors: the geographical reality and its relationship with politics and strategy could not be ignored for too long and thus spread once again beyond the mere entourage of military circles.

[3.44]   At the same time, a new geopolitical current arose in France thanks to Yves Lacoste and his magazine *Hérodote*. This new school of thought believed in the geopolitical relevance of other internal and external actors besides traditional states, ranging from ethnic groups to local authorities, multinationals, and the mass media. The recognition of the multiplicity of political actors, along with a less deterministic approach and the attention to the various non-physical spaces such as the telecommunications networks or financial flows would be one of the main characteristics of contemporary geopolitics.

[3.45]   Parallel to the French School, a "neoclassical" geopolitical current appeared, aiming at rediscovering and modernizing the teachings of the classic thinkers (particularly Mahan, Mackinder, Haushofer, and Spykman). Among the prominent members of this current are the Anglo-Saxons Colin S. Gray, Geoffrey Parker, Geoffrey Sloan and Zbigniew Brzezinski, the French Aymeric Chauprade and François Thual, and the Russian Aleksandr Dugin.

[3.46]   Finally, another geopolitical current known as "critical geopolitics" appeared in Anglo-Saxon countries, whose founder may be considered the Irish Gearóid Ó Tuathail. Critical geopolitics is closely linked to post-modernist instances, and its main interest lies in deconstructing the geographical bases of geopolitical discourses, describing geography as a minor fact in determining the political conception, but rather believing that the political conception plays a significant part in influencing the interpretation of the geographical facts. The most important thesis of the critical school is that no connection exists between politics and geography that may be scientifically investigated. Rather than searching for a connection between politics and geography and between international relations and political geography, what is more valuable when dealing with international affairs and crises is instead to deepen the analysis of non-state actors like the mass media, think tanks, civil society, and pressure groups or lobbies.[21]

This current has played a valuable role in promoting contextualization [3.47] and critical analysis of the geopolitical argument, though lacking a truly solid and constructive theoretical framework. Reintroducing geopolitics in the context of a post-modern globalized environment appeared as a contradictory and often conflicting task.

In conclusion, contemporary geopolitics witnesses the contraposition of [3.48] its two main families: that of "neo-classical" authors and that of "critical" thinkers. The doctrine of Eurasianism and its supporters clearly align with the former current.

CRITICISM OF THE THEORY OF GEOPOLITICS [3.49]

Geopolitics has been subject to several kinds of criticism in contemporary [3.50] debates. The main criticism refers to its overestimation of the geographical factor in interpreting the reality of international relations. Critics of geopolitics questioned whether a theoretical framework built upon geographic determinism could have a real validity in the context of globalism and of the abolition of rigid state borders. The idea of the pursuit of national interests from within the confines of strict geographical borders has been perceived as obsolete and in contrast with the potential rise of global governance and of meta-state institutions that tend to diminish the weight of national states. Many IR scholars believe that international relations cannot be explained referring to geopolitics alone, omitting other variables like domestic politics, interdependent economies, trade, political ideologies, constructivist worldviews, religion, psychology, and so on. For instance, in electoral democracies some foreign policy decisions could aim at gaining electoral consensus or downsizing domestic crises. At the same time, commercial interests of economic lobbies could lead to international policies that contrast with national interest. Also, ideologies and religions could play a decisive role in inspiring a country's foreign policy, especially in a constructivist perspective.

Geopolitical theories tend to display models that show how to gain global [3.51] power and ultimately world supremacy: in this sense, geopolitics has been accused—especially by liberals and Marxists—of propagandizing imperialism, militarism and colonialism. The itineraries of power that geopolitics pursues are often perceived as hyper-realist and hyper-determinist, following an immoral—or at least amoral—rhetoric. It is a tempting allure to generalize the nature of geopolitics, linking it to imperialism, power politics (*Machtpolitik*) or even fascism.

[3.52]   One of the main weaknesses of geopolitical models is that they often underestimate the role of domestic factors and individuals, considering the state the chief subject of international relations. If this state-centric vision could bear meaningfulness during the 19th and first half of the 20th century, it is uncertain whether it may be considered still valid after the end of the Second World War and, especially, after the end of the Cold War. During the second half of the 20th century, the rapid appearance of meta-state institutions and organizations like the United Nations or the European Union, as well as the increased role of civil society, international regimes, and global networks have clearly resized the role of the state as sole international actor.

[3.53]   In academic debates, some scholars have shown skepticism towards the utility of classical notions of geopolitics, such as those advocated by Mahan, Mackinder and Spykman and on those who make use of those theories today, including Robert Kaplan and Colin Gray.

[3.54]   Some scholars believe that geopolitics fails in relation to three main theoretical aspects: in the description of the way in which the world works; in the prediction of how future events will truly develop; and in the potential plausibly offer guidance to policymakers in the face of a crisis. [22]

[3.55]   Geopolitical studies would not employ the scientific method and many theories would not be confirmed by empirical evidence. The lack of a positivist approach would endanger geopolitical studies with the risk of making them appear unscientific. Accordingly, it is assumed that geopolitics as a descriptive research program did not adapt to the behavioral revolution in political science.

[3.56]   These scholars detect that the major part of the geopolitical analysis is founded in the tradition of classical realism, sharing the basic norms of that school of thought, including that of an unchanging international order based on anarchy and everlasting conflict between states. Apparently, the contemporary international stability granted by the United Nations and by international law seems to contradict geopolitics and its warlike logic. Geopolitics may lose all its relevance in international relations if wars will gradually disappear in favor of other phenomena like the free market or globalism. When the will of forging empires disappears, geopolitics is doomed to a similar fate. Critics of geopolitical theory argue that geopolitical analysis has always tended to inspire confrontational and aggressive behavior. Geographical maps are tools that boost the emergence of competitive or even belligerent strategies. Staring at maps seems to promote the idea of gaining possession of lands and that the geopolitical system is a zero-sum game where the goal is not to coexist or cooperate but to conquer and dominate. To the extent that geopolitics acts as an aid to statecraft, it advises expansive policies and bellicose strategies. When leaders adopt a geopolitical mindset, the likelihood of the occurrence of conflicts would increase significantly.

Moreover, one of the fundamental failures of geo-strategic thought would   [3.57]
be its incapacity to recognize the contributions of technology in overcoming
the restrictions related to the planet's shortages (availability of land, quality
of soil, distribution of resources, etc.). Progresses in the field of transportation—especially in relation to aircraft—made geopolitics lose more of its
ability to interpret international processes. In other words, geopolitical thinkers are accused of underestimating the impact that technology has had in
relation to geography. The interaction between geography and state behavior
seems to have undergone a diminishing influence in recent decades.

The end of the Cold War has generated different descriptions of the   [3.58]
international order that—following the logic of the unipolar model—essentially decree the demise of geopolitics.

Among these descriptions is the post-Cold War theory of the "end of   [3.59]
history" as espoused by Francis Fukuyama, which claims that the end of the
Cold War represented the undisputed victory of liberal democracy over its
twentieth-century ideological contenders, fascism and communism.[23]

Other descriptions include the idea of world interdependence due to glo-   [3.60]
balism, global governance, and the free market. The advocates of such theses
believe that the classic pursuit of power through geographical means has
been replaced by liberal economic cooperation and trade. The gradual expansion of the global village and market would ultimately lead to borderless
economic interrelation and to the end of the nation-state.

The neo-Marxist tradition has also proposed a non-geopolitical explana-   [3.61]
tion of contemporary international relations. According to this school of
thought, the capitalist world economy created a single global unit generating
fundamental inequalities such as the traditional class disparity between bourgeoisie and proletariat, and the spatial discrimination between developed
capitalist countries (Core) and underdeveloped exploited states (Periphery).[24]
Consequently, the international analysis should focus on overcoming these
inequalities rather than on the imperialistic pursuit of geopolitical hegemony.

The center-periphery model can also be applied to schools of thought that   [3.62]
do not necessarily belong to the Marxist tradition, like structural realism.
Structural realists believe that multipolarity is now appearing due to the
emerging of great powers that have embraced capitalism—chiefly China.
However, they also claim that the (liberal) ideological harmony within the
center has lessened the relevance of military power among states that belong
to the center, but not between the center and the periphery.[25]

Other analysts believe that geo-economics is quickly supplanting geopoli-   [3.63]
tics. Geo-economics represents that specific branch of geopolitics that proposes to interpret international relations in light of transnational economic
factors. Those that stick to the primacy of economic aspects in international
affairs believe that today's trade is superseding traditional warfare and that
states are reorienting themselves towards the pursuit of the maximization of

the economic profit for them and for their national enterprises and companies. In other words, in a geo-economic global competition, the logic of conflict will be expressed in the declination of commerce.[26] The corollary of the geo-economic criticism towards geopolitics asserts that the pursuit of welfare and prosperity is displacing the quest for power, making classical geopolitical theories obsolete.

[3.64]   Finally, other critics highlight the fact that the advances in technology and the rise of airpower, space power, and nuclear power constitute a huge downsizing of the geographic factor in international analyses.[27]

[3.65]   On the other hand, other scholars have challenged the opponents of classical geopolitics.[28] Specifically, a counter-criticism to the idea that technological progress and international economic relations would supplant geopolitics led to the statement that, in fact, technology and economics are not at all extraneous to geopolitical analysis but rather an integral part of it. For instance:

[3.66]   "The shift in ship propulsion from sail to coal to oil to nuclear power significantly changed the geopolitical landscape, as did the railroad and the development of air power. Some analysts suggested that nuclear weapons spelled the end of geopolitics; some make that claim now on behalf of information technology and cyberspace. However, while technological advances can alter the importance of the geographic determinants of policy and strategy, they do not negate it. The same is true of economic development; the infusion of capital may modify but not negate the importance of a particular geographic space."[29]

[3.67]   Geopolitics would not reflect geographic determinism but trust in the idea that geography defines limits and opportunities in international politics. States can realize their geopolitical opportunities or become the victims of their geopolitical situation: geopolitics is a dynamic subject, not a static one. Being chiefly close to the realist school of international relations, geopolitics reflects international realities and the global constellation of power arising from the interaction of geography on the one hand and technology and economic development on the other. Technology and the infusion of capital can modify, though not negate, the strategic importance of a specific geographic space, which is an everlasting physical reality.

[3.68]   THE FOUNDATIONS OF GEOPOLITICAL ANALYSIS
                     ACCORDING TO ALEKSANDR DUGIN

[3.69]   Geopolitical analysis may help in understanding how variables like economic needs, demography, strategic priorities, and geography converge to influence future international trends. The study of these convergences and interactions are the core of geopolitical analysis. A careful application of the precepts of geopolitical analysis could provide an insight into unfolding international events, and possibly lead to predictions of future outcomes.

Generally, geopolitical analysis considers three main elements: geography, culture and history, and national interest.   [3.70]

Geography is perhaps the most important feature when considering the geopolitics of a nation. A nation's geography inevitably affects its foreign policy and its strategic policies. The examination of the geographic factor of a nation considers elements like the country's natural resources, its ease of access to the outside world, and its internal transportation systems. For instance, nations that have a limited access to natural sources of energy have a permanent concern of how to secure the supply of these resources. Land-locked nations have fewer opportunities for trading compared with those that have access to seas and oceans. Nations that do not possess overseas territories and depots or that do not benefit from international connections and communication lines are less advantaged than those that possess these benefits. Moreover, countries with articulated internal water transportation like navigable rivers that flow from north to south and from east to west grant them a permanent cost advantage compared to those that lack this condition, since water transportation is much less costly than overland transport. Geography also either blesses or curses nations with neighbors: the historical relations with neighboring countries may lead either to alliances or to rivalries nourished by territorial irredentism. Overall, it is the geography of a nation to provide almost unalterable advantages or disadvantages, and geopolitical analysts use the unchanging reality of geography to provide high levels of predictability.   [3.71]

The second element that geopolitical analysis takes into account is the civilization and history of nations and of different ethnic groups within nations. Geopolitics studies culture and history as living and dynamic entities, not static ones. Often, past relations among nations and peoples are undifferentiated from the flow of current events and present some fixed constants that reappear in the unfolding of historical development. Alignments and differences between civilizations often follow cultural and historical courses that are hundreds of years old. Knowing the history of countries and peoples assures a higher level of predictability in geopolitical analysis.   [3.72]

Finally, the third element is national interest. National interest implies the needs, expectations, and strategic imperatives of a country: it includes a country's economic, military, and cultural goals and ambitions. For instance, the national interest and basic needs of Russia include its famous need for access to warm waters during the winter, and this exhibits one of the reasons why Russia has a chief interest for expanding its influence over Ukraine: "Ukraine's location constrains Russia's access to the oceans and thus its ability to trade and project power globally. Additionally, because the border between Russia and Europe is a vast plain, Russia requires buffer states to   [3.73] secure its national boundaries. So, if Ukraine is not in Russia's orbit, access to Russia's heartland will be largely unobstructed by geographic obstacles, such as mountains."[30] Similarly, Serbia needs to have solid connections with Montenegro in order to enjoy an access to the Mediterranean Sea and with Bosnia-Herzegovina to avoid a marginalization in the Balkan Peninsula.

[3.74]   Therefore, "geopolitical analysis treats a nation's politics as almost entirely determined by its unmoving geography, its unchangeable history, its long-lived cultural distinctions, and the expectations of people about what qualifies as basic needs."[31]

[3.75]   Aleksandr Dugin builds his neo-Eurasianist political doctrine upon geopolitical analysis. The chief work that exposes the use of geopolitics as tool and method for explaining international relations is *Osnovy Geopolitiki: Geopoliticheskoye Budushcheye Rossii* ("The Foundations of Geopolitics: The Geopolitical Future of Russia") (1997). The book, which has had a large influence within the Russian military, police, and foreign policy elites and was probably used as textbook in the General Staff Academy of Russian military, was co-authored by General Nikolai Klokotov of the General Staff Academy; moreover, Colonel General Leonid Ivashov, head of the International Department of the Russian Ministry of Defense, apparently advised in the project. "The Foundations of Geopolitics" provides a political plan based on geopolitical analysis aimed at creating a powerful Eurasian unified polity under the hegemony of Russia in Euro-Asia and a German-French axis in Europe. Dugin claims that the "Eurasian Empire" will be fabricated on the fundamental principle of the common enemy, i.e. the rejection of Atlanticism, the end of strategic control by the West, and the refusal to allow liberal values to dominate it.

[3.76]   Dugin claims that geopolitics is a method of politics based on considering geography as a cause and condition of political actions, encompassing a wide spectrum of social, economic, political, and military decisions; in this sense, every unit of international politics has, or should have, an ability to make geopolitical decisions. Dugin considers geopolitics as an ideology, like Marxism or Liberalism:

[3.77]   "Geopolitics is a worldview and as such it is not prudent to compare it to science but to the system of sciences. It is on the same level with Marxism, Liberalism, etc., that is: explanatory systems of society and history that extrapolate the most important principle as their criteria and then reduce all innumerable aspects of man and nature to it. [. . .] In contrast with "economic ideologies" it is founded on the thesis: "geographical conditions as destiny." Geography and space in geopolitics serve the same function that money and means of production serve in Marxism and Liberalism—all fundamental aspects of human being are reduced to them, they are the main method of explaining the past, the main factors of human being, around which all other aspects of existence are being organized."[32]

Furthermore, Dugin believes that geopolitics, unlike other ideologies, is not a   [3.78]
"mass" ideology, since its comprehension can be fully understood only by
the governmental establishment and not by the common people: Geopolitics
is a discipline belonging to political elites that represents a sort of "comprehensive handbook of the overlords" and the science of how to rule.[33]

Geopolitics as political and state ideology transcends Marxism and Liber-   [3.79]
alism because it is as far removed from the common human being and as
close to the elites as possible. It can be considered a hyper-ideology in the
sense that it can be implemented only by the self-directed will of the rulers.
In Dugin's view, geopolitics bears a universal scope, since it serves the
purposes of forging global empires. Hence, there cannot be any regional,
national, or federal geopolitics since its very nature is not that of a science or
technique but that of a worldview for those who hold or strive for absolute
power granted them primarily by geographical factors. The essence of geopolitics is global in its scope, because it considers only "destiny-making"
decisions, which affect not only some portion of space but all the spaces of
the planet.

The Russian philosopher uses the classical geopolitical schemas of Heart-   [3.80]
land, Rimland, and World-Island to explain contemporary international
events. In this sense, the expansion of NATO towards Eastern Europe is
viewed through lenses that display the Atlanticist will of enlarging the Rimland for the benefit of thalassocracy. At the same time, a possible agreement
between Germany and France on creating an independent, unified European
army would signify a step towards the creation of a continental might for the
benefit of tellurocracy.

Dugin argues that geopolitical realities are unchangeable and always val-   [3.81]
id, presenting a continuous struggle between sea power—incarnated by the
Leviathan—and land power—incarnated by the Behemoth: this historical
constant would date back centuries, at least since the times the thalassocratic
Greeks were struggling against the tellurocratic Persians. Dugin's thought
presents a marked eschatological formulation, being founded on the eternal
struggle by impersonal forces of history, i.e. by the apocalyptic clash between the two pillars of Sea and Land.

Like Marxism, the geopolitical ideology is based on a Hegelian dialectic   [3.82]
struggle between tellurocracy and thalassocracy, whose synthesis is represented by the advent of the global empire. Therefore, geopolitical analysis
rests on an eternally valid dual principle based on the confrontation of sea
power against land power:

> "The affirmation of primordial duality displayed by geographical structure of   [3.83]
> the planet and historical typology of civilizations is the basic law of geopoli-
> tics. This duality is being expressed in the opposition between "Tellurocracy"
> (land power) and "Thalassocracy" (sea power). The character of this opposi-

tion is being reduced to a conflict between mercantile civilization (Carthage, Athens) and military-authoritarian civilization (Rome, Sparta) or, in other words, to a duality between "democracy" and "ideocracy." Fundamentally, this duality possesses the character of enmity of its constitutional poles [. . .]. Therefore, the history of human societies is said to be constituted by two torrents—"water" ("fluid," "unstable") and "land" ("solid," "stable")."[34]

[3.84]   Hence, the different forms of civilizations and all that Dugin subsumes unto them, i.e. religion, philosophy, art, economics, etc. (superstructures), would be mere expressions of this primal geographical clash of the elements of sea and land (structure). Dugin also claims that the "geopolitical outlook on history is a model of the development of planetary duality to its final extremes. The Land and the Sea expand their primordial conflict onto the whole world. The history of humankind is nothing else but the expression of this struggle and the path towards making it absolute."[35]

[3.85]   The history of geopolitics reproduces the expansion of the primordial geographical contraposition to the point of final global conflict, a kind of ultimate Armageddon. Indeed, on the most elementary basis, geopolitics is evolutionary and apocalyptic, and its dogmatism moves towards the conscious reduction of all human accomplishments in the spheres of art, religions, politics, and science to the last, total war of the geographical determinants of Land and Sea. Therefore, the method of geopolitics is—in Hegelian terms—its history, since it cannot be observed outside the evolution of the historical and civilizational path of nations.

[3.86]   The framework of geopolitical principles has been reached in antiquity, after the Punic wars and "acquires its full meaning in the period when England becomes the great maritime power—from the 16th to the 19th century."[36] The age of the great geographical explorations and discoveries serves as an overture to globalize the dialectics of the conflict, being the moment when Thalassocracy finally split from Tellurocracy as "a self-sufficient planetary formation detached from Eurasia and its shores, fully concentrated in the Anglo-Saxon world and its colonies. The 'New Carthage' of Anglo-Saxon capitalism and industrialism has been molded into something unique and wholesome, and from then on geopolitical duality acquired clearly recognizable ideological and political forms."[37]

[3.87]   In Dugin's view, this duality between Land and Sea had reached its fullness during the Cold War, when the two cultural-political forms of Marxism and liberalism perfectly fit Mackinder's schema, the former holding the Heartland and the latter the Outer Crescent of the World-Island. Following Mackinder, Dugin depicts the geopolitical map of the world in three zones: the inner continental Eurasian spaces represent an "immobile platform" that Mackinder called "Heartland" or "geographical pivot of history" and constitute the stable landmass for the projection of telluric power; the inner or continental crescent, or "zone of the shores," which coincides with Spykman's Rimland, is characterized by an intense civilizational development and presents notable thalassic features that nonetheless are balanced by numerous telluric impulses; the outer or insular crescent, which represents the lands that can only be reached by sea, embodies the core for the projection of thalassic power over the rest of the world.[38]

Dugin's notion of geopolitics appears extremely deterministic in its reductionism claiming that there are two powers, the power of the Land and the power of the Sea, that expand unlimitedly until they ultimately clash in a final, global war. The greatest possible spatial expansion of Thalassocracy and Tellurocracy coincides with the inevitable confrontation on global scale between the two forces. [3.88]

In "The Foundations of Geopolitics," Dugin locates Russia at the center of the global Eurasian Empire. Russia and the Russians bear a geopolitical "manifest destiny" that should lead them to the unification of the Eurasian landmass and to replace Western liberal principles with more conservative values; if Russians fail in doing so, this treachery would end up only in the disappearance of Russia itself: "If we [. . .] repress this vector [i.e. the building of the Eurasian Empire], we will pierce the very heart of Russian people, we will deprive them of national identity, turn them into historical rudiment and we will prevent the global, teleological, eschatological process."[39] [3.89]

Per Dugin, Russia possesses the quality and legitimacy to forge a universal empire, since its destiny rests entirely on an imperial vocation inherited with the appropriation of the title of Moscow as Third Rome. He argues that unlike Imperial Rome, Imperial Russia possesses deep teleological, eschatological meaning, which he connects to Hegel's notion about the Absolute Idea manifested in the self-conscious realization of the Prussian state. However, both Prussia and then Germany did not fully fulfil this concept, whereas Russia, the Third Rome, would be perfectly fit to accomplish it in a historical, religious, cultural, geographical, and strategic sense. The Hegelian concept of Absolute Idea applied to the Russian case would imply the civilizational conquest of the Eurasian continent, beyond the notion of "nation state."[40] [3.90]

Dugin believes firmly that Russia and the Russian people bear a special "messianic" mission of planetary importance, which should replace Atlanticist liberalism with Eurasian conservatism.[41] [3.91]

In a rather reductionist fashion, the Russian philosopher believes that the only thing that matters for Russia and the rest of the world is the clash of the Eurasian land-based empire—an "invisible empire" that only Eurasianists perceive—with the US-led Atlanticist political bloc. Through the lens of geopolitical analysis, Dugin brings back all events that concern politics, culture, and religion to shadows of this great conflict between land power and [3.92] sea power, which would ultimately lead to the creation of a great empire and the fall of another. Within this context, Russia's specific role is to lead the world in forging a new multipolar order that would replace the unipolar global model.

[3.93]   Dugin foresees four possible outcomes of the geopolitical struggle between Sea and Land.[42]

[3.94]   The first possibility is the victory of Thalassocracy, which would annihilate the civilization of Tellurocracy. This would imply that the entire planet would adopt the liberal-democratic model and subdue to the United States and Western allies. The consequence of this outcome would also represent the end of geopolitical history, with the overwhelm of the rule of the Land—incarnating the traditional world—and the triumph of the rule of the Sea—personifying the modern world. This scenario corresponds to the radical messianic viewpoint of fundamentalist neocons. In Dugin's thought, which is heavily influenced by occultist and eschatological elements that follow some ideas proposed by Julius Evola, Herman Wirth, and René Guénon, tradition and modernity are totally opposed as two geographical opposites: thus, the philosopher's world is divided into a Russian-led ideocratic, conservative, and stable Empire of the Land and the US-led democratic, liberal, and progressivist Empire of the Sea.

[3.95]   The second possibility is that the victory of Thalassocracy would end the cycle of conflict between the two civilizations but does not spread its liberal-democratic model upon the rest of the world, though ending geopolitical history. This outcome would coincide with Francis Fukuyama's vision of "end of history" in the ambiguous notion of liberal democracy and a dynamic headway towards a free market economy throughout the world.

[3.96]   The third possibility is that the defeat of global Tellurocracy occurred after the demise of the Soviet empire is only momentary since Eurasia will return to its pan-continental mission under a new form. The consequence would be the world's return to a bipolar system, though differing completely from the Cold War era.

[3.97]   Finally, the last possibility is given by the victory of Tellurocracy, which would base the international system on a civilizational model and enclose the cycle of history. The whole world, through a conservative revolution, would be transformed into a multipolar system and ideocracy would rule everywhere. The ideocratic Land power emerging from the World-Island would be the Pan-Eurasian Empire, a dominant actor unified "from Dublin to Vladivostok," in the frame of a multipolar world.

[3.98]   NOTES

[3n1]   1. Nicholas J. Spykman, Helen R. Nicholl, and Frederick S. Dunn, *The Geography of the Peace* (New York: Harcourt, Brace and Co., 1944), 41.

2. Colin S. Gray, "The Continued Primacy of Geography," *Orbis* 40, no. 2 (1996): 248–49, doi:10.1016/s0034387(96)90063-0.   [3n2]

3. Saul B. Cohen, *Geography and Politics in a World Divided* (New York: Oxford University Press, 1975), 3.   [3n3]

4. Ibid, 29.   [3n4]

5. Geoffrey Parker, *Geopolitics: Past, Present and Future* (London: Pinter, 1998).   [3n5]

6. Saul B. Cohen, *Geopolitics: The Geography of International Relations* (Lanham, MD: Rowman & Littlefield, 2015).   [3n6]

7. Yves Lacoste, *Géopolitique: La Longue Histoire D'Aujourdhui* (Paris: Larousse, 2006).   [3n7]

8. Gerard Kearns, *Geopolitics and Empire: The Legacy of Halford Mackinder* (Oxford: Oxford University Press, 2011), 3–4.   [3n8]

9. Friedrich Ratzel (30 August 1844—9 August 1904) was born in Karlsruhe, in Baden-Württemberg. A prominent geographer and ethnologist, Ratzel was the founder of the so-called "anthropogeography," which is a branch of science that studies the distribution, localization, and spatial organization of human beings. He was the first to coin the expression "living space" (*Lebensraum*), which would have had much following and relevance in demographic studies. He also highlighted the fundamental contributions of ethnic groups to the establishment of historical civilizations. In the early years of his life he worked mainly in the Mediterranean area, and then—from 1874 to 1876—he lived in North America, Cuba, and Mexico, where he studied the distribution of German ethnic groups that had migrated in these countries in the previous decades. When he came back to Germany, he undertook an academic career, holding lectures at the universities of Munich and Leipzig, and publishing significant works related to geography, anthropology, and ethnography. His main works are *Vorgeschichte des Europäischen Menschen* ("Prehistory of Europeans") (1875), *Anthropogeographie* ("Human Geography") (1882–1891), *Volkerkunde* ("Human Races") (1885–1888), *Politische Geographie* ("Political Geography") (1897), and *Die Erde und das Leben* ("The Earth and Life") (1902).   [3n9]

10. Robert D. Kaplan, *The Revenge of Geography: What the Map Tells Us about Coming Conflicts and the Battle against Fate* (New York: Random House Trade Paperbacks, 2013), 80–81.   [3n10]

11. Rudolf Kjellén (30 August 1848—9 August 1922) was born in Torsö, Sweden, and is considered the founding father of geopolitics. After teaching geography for several years, he then became professor of political science and statistics at the university of Göteborg and Uppsala. Kjellén would highly influence the German school of *Geopolitik*. His major works include *Samtidens Stormakter* ("Contemporary World Powers") (1914), *Världskrigets Politiska Problem* ("The Political Issues of the World War") (1915), and *Staten som Livsform* ("The State as Life Form") (1916).   [3n11]

12. Kaplan, *The Revenge of Geography*, 81.   [3n12]

13. Ibid.   [3n13]

14. Emidio Diodato, *Che Cos'è La Geopolitica* (Rome: Carocci, 2011), 13.   [3n14]

15. Paolo A. Dossena and Giorgio Galli, *Lo Scienziato e Lo Sciamano: Mackinder, Hitler e L'Isola Del Mondo* (Turin: Lindau, 2011), 171.   [3n15]

16. Alfred Thayer Mahan (27 September 1840—1 December 1914) was an American naval officer and historian whose strategic thought would have deep impact in military circles. In his studies, he focused on the role of maritime and naval power. He believed in the contrast between continental and sea powers, arguing that the latter presented some characteristics that made them intrinsically stronger in the competition. Mahan analyzed the development of the navy in the late 17th century and early 19th century, when the great colonial powers of France and Great Britain confronted each other. He firmly believed that geographical factors could influence the course of history, and that maritime power could assure more easily the freedom of the seas and, accordingly, international trade. Among his main works are *The Influence of Sea Power Upon History, 1660–1783* (1890), *The Influence of Sea Power upon the French Revolution and Empire, 1793–1812* (1892), *The Interest of America in Sea Power, Present and Future* (1897), and *Naval Strategy: Compared and Contrasted with the Principles and Practice of Military Operations on Land* (1911).   [3n16]

17. Kaplan, *The Revenge of Geography*, 103.   [3n17]

18. Diodato, *Che Cos'è La Geopolitica*, 51–54.   [3n18]

[3n19]   19. Carl Schmitt (11 July 1888—7 April 1985) was a German jurist and political theorist. He wrote extensively about the effective wielding of political power. His work has influenced the subsequent political theory, legal theory, continental philosophy, and political theology. His ideas related to the contraposition between sea power and land power were expressed in the work *Land und Meer. Eine Weltgeschichtliche Betrachtung* (Land and Sea. A World-historical Meditation) (1942).

[3n20]   20. Kaplan, *The Revenge of Geography*, 80.

[3n21]   21. Diodato, *Che Cos'è La Geopolitica*, 16–19.

[3n22]   22. Christopher J. Fettweis, "On Heartlands and Chessboards: Classical Geopolitics, Then and Now," *Orbis* 59, no. 2 (2015).

[3n23]   23. Francis Fukuyama, *The End of History and the Last Man* (New York: Free Press, 1992).

[3n24]   24. Immanuel Wallerstein, *The Capitalist World-economy* (Cambridge: Cambridge University Press, 1979).

[3n25]   25. Barry Buzan, Charles A. Jones, and Richard Little, *The Logic of Anarchy: Neorealism to Structural Realism* (New York: Columbia University Press, 1993).

[3n26]   26. Edward N. Luttwak, "From Geopolitics to Geo-Economics: Logic of Conflict, Grammar of Commerce," *The National Interest*, no. 20 (1990): 17, 19.

[3n27]   27. Robert J. Art, "A Defensible Defense: America's Grand Strategy after the Cold War," *International Security* 15, no. 4 (1991): 10–11. doi:10.2307/2539010.

[3n28]   28. Mackubin T. Owens, "In Defense of Classical Geopolitics," *Orbis* 59, no. 4 (2015).

[3n29]   29. Ibid.

[3n30]   30. Jason Voss, "The Value of Geopolitical Analysis," *CFA Institute Magazine* 25, no. 3 (2014): 18.

[3n31]   31. Ibid.

[3n32]   32. Aleksandr Dugin, *Osnovi Geopolitike. Geopolitička Budućnost Rusije* (Zrenjanin: Ekopres, 2004), 23–24.

[3n33]   33. Ibid, 24–25.

[3n34]   34. Ibid, 26.

[3n35]   35. Ibid, 29.

[3n36]   36. Ibid, 27.

[3n37]   37. Ibid.

[3n38]   38. Ibid.

[3n39]   39. Ibid, 175.

[3n40]   40. Ibid, 174–75.

[3n41]   41. Ibid, 167–69.

[3n42]   42. Ibid, 30.

Chapter Four

The Foundations of Eurasian Power

*The Strategic Role of the Heartland
Region in Geopolitical Thought*

[4.0]   INTRODUCTION

[4.1]   Sir Halford J. Mackinder[1] is often considered the father of modern-day geopolitics.[2] It is not per chance that his geopolitical thought, highlighting the
strategic relevance of Eurasia for world hegemony—albeit from an antagonistic point of view—, is considered fundamental by the neo-Eurasianist
movement. Aleksandr Dugin himself places Mackinder among the major
thinkers that have influenced the geopolitical conceptions of Eurasianism and
that have helped to build the framework of the new multipolar world order
Eurasianists seek to build. Dugin spends many pages of his works quoting
Mackinder's geopolitical theories and their implications for Eurasia. Indeed,
Mackinder was one of the first thinkers to understand the strategic relevance
of the Eurasian landmass for the purposes of world rule. His geopolitical
thought, chiefly expressed in the theory of the pivotal region—or Heartland—of the Eurasian continent, describes through the principle of geographic reality how to achieve control of Eurasia—or World-Island—and thus of
the entire planet. The core of this conception is embodied by Mackinder's
famous dictum according to which who controls Eastern Europe controls the
Heartland, who controls the Heartland controls the World-Island, and who
controls the World-Island ultimately controls the rest of the world. The main
feature that grants a strategic superiority to the Heartland would be its natural
inaccessibility by sea power. Mackinder's main concern was that of a single
power—or of an alliance of powers—that would eventually unite Eurasia
into a single geopolitical empire strong enough to act as a hegemonic global

player.[3] The existence of such a mighty domain would have clearly put at stake the existence of sea powers, and primarily that of the thalassocratic British Empire.[4]

Mackinder recognized that continents represented landmasses emerging from the waters each bearing a different strategic weight, and that a clear distinction existed between sea powers and continental powers, as Alfred Mahan had already acknowledged.   [4.2]

The British geographer decided to name the continental landmass that forms Eurasia "World-Island." This vast area included on the outside the highly populated and developed sea countries of the Eurasian peripheral rim and on the inside enormous territories scarcely populated but filled with resources. The very core of the World-Island is represented by what he initially called the world's pivotal region or "geographical pivot of history" and later the Heartland.   [4.3]

Mackinder's geopolitical worldview highlighted some truly significant aspects like the repartition of lands and seas as essential factor in the historical and cultural evolution of nations, the relevance of maritime navigation in the history of civilization, and the strategic organization of big inner spaces as nuclei for political might.   [4.4]

Mackinder's ideas and observations would have thoroughly influenced the German *Geopolitik* school of thought, embodied by strategists like Karl Haushofer,[5] and somewhat the Nazi logics of territorial expansionism and plans of conquest. Likewise, his influence would have been significant for the Cold War era, especially for the US containment strategy against the USSR, the Heartland-holder. Moreover, Mackinder's thought would have been studied and improved by strategists like Nicholas Spykman, who would retort the Briton's theory by suggesting the strategic superiority of the Inner Crescent—or "Rimland"—rather than that of the Heartland.   [4.5]

It is paradoxical that Mackinder, a strategist that belonged to a sea-power and that wrote for the benefits of imperial Britain, in fact contributed in creating some useful strategic principles for the rival continental powers of Germany and Russia.[6] The description of the strategic value of the Heartland and of the Eurasian landmass turned Mackinder ironically into a chief master for continental pan-Eurasianists, from Karl Haushofer to Aleksandr Dugin.   [4.6]

MACKINDER'S "NEW GEOGRAPHY"   [4.7]

Mackinder's strategic thought pivots on the principles dictated by geographical realities. The unchanging geographical realities would lead to the geopolitical destiny of nations. In this context, human beings would represent biological elements that interact in harmony with the geological soil, the natural environment, and the climatologic features of their land, becoming   [4.8] natural parts of a geographic reality. Geographical reality is strictly linked to Darwinism and determinism, and it influences the historical and civilizational development of peoples.

[4.9]   In the year 1887, Mackinder published, for the benefit of the Royal Geographical Society, an innovative article entitled *On the Scope and Methods of Geography*. This article introduced the concept of "New Geography."[7] The issue that Mackinder wished to raise was fundamental for the knowledge and teaching of the science of geography, which was highly criticized and considered with skepticism by British academia. He asked himself and his audience what geography truly represented and whether it could have been transformed into a proper discipline rather than just a mere body of information. To answer these questions, Mackinder believed it necessary to understand what the true scopes and methods of the geographic science were. With his article, Mackinder attempted to demonstrate that not only geography represented a proper discipline, separate from geology and history,[8] but that it was also necessary for the natural evolution and progress of many others.

[4.10]   Mackinder began his dissertation describing the role that geographical societies played, especially during the 19th century, in actively promoting the exploration of the world. Thanks to the helpful support of these societies, explorers, merchants and travelers had been able to discover, for the profit of all humankind, an increasing number of new lands and countries. The result had been the global discoveries that led to the unveiling of the world's entirety. Thanks to global discoveries the world became a closed geographical—and thereby political—system.[9] The gradual exploration of the world therefore led to "the natural result [. . .] that we are now near the end of the roll of great discoveries."[10] Indeed, when the article appeared, the only lands that still needed a thorough and systematic exploration were the Polar Regions, some areas in New Guinea, Central Africa and Central Asia, and the Tibetan peaks. This uninterrupted effort by the geographic societies and by the pioneers of world discoveries self-evidently shows the value of the study of the geographical discipline.

[4.11]   The second issue that Mackinder raised referred to the nature of geographical studies. He questioned whether geography should have been considered as one single subject or rather as the sum of several others. In other words, Mackinder enquired whether political geography and physical geography were to be considered as two separate subjects or not. Moreover, he also posed the question whether they were to be recognized as self-existing and self-sufficient or like mere appendices of other subjects, respectively of history and geology. In answering, Mackinder argued that men are the creatures of their environment and that people and territory combine into a single self-sustainable subject known broadly as geography. This does not exclude the fact that within geographical studies different branches may exist, but this fact does not interfere with the general acknowledgment of geography as one coherent philosophical and epistemological system. Each sector of the entire geographical scheme deals with a specific matter. For instance, the function of physical geography is to trace the interaction between humankind and natural environment. In fact, it is a specific characteristic of geography to suggest the influence of locality, or best to say, the change of anthropological variations in contact with environmental diversities. If physical geography fails in doing so, then it turns into mere physiography, a sub-subject of geography itself.

The definition that Mackinder gives to geography is the following: the [4.12] science whose main function is to depict the interaction of man in society and so much of his environment as varies locally.[11] This explanation allows us to comprehend the general definition that may be given, instead, to geopolitics, that of "expression of political power over landscape." The elements that interact here are two:

1. The varying natural environment. [4.13]
2. The communities of men that struggle for existence more or less fa- [4.14] vored by their specific environments.

As for political geography, the discipline could not exist if not built upon [4.15] physical geography. The function of political geography is to detect and demonstrate how much the natural environment interferes in forging the destinies of an entire nation or race of human beings, and how relevant it is to understand the strengths and weaknesses of a country. What counts more is to avoid considering physical geography as a younger sister, if not a maiden, of geology, and political geography that of history. Mackinder clearly perceived the huge gap that still existed between the natural and social sciences and suggested that the geographer, being the master of a half-humanistic and half-scientific subject, could build the bridge over such abyss, linking together the two branches of knowledge.

As already noted, geography itself too divides in several sub-categories, [4.16] although it ought to be studied and considered as a whole. The distinction, in Mackinder's overview, between geology and geography is that the geologist looks at the present in order to interpret the past, and the geographer looks at the past so that he may interpret the present. Physiography asks for a given feature, "Why is it?"; topography, "Where is it?"; physical geography, "Why is it there?"; political geography, "How does it act on man in society, and how does it react on it?"[12]

According to Mackinder, three elements influence the natural environ- [4.17] ment:

1. The configuration of the Earth's surface. [4.18]
2. Meteorology and climate. [4.19]

[4.20]   3. The outputs that countries offer to human industry.

[4.21]   To fully understand how environment affects the history of civilization and political destiny of a race of men, Mackinder offered the example of the influence of England's south-eastern physical geography in molding the English historical character. With accurate descriptions, following the historical periods of the Celtic, Roman and Anglo-Saxon rule over Britain, the English geographer exposed exhaustively how geography influences in a decisive way human settlements and history. The results of these geographical studies are that "from a consideration of the folding of the chalk and of his hardness as compared with the strata above and below it, may be demonstrated the causes of the two great promontories, the two great inlets, and the three great upland openings which have determined the positions, the number and the importance of the chief cities [including London] and divisions of South-eastern England."[13] The same methodological approach could be applied to describing any other geographical region and geo-historical evolution.

[4.22]   Geography, Mackinder continued, must benefit from a separate sphere of work from other subjects, although some may closely be linked to it. In fact, all other subjects involved in geographical reasoning should be analyzed in order to understand whether they are truly pertinent to the main line of geographical argument. It is true, however, that the bounds of all sciences must naturally be compromises, especially when considering geography, which includes features belonging to geology, paleontology, zoology, botany, meteorology, anthropology, history, demography and sociology. As Mackinder stated, "knowledge is one, but its division into subjects is a concession to human weakness"![14]

[4.23]   As for the relations of geography with history, the geographer must turn to history for verifying the relations that he suggests. The historian finds full occupation in the critical and comparative study of original documents, having no time—or will—left to scan science for himself with a holistic view to selecting facts and ideas which he requires: and this is, in fact, the geographer's own duty.

[4.24]   Environment and community are the two main topics to consider and combine when approaching the study of geography. What definitions can be attributed to them?

[4.25]   "Environment" is a term that refers to a natural, exclusive, and locked region. The smaller the area included within it, the greater the number of similar conditions will be. Thus, there are environments of different orders, whose extension may vary.

[4.26]   On the other hand, "community" is a term that refers to a group of men bearing certain characteristics in common. Even here, the smaller the community is, the greater the number of common characteristics tends to be.

Community can also differ in terms of orders and species: there are self-sustaining communities expressed by races, nations, provinces, and towns.

Geography should then question what the effects would be of exposing, for instance, two communities to one environment—e.g. two different ethnic groups dwelling within the same territory—or one community to two environments—e.g. the Anglo-Saxon race into the three different environments of Britain, America, and Australia.   [4.27]

Mackinder firmly believed that at all latitudes and in all ages, all political questions could be answered by physical geography.[15] He attempted to demonstrate that certain conditions of climate and soil are needed for the aggregation of dense populations. A certain density of population seems necessary to the development of civilization. Wide plains, for instance, seem especially favorable to the development of homogeneous races, whereas heterogeneous landscapes tend to encourage a variegated racial offspring. The course of history at every given moment, whether in politics and economics or in any other social human activity and behavior, is the result of the interaction between the natural environment and human society. In Mackinder's words, "the course of history at a given moment, whether in politics, society, or any other sphere of human activity, is the product not only of environment but also of the momentum acquired in the past."[16]   [4.28]

Mackinder noticed that two environmental conditions are somewhat favorable to the development of civilization: the density of population and the ease of communication. The example he uses is that of the Ganges valley for the further development of the Hindu civilization. Of course, a wealthy civilized country is a regional temptation for a conqueror, either if it commands a sea power or a continental power: this one too is a geographical constant. "Geographical selection" leads statesmen and peoples to choose the best geographical locations to build harbors, commercial warehouses, cities, metropolises, fortresses, and so on: the term bears the same meaning as "natural selection" in biology. This statement should not surprise, since Mackinder was heavily influenced by the Darwinian theory of evolution. Neo-Lamarckism and Darwinism offered Mackinder a theoretical framework for constructing his conception of geography and for forging his worldview: the British geographer was essentially a social-Darwinist who accounted history as a struggle for the survival amongst different human groups.[17]   [4.29]

Thanks to the paper *On the Scopes and Methods of Geography*, Mackinder helped the learned men of his time to render to geography its honorable merit. The discipline's chief value and achievement relied on its inherent and holistic breadth; geography satisfied at once the practical requirements of the statesman and merchant, the theoretical requirements of the historian and scientist, and the intellectual requirements of the teacher: [4.30]

[4.31]   "To me it seems that geography combines some of the requisite qualities. To
          the practical man, whether he aim at distinction in the State or at the amassing
          of wealth, it is a store of invaluable information; to the student it is a stimulat-
          ing basis from which to set out along a hundred special lines; to the teacher it
          would be an implement for the calling out of the power of the intellect [. . .].
          All this we say on the assumption of the unity of the subject. The alternative is
          to divide the scientific from the practical. The result of its adoption will be the
          ruin of both. The practical will be rejected by the teacher and will be found
          indigestible in after life. The scientific will be neglected by most men, because
          it lacks the element of utility in every-day life. The man of the world and the
          student, the scientist and the historian, will lose their common platform. The
          world will be the poorer." [18]

[4.32]   ## THE GEOPOLITICAL AWARENESS OF BRITISH MIGHT

[4.33]   In 1902, Mackinder published a significant geographic digest on the descrip-
          tion of the regions of the world. This work included the account of all
          geographic areas divided into the following volumes: Britain and the British
          Seas; Western Europe and the Mediterranean; Central Europe; Scandinavia
          and the Arctic Region; the Russian Empire; the Nearer East; Africa; India;
          the Farther East; North America; South America; Australasia and Antarctica.

[4.34]   The first of these volumes, that regarding Britain, was written by Mack-
          inder himself and it represents a wonderful example of how geographical
          features influence the history, the political system, the philosophical mental-
          ity, and the ethnography of a country.

[4.35]   Mackinder begins his description of Britain focusing on its position on
          the map. He admits that before the great geographical discoveries of the 15th
          and 16th centuries, the known lands laid almost wholly in the Northern
          Hemisphere and spread in a single continent, from the shores of Spain to
          those of China. Therefore, Britain was then at the end of the world, being the
          utmost corner of the West: "Before the great geographical discoveries of the
          fifteenth and sixteenth centuries, the known lands lay almost wholly in the
          Northern Hemisphere and spread in a single continent from the shores of
          Spain to those of Cathay [China]. Britain was then at the end of the world
          almost out of the world." [19]

[4.36]   Consequently, during two thousand years, Britain was at the margin, not
          in the center, of the theatre of politics, and, for most practical purposes, its
          position was accurately shown in the maps of the Greek geographers and in
          the fantastic charts of the medieval monks:

[4.37]   "In pre-Columbian times, then, Britain lay off the western shore of the world,
          almost precisely midway between the North Cape and the coast of Barbary, the
          northern and southern limits of the known. Northward and westward was the
          ice; south-westward lay a waste of waters; southward, beyond the Mediterra-

nean, was the great [Saharan] desert. Only eastward and southeastward did the
world of men spread far through the known into the half-known, and only in
those directions was Britain related to opposing coasts."[20]

Notwithstanding, the Columbian discoveries of the Americas radically mod-   [4.38]
ified the geopolitical position and meaning of the British Isles in the world.
After the finding of the Americas and the circumnavigation of Africa, Britain
suddenly appeared to be in the very midst of the world, standing almost half
the way from the old Eurasian continent and the lands of new discovery.
Britain was now the center of the world because, due to its maritime position,
it could project power along different trajectories: towards America, towards
Africa, and towards Eurasia.

Accordingly, Mackinder believed that Britain possessed two geographical   [4.39]
qualities, which were complementary rather than antagonistic: insularity and
universality. Before Columbus, the insularity was more evident than the
universality; but after Columbus, Britain's significance began to rely on the
oceanic links, which are in their nature universal.[21] The oceanic routes led
Britain to rule the waves and to become the dominant sea power in modern
history. The dualistic position of Britain—partly in Europe and partly in the
Atlantic Ocean—dragged the island country to roll away from the European
continent and to expand beyond the sea. The seas preserved its liberty, and
allowed the rise of private initiative, as well as more liberal forms of government since freedom is the natural privilege of islanders. Moreover, Britain
owes to the submarine platform the currents and tidal fluctuations that have
shaped the detail of its coastlines, increased the value of its estuarine harbors,
contributed to the motive power of its shipping, determined the position and
seasons of its fisheries, and ultimately pushed the country to develop maritime power.

According to Mackinder, the British environment is characterized by six   [4.40]
essential qualities:

> "1) Insularity, which has tended to preserve the continuity of social organiza-   [4.41]
> tion; 2) accessibility, which has admitted stimulus from without, and prevented
> stagnation; 3) division into a more accessible east and a less accessible west,
> which has made for variety of initiative and consequent interaction; 4) produc-
> tivity of soil and climate, the necessary basis of a virile native growth; 5)
> possession of a vast potential energy stored in deposits of coal, the mainspring
> of industrial life; and 6) interpenetration by arms of tidal sea, giving access to
> the universal ocean-road of modern commerce."[22]

In terms of the dynamic aspects of British geography—i.e. its strategic geog-   [4.42]
raphy—the role of controlling the seas is the main element for safeguarding
Britain's power. Mackinder believed that strategic geography represents that
branch of geography that deals with the larger topographical conditions of

offence and defense, and that defense is essentially the protection of the means of economic subsistence. Accordingly, he affirmed that the defense of Britain rests fundamentally upon the theory implied in the command of the sea.[23]

[4.43]   Mackinder speculated that in a military sense a country has command of the sea, as against another country with which it is at war, when it has destroyed the enemy's fleet or securely blockaded it and has thus carried the national frontier for the purpose of the war and for that purpose only, to the enemy's coast. By way of example, he surmises that had Britain obtained command of the sea in a war with France, the effect would be to carry the British frontier to the coast of France, and to add the Channel to Britain as a part of the globe within which the commanding country could prepare an attack against the enemy. Under such circumstances, England would be safe from invasion by sea, and France would be liable to it. That famous English expression stating that the navy is Britain's shield and the army its spear summarizes well British strategic strengths. In terms of projection of power over the coastline, Mackinder believes that the enemy's coasts are the utmost limit of sea power, whose final office is to give freedom in the selection of the point at which to deliver an attack with land forces. The opposite example given is the following: Had France obtained command of the sea, France would move freely in the Channel, and would deliberately choose its anchorage for the invasion of Britain. Viewed from this perspective, Mackinder reckoned that the defense of Britain resolved into three problems: "1) The retention of the command of the sea, or rather, of the power of taking that command should occasion demand it; 2) the defense of Great Britain should the command of the sea be temporarily lost; 3) the separate defense of Ireland in the same contingency, for under such a condition the prompt and certain reinforcement of the army in Ireland would not be practicable."[24]

[4.44]   According to Mackinder, the most threatened regions of Britain were those closest to the continental angle and the Channel entries. At the time Mackinder was writing, all the chief bases of naval power laid within Metropolitan England, near the shores of the Narrow Seas. Chatham, Sheerness, Portsmouth, and Devonport were the dockyards, standing opposite to the Rhine mouths, to Cherbourg, and to Brest. Harbors of refuge laid between them at Portland, at Dover, and at Harwich. The great naval arsenal was at Woolwich. The naval schools were at Dartmouth, Portsmouth, and Greenwich. Walmer, on the coast of Kent, was the depot of the marines, and the three divisions of the marines ashore were stationed at Chatham, Portsmouth, and Devonport. The dockyards of Pembroke in Wales, and Queenstown in the south of Ireland, were the only important naval stations beyond the limits of Metropolitan England, and their position had an obvious bearing on the defense of the ocean roads where they enter the St. George's and the Bristol Channels. The exercise ground of the navy, on the other hand, was often to the west of Ireland, clear of the steam lanes of commerce, in waters where seamanship could practice in oceanic weather. Moreover, the centers of the mobile army in England were at Aldershot and on Salisbury Plain, on the flank of an enemy's line of march from the south coast to London, and in a position to relieve Portsmouth and to repel attack either from the Devonian Peninsula or the Bristol Channel. They were also convenient for the shipmen of an army going overseas from Southampton, London, and Bristol. Colchester was the prepared basis for the defense of the Metropolis from attack on the east. Dover, Chatham, Portsmouth, and Devonport had garrisons, but Portsmouth was probably the only first-class British fortress. There used to be a small garrison at Portland, and there were large depots at Winchester and Canterbury. There were Guards at Windsor, and Cavalry at Hounslow, in the western outskirts of London. Woolwich was the chief station of the Artillery, and Chatham of the Engineers. At Woolwich, Sandhurst, and Camberley were the institutions for military education. At Waltham and Enfield on the Lea were the factories of explosives and small arms, and at Pimlico the clothing factory. In Industrial England and in Scotland the main military centers were at York and at Edinburgh; but the troops stationed in these districts remote from the Continent were but a few thousand for recruiting purposes and for the support of the police. They consisted usually of regiments lately returned from Foreign Service, whereas those preparing to go abroad were concentrated at Aldershotand on Salisbury Plain. As in the case of the Navy, there were private works in Industrial England, which formed an ultimate reserve for the manufacture of weapons. In Ireland, the location of the military forces was analogous to that in the greater island, and for somewhat similar reasons. Strategy in Ireland turned necessarily on Dublin, and on the roads in rear of the Wicklow mountains, which communicate between Dublin, on the one hand, and Waterford and Cork on the other. The chief military station, apart from Dublin, was the Curragh, the Irish Aldershot, near Kildare on the Liffey, where the roadways branch which led down the valley of the Barrow to Waterford, and across the plains of Queen's County and Tipperary to Cork and Limerick. Most of the remaining troops were distributed among several small stations within and about the triangle Waterford-Limerick-Cork. In the north and west were but a few scattered units, comparable to those commanded from York and Edinburgh, used for recruiting purposes. In conclusion, the effective forces were within and about the continental angle, but the reserves of men and constructive power, both military and naval, were distributed through Industrial England, Scotland and Ireland.[25]

In considering the British Empire, Mackinder—a convinced imperialist—affirms that the reason behind British imperial expansionism was to be found in the upholding of the idea of supporting a trade that would have been opened to the entire world. The reasons for British expansion were very [4.45] clear: when order broke down, or foreign interference was threatened in a land in which large British interests were at stake, Britain was often compelled to add it to its possessions by assuming authority among an alien and distant population. The British imperial strategy was focused on the need to supersede the imperial rivals' trade:

[4.46]   "Britain undertook the conquest of India in the course of trade-competition with France; she extended her Indian domain to prevent interference with her rule from without; she became mistress of Egypt and of the Cape because they command the roads to the Indies; she conquered the Sudan for the purpose of ensuring the water supply of Egypt; she has annexed Rhodesia and the Transvaal in order to protect her position at the Cape. Thus, and by similar processes, has Britain incurred vast Imperial responsibilities both in Asia and Africa. Internal and external peace and just administration are the returns made to India for freedom of trade and security of capital."[26]

[4.47]   According to Mackinder, the Empire rested on two fundamental pillars: the federation of different countries into a British Commonwealth, and the British rule among diverse peoples: "Thus Empire has for Britain two meanings: the federation, loose or close, of several British commonwealths, and the maintenance of British rule among alien races."[27]

[4.48]   The entire reason for British imperial building was due, of course, to economic purposes and specifically to the need for preserving the international oceanic commercial routes. Mackinder considered the British Empire as the most enlightened and well governed of the time. The natural separation of the British colonies by the oceanic waters somewhat safeguarded the Empire from social upheavals and racial tensions: "For of all empires in the world's history, the British is probably the best calculated to preserve the dominant nation from the destruction of its own liberties. The intervening ocean holds wide apart the masses of the ruling and of the subject peoples."[28]

[4.49]   Regarding British maritime empire, the British fleet in the Mediterranean, based on the control of the small territories of Malta, Gibraltar and Cyprus, was one of the most extraordinary historical examples of detached imperial power. The English maritime control of the Mediterranean strategic waterways found its main purpose on the protection of the routes to the Indies against a potential threat given for instance by Russian expansion towards the Ottoman Empire, in the Balkans and in the Near East:

[4.50]   "The ships were there primarily for the defense of the road to India, but owing to the fact that both France and Russia had coasts on the Northern Seas and on the Mediterranean, the British Mediterranean fleet acted incidentally for the defense of London. Were Malta abandoned and the ships withdrawn to the English Channel, France and Russia would be free to concentrate a larger part of their naval strength in northern waters. Thus the Mediterranean fleet, while maintaining the imperial road, served also the purpose of the defense of the island. Owing to the continuity of the ocean and to the consequent mobility of sea power, the same may be said of every British squadron, whether in the Indian Ocean, at the Cape, in the China Seas, in the Australian Seas, off the Pacific Coast of America, in the West Indies, or at the Falkland Islands. The strength of each is adjusted to the number of foreign ships in the same waters, because each foreign ship in a distant sea is absent from the neighborhood of Britain itself. Even the army in India, maintained always on a war footing, is a school for the training of officers and men, who, on their return to Britain, form reserves, whether officially recognized or not, tending to reduce the risk of invasion, and helping to avert the political dangers of a great standing army at home."[29]

Nonetheless, Mackinder already foresaw the elements of instability of the British Empire and depicted the potential portrait of Great Britain without its world empire: foreign markets would have been lost, and employment for British workers reduced; capital may have been repaid by debtor countries, and the annual interest may have ceased to be received; the carrying trade may have dwindled, and shipping be transferred to other flags; the preference of later generations of colonists may have grown weaker, and they may have bought more impartially from the competitors of the mother country; finally, the coalfields at home may have been exhausted, and no fresh supply of energy would be available.[30]   [4.51]

In terms of imperial rivalry, Mackinder perfectly understood that at the beginning of the twentieth century, a new balance of power was being wrought, and already only five great world powers existed: Britain, France, Germany, Russia, and the United States of America. Their expansion was a clear threat to world peace. France and Germany were obliged to maintain great armies, and could not afford supreme fleets, although possessing vulnerable colonies. The United States had sacrificed an impregnable isolation and had to care for the defense of the ocean paths to its new possessions. Even Russia had come down to the coast at points accessible to sea power. All of them had emerged from continental seclusion and had made themselves neighbors of Great Britain in the Ocean. All Britons were threatened by the recent expansion of other European powers, and all were ready to share in the support of the common fleet, as being the cheapest method of ensuring peace and freedom to each. Thus, the chief dangers for the British Empire were not the subjugated colonies, but rather the colonial and imperial rise of other countries. This fact compelled Britain to maintain a fleet at least equivalent to those of the United States and Russia. Mackinder already forecasted two of the main reasons for the outbreak of World War One: the naval arms race on one hand, and the rivalry for colonial expansionism on the other.   [4.52]

[4.53]   THE WORLD'S PIVOTAL REGION

[4.54]   In April 1904, while he was Reader in Geography at the University of Oxford and Director of the London School of Economics and Political Science, Mackinder published a fundamental article in the Geographic Journal of the Royal Geographical Society entitled *The Geographical Pivot of History*. This original work introduced for the first time the idea that within Eurasia laid a vast pivotal region whose possession would have allowed the rule over the rest of the Eurasian continental landmass. This theory—which would evolve in 1919 into the idea of the Heartland—affirms that the rule over the pivotal area is inevitable for gaining supremacy over the World-Island—i.e. Eurasia. At the same time, the control of Eurasia would allow the rule of the rest of the world by creating a hegemonic global empire capable of blending telluro-cratic and thalassocratic power, and of transforming the rest of the peripheral continents into secondary global actors, economically and strategically dependent upon the Eurasian continental block.

[4.55]   To introduce the concept of the Eurasian pivotal region, Mackinder begins his argument with a lengthy historical dissertation on the European geographical discoveries that commenced in the 15th–16th centuries to show how they had affected on the political quest for world hegemony. At the beginning of the 20th century, Mackinder argues, the entire world had been completely discovered and conquered, and no land was left to possess because undiscovered.[31] The beginning of the world's "discovery" followed two precise directions: while Western European sea powers, from Vasco da Gama onwards, started exploring the oceans and maritime routes that connected the continents, creating trade posts and colonies in all continents, at the same time Russian land-power, thanks to Yermak and his Cossacks, began its exploration of Siberia and Inner Asia, soon expanding till the Pacific shores and reaching—with the crossing of the Bering Strait—Alaska and America. In other words, the world had been explored and carried to geographical unity at the same epoch, both by sea and by land. Therefore, in the post-Columbian age, nations were bound to deal with a closed political system of worldwide scope.[32] Indeed, the post-Columbian age managed to transform the world into a worldwide closed political system, thus leading all international actors to confront each other: international relations could finally become organic and systemic. During the time the author wrote, at the beginning of the 20th century, a correlation linked together all larger geographical and historical generalizations. It was already possible to consider the world's events as a whole in terms of geographic width: history and geography already intermingled. This closed international system offered a correlation between the larger geographical and the larger historical generalizations and offered the faculty to formulate some general theories of geographical causation in universal history that would expose the competing forces in current international politics.[33] Within this perspective, the aim of Mackinder's study was to describe the physical features of the world that had been—and still were—most coercive of human action and to present the chief phases of history as originally linked to them. This, in other words, meant nothing more than exhibiting human history as part of the life of what was considered the "world organism."[34] The idea of world organism strongly recalls the geographical determinism of Ratzel, of whom Mackinder was a close reader and shared his organic conception of the state.[35]

Social Darwinism, determinism, biological racism, and imperialism had had a remarkable philosophical impact in late 19th century European societies, and Mackinder was accused—often correctly—of being a promoter of these ideologies.[36] Indeed, following a Darwinian pattern, Mackinder stated that the birth of nations was the result of the pressure of a common tribulation. He believed that nations were wrought under a common need to resist against outer forces, and his historical determinism, that made historical facts depend on a principle of causality, led him to affirm that: [4.56]

> "The idea of England was beaten into the Heptarchy by Danish and Norman conquerors; the idea of France was forced upon competing Franks, Goths, and Romans by the Huns at Chalons, and in the Hundred Years' War with England; the idea of Christendom was born of the Roman persecutions, and matured by the Crusades; the idea of the United States was accepted, and local colonial patriotism sunk, only in the long War of Independence; the idea of the German Empire was reluctantly adopted in South Germany only after a struggle against France in comradeship with North Germany."[37]   [4.57]

According to the British geographer, Europe's entire destiny and development, for the good and for the bad, relied wholly on its relationship with Asia. In other words, European history was subordinate to Asiatic history since European civilization represented the outcome of the secular struggle against Asian invasions.[38] This revolutionary—yet almost obvious—idea is one of the foundations on which Mackinder's thought rests and is essential to understanding all further implications of his theory.   [4.58]

As a geographical entity, Europe presents a remarkable contrast that splits it up into two distinctive parts: Russia occupies half the continent, connecting the European peninsula with the Asiatic landmass, and the Western powers the remaining territorial appendices, which stretch like branches in the sea. This partition shows a physical contrast between the unbroken lowland in the East and the land variety in the West, and some may consider the existence of a possible correlation between natural environment—its flatness or diversity—and political organization—more representative and centrifugal regime on one hand, or more despotic and centripetal on the other. As far as Eastern Europe is concerned, a separation line exists that cuts the region into two distinct areas: the forest and marsh region in the north, from the Baltic region   [4.59] to the Urals, and the steppe region, from Western Ukraine to Turkistan, in Central Asia. Beyond this line, moving westwards, lays peninsular Europe, which commences with three distinguishing natural environments next to its eastern borders: the Hungarian great plain—or *Puszta*; the Carpathian Mountains; the German woods. The above-mentioned separation between forest/marsh and steppe regions slowly diminished during the 19th century because of Russian cultivations, but it had been formerly very harsh for humankind to inhabit.

[4.60]   The geographical division of Europe and Eurasia into areas of either forests/marshes or steppes determined their historical destiny, since the landscape either encouraged or discouraged migrations of peoples, raids and invasions throughout time:

[4.61]   "For a thousand years a series of horse-riding peoples emerged from Asia through the broad interval between the Ural Mountains and the Caspian Sea, rode through the open spaces of Southern Russia, and struck home into Hungary in the very heart of the European peninsula, shaping by the necessity of opposing them the history of each of the great peoples around—the Russians, the Germans, the French, the Italians, and the Byzantines Greeks."[39]

[4.62]   The arrival in the European peninsula of the Turanian peoples (5th–16th centuries)—a historical phenomenon that started manifesting with the Hunnish invasion led by Attila and continued with that of the Avars, Bulgars, Magyars, Khazars, Patzinaks, Cumans, Mongols, and Kalmyks—gave birth to the secular struggle between nomadic Asians and settled Europeans. Through the vast gateway between the Urals and the Caspian Sea, thousands of these horsemen, originally residing in Mongolia and Turkistan, flooded into the fertile and rainy European lands, giving shape to the idea of a common European fellowship united against the Asiatic invaders. Indeed, these continuative nomadic invasions and raids influenced the birth of Western European nations, settling them in their current lands, creating a common European identity, and uniting the European kinsmen after centuries of brotherly struggles against each other. For example, the birth of France is strictly linked to the expulsion of the Huns from the lands of Gaul, and that of Austria—formerly *Ostmark*, i.e. "eastern frontier"—relies on the foundation of a marchland by Charlemagne conceived as a bulwark against the oriental invasions. Even the birth of Muscovy—which later absorbed the other Russian principalities and gave birth to the Russian Empire—is a close consequence of the so-called "Tatar yoke,"[40] which Mackinder considered as a dominant factor for Russia's inferior development compared to the rest of Europe: "Russian development was thus delayed and biased at a time when the remainder of Europe was rapidly advancing."[41] Moreover, the Turanian—or Ural-Altaic—pressure from central Eurasia towards Europe forced the European people to cram in the peninsular rims of the continent, thus stimulating a thrust to sail across the seas in search for new vital space and to begin a rise as sea powers.

Parallel to the mighty threat of the Asiatic horsemen, another rival mobility power emerged through the riverways and seaways and waged war against Europe: that of the Vikings in the North and of the Saracens in the South. Whereas the nomadic Asians forced the European frontier in the East, the Norsemen and the Saracens began raiding the continent's coasts and towns from all other directions—West, North, and South. The European settled peoples, gripped between these two pressures, tried to answer with a major cohesion and unity amongst them: both pressures turned to be stimulating, in a way or in another, leading some countries to unite, like France or England, and others to divide, like Italy and Germany.   [4.63]

The Asiatic invasions, among which the most devastating had been that of the Mongols (13th–15th centuries), had left enduring traces in the racial anthropology of numerous European regions. One of these was for instance the spread of individuals with brachycephalic skulls and broad faces from Eastern and Central Europe till France, in contrast with much of the dolichocephalic skulls and narrow faces in the Northern, Western, and Southern European peripheries.   [4.64]

Indeed, the Asiatic nomadic invaders did not just raid the European peninsula. In fact, different Mongolic hordes originating from the easternmost Asian steppes of Turkistan and Mongolia repeatedly struck all the rich peripheral regions of Eurasia, often creating some tributary or vassal states, if not some real dominating dynasties in Europe, the Middle East and China. Eventually, Russia, Persia, India—despite the natural Himalayan barrier—and China either became tributary of the Mongol/Tatar stocks or had to accept the direct Mongol rule. The Seljuk Turks, for instance, overthrowing the Saracen dominion of the Middle East from Baghdad and Damascus—giving a pretext for the beginning of the crusades and the unification of the Christian nations of Europe—managed to spread their power over those water basins that Mackinder called the "Five Seas": the Caspian, the Black, the Mediterranean, the Red and the Persian seas.   [4.65]

As for demography, Mackinder noticed that much of the world's population settled along the relatively small margins of the Eurasian continent closely related to rainfalls, i.e. Europe, China and India: "It is obvious that, since the rainfall is derived from the sea, the heart of the greatest landmass is likely to be relatively dry. We are not, therefore, surprised to find that two-thirds of all the world's population is concentrated in relatively small areas along the margins of the great continent—in Europe, beside the Atlantic Ocean; in the Indies and China, beside the Indian and Pacific Oceans."[42]   [4.66]

In trying to define the borders of Eurasia, Mackinder considered the Sahara Desert as the natural, impenetrable, southern border of Europe, rather than the Mediterranean Sea: "In fact, the Southern boundary of Europe was and is   [4.67] the Sahara rather than the Mediterranean, for it is the desert which divides the black man from the white."[43] At the same time, the Oceans separated Eurasia from the Americas and the Australasian archipelago. Thus, in other words, Eurasia had been severed for many centuries from Central and Southern Africa, from the Americas and from Oceania: this meant that Eurasia represented for a long time a closed system focused on the interaction of the populations of its crowded but limited outskirts with the relatively underpopulated but vast inner core.

[4.68]   This continuous and apparently endless Eurasian landmass represents half of all the dry lands of the globe (more than 54,000,000 square kilometers). The core of Eurasia, although mottled with desert patches, which from Syria reach Manchuria passing through Persia, is overall a steppe-land entirely unpenetrated by waterways from the ocean. It is also characterized by a very remarkable distribution of river drainage, with six of the greatest rivers in the world: "Throughout an immense portion of the center and north, the rivers have been practically useless for purposes of human communication with the outer world. The Volga, the Oxus, and the Jaxartes drain into salt lakes; the Obi, the Yenesei [*sic*], and the Lena into the frozen ocean of the north."[44]

[4.69]   The most remarkable feature that characterizes the core of Eurasia, as we will see, is its distance from the oceanic waterways, which makes the region impenetrable by sea power.[45]

[4.70]   Wide steppes that are perfectly appropriate for the maintenance of sparse horse-riding nomads—that, as previously affirmed, have continuously raided throughout medieval and modern history the rich Eurasian marginal peripheries—spread continuously from the Hungarian *Puszta* to the Little Gobi of Manchuria and except for their westernmost extremity, they are untraversed by rivers which drain to an accessible ocean. Each of the Eurasian steppes, which can be classified as the Magyar, the Ukrainian, the South-Russian, the Turkestanian and the Mongol, present essentially the same characteristics and offer a common landscape so that Eurasianists claimed that the unity of Eurasia was justified not only from a political point of view but even from a naturalistic and geographic one.[46]

[4.71]   Mackinder describes Eurasia as a continuous land, surrounded by ice in the north, surrounded by water elsewhere, with an extension that is three times that of North America, whose center and north have no available waterways to the oceans but, except for the sub-Arctic forest, are favorable to the mobility of horsemen and camel-men. The area that represents the core of this huge landmass represents the Heartland of the continent.

[4.72]   According to the British geographer, to the East, South and West of the Eurasian Heartland are some marginal regions, ranged in a vast Crescent that is accessible by shipmen and reachable by sea power.[47] These rim regions representing the Crescent are four, according to their physical conformation, and each of them, interestingly, embrace a different majoritarian religion or creed:[48]

> 1) The Indian Subcontinent; 2) Eastern China and Indochina; 3) The European Peninsula; 4) The Nearer East.   [4.73]

The first two are strongly influenced by the monsoons and may be considered monsoon lands: together with the third region, they host two-thirds of the world population. The fourth area, though thinly populated, includes the abovementioned "Five Seas" region[49] and its geostrategic relevance rests on the fact that it partakes of the characteristics both of the marginal belt and of the central core of Eurasia; both its weaknesses and strengths originate from its sea-gulfs and oceanic rivers that lay it open to sea power influence and projection.   [4.74]

In considering the historical evolution of sea power and land power, Mackinder stated that, before being severed, the Isthmus of Suez had been historically dividing the world sea power into two parts without a continuity line. Until the age of discoveries, the Western sea power of the Mediterranean Sea and the Atlantic Ocean had been for centuries segregated by the Eastern sea power of the Indo-Pacific greater oceanic region. At the same time, the wasteland of Persia, vertically extending from Central Asia to the Persian Gulf, separated due to nomad-power India and China from the Mediterranean world. Since the beginning of historical ages, when for instance the civilized ancient oases of Babylonia, Assyria and Egypt were weak, the steppe-peoples could treat the open tablelands of Persia and Asia Minor as forward posts from which to strike through the Punjab into India, through Syria into Egypt, and through the Straits into the Balkans and Central Europe: [4.75]

> "Here is the weakest spot in the girdle of early civilizations, for the isthmus of Suez divided sea power into Eastern and Western, and the arid wastes of Persia advancing from Central Asia to the Persian Gulf gave constant opportunity for nomad-power to strike home to the ocean edge, dividing India and China, on the one hand, from the Mediterranean world on the other. Whenever the Babylonian, the Syrian, and the Egyptian oases were weakly held, the steppe-peoples could treat the open tablelands of Iran and Asia Minor as forward posts whence to strike through the Punjab into India, through Syria into Egypt, and over the broken bridge of the Bosporus and Dardanelles into Hungary. Vienna stood in the gateway of Inner Europe, withstanding the nomadic raids, both those which came by the direct road through the Russian steppe, and those which came by the loop way to south of the Black and Caspian seas."[50]   [4.76]

The Turanian peoples of inner Eurasia, who embodied horse-mobility but lacked any kind of sea-mobility, found their natural rivals in the maritime power of the Marginal Crescent dwellers. The Saracens, for instance, repre-   [4.77] sented an example of sea power combined with camel/horse land power. Thanks to this fortunate blend, they could forge a vast empire in the central strategic position between the western and eastern oceans and within the geographical Eurasian southern hub. At the same time, the sea power of western European nations managed to encircle the African and Eurasian landmass through the ocean-ways, thus founding colonial bridgeheads in the marginal rims of these continents, from the African shores to the Indonesian archipelago.

[4.78]   Mackinder does not ignore of course the relevance of riverways for the rise of civilizations. According to him, the beginning of all the greater civilizations relied on two main geographical elements: the navigation of riverways connected with the oceans (e.g. China/Yangtze; India/Ganges; Babylonia/Euphrates; Egypt/Nile), or the thalassic power given by navigation (e.g. the Greeks; the Romans; the Vikings; the Saracens).

[4.79]   The chief result of the Western powers that managed to double the Cape of Good Hope—and thus to reach the Eastern Indies bypassing the Islamic continental world—was that of connecting the western and eastern coastal navigation around Eurasia. This fundamental event succeeded in neutralizing the strategic advantage of the central position of the steppe-nomads by pressing upon them in the rear, thus delineating neatly the contraposition between land power and sea power, which would have represented the foundation of all subsequent rivalry of powers for the hegemony over Eurasia.

[4.80]   Moreover, the discovery of the Americas, or Western Indies, reversed the relation of Europe and Asia: whereas in the Middle Ages Europe was caged between an inaccessible desert to the South—the Sahara—, an unknown ocean to the West—the Atlantic—, and icy or woody wastes to the North and North-East, and was always threatened in the East and South-East by the pressure of nomadic horsemen, now it emerged upon the world, wrapping its influence around the Eurasian land power that had always menaced its very existence. Before 1492, England and the British Isles were nothing more than the furthest outskirts of Eurasia, located at the end of the world; afterwards, they assumed a central position, becoming in fact the very center of the world, laying just in-between the oceanic connections of the Old World with the New one. After 1492, as new lands and continents were slowly discovered, the Americas, Australasia, Trans-Saharan Africa and the Japanese archipelago became a ring of outer or insular bases for the propagation of sea power. Their position and rulers turned them inaccessible for trade by the land powers of central Eurasia. Thanks to the Columbian Age, the European seamen accomplished the task of uniting the oceans of the world into a single entity that Mackinder calls "World Ocean," in fact encircling by sea the Eurasian Heartland.[51] Thanks to the European navigations of the 15th–18th centuries, the globe had been connected by sea power. The Columbian Age led the Europeans littoral populations to discover and occupy the lands of the

Outer Crescent: Pan-America, Sub-Saharan Africa, and Australasia. Through the control over the World Ocean, Western Europe now ruled the Earth, outflanking and marginalizing the Heartland. The Turanian nomad mobility was now contrasted by the faster mobility of European sailors, who controlled the sea through their control of the coastlands of the Inner Crescent: Europe, Arabia, the Asiatic peninsulas of the Indian and Pacific Ocean.[52]

However, during the Tudor Age, while Western Europe began its expansion over the seas, at the same time Russian power started carrying from the principality of Muscovy a tireless expansion through Siberia thanks to Cossack explorers and settlers. If until then it had been the Turanian tribes to strike westward towards Europe, now the European Russians—coming out from their northern forests used for centuries as shelters—began to expand eastward, holding the control of the Heartland against the Tatars.[53] Such striking momentum would quickly expand the Russian rule from Eastern Europe to the shores of the Pacific Ocean and Alaska within less than three centuries.   [4.81]

The western seaward-oriented and the eastern landward-oriented expansion of the modern age somewhat resembled the continuation of the ancient opposition between Romans and Greeks, exemplified in the political—and religious—separation of the Roman Empire into two parts. As Teutonic folks were overall civilized and Christianized by the Romans, so were the Slavic by the Greeks. Things being so, the Romano-Teutonic European stock embarked upon the ocean enforcing sea power whilst the Greco-Slavic rode over the steppes, focusing on land power, and conquering the Turanian lands.[54]   [4.82]

During the 19th century, Russian railways had subjugated the Eurasian steppes, linking together and rationalizing these vast landscapes. Between 1891 and 1904, Russia concluded the Tran-Siberian railway, the longest on Earth. Therefore, immense continental railways replaced the horse and the camel as faster means to cross Eurasia. With this doubled mobility, it was now possible for Russia to strike Europe, the Middle East and the Far East.[55] The Russian army in Manchuria, whose deployment was possible thanks to railway communications, embodied an example of mobile land power, whereas the rival British army arranged in South Africa showed evidence of mobile sea power.   [4.83]

Thanks to the connection of the Eurasian core made possible by Russian railways, Mackinder already predicted the birth of a Eurasian economic zone. The richness of the resources of the Russian Empire and Mongolia were so big that the creation of a more or less separated world economy would be inevitable; being unhooked by the oceanic seaways, this zone would be inaccessible to oceanic commerce and therefore self-sufficient: "The spaces within the Russian Empire and Mongolia are so vast, and their potentialities in population, wheat, cotton, fuel, and metals so incalculably great, that it is   [4.84] inevitable that a vast economic world, more or less apart, will there develop inaccessible to oceanic commerce."[56]

[4.85]   According to Mackinder, the Eurasian utter strategic zone was that geographical area designated as the "pivot region of the world's politics."[57] Protected from the attacks of maritime powers, the pivotal area appeared as an ideal strategic zone that could enable the continental power that controlled it to dominate the world. In Mackinder's schema, the pivot region is represented by that vast inner continental landlocked area of Eurasia inaccessible to ships, that was by that time covered by railways but had previously lain open to the horse-riding nomads. This region was landlocked—or better said seasonally landlocked—since of its only coastline bordered the northern icy sea adjacent to the Arctic Ocean.

[4.86]   To analyze the distribution of global geopolitical power, Mackinder divided the world into five parts:

[4.87]   1) Pivot area or Heartland: wholly continental, it includes the major part of Russia—specifically Central Russia and Siberia—, the eastern part of Caucasia, most of Persia, the whole of Turkistan—from present-day Kazakhstan to the land of the Uyghurs in Chinese Xinjiang—, Afghanistan and Mongolia.[58]

[4.88]   2) Outer or Insular Crescent: it is wholly oceanic and includes the Americas, the British Isles, all Sub-Saharan—i.e. Black—Africa, the whole of Oceania including the Indonesian archipelago and Australasia, the Japanese Isles and Alaska.

[4.89]   3) Inner Crescent or Marginal Crescent:[59] it is partly continental and partly oceanic and includes all Western and Central Europe, the majority of Eastern Europe, Ukraine, the western part of Caucasia, the Anatolian peninsula, the northern part of the Near East, the Persian coast, the entire Indian Subcontinent, Tibet, northern, southern and eastern China—but not the western one–, Indochina, Manchuria and the Kamchatka Peninsula.

[4.90]   4) The Desert: it is inaccessible and includes the wastelands of the Sahara and of the Arabian Peninsula.

[4.91]   5) The Icy Sea: it is inaccessible—at least during the winter—and it coincides with the Arctic Ocean.

[4.92]   Given its position as principal holder of the pivotal area, Mackinder considers Russia—i.e. the former Russian Empire—the potential hegemonic ruler of the world, though penalized by the lack of sea power. The author believes that just like the Mongol Empire in the past, Russia had the power and the possibility to threaten and pressure all of its rims: Scandinavia, Eastern Europe, Turkey, Persia, India, and China. Considering the world at large, the Russian czardom occupied a central strategic position like the one that the

German kaiserdom held at the time in Europe. Its special position offered Russia the faculty to strike on all sides, but also the risk of being sieged from all directions, save from the north.[60]

Looking at things with the eyes of a sophisticated strategist, Mackinder's [4.93] main concern was the potential combination of land and sea power by a single ruler or an alliance of states that would adjoin the core Eurasian region with its marginal rims. An expansion of the holder of the pivotal area—at the time Russia—on the marginal lands of Eurasia represented by the Inner Crescent would represent a serious threat for the sake of international equilibrium and balance of power, and specifically a mortal danger for the British Empire. Indeed, if Russia would add its continental resources with the possibility to use them for the construction of a world fleet, uniting land power with sea power, then the ultimate world empire would rise:

> "The oversetting of the balance of power in favor of the pivot state, resulting in [4.94] its expansion over the marginal lands of Euro-Asia, would permit of the use of vast continental resources for fleet building, and the empire of the world would then be in sight. This might happen if Germany were to ally herself with Russia. The threat of such an event should, therefore, throw France into alliance with the over-sea powers, and France, Italy, Egypt, India, and Korea would become so many bridgeheads where the outside navies would support armies to compel the pivot allies to deploy land forces and prevent them from concentrating their whole strength on fleets."[61]

Mackinder's strategic conclusions represent the foundations of all further [4.95] theories that wish to demonstrate the geopolitical importance of Eurasia. The unification of the Heartland/pivotal area with the Rimland/Inner Crescent under the rule of a single power or block of powers would easily lead to the birth of a hegemonic world empire: this statement would have been taken extremely seriously by German geopoliticians, of both the Wilhelminian and Nazi ages, by the Soviets, and by American and NATO strategists.

As a geographical entity, the pivotal region would always bear a strategic [4.96] relevance, no matter which power would control it. Was it to be controlled by China, for instance, China would become a real threat to the world by fusing together the ocean frontage with the exploitation of the inner resources of the vast Eurasian continent, what Russia could not yet do.[62]

THE HEARTLAND THEORY   [4.97]

After the traumatic experience of World War One, Europe lay in material and [4.98] moral ruins. In 1919, the same year the Versailles Peace Conference took place, Mackinder published his major geopolitical essay *Democratic Ideals and Reality*. In this fundamental study, he broadened both qualitatively and quantitatively the scope of the concept of "Pivot area," which he renamed "Heartland." Mackinder describes the concept of the Heartland as the geographical landlocked region inaccessible to maritime power located in the core of Eurasia, surrounded by semi-circular rim regions—or Crescents—, whose political and strategic control would lead to the dominion of the Eurasian continent—or World-Island—, whose control, in turn, would lead to the dominion of the entire world. The unchanging reality of geography makes Mackinder's concept of the Heartland always relevant, still today often serving as a basis for discussion in geopolitical explanations of world events. Also, the German attempt during the two world wars of invading Eastern Europe, turning it into a bridgehead for further expansion into the Russian-held pivotal region, seemed to confirm Mackinder's view on the strategic importance of the Heartland for world rule.

[4.99]   After 1918, also due to the punitive peace decisions, Mackinder was concerned about the potential resurgence of a revanchist Germany. The most important contribution that Mackinder gave with the essay *Democratic Ideals and Reality* was the need for creating a tier of buffer states between Germany and Russia in order to prevent them from either coalescing or striking each other in the relevant area of Eastern Europe, from where the Heartland may be controlled. Mackinder believed that the future world peace would be achieved only combining idealism (democratic ideals) with geopolitical realism (reality): this combination would be incarnated by the development of the newly born League of Nations on one hand, and on the other by the creation of buffer states in Eastern Europe that would prevent the rise of continental powers against littoral nations of the Inner or Outer Crescent.

[4.100]   In *Democratic Ideals and Reality*, Mackinder makes a clear distinction between thalassocratic power, represented by the seaman's point of view, and tellurocratic power, represented by the landsman's point of view.[63] Apparently, rival sea power and land power are strategically irreconcilable, and a possible interpretation of the world's history is given by the never-ending clash between Sea and Land. The essay describes the historical contraposition between land powers and sea powers starting from Ancient Egypt.[64] Sea power rose with the settlement of the first civilizations either in areas crossed by rivers connected to the major seas of the past or in insular and peninsular bases from which they could radiate their power elsewhere. The main goal that sea power aims at is that of transforming a water basin into a "closed area," completely under the rule of a single polity. For instance, Egypt owed its civilization to the combination of physical advantages and manpower: the fertility of the Nile Valley, its line of communications with the Mediterranean Sea, and propitious winds combined with the massive employment of slaves as manpower granted it a fast rise. As soon as Egypt managed to unite the river Nile and to carry it unto its own leadership, it created a "closed river-system" that allowed its rise as a sea power: "At last, the whole length of the valley was brought under a single rule, and the kings of all Egypt established their palace at Thebes. Northward and southward, by boat on the Nile, traveled their administrators, their messengers and their magistrates. Eastward and westward lay the strong defense of the deserts, and at the northern limit, against the sea pirates, a belt of marsh round the shore of the Delta."[65]

As for the Mediterranean Sea, its early history describes its gradual transformation into a closed water system held by a single power. The Mediterranean first center of civilization was that of Crete in the pre-Greek Aegean Sea. Crete offered the first historical example in Western history of an island that acted as a natural base for the propagation of sea power: the Minoan thalassic power could blend sea power with a solid insular base fertile enough to nourish its manpower.[66]   [4.101]

Later, the rise of post-Cretan Greek power began with Indo-European horse-riding tribes coming down from the north into the Hellenic peninsula, colonizing it and advancing into its Peloponnesian terminal limb. From the peninsular sea-base, the Hellenic tribe of the Dorians could conquer Crete, thus gaining sea power from a small but completely insular base. The settlement of colonists both in the southern-Italian shores and in the Anatolian-Mediterranean littoral of Asia Minor transformed the Hellenic peninsula into a "citadel in the midst of the Greek sea-world" and thus completed the "enclosure" of the Aegean Sea.[67]   [4.102]

Greek sea power could flourish until challenged by the invasions of the Persian continental power, but the efforts of the Persian kings failed one after the other, so that the unity of the Aegean Sea was maintained, and the freedom of Greek city-states confirmed.[68]   [4.103]

The successive wars of Alexander the Great led to the unification of the Greek world, to the demise of the Persian Empire and to the creation of an immense domain—albeit partitioned after the death of its founder—that included both sea power and land power. Alexander managed to transform the entire Eastern Mediterranean into a "closed sea" by depriving both Greeks and Phoenicians of their bases.   [4.104]

While Greeks and Macedonians were enclosing the Eastern Mediterranean Sea, in the Western Mediterranean the power of Rome was rapidly ascending. From their peninsular sea base of Latium, after having subjugated the neighboring Italic folks, the Romans resorted to expanding towards the sea, thus entering in contraposition with the Carthaginians. The result of the Roman-Carthaginian sea power rivalry in the Western Mediterranean was the outbreak of the Punic Wars. The outcome of the first granted to the Romans the control of the sea and the preconditions to become a sea power whilst continuing the expansion on peninsular Italy. The second was characterized by Hannibal's attempt to outflank Roman sea power by marching around it, from Africa into Spain and Southern Gaul, penetrating Italy from the Alps.[69]   [4.105]

Thanks to the strategic genius of Scipio, who decided to carry the war in Africa, Hannibal's troops were defeated, and Rome could gain control of the Mediterranean coasts of Spain and Gaul. Finally, after winning the Third Punic War and destroying Carthage, the Romans would transform the Western Mediterranean into a "closed sea" held by a single land power.

[4.106] The further stage of the Mediterranean Sea's enclosure was represented by the unification of its western and eastern parts. This process began with the gradual annexation by the Roman Republic of the Hellenistic realms that followed the demise and partitioning of Alexander's Macedonian Empire. One by one, Rome managed to subjugate and annex Hellenistic Greece, Anatolia, the Near East, and Egypt.

[4.107] However, the Roman age of civil wars still saw the contraposition between a Latin West and a Greek East, until the decisive battle of Actium (31 B.C.) would finally concur to unify the entire Mediterranean basin and to transform Rome into an empire with an epicenter in this sea:

[4.108] "There remained the task of uniting the controls of the western and eastern basins of the Mediterranean, connected by the Sicilian Strait and the Strait of Messina. The Roman legions passed over into Macedonia and thence into Asia, but the distinction between Latin West and Greek East remained, as was evident when civil war came to be waged between the Roman governors of the West and the East, Caesar and Antony. At the sea-fight of Actium, one of the decisive battles of the world's history, the Western fleet of Caesar [Octavian Augustus] destroyed the Eastern fleet of Antony. Thenceforth for five centuries the entire Mediterranean was a 'closed sea'; and we think in consequence of the Roman Empire as chiefly a land-power. No fleet was needed, save a few police vessels, to maintain as complete a command of the arterial sea-way of the Mediterranean as ever the kings of Egypt exercised over their Nile way. Once more land-power terminated a cycle of competition upon the water by depriving sea-power of its bases. True that there had been the culminating sea-battle of Actium, and that Caesar's fleet had won the reward of all finally successful fleets, the command over all the sea. But that command was not afterwards maintained upon the sea, but upon the land by holding the coasts."[70]

[4.109] After Actium, and despite the final demise of the Western Roman Empire and its substitution with Germanic "Romanized" kingdoms, the Mediterranean would stay a Roman—or rather German-Roman—and later Byzantine lake until the Arab-Islamic invasions of the 7th–8th centuries and the Norman raids of the 10th–11th centuries.

[4.110] After the consolidation of the Roman dominion, with its frontiers given by the Hadrian's Wall in Britain, the rivers Rhine and Danube in Europe, the Middle Eastern wastelands eastward and the Sahara Desert southward, a long transitional epoch followed during which the oceanic expansion was gradually preparing. The consequence of Rome's enlargement in the Celtic regions of Gaul and Spain led to the birth of the "Latin" portion of the Empire, which included Italy, Gaul, Spain, and former Carthaginian Africa. Mackinder affirmed that the "Latin" imperial half came to be based on two geographic features: the Latin Sea—i.e. the Western Mediterranean—and the Latin Peninsula—which covered the western part of Europe, from the river Rhine to Portugal.[71] Moreover, the Roman conquer of Britain had averted the rise of a potential Celtic sea power off the coasts of Gaul; thus, the Romans managed to transform the English Channel into a closed waterway controlled by legionary land power.

The massive invasion of Germanic folks in Britain—Angles, Saxons, Jutes—led to the end of the closed system of the English Channel, and that of the Vikings around the shores of the Latin Peninsula led to the end of the closed system of the seas of the Latin Peninsula: the Norsemen enveloped with their sea power the whole great peninsula, including its Mediterranean part. [4.111]

While Normans were encompassing Europe's shores from the north, at the same time the Saracens managed to occupy the southern Mediterranean provinces of the Byzantine Empire: once again, the Mediterranean would not be a closed sea anymore. Since the Saracen invasion of North Africa, Spain and Sicily, "the Mediterranean ceased to be the arterial way of an empire, and became the frontier moat dividing Christendom from Islam."[72] [4.112]

Later, the Carolingian Empire would somewhat give birth to the geographical and spiritual concept of Europe. Charlemagne's dominion over continental Europe once again compacted the core European lands in an organic way. The unification of Europe under the scepter of the Holy Roman Empire helped to define the borders of the heart of the continent, but soon after the death of Charlemagne, his successors once again fragmented Europe into smaller political entities that would be the cradle of future European nations. [4.113]

Afterwards, from the seaman's point of view, the age of the Crusades would represent an attempt to once again "enclose" the Mediterranean Sea for the benefit of Christian Europe, but their ultimate failure transformed this sea into a zone of contraposition for several centuries, until some hegemonic actors would gain rule over it.[73] [4.114]

The turning point for sea power occurred with the age of the oceanic discoveries. This epoch began with Prince Henry the Navigator who inaugurated the beginning of Portuguese overseas navigation for the purpose of reaching the rich Indies from a different direction, bypassing the Islamic world. Vasco Da Gama managed to discover the waterway to the Indian Ocean by circumnavigating Africa. Before that, the Suez Isthmus detached the European system of waterways from the Indian Ocean, and thus Europe—despite its terrestrial border with the forests and steppes of Eurasia—was a world apart. The discovery of the seaway to the Indian Ocean via Cape [4.115] of Good Hope had taken the Islamic world in rear: it had sailed around the Muslim foe, just like Xerxes, Alexander, Hannibal, and the Crusaders, had marched round to the rear of the sea. From Vasco Da Gama's circumnavigation of Africa and voyage to India until the opening of the Suez Canal (1869) the European seamen continued in ever-increasing number to round the Cape and to sail northward on the eastern oceans as far as China and Japan.

[4.116]   From the point of view of the traffic to the Indies, the world represented a vast landmass that included the triple continent of Europe, Asia, and Africa—or Eurafrasia—that Mackinder renamed the "World Promontory"[74] , which "was enveloped by sea-power, as had been the Greek and Latin promontories beforehand: all its coasts were open to ship-borne trade or to attack from the sea."[75]

[4.117]   Within the World Promontory—or great island of Eurafrasia—, the Europeans enjoyed some relatively well-defined borders:

[4.118]   "Europe is but a small corner of the great island which also contains Asia and Africa, but the cradle land of the Europeans was only a half of Europe—the Latin Peninsula and the subsidiary peninsulas and islands clustered around it. Broad deserts lay to the south, which could be crossed only in some three months on camel back, so that the black men were fended off from the white men. The trackless ocean lay to the west, and to the north the frozen ocean. To the northeast were interminable pine forests, and rivers flowing either to ice-choked mouths in the Arctic Sea or to inland waters, such as the Caspian Sea, detached from the ocean. Only to the southeast were there practicable oasis routes leading to the outer world, but these were closed, more or less completely, from the seventh to the nineteenth century, by the Arabs and the Turks."[76]

[4.119]   Due to their small commercial colonies spread throughout the Indian Ocean, the European seamen, thanks to their greater mobility, maintained for some four centuries advantages over the landsmen of Afro-Asia. The discovery of the Americas—i.e. Western Indies—and the maritime traffic towards the Eastern Indies made European sea powers compete for hegemony. The Treaty of Tordesillas (1494) prevented Spaniards and Portuguese seamen from quarreling. By the end of the 16th century, five contending oceanic and colonial powers arose: Portugal, Spain, France, Holland, and England.

[4.120]   In the long term, the sea power that would gain supremacy would be the English, unchallenged until the end of the 19th century. The rise and affirmation of British sea power took three centuries. Its consolidation passed through at least two fundamental events: the defeat of the Spanish Armada (1588) and the defeat of the French at Trafalgar (1805). After Trafalgar, British sea power definitely enveloped the Latin Peninsula, also through subsidiary bases in Gibraltar, Malta, and Helgoland—and later Cyprus: thus, "the continental coast line became the effective British boundary."[77] Later,

Britain would enfold through sea power the totality of the World Promonto-ry, while English capitalism would become the tool for the maintenance of the rule on the colonies and on the sea. [78] In the path to building its empire, by means of sea-borne armies, Britain could establish local powers in India, Egypt, Southern Africa, Canada, and Australasia. [79] In the 19th century, the Indian Ocean would become a closed English sea, and Great Britain would possess or protect the major part of its littorals. Like the Roman Empire had controlled the inner European land from their closed Mediterranean Sea with the deployment of legions along the Rhine, so the Brits, with a closed Indian Ocean, could control the inner land power of Eurasia through their troops located in the northwestern part of the Indian Raj: the bases of maritime power were outflanking and controlling the land. [80]

Until the end of the 19th century, Britain possessed the unrivaled single mastery of the seas. Having neutralized the Black Sea after the Crimean War (1853–1856), Britain avoided the rise of Russian sea power in the Mediterra-nean Sea and Atlantic Ocean. However, the foundation of the German Sec-ond Reich (1871), which under Kaiser Wilhelm II would look for colonies and start to build up fleets, and the rise of the Japanese and American sea might—the former consecrated with the result of the Russo-Japanese War (1904–1905), the latter with the Spanish-American War (1898)—would compel Britain to face new rivals. Specifically, the outcome of the Spanish-American War resulted in huge benefits for the United States of America, since now America possessed detached possessions in both the Atlantic and Pacific Oceans. Furthermore, the undertaking of the construction of the Pana-ma Canal (1907–1914) would offer to the US the advantages of insularity for the mobilization of its warships from one ocean to another. [4.121]

The 20th century coincided with the end of the age of discoveries and with the entrance into the Post-Columbian Age, an era characterized by a globally closed geographical system. [81] The outbreak of World War One in 1914 thus appeared as a war between islanders and continentals, between thalassic power and telluric power: [82] The insular powers of Great Britain and its Dominions, the United States, and Japan—supported by the peninsular powers of France and Italy and by the advanced continental bulwarks of Russia, India and China—confronted the continental powers of Germany, Austria-Hungary, and Turkey. The outcome of the war saw the affirmation of the natural superiority of sea power, which thanks to the unity of the ocean proved to have the last word in the rivalry with land-power. [83] [4.122]

Parallel to the seaman's point of view, Mackinder focused on the lands-man's point of view, which led him to conjecture the Heartland theory. [4.123]

In order to recognize the relevance of the Heartland, it is important to understand what, according to Mackinder, the "World Island" would repre-sent. The British geographer uses the term "World Island" to indicate the three continents of Europe, Asia, and Africa, which jointly create the single [4.124] landmass of Eurafrasia. Until the cut of the Suez Isthmus, this enormous landmass constituted a single block. Was it not for the icy Arctic Sea that impedes naval mobility, the World Island would be a proper island that could be wholly circumnavigated:

[4.125]
"One reason why the seamen did not long ago rise to the generalization implied in the expression 'World-Island', is that they could not make the round voyage of it. An ice-cap, two thousand miles across, floats on the polar sea, with one edge aground on the shoals off the north of Asia. For the common purposes of navigation, therefore, the continent is not an island. The seaman of the last four centuries [16th–19th] have treated it as a vast promontory stretching southward from a vague north, as a mountain peak may rise out of the clouds from hidden foundations. Even in the last century [20th], since the opening of the Suez Canal, the eastward voyage has still been round a promontory, though with the point at Singapore instead of Cape Town [. . .]. Were it not for the ice impediments to its circumnavigation, practical seamen would long ago have spoken of the Great Island by some such name, for it is only a little more than one-fifth as large as their ocean."[84]

[4.126]   In antiquity, Eurafrasia—or at least the portions of it that had been already discovered—was known as the "Ecumene" and most commonly known since the Age of Discovery as the "Old World."

[4.127]   In geographical terms, Eurafrasia is the largest landmass on Earth, spreading primarily in the Northern and Eastern Hemispheres, and its term derives from a combination of its constituent parts: Africa and Eurasia, the latter divided into Europe and Asia. This supercontinent encompasses almost 85 million square kilometers and today has a population of approximately 6 billion people—roughly 85 percent of the world population. Its westernmost limit is given by Portugal, the southernmost by South Africa, the northeasternmost by the Chukotka Peninsula, and the southern-easternmost by the Strait of Malacca. The British Isles and Iceland in the West and the Japanese archipelago in the East are its insular satellites located in the Inner Crescent. Like the New World, which is divided into the two peninsulas of North and South America, the World Island too is divided into the two peninsulas of Eurasia and Africa. Mackinder suggests that the geographical separation between Eurasia and Africa is given by the Sahara Desert rather than by the Mediterranean Sea, because "the northern and northeastern shores of Africa for nearly four thousand miles [approximately 6400 kilometers] are so intimately related with the opposite shores of Europe and Asia that the Sahara constitutes a far more effective break in social continuity than does the Mediterranean."[85] The third supercontinent along with Pan-America[86] and Eurafrasia is Oceanian Australasia, which, according to Mackinder represents a number of peripheral islands of the World Island, the largest of which is Australia. Pan-America too constitutes the world's major geographical satellite of Eurafrasia: "Thus, the three so-called new continents are in point of area merely satellites of the old continent. There is one ocean covering nine-twelfths of the globe; there is one continent—the World-Island—covering two-twelfths of the globe; and there are many smaller islands, whereof North America and South America are, for effective purposes, two, which together cover tile remaining one-twelfth."[87]

Indeed, Mackinder acknowledges the strategic weight of the World Is-   [4.128] land, and chiefly its incomparably great advantages in terms of manpower, natural resources, and territorial extension. The greatest fear of Mackinder, as already anticipated, was represented by the potential unification of the World Island under a continental power that would use it as a base of sea power. The unification of land power projection with a sea power base would create the world's strongest empire. If this scenario would occur—and Mackinder was thinking of Germany—the insular powers of the Outer Crescent— e.g. Great Britain, Japan, or the United States of America—would not be able to contain what would become a Eurasian unbeatable empire: "What if the Great Continent, the whole World-Island or a large part of it, were at some future time to become a single and united base of sea-power? Would not the other insular bases be outbuilt as regards ships and out-manned as regards seamen? Their fleets would no doubt fight with all the heroism begotten of their histories, but the end would be fated."[88]

Mackinder's immediate concern about the creation of the combined Eur-   [4.129] asian land and sea power empire was for Germany. Germany already possessed a self-sufficient European continental base and was striving to develop sea power through the creation of a fleet. If Germany would have managed to defeat Russia and control the Heartland, it could have easily gained world hegemony: "Even in the present war [World War One], insular America has had to come to the aid of insular Britain, not because the British fleet could not have held the seas for the time being, but lest such a building and manning base were to be assured to Germany at the Peace, or rather Truce, that Britain would inevitably be outbuilt and outmanned a few years later."[89]

But what is it that makes the World Island so strategically important?   [4.130] Why, according to Mackinder, does the control of its pivotal inner region make it so relevant for the domain over the rest of it? To answer these questions, we must introduce Mackinder's Heartland theory identifying ourselves with the landsman's point of view.

The Heartland is a vast Eurasian inner area inaccessible to navigation   [4.131] from the oceans. Its borders are all segregated by international water communications. From North to South, the Heartland includes Siberia, Central Asia, and the Iranian Plateau; its eastern border are western Mongolia and eastern Turkestan; its 1904 western border are Caucasia, eastern Ukraine, and European Russia, and in Mackinder's 1919 view, for the purpose of strategic thinking, the western borders are extended with the inclusion of Eastern

Europe, Anatolia, and the inner basins of the Baltic and Black Seas: "That whole patch, extending right across from the icy, flat shore of Siberia to the torrid, steep coasts of Baluchistan and Persia, has been inaccessible to navigation from the ocean [. . .]. Let us call this great region the Heartland of the Continent."[90]

[4.132]   The Heartland's northern boundary is entirely constituted by the Arctic Ocean, that Mackinder renames Icy Sea, which is characterized by a virtually inaccessible coast all year long—although ice breakers are now changing this reality. The main Siberian rivers, streaming northward and reaching the icy coast of the Arctic shores represent hydrographic basins detached from the other world's fluvial and oceanic navigation. Likewise, south of Siberia the Eurasian rivers flow into salt lakes with no connection with the oceans, forming inner continental basins:

[4.133]   "The northern edge of Asia is the inaccessible coast, beset with ice except for a narrow water lane which opens here and there along the shore in the brief summer owing to the melting of the local ice formed in the winter between the grounded floes and the land. It so happens that three of the largest rivers in the world, the Lena, Yenisei, and Obi, stream northward through Siberia to this coast, and are therefore detached for practical purposes from the general system of the ocean and river navigations. South of Siberia are other regions at least as large, drained into salt lakes having no outlet to the ocean; such are the basins of the Volga and Ural Rivers flowing to the Caspian Sea, and of the Oxus and Jaxartes to the Sea of Aral."[91]

[4.134]   Beneath the Arctic region rests an immense vast plain that Mackinder calls "Great Lowland":

[4.135]   "The north, center, and west of the Heartland are a plain, rising only a few hundred feet at most above sea level. In that greatest lowland on the globe are included Western Siberia, Turkestan, and the Volga basin of Europe, for the Ural Mountains, though a long range, are not of important height, and terminate some three hundred miles north of the Caspian, leaving a broad gateway from Siberia into Europe. Let us speak of this vast plain as the Great Lowland."[92]

[4.136]   The southernmost area of the Heartland consists in what Mackinder calls the "Iranian Upland," which includes Persia, Baluchistan, and the major part of Afghanistan: "Southward the Great Lowland ends along the foot of a tableland, whose average elevation is about half a mile, with mountain ridges rising to a mile and a half. This tableland bears upon its broad back the three countries of Persia, Afghanistan, and Baluchistan; for convenience we may describe the whole of it as the Iranian Upland."[93]

Thus, the Heartland intended as the region of Arctic and Continental drainage includes most of the Great Lowland and most of the Iranian Upland.[94] [4.137]

In North Africa, Eurafrasia finds a natural barrier that separates its Euro-Asian part from the African one in the Sahara Desert, which is "the most unbroken natural boundary of the world."[95] Between the Sahara Desert and the Heartland is a broad gap occupied by the Arabian Peninsula. The Arabian wastelands and dry steppes are traversed by three great waterways in connection with the ocean: the Nile, the Red Sea, and the Euphrates. A huge belt inaccessible by sea power thus cuts the World-Island into two parts, from the Sahara to the Heartland: [4.138]

> "The Heartland, Arabia, and the Sahara together constitute a broad, curving belt inaccessible to seafaring people, except by the three Arabian waterways. This belt extends completely across the great continent from the Arctic to the Atlantic shores. In Arabia it touches the Indian Ocean, and, as a consequence, divides the remainder of the Continent into three separate regions whose rivers flow to the ice-free ocean. These regions are the Pacific and Indian slopes of Asia; the peninsulas and islands of Europe and the Mediterranean; and the great promontory of Africa south of the Sahara."[96] [4.139]

According to Mackinder, the interior of Africa south of the Sahara is a second Heartland, which he calls "Southern Heartland" in contraposition to the Northern Heartland in the Euro-Asian part of Eurafrasia.[97] [4.140]

> "The Southern Heartland also has its wide open grasslands, which in the Sudan gradually increase in fertility from the edge of the Sahara towards the tropical forest of the Guinea Coast and the Congo. The forests do not spread completely across to the Indian Oceans but leave a belt of grassy upland which connects the grasslands of the Sudan with those of South Africa, and this immense, open ground, thus continuous from the Sudan to the Cape Veldt, is the home of the antelopes, zebras, and other large hoofed game, which correspond to the wild horses and wild asses of the Northern Heartland. Though the zebra has not been successfully domesticated and the South African natives had no usual beast of burden, yet the horse and the one-humped camel of Arabia were early introduced into the Sudan. In both Heartlands, therefore, although to a greater extent in the Northern than in the Southern, mobility by the aid of animals has been available to replace the riverwise and coastwise mobility of the ships of the Atlantic and Pacific coastlands."[98] [4.141]

The Southern Heartland adjoins at its northeastern corner in Abyssinia and Somaliland. The Arabian steppes serve as a passage-land between the Northern and Southern Heartland. Therefore, the Eurasian Heartland, Arabia, and the African Heartland provide a broad way for horse and camel mobility from Siberia through Persia, Arabia, and Egypt into Sudan. [4.142]

[4.143]   According to Mackinder, the World Island can be divided into six natural regions: 1) the Heartland; 2) the Southern Heartland; 3) the Sahara Wasteland; 4) the European Coastland; 5) the Arabian Peninsula; 6) the Monsoon Coastland.[99] The last three represent the regions that Spykman would call the Rimland.

[4.144]   Differently from the 1904 schema, in 1919 Mackinder extended the strategic borders of the Heartland by adding the two "closed" Black and Baltic Seas:

[4.145]   "Within the Heartland, the Black Sea has of late been the path of strategic design eastward for our German enemy [. . .]. The Baltic is a sea which can now be 'closed' by land-power [. . .]. It is of prime importance in regard to any terms of peace which are to guarantee us against future war that we should recognize that under the conditions of to-day [. . .] the fleets of the islanders could no more penetrate into the Baltic than they could into the Black Sea."[100]

[4.146]   Other regions included in the 1919 version of the Heartland were the navigable Middle and Lower Danube, as well as central Transcaucasia, the Tibetan heights, and the Mongolian steppe. Thus, the Heartland included the three continental empires of Prussia, Austria-Hungary and Russia:

[4.147]   "The Heartland for the purposes of strategic thinking, includes the Baltic Sea, the navigable Middle and Lower Danube, the Black Sea, Asia Minor, Armenia, Persia, Tibet, and Mongolia. Within it, therefore, were Brandenburg-Prussia and Austria-Hungary, as well as Russia a vast triple base of man-power, which was lacking to the horse-riders of history. The Heartland is the region to which, under modern conditions, sea-power can be refused access, though the western part of it lies without the region of Arctic and Continental drainage."[101]

[4.148]   Mackinder considers the Heartland—especially when including its strategic East European extensions—the core region from which world wars break out:

[4.149]   "It is evident that the Heartland is as real a physical fact within the World-Island as is the World-Island itself within the ocean, although its boundaries are not quite so clearly defined. Not until about a hundred years ago, however, was there available a base of man-power sufficient to begin to threaten the liberty of the world from within this citadel of the World-Island. No mere scraps of paper, even though they be the written constitution of a League of Nations, are, under the conditions of to-day, a sufficient guarantee that the Heartland will not again become the center of a world war. Now is the time, when the nations are fluid, to consider what guarantees, based on geographical and economic realities, can be made available for the future security of mankind."[102]

The outbreak of World War One in Bosnia and that of World War Two in   [4.150]
Poland seem to have offered empirical evidence to this statement.

The Great Game, i.e. the Anglo-Russian rivalry of the 19th century in   [4.151]
their respective Asian colonies, is one of the clearest examples of a concealed
struggle for the rule over Eurasia and of contraposition between sea power
and land power. After the battle of Trafalgar (1805), Britain could envelop
Europe with its sea power insofar as it could intervene in the Eastern Mediterranean to safeguard the communication lines with India. Likewise, British
sea power also encircled the world-promontory, from South Africa to Hong
Kong: operating from the seafront of the Indies, it naturally came into rivalry
with the Russian Empire's expansion in Central Asia, which was gradually
completing its hold on the Heartland and thus threatening the British Raj
beyond the northwestern Indian frontier. By the second half of the 19th
century, Russia was in command of almost the entirety of the Heartland,
from which it pressed at the gates of the British Indies. At the same time,
Britain had completed its envelopment of the Indian Ocean with its colonial
possessions in the Arabian Peninsula, in the Indian Subcontinent, and in
Indochina, and was pressing China to open its markets. Therefore, while
Russian manpower was quickly heading southwards, closely approaching the
frontier with the British Empire—Persia, Afghanistan—,[103] Britain was
enveloping the Eurasian continent from the Indian Ocean's sea bases.
Whereas the Russian rule in the Heartland was based on its Eastern European
manpower and was carried to the border with India by the mobility of Cossack cavalry, English sea power relied upon the manpower of the British
Isles and was transported into the Indies by the mobility of the British
fleet.[104]

The rivalry between empires would always meet its utter manifestation in   [4.152]
Eurasia: the World Island and the Heartland would represent the final geographical realities concerning sea power and land power. In considering
Eastern Europe as a strategic part of the Heartland, Mackinder summarizes
his theory in 1919 by affirming that: "Who rules East Europe commands the
Heartland; who rules the Heartland commands the World-Island; who rules
the World-Island commands the World."[105]

This famous statement somewhat resembles the shape of a Russian ma-   [4.153]
tryoshka doll, where the smaller one is contained in the bigger one in ever
increasing formats. The scope of this statement would have influenced the
successive history of international relations, alluring the Nazis to expand
eastwards and later contributing to shaping the NATO-Soviet contraposition
in Europe during the Cold War.

In Mackinder's view, World War One represented a struggle between the   [4.154]
Islanders of the Outer Crescent with some ally of the Inner Crescent against
the Continentals for the rule over the World Island. The sea powers won, but
if Germany would win "[it would have] established her sea-power on a wider

base than any in history, and in fact on the widest possible base."[106] Given the immense territorial, demographic and economic potential of the World Island, if it became the base of combined sea and terrestrial power it would easily crash any outer maritime power.[107]

[4.155]   Mackinder proclaimed that the salient elements to take into consideration for geographic hegemony were four: 1) the oceans form a whole water mass that envelops all lands; 2) the atmosphere is a unique and indivisible entity; 3) sea-power and airpower depend on land bases from where they project their might, whereas land-power rests just on itself (is thus self-sufficient); 4) the rule of the vast continental mass of Eurafrasia grants the world dominion.[108]

[4.156]   The corollary to Mackinder's theory implies the atomization of Eastern Europe so as to avoid its possession by a single continental power or by an alliance of continental powers. Given the strategic relevance of Eastern Europe for the rule of the Heartland, Mackinder believes that the only solution to grant European peace is through its division into the two regions of Western and Eastern Europe creating a buffer of small self-contained nations. In other words, it was necessary to separate Germany from Russia—thus putting an end to the secular rivalry between Germans and Slavs—with the creation of buffer national states that covered the area that stretches from the Baltic Sea to the Black Sea. It was also necessary to prevent Germany or Russia from obtaining a demographic and territorial advantage over other European countries. Finally, it was necessary to encourage the birth of a League of Nations—of which Mackinder would be a promoter—that would safeguard the rights of all nations.[109] The chief event to avoid was the unification of the Russian and German spaces since such a merger could have led to a pan-European—or even global—domination.[110]

[4.157]   Mackinder believed that after the outcome of World War One the conditions of stability could appear only by creating a tier of independent states between Russia and Germany that he named "Middle Tier": "The condition of stability in the territorial rearrangement of East Europe is that the division should be into three and not into two state systems. It is a vital necessity that there should be a tier of independent states between Germany and Russia."[111]

[4.158]   The final dispositions of the peace conference of Versailles, the birth of the Little Entente and Clemenceau's *"Cordon sanitaire"* policy seem to follow Mackinder's reasoning. The buffer states that Mackinder kept in mind were Poland, Czechoslovakia, Yugoslavia, Romania, and Greece on the side of the winners, and Hungary and Bulgaria on the side of the defeated.

[4.159]   Assuming that the unification of Eastern Europe under a single power would have implied the control of the Heartland, the best way for Western sea powers to keep in balance Europe was to sever its eastern and western parts by creating independent and self-sufficient nations. The major strategic goal was thus separating Germany and Russia through the creation of a tier of states: "It is a vital necessity that there should be a tier of independent states between Germany and Russia."[112] Therefore, a chain of non-German folks should have created seven independent states between the Baltic and the Mediterranean to separate Germany from Russia: the Poles, the Czechs, the Hungarians, the Yugoslavs, the Romanians, the Bulgarians, and the Greeks. This tier of states would act as "third power" in Eastern Europe and as a shield to avoid both German and Russian expansionism. Mackinder's idea implied forced emigration or assimilation, people's exchange, and the need for Polish access to the Baltic Sea—one of the chief causes of the deflagration of World War Two.

The adequate subdivision of Eastern Europe in the Middle Tier would prevent a single nation from becoming dominant in the Heartland. The Middle Tier, supported by the outer nations of the League, would lead to the subdivision of Eastern Europe into more than two state-systems—i.e. Germany and Russia—and these states, equal in power, would put an end to the continental Teutonic-Slavic rivalry both by separating Germany from Russia and preventing one of the two powers from controlling Eastern Europe, and consequently of the Heartland, of the World Island, and of the rest of the planet: [4.160]

> "Any mere trench-line between the German Powers and Russia [. . .] would   [4.161]
> have left German and Slav still in dual rivalry, and no lasting stability could
> have ensued. But the Middle Tier, supported by the outer nations of the World
> League, will accomplish the end of breaking-up East Europe into more than
> two state-systems. Moreover, the states of that Tier, of approximate equality of
> power, will themselves be a very acceptable group for the recruitment of the
> League [of Nations]."[113]

The need to avoid the unification of the Russian and German spaces was compulsory and vital to avert a pancontinental rule over Europe and over the entire World Island. The major risk for Great Britain was that Russia, the "pivotal state," possibly through an alliance with Germany, could expand towards the rims of Eurasia and exploit the vast resources of the continental mass to build fleets capable of forging a global empire.[114] Therefore, Britain's role consisted in avoiding this eventuality by supporting from the sea France, Italy, Greece, Egypt, India, and Korea, which all represented bridgeheads of sea power. Furthermore, Great Britain and Japan had to act respectively upon the western and eastern marginal regions of Eurasia maintaining a balance of power against expansive continental forces—e.g. Germany, Russia, and China.   [4.162]

Finally, the tier of states would bear the function of representing an ideological sanitary cordon that divided communist Russia from Germany and western democracies.   [4.163]

[4.164]   Mackinder did not refuse the democratic ideal, mainly because he had seen that the coldhearted efficiency and technocracy of the German "organizer" that resulted in two bloody world wars. The democratic idealism of Wilsonian fashion was thus important to him, but not yet enough. If democracies wished to survive, they were to create a stable international order that paid attention to geographic realities but that would also encourage the division of world labor and the establishment of a sustainable mixed economy.[115]

[4.165]   German *Geopolitik* would interpret Mackinder's "Middle Tier" project in two ways. On one hand, thinkers like Karl Haushofer believed in the need for concluding a German-Russian alliance and to create a mighty "Fortress Eurasia" demarcated by a *Kontinentalblock*.[116] On the other hand, other strategists believed that invading Russia, and subtracting its Heartland could more easily lead to an expansion of Germany's vital space, allowing it to gain control over Eurasia: this second option—that would unfortunately prevail—would lead to the catastrophic Nazi invasion of the USSR with the Operation Barbarossa.[117]

[4.166]   When glancing at Europe's history of the last two hundred years we may notice that the attempt to rule Eurasia through the Heartland and Eastern Europe was carried out at least four times by Napoleon, Kaiser Wilhelm II, Hitler, and the Soviet-led powers of the Warsaw Pact: all attempts, however, were prevented by the maritime powers of Britain and America. In the case of the Soviet Union, were it not for the US and NATO containment in the Inner Crescent—specifically in Germany, Greece, Turkey, Indochina, and Korea—the USSR, possibly allying with communist China, would have probably gained control over the totality of Eurasia.

[4.167]   Overwhelmed by his anxiety for the rise of continental powers, Mackinder believed that the age of naval power was about to end in favor of terrestrial might. In 1919, despite Britain's victory in World War One, the geographer already expected Great Britain's decline as world power and the birth of an irresistible continental power over the Eurasian landmass—be it Russia or Germany—as world hegemon.[118] It is true, however, that the outcome of World War Two and the collapse of the USSR after the Cold War would in fact contradict Mackinder's prediction, since the world hegemon would eventually stay a maritime peripheral power located in the Outer Crescent: the United States. Still, American hegemony has lasted only until the beginning of the 21st century. Some claim that today humankind is entering in the so-called "post-American world"[119] in which new continental Eurasian and Asian countries are rising or reaffirming themselves. Hence, could the rise of a multipolar world revalidate Mackinder's beliefs and worries?

THE EVOLUTION OF THE HEARTLAND THEORY
UNDER THE CIRCUMSTANCES OF WORLD WAR TWO

[4.168]

In July 1943, while the Second World War was still crudely unrolling and its outcome was not clearly certain, Mackinder published an article in "Foreign Affairs" entitled *The Round World and the Winning of the Peace*. The main purpose of this publication was to detect whether the strategic concept of the "Heartland" had lost its significance under the conditions of modern warfare, especially in relation to the rise of airpower. In this sense, the concept of the Heartland, firstly introduced in 1904, finds a final and definitive theorization in 1943.

[4.169]

Mackinder begins his updated thesis by rebuilding the entire idea of Heartland, once again underlining its intrinsic and everlasting strategic relevance. He begins recalling his childhood memories on what had meant for the English public opinion the French defeat at Sedan (1870) by the Prussian army. Though being only a young boy at the time, Mackinder remembers England's deep concern for what represented a total victory of the new Prussian/German warfare machine against the continental nation of France, which some sixty years before had been stopped by the British with difficulties and sacrifices at Trafalgar (1805) and Waterloo (1815). In 1870, the importance of the Prussian victory was not yet clear enough and Britain would fully understand its consequences when its supremacy over the seas would be at stake. At that time, the only danger Britain feared for its overseas empire was the Asiatic expansion of imperial Russia, which year after year was getting closer to the Indian frontier: British sea power on one hand and Russian land power on the other held the center of the international stage.

[4.170]

However, things changed at the turn of the 20th century when the newly born Second German Reich began to build a high seas fleet: this sudden event could truly challenge Britain's supremacy on the oceans.[120] It also meant that the German nation, already owning the greatest well-organized European territory and occupying a strategic central position in Mitteleuropa, was about to add to its terrestrial warfare machine a sea power strong enough to compete with the British one. Moreover, in those years the United States of America were also arising as to become one of the world's Great Powers, especially after the successful war against Spain in 1898. Thus, Germany and the United States were quickly coming up alongside Britain and Russia on the imperial scene.[121]

[4.171]

At this point, Mackinder considers the events from which the idea of the Heartland emerged, which were two: the Anglo-Boer War (1899–1902) and the Russo-Japanese War (1904–1905). The contrast presented by the British wars against the Boers fought in South Africa and the war fought by Russia in Manchuria across the land breadth of Asia naturally suggested a parallel contrast between the western European rounding of the Cape of Good Hope

[4.172]

The Foundations of Eurasian Power

towards the Indies and the Russian penetration into Siberia. This comparison, in turn, led to a review of the long succession raids made by the nomadic Turanian folks of Central Asia through classical antiquity and the Middle Ages upon the settled inhabitants of the Marginal Crescent of the Eurasian subcontinents: Europe, the Middle East, the Indies, and China proper. Indeed, the word "Heartland" occurs for the first time in Mackinder's thought in 1904, although at the time the meaning of the term was more descriptive rather than technical. The author preferred to expose his geopolitical theories using other expressions such as "Pivot Area" or "Pivot State" to describe what would have later become the Heartland. In his *Geographical Pivot of History*, Mackinder had introduced the issue of the strategic relevance of the world's pivotal area in the following terms:

[4.173]   "The oversetting of balance of power in favor of the pivot State, resulting in its expansion over the marginal lands of Eurasia would permit of the use of vast continental resources for fleet-building, and the empire of the world would then be in sight. *This might happen if Germany were to ally herself with Russia* [. . .]. In conclusion, it may be well expressly to point out that the substitution of some new control of the inland area for that of Russia would not tend to reduce the geographical significance of the pivot position. Were the Chinese, for instance, organized by the Japanese, to overthrow the Russian Empire and conquer its territory, they might constitute the yellow peril to the world's freedom just because they would add an oceanic frontage to the resources of the great Continent [Eurasia] [Emphasis added]." [122]

[4.174]   As already mentioned, the power who controlled the Heartland would be able to rule the rest of the world specifically by uniting the sea power that radiates from the Marginal Crescent with the inner land power of the Heartland itself.

[4.175]   Later, in the year 1919, at the end of World War One, Mackinder reformulates his theories in the well-known essay *Democratic Ideals and Reality*. At that time, the "pivot" label was no longer adequate to the international situation as it had emerged from the events of that first common global crisis and war. The entire idea of "Pivot Region" hence changed in a subtler and more complicated concept that did not merely describe a geographical reality. In 1919, the name "Pivot area" was replaced with that of "Heartland," but both notions described the same unchanging reality: the power that controlled this area would ultimately obtain world hegemony.

[4.176]   While describing once again the geographical breadth of the Heartland, in 1943 Mackinder modifies its borders by including all the northern part and the interior of Eurasia and by extending them from the Arctic coast down to the central deserts, with their western limits given by the broad isthmus that separates the Baltic Sea from the Black Sea, from Poland to Bulgaria. Aware of adjusting more than once its boundaries, the British geographer explains that the very concept of the Heartland area cannot bear a precise geographi-

cal definition on the map, although it includes three clear physical-geographical features: [123]

1. This region includes by far the widest lowland plain on the globe. [4.177]
2. Navigable rivers flow across this broad plain, some of which run [4.178]
   northwards to the Arctic Sea and are inaccessible from the oceans
   because of its perennial glaciation, and others run towards the inland
   waters of closed water basins like the Caspian Sea, with no access to
   the ocean.
3. The area comprises a vast grassland area that until the latter half of the [4.179]
   19th century presented the ideal conditions for the development of
   quick nomadic mobility of camel-men and horsemen.

In 1943, Mackinder could finally affirm that the territory of the Soviet Union [4.180]
corresponded in principle to that of the Heartland. He believed however that
this statement was true save for Eastern Siberia. In fact, the area around the
River Lena, which he called "Lenaland," represented a vast region not included in the Russian Heartland, which rested instead west of the River
Yenisei. [124]

The idea that the Heartland was fully encompassed within the Soviet [4.181]
Union would later raise the strategic consideration that thanks to the Warsaw
Pact the Soviet Union had assumed also the characteristics of being a sea
power by adjoining portions of the territories laying on the Marginal Cres-
cent, confirming Mackinder's statement according to which the ruler of East
Europe would rule the Heartland and consequently the World Island.

In order to understand the strategic values of the Soviet Heartland, Mack- [4.182]
inder confronts this area with France. [125] France, he says, has a sufficient
space both for defense in depth and for strategic retreat, and—except for its
north-eastern borders—it is safely enclosed by natural frontiers given by the
seas, the river Rhine, the Alps, and the Pyrenees. Similarly, Russia repeats
the pattern of France but on a greater scale: in its rear lies the vast plain of the
Heartland, useful for defense in depth and strategic retreat; away back this
plain recedes eastwards into the natural bulwarks of the inaccessible Arctic
shores, the Lenaland wilderness behind the Yenisei, and the fringe of mountains from the Altai to the Hindu Kush, backed by the wastelands of Gobi,
Tibet, and Iran. Indeed, the cited natural barriers possess such a breadth and
substance that by far exceed in defensive value the coasts and mountains that
surround France. It is true, notes Mackinder, that today icebreakers can be
able to transform the Arctic Sea into a navigable seaway, but it is also true
that it is unlikely to consider a complete land invasion from that direction
feasible.

In *The Round World and the Winning of the Peace*, Mackinder introduces [4.183]
the geopolitical premises for the birth of the Atlantic Alliance between An-

glo-Saxon naval powers. He also presents the idea of a new American Heartland with its epicenter in Missouri. The North-Atlantic Ocean and its surrounding waters and basins become an enclosed sea amongst the lands of America, Europe, and Africa: Mackinder calls this new closed water system the "Midland Ocean," strategically united by the North-Atlantic military alliance. Thus, the planet now appears divided into two axes: the Siberian River Yenisei (the old Heartland) and the Missouri River (the new Heartland). [126]

[4.184]   Two years before the end of World War Two, Mackinder foretold that if the USSR would have conquered Germany it would have become the world's greatest land power, as well as the state in the strategically strongest defensive position thanks to the total control of the Heartland, which represents the greatest natural fortress on Earth. The control of the Heartland implied the rule over the most impenetrable citadel of land power on Eurasia, the greatest mainland of the world. What the author foresaw would become even more realistic after the split of Germany into the two German republics and after the creation of the Warsaw Pact alliance system in 1955.

[4.185]   In the case that the Allies came to victory, Mackinder believed in the idea of forging a new world order based upon a cooperation of western sea powers with the Soviet land power in order to encircle Germany and to compel it to fight continually on two fronts. For the purposes of the future peace, the geographer stated that the Germans had to realize that every further war fought by Germany would be against two unshakable fronts: land power to the east in the Heartland, and sea power to the west in the North Atlantic basin. In considering the western system of alliance, Mackinder divided the roles of sea power democracies within the frame of a very sharp strategic concept. He believed that within the western fellowship of sea powers the United States and Canada would represent the area useful for strategic retreat or deep defense, Britain a kind of moated forward stronghold—like Malta on a greater scale—, and France the defensible bridgehead on the European continent. Mackinder also reckoned that "sea power must in the final resort be amphibious if it is to balance land power," [127] and this statement reveals the strategic role that France would bear within the alliance. Finally, he believed that the three—four with Canada—western powers should cooperate with Russia to avoid a new German awakening in the future.

[4.186]   At that time of history, Mackinder was aware of the relevance of airpower as a disturbance factor for his land power versus sea power theoretic scheme. Though fully understanding the potential changes in geo-strategy given by the fast and ubiquitous mobility of airpower, he still considered the principles of his theories totally valid.

[4.187]   In *The Round World and the Winning of the Peace*, Mackinder also presents an extremely important geographical description—absent in his previous writings—of a global geographical girdle. [128] This girdle can be considered as a new geographical interpretation of Mackinder's world map, and it is, we believe, the lawful evolution of the previous interpretative map based on the concepts of World-Island-Marginal Crescent-Heartland. Moreover, the idea of a world's geographical girdle, or belt, can be fully understood only with the rise of airpower and with the affirmation of the new international system that came out after World War Two, with the fundamental role played by the United States and the Northern Atlantic Ocean. In Mackinder's words, a girdle revolves around the northern Polar Regions: it begins with the Saharan Desert, follows with the Arabian, Iranian, Tibetan and Mongolian deserts, and then extends in the wildernesses of the Lena region—or Lenaland—, Alaska and the Laurentian shield of Canada to the sub-arid belt of the western United States. This girdle of deserts, wastelands and wildernesses represents a key element in global geography since it comprises two important regions:

> 1) The Heartland, which is set in a girdle of broad natural defenses: the ice-clad Polar Sea, the forested and rugged Lenaland, and the Central Asiatic mountainous and arid tableland. The Heartland girdle is nonetheless incomplete because of the open gateway that goes from Peninsular Europe into the inner plain through the broad isthmus that separates the Baltic Sea from the Black Sea.   [4.188]
>
> 2) The basin of the Midland Ocean—i.e. the North Atlantic—with its four subsidiaries seas: the Mediterranean, the Baltic, the Arctic, and the Caribbean.   [4.189]

Outside the girdle is the Great Ocean, which includes the Pacific, the Indian and the Southern Atlantic, and the lands that drain to it: the Asiatic Monsoon regions, Oceania, South America, and Africa south of the Sahara. [129]   [4.190]

After giving birth to this completely new subdivision of the world's map, Mackinder ends his article considering two more elements: the new role of Germany in the international system and the geographical concept of the "Midland Ocean."   [4.191]

As far as Germany is concerned, Mackinder suggests that this nation should be discouraged in the future from waging new wars by the new threat given by the continuous possibility of a clash on two fronts against the amphibious nations of America, Britain and France on one hand and the land power of the USSR on the other.   [4.192]

As for the "Midland Ocean," this expression represents nothing more than the North Atlantic Ocean itself, of fundamental strategic interest after World War Two, especially in the context of the newly born North Atlantic Treaty Organization (1949). The Midland Ocean includes some dependent seas and river basins and should be controlled by the amphibious powers, each of them with a proper strategic role, as anticipated previously: [4.193]

> 1. France would be the bridgehead of the North Atlantic sea power fellowship in the European continent.   [4.194]

[4.195]   2. Great Britain would be a kind of moated aerodrome forward stronghold.

[4.196]   3. The United States and Canada would represent the territorial reserve
of manpower and the supply of agricultural and industrial outputs.

[4.197]   Relying on this post-World War Two frame, Mackinder believes that China
and India should bear the role of counterbalancing the other world powers
and play a central part in developing the Southern Hemisphere's populations.

[4.198]   In short, what Mackinder truly prescribes for the future global peace is the
idea of balancing the world powers, in order to make the peoples of the world
free. Doubtlessly, we can affirm that Mackinder's political and social thought
directly descends from the historical British notion of balance of powers.
What Mackinder ultimately was seeking for was a balance of global power
that would guarantee peace and freedom for all: in his words, a "balanced
globe of human beings. And happy, because balanced and thus free."[130]

[4.199]   ## HAUSHOFER'S APPROPRIATION OF MACKINDER'S THEORY:
THE *KONTINENTALBLOCK* PROJECT AND THE UNIFICATION
OF EURASIA THROUGH A RUSSO-GERMAN ALLIANCE

[4.200]   Karl Ernst Haushofer[131] can be considered the main exponent of German
Geopolitik. According to Haushofer's school of thought, the state is a living
organism that includes all human sciences and activities and that takes into
account not only the geographical factors, but also the ethnic structure, the
migratory movements, the social classes, the density of population, the private economy, the trade, and the international communications of a society.
In this perspective, state borders are perceived as dynamic and flexible, expanding in relation to the need of human beings to survive: frontiers are
perceived as temporary itineraries.

[4.201]   Deeply influenced by Ratzel, Kjellén, and Mackinder, Haushofer perceived geopolitics as a subject aimed at determining the chief factors of the
political life that are linked to the geographical environment and that are
scientifically extractable from the historical experience. The geographical
environment (*Erdgebundenheit*) is studied in relation to its importance for
the survival and enforcement of the state. The geographical factor of a given
territory on which the state exercises its sovereignty shapes its political life,
which is strictly bound to the geographical conformation of its territory. This
bond between polity and geography is studied in the light of the historical
evolution of the state and of its nation. The geographical variables that Haushofer takes into consideration—e.g. rivers, access to the sea, orography,
nature of the coasts, islands, inner seas, climate, natural resources, quality of
the soil, etc.—are closely related to the demographic factor—growth or de-

cline of the population's rate, immigration, emigration, health—and to the anthropological one—social, cultural, racial, economic, and religious features of nations. Geopolitics studies the ties that link political events to the soil, using the hermeneutical tool of physical and political geography.

In his famous essay *Weltpolitik von Heute*,[132] Haushofer illustrated the need for a German expansion in Central Europe as a necessary condition to allow normal standards of living to the overcrowded German folk. Germany must evolve from a great power into a world power. In doing so, it must seek for living space in the East and rebuild a new mighty war fleet. Haushofer believed that to become a dominant power in Mitteleuropa Germany had to conquer more space and to widen its borders. The Germans could not fully develop within the limited and imposed frontiers established by the Treaty of Versailles. The solution to this issue was to follow a pan-Germanist pattern, integrating all Germanic stocks into a common polity. In the quest for vital space, Germany could have counted on some allies among which Japan, Italy, and eventually the Heartland-holder USSR.   [4.202]

Haushofer believed that the international order should have been built through great areas of expansion that he nominated pan-regions, which would have been divided following the meridians of the Earth's map. The pan-region concept is described in Haushofer's thought as a geographic macro-area that includes a dominant power in the role of hegemonic actor and other actors that are in a condition of economic, political and cultural dependency towards it; the dominant power considers the macro-area as belonging to its own sphere of influence, thus partitioning the world with other dominant world powers into several spheres of influence. Haushofer auspicated the birth of four pan-regions: the American pan-region, dominated by the US; the European pan-region, dominated by Germany; the Eurasian pan-region, including Central Asia and the Indian Subcontinent, dominated by Russia; and the Asiatic-Pacific pan-region dominated by Japan. Haushofer's new world order envisioned the creation of four self-sufficient big spaces: Pan-Europa with Greater Germany as hegemon, with a preponderant influence shared partly with Italy in the Near-Middle East and Africa; the Pan-Pacific zone headed by Japan including the rule over the Pacific Ocean, the control of China, Manchuria, Korea, Indochina, Indonesia, and Australasia; Pan-America, including all Americas and guided by the United States; and the Eurasian big space, with the Soviet Union as dominant superpower, replacing Britain in the rule of India. The hegemony over a macro-area, or Pan-region, created a relationship of dependency of the subdued nations towards their specific dominant power, which exercised an influence over them. This relationship based on dependence implied a form of economic, political and cultural subjection and a remarkable loss of sovereignty for the subdued nations of the pan-region. The general idea of the geopolitical thinker was to create a new balance of power in which the United States, Germa-   [4.203] ny, Japan and Italy would act as regional dominant powers, creating spheres of influence in the subdued areas of their respective pan-region: "The German new world order presupposed the birth of a Greater East Asia under Japanese hegemony, a U.S.-dominated "Pan-America," and a German-dominated Eurasian Heartland with a "Mediterranean-North African sub-region under the shadow rule of Italy."[133]

[4.204]   Not surprisingly, Haushofer's entire project was mainly conceived in an anti-British spirit and did not exclude the possibility of Soviet participation as a further dominant world power that could expand its sphere of influence over British India. Also, Haushofer's pan-regional plan served as part of theoretical basis from which the idea of the Tripartite Pact (1940) was conceived. The concept of pan-region stemmed from Haushofer's theory of pan-ideas, which implied the overcoming of nation-states in favor of common cultural big spaces.[134]

[4.205]   Haushofer also stressed his attention on the struggle between land powers and sea powers. Haushofer believed in the need that the state (perceived as a living organism) should have expanded towards a "great space" (*Grossraum*) in order to be a world power (*Weltmacht*). Moreover, he managed to link the theme of the great spaces to the contraposition between territorial power (*Landmächte*) and maritime-mercantile power (*Seemächte*).

[4.206]   Having thoroughly analyzed Mackinder's thought and the benefits that Germany could obtain from it, he exploited Mackinder's views of the Heartland for the purposes of German expansionism: Haushofer wished the opposite of what Mackinder feared. i.e. the Eurasian unification. The same fear that Mackinder showed towards Germany, Haushofer expressed towards Great Britain, which he believed was strangling the German Reich and its right to survive. After the Treaty of Versailles, Haushofer used the Heartland concept to denounce the aggressiveness of British aggressive imperialism and to defend revisionism, pan-Germanism, and the need for a German *Weltpolitik*. Haushofer made use of Mackinder's ideas about the strategic relevance of Central and Eastern Europe reversing his political conclusions: whereas the British geographer had advocated a fragmented and independent tier of Eastern European states guaranteed by the League of Nations, that would guarantee the separation between Germany and Russia and avert the risk of continental pan-Eurasian unification, Haushofer supported the alliance between Germany and Russia, attributing to Germany the control over Mitteleuropa and a living space for all Germanic folks.[135] Thus, Haushofer developed the ideas of Ratzel, Kjellén, and Mackinder in a program targeted to a German domain over Eurasia against the Anglo-Saxon maritime power.[136]

[4.207]   The theory of the Heartland helped in shaping the decision of a German rule over Russia.[137] In relation to Germany's *Machtpolitik*, the Heartland theory could have two possible consequences: either the alliance between

Germany and Russia, like Haushofer favored, which was taking shape thanks to the Molotov-Ribbentrop non-aggression pact and by the negotiations for the inclusion of Russia in the Tripartite Pact; or the German incorporation of Russia, which was the plan supported by Hitler. Mackinder believed that the German domination of the Heartland could have been reached not only through a war of conquest, but also through an alliance and a peaceful penetration. Therefore, Haushofer interpreted Mackinder's thought in the sense of an alliance between Berlin and Moscow and focused on the need for the struggle against British sea power. However, Adolf Hitler wished the exact opposite: an agreement with Great Britain and the invasion and destruction of the Soviet Union. [138] In other words, Haushofer would interpret the Heartland theory in the sense of an alliance between Berlin and Moscow, but Hitler as the need for the German invasion of Russia for the direct domination of the great resources of the Heartland, in the quest for more vital space for the crammed Third Reich.

Haushofer was convinced that Germany's main enemy was represented by British maritime power. In this sense, he continuously advocated for a strong Eurasian continental alliance that included Germany, Russia, and Japan with its bridgeheads in Korea, Manchukuo, and China. [139] This continental alliance should have taken the shape of a *Kontinentalblock*. [140] A common border between Germany and Russia would have realized, with the help of Japan's bridgeheads in continental Asia, a continental block that would have granted the full domain of the Eurasian landmass and would have countered and isolated the sea powers of Britain and the US. Therefore, unlike Mackinder, Haushofer wished to dissolve that tier of states in Eastern Europe created after World War One that served the purpose of separating Germany from Russia and that implied the division of Eurasia. The purpose of the continental block formed by Mitteleuropa, Eurasia and Greater Japan was that of avoiding potential future conflicts and grant the final isolation and marginalization of sea powers. This alliance would skip the control of thalassocracies, which practiced what Haushofer called the anaconda strategy by squeezing other powers and suffocating them to death. The Eurasian landmass, when united and organized, would have represented too large a prey to be suffocated by the Anglo-American anaconda. Therefore, Haushofer accepted with satisfaction the Molotov-Ribbentrop Pact, believing that Mackinder's nightmare of the exclusion of the maritime powers of Great Britain and the United States from the World-Island had finally occurred.

[4.208]

Haushofer's ideas would have intensely influenced National-socialist geopolitics and Hitler's personal foreign policy agenda. Haushofer proposed the dissolution of Eastern Europe into small buffer states, the demise of the British Empire and the crash of Bolshevism in Russia, while supporting the birth of a Greater German empire allied with Imperial Japan. Similarly, he offered the Germans—specifically the Nazis—a coherent imperial doctrine,

[4.209]

overturning Mackinder's balance of power geopolitics and considering the need to wipe out all frontiers and to build roads for the master folk instead. In Haushofer's point of view, German *Geopolitik* was obliged to serve the purpose of leading an everlasting warfare in search of space for the cramped Teutonic nation. Nonetheless, Haushofer approved, as said, the signing of the Molotov-Ribbentrop Pact and was skeptical towards the successive German invasion of the Soviet Union, although he was clearly aware of the importance for Germany to gain control over the Soviet-controlled Heartland.

[4.210] Believing in a never-ending state of war amongst nations, Haushofer's political thought can be somewhat linked to that of Thomas Hobbes and Charles Darwin. His whole analysis takes the move from the idea that nations suffer from a crisis of room that compels them to expand in order to survive: a lack of expansion and a territorial stagnation would lead a folk to natural death. Haushofer's geopolitical thought depicted a form of perpetual warfare for space, in Darwinian, deterministic, and nihilistic fashion.

[4.211] Whereas Mackinder imagined the future in terms of a balance of power capable of protecting freedom and avoiding the birth of an imperial hegemonic superpower, Haushofer was willing to overthrow the balance of power—which he considered useful only for weak and small nations—, replacing it with the creation of big spaces, thus perverting geopolitics into a tool for expansion and domination. He believed that only nations in decline looked for stable borders and only decadent ones desired to protect their borders with permanent fortifications, "for frontiers are living organisms."[141] In his opinion, virile nations would build roads, not walls.

[4.212] Haushofer's geopolitical thought can be summarized into three main points:[142]

[4.213] 1. The Pacific Ocean was perceived as the future arena of strategic confrontation for the global domain, with the two powers of the US and Japan contending their hegemony in the area.

[4.214] 2. Eurasia possessed the same importance that Mackinder attributed to it. However, unlike Mackinder, who perceived the Eurasian unification as a threat, Haushofer believed that Central Europe should possess the Heartland so to avoid the encirclement and strangulation by the Anglo-Saxon sea powers of US and UK, plus France. In his view, only the alliance between Germany, Russia, and Japan could have avoided this mortal squeeze through the creation of a *Kontinentalblock* epitomized in the *Dreimächte Pakt* (Tripartite Pact) with the further inclusion of Russia.

[4.215] 3. A new world order would have appeared, following the axis North-South, embodied in the pan-regional system, with a dominant power projecting its influence over the subdued ones: the balancing of these poles gravitating around Berlin, Tokyo, Washington, and Moscow would have assured a freer and just global equilibrium.

SPYKMAN COUNTERING MACKINDER: THE RIMLAND THEORY

[4.216]

Nicholas J. Spykman[143] is famous for having contributed to expanding Mackinder's Heartland theory shifting the strategic relevance of Eurasia from its core to its marginal, surrounding crescent.   [4.217]

Spykman can be considered one of Mackinder's major critics. In developing his theory, Spykman renamed Mackinder's Inner crescent the "Rimland." While accepting Mackinder's description of the World Island, the Heartland, and the Inner and Outer crescents, his Rimland theory gave opposite strategic values to the Eurasian zones, giving priority to the rims rather than to the core. Whereas Mackinder was skeptical towards democratic ideals and focused mainly on the "autocratic" continental states and on their potential offensive use of their land power, Spykman's focus was on the peripheral democracies that based their strength on sea power. These nations on the periphery of the World Island served the defensive purpose of restraining the Heartland holder—be it Nazi Germany or Soviet Russia. The idea of restraining the Heartland-holder would be concretely realized during the Cold War thanks to George Kennan's and Harry Truman's containment strategy.   [4.218]

Spykman accused Mackinder of failing in recognizing the strategic importance of the Rimland and of the Offshore Islands—i.e. North and South America, Britain, Japan, and Australia. But the American political scientist was right as far as the United States and its satellites had possessed during the Cold War enough resources of their own capable of preventing the Soviet Union in the Heartland from achieving domination beyond its continental borders. The containment strategy had no other purposes than preventing the USSR from gaining the resources needed to become equal or even more powerful than the US.   [4.219]

Spykman's approach to geopolitics reproduced Mackinder's conceptual dialectic and vocabulary. However, he argued that from a strategic point of view based on an analysis of power politics Mackinder's famous slogan needed to be recast as "Who controls the Rimland rules Eurasia; who rules Eurasia controls the destinies of the world."[144]   [4.220]

Spykman considered the United States of America as the country with the best geostrategic location in the world. He upheld the idea that international relations rely on anarchy and therefore the quest for power incarnates little more than a mere need to survive: "The search for power is not made for the achievement of moral values; moral values are used to facilitate the attainment of power."[145] Unlike Haushofer, however, Spykman did not believe in   [4.221] domination but rather in the safety of equilibrium and in the balance of power in international relations. He believed that history could develop only in temperate latitudes included in the Northern Hemisphere between the 20th and 60th parallel north, an area that comprises North America, Europe, the Greater Middle East and North Africa, most of Russia, China, and the bulk of India.[146]

[4.222]   Whereas Mackinder held a Eurasian-centric view, Spykman possessed a worldwide American-centric one. In considering the regional hegemony of the US in the Western Hemisphere, he noted that America built its hemi-spherical power through the control of the Caribbean basin; the geo-strategic heart of the New World was therefore the Greater Caribbean, including the Gulf of Mexico, of which the US had gained hegemony on after the victori-ous Spanish-American War of 1898.[147] America's strategically advantageous position is made possible by the fact that the US represents the regional hegemon in the Western Hemisphere capable of projecting its power outside the New World, thus affecting the balances in the Eastern Hemisphere.[148]

[4.223]   While Mackinder considered the struggle for the Heartland as a contrapo-sition between land power and sea power, with a Heartland-based land power in the better position, Spykman believed the exact opposite, stating that sea powers reside in a far better position. In considering Russian encirclement, he stated that "for two hundred years, since the time of Peter the Great, Russia has attempted to break through the encircling ring of border states and the reach the ocean. Geography and sea power have persistently thwarted her."[149]

[4.224]   According to Spykman, the Heartland was contained within a belt of mountains that run from the Carpathians to the Korean peninsula: this was a strip of land that people would have always fought for. Also, for Spykman the Heartland roughly coincided with the Soviet bloc: it bordered to the north with the ice-blocked Arctic Sea, between Norway and the Russian Far East; and was ringed to the south by mountains, from the Carpathians in Romania to the plateaus of Anatolia, Persia, and Afghanistan, turning northeastward to the Pamir Knot, the Altai Mountains, Mongolia, Manchuria, and finally to the Korean Peninsula. To the south and outside of this belt of mountains and flatlands was located the highly-populated land of the Rimland. As already mentioned, "Rimland" was the name given by Spykman to the land-ring encircling the pivotal Heartland that included Europe, the Middle East, Southern Asia, Southeastern Asia, China, and the Japanese archipelago.[150] The concept of Rimland was described as the strip of land resembling the shape of a crescent that included all the marginal areas of the Eurasian continent, which, being deeply influenced by maritime power, radiated pow-er over both Eurasia and the outer world and whose control would lead to the dominion of the Eurasian continent, whose control, in turn, would lead to the dominion of the entire world.

The control of the Rimland opened the door to world power: the reason   [4.225]
was that while Mackinder's Heartland could only radiate power over Eurasia,
the maritime-oriented Rimland could cover a range of power over both Eurasia and the outer marginal world. Within the Rimland dwelled highly developed populations, economically advanced and with high demographic rates.

During World War Two, the USSR had full control over the Heartland   [4.226]
and the Axis powers an increasing dominion over the Rimland at the expenses of Britain and the United States. By stopping the Axis territorial
expansion in North Africa, the Pacific Ocean and Indochina, the Anglo-
Saxon thalassocracies managed to re-affirm their own hegemony on the Rimland. After the conflict, the competition for the Rimland continued throughout the Cold War. Under these circumstances, the containment strategy enunciated in 1946 by George Kennan in his Long Telegram was an attempt of
Anglo-Saxon sea powers to marginalize Soviet land power. In this context,
the defense of Western Europe, Israel, some Arab states, and Persia, as well
as the war in Korea and Vietnam served the purpose of preventing the Soviet
empire from extending its control from the Heartland into the Rimland. On
the other hand, to oppose the containment strategy, the Soviets interacted
with Rimland countries, going so far to support militarily filo-Soviet governments in the Greater Middle East, the Korean Peninsula, and Indochina. Even
the 1979 Soviet invasion of Afghanistan epitomized the Russian attempt to
combine land power and sea power, when a Heartland-dominating superpower tried to gradually control the Rimland and its seashores starting from
the Afghan pivotal region. At the same time, the Iranian Revolution of 1979
represented for America the loss of a fundamental ally in countering the
Soviet penetration in the Rimland.

The Rimland represented the main area of opposition between the United   [4.227]
States and the Soviet Union during the Cold War,[151] as well as the area
where the two superpowers held buffer States under their direct or indirect
influence.

This being the case, containment is the name used by peripheral sea   [4.228]
powers for what the Heartland powers call encirclement.

Spykman recognized some of the chief foundations of state power: "The   [4.229]
factors that condition the policy of states are many; they are permanent and
temporary, obvious and hidden; they include, apart from the geographic factor, population density, the economic structure of the country, the ethnic
composition of the people, the form of government, and the complexes and
pet prejudices of foreign ministers."[152]

However, his position was not that of a geographical determinist, believ-   [4.230]
ing that geography was important, but not the only important factor of international politics and power relations: "The geography of a country is rather
the material for, than the cause of, its policy, and to admit that the garment
must ultimately be cut to fit the cloth is not to say that the cloth determines

Sea power = Containment	versus	Heartland power = Encirclement

↓

In relation to the control over the Rimland

↓

Sea power's interest = to avoid that Heartland and Rimland coming under the same ruler and thus to ensure the control of bridgeheads on the Rimland

Heartland power's interest = to break the sea power encirclement by gaining control over parts of the Rimland

[4f1]

either the garment's style or its adequacy. But the geography of a state cannot be ignored by men who formulate its policy. The nature of the territorial base has influenced them in that formulation in the past and will continue to do so in the future."[153]

[4.231]   Spkyman's geopolitical methodology was based in long-term historical analysis. He devoted the theoretical frame of his geopolitical thought to the effects of territory size and location upon a state's political and strategic history. Size, he believed, represented a potential strength of countries, yet not the only relevant one: territorial extension denoted strength insofar as it was equivalent to arable land and therefore to manpower. Based on this assumption, Spykman believed that land powers possessed a natural inclination towards expansion originated by the search for fertile lands outside their territory. Often this need for expansion would be dictated by demographic factors: the augmentation of a country's population would necessarily lead towards the seek for new lands to cultivate and exploit. However, since the times of the Industrial Revolution, a state's strength was identified with its industrial potential, which pivoted on the supply of raw materials for industrial production. Despite the industrial development, Spykman believed that the spatial factor did not lose its overall relevance, since a larger geographical area would always offer better chances of hosting different climatic ranges, natural habitats and varied resources.[154] The territorial size and resources of a country, when combined with technological might, would project a state or an alliance of states to the rank of great power.

[4.232]   Mackinder and Spykman were both concerned with the possibility of a single land power that would dominate Eurasia by adjoining the Rimland to the Heartland, and with the possibility of a single sea power that would control the Eurasian Rimland from its Motherland headquarters and through the rule over the seas. In other words, the major geopolitical threat was represented by the unification of the Heartland and the Rimland under the rule of the same world power: this event would lead to the breakdown of trade and economic growth for all other countries in the "Periphery islands." Eurasia would therefore turn into a huge self-sufficient stronghold, defended by the water of the oceans that border it and in a hegemonic position in relation to the countries that reside on the outer crescents. As history has shown, the control of the Rimland had been the main goal of all those powers in search of global supremacy: Napoleonic France, Wilhelminian Germany, Hitlerite Germany, US-led NATO military alliance, and USSR-led Warsaw Pact military alliance. However, the Rimland's natural fragmentation made it more difficult for it to fall under the control of a single power, encouraging instead forms of balanced power—which Spykman strongly advocated.

In relation to Europe, Spykman opposed all forms of pan-European unifi-   [4.233]
cation for the sake of safeguarding the balance of power. Thus, the idea of a federal Europe was perceived as an alteration of the United States' predominance over the Atlantic Ocean and a weakening of its position in the whole Western Hemisphere and within the context of the NATO alliance. Spykman opposed the idea of a German or Russian domination of Europe, as well as the unification of the continent under whatsoever condition. According to him, maintaining a European fragmentation was one of the key US strategic goals: a true European super-state with united armed forces and a single foreign policy would represent a major US competitor, as well as the potential dominant power in the equidistant zone of South America.[155]

Spykman can be included among the theoretical developers of strategic   [4.234]
Atlanticism, advocating the engagement of the US in the Pacific area and in the rest of the world.[156] He believed in the need for the US to assume global responsibilities due to the immense size of the country and to its particularly favorable geographic location. Along with the Soviet Union, China, and India, the US could exercise an effective political control over vast areas. However, the US possessed a strategic factor that the other three extended nations did not have: a favorable position of continental insularity, granted by two oceans from which the country could project its sea power. Moreover, the US did not have to fear regional threats to security due to the bordering with "friendly" countries like Canada and Mexico.

In relations to various areas, the US enjoyed several points of strength. In   [4.235]
the western hemisphere, American hegemony was granted by a lack of fragmentation and by the ideals of pan-Americanism. In relation to the trans-Atlantic area, the strength of the US was given by the weakness and fragmentation of Europe, which could easily be controlled through a strategic partnership with some of its western nations. The major threat here was given by Germany when it presented itself as capable of controlling the strip of land from Eurasia to the Atlantic Ocean, weakening Britain's role as balancer. In relation to the trans-Pacific area, the nation that had threatened American interests with its attempt to control the strip between Eurasia and the Pacific

Ocean had been Japan, but its defeat and alignment with the US after World War Two granted US hegemony over the Pacific. Finally, in relation to the rest of the world, after controlling respectively the trans-Pacific and trans-Atlantic areas that surround the Eurasian landmass, the US could easily project a global hegemony in the remaining peripheral lands. In other words, by controlling the Rimland, from Great Britain to Japan, the US could achieve world hegemony, encircling the Eurasian Heartland held by the Soviets.[157]

[4.236]

NOTES

[4n1]   1. Sir Halford John Mackinder (15 February 1861–6 March 1947) was born in Gainsborough, Lincolnshire. His life was characterized by eclecticism: he was a geographer, an academic, a Member of Parliament, the first Principal of University Extension College of Reading—which later became the University of Reading—, the Director of the London School of Economics, and an explorer, being the first man to climb the top of Mount Kenya. He is unanimously acknowledged as one of the founding fathers of geopolitics and geo-strategy. Among his main works that highlight the author's geopolitical considerations are *On the Scopes and Methods of Geography* (1887), *Britain and the British Seas* (1902), *The Geographical Pivot of History* (1904), *Democratic Ideals and Reality: A Study in the Politics of Reconstruction* (1919), and *The Round World and the Winning of the Peace* (1943).

[4n2]   2. Kaplan, *The Revenge of Geography*, 62.
[4n3]   3. Mackinder's immediate concern was related to Germany and only secondarily to Russia.
[4n4]   4. Daniele Scalea, *Halford John Mackinder : Dalla Geografia Alla Geopolitica* (Rome: Fuoco Ed., 2013), 296–97; Dossena, *Lo Scienziato e lo Sciamano*, 159–160.
[4n5]   5. See Karl Haushofer, *Il Giappone Costruisce il Suo Impero.* (Parma: All'Insegna del Veltro, 1999), 377–78.
[4n6]   6. Dossena, *Lo Scienziato e lo Sciamano*, 10.
[4n7]   7. Scalea, *Halford John Mackinder*, 205–43.
[4n8]   8. Ibid, 214.
[4n9]   9. Mackinder, "The Geographical Pivot of History," 422.
[4n10]   10. Halford J. Mackinder "On the Scope and Methods of Geography," *Proceedings of the Royal Geographical Society and Monthly Record of Geography* 9, no. 3 (1887): 141. doi:10.2307/1801248.
[4n11]   11. Ibid, 143.
[4n12]   12. Ibid, 147.
[4n13]   13. Ibid, 153.
[4n14]   14. Ibid, 154.
[4n15]   15. Ibid, 157.
[4n16]   16. Ibid.
[4n17]   17. Scalea, *Halford John Mackinder*, 243.
[4n18]   18. Mackinder, "On the Scope and Methods of Geography," 160.
[4n19]   19. Halford J. Mackinder, *Britain and the British Isles* (London: Heinemann, 1902), 1.
[4n20]   20. Ibid, 9.
[4n21]   21. Ibid, 11.
[4n22]   22. Ibid, 178–79.
[4n23]   23. Ibid, 309.
[4n24]   24. Ibid, 310.
[4n25]   25. Ibid, 311–14.
[4n26]   26. Ibid, 344.
[4n27]   27. Ibid, 345–46.
[4n28]   28. Ibid, 349.

29. Ibid, 349–50.   [4n29]
30. Ibid, 350.   [4n30]
31. The only regions yet to be discovered were the Arctic regions and the Arabian Desert.   [4n31]
32. Mackinder, "The Geographical Pivot of History," 422.   [4n32]
33. Ibid.   [4n33]
34. Ibid.   [4n34]
35. Kearns, *Geopolitics and Empire*, 4.   [4n35]
36. Dossena, *Lo Scienziato e lo Sciamano*, 72.   [4n36]
37. Mackinder, "The Geographical Pivot of History," 423.   [4n37]
38. Ibid.   [4n38]
39. Ibid, 427.   [4n39]
40. Then expression Tatar or Mongol yoke indicates the historical epoch of the Mongol rule   [4n40]
over Kievan Rus' (1237–1480).
41. Mackinder, "The Geographical Pivot of History," 427.   [4n41]
42. Ibid, 428.   [4n42]
43. Ibid.   [4n43]
44. Ibid, 429.   [4n44]
45. Scalea, *Halford John Mackinder*, 282.   [4n45]
46. Cf. Gumilëv, "Zametki Poslednego Yevraziitsa," in *Ritmy Yevrazii*.   [4n46]
47. Mackinder, "The Geographical Pivot of History," 431.   [4n47]
48. Respectively Buddhism, Brahmanism, Islamism, and Christianity.   [4n48]
49. This region includes the Eastern Mediterranean Sea, the Southern Black Sea, the South-   [4n49]
ern Caspian Sea, the Red Sea, and the Persian Gulf.
50. Mackinder, "The Geographical Pivot of History," 431–32.   [4n50]
51. Dossena, *Lo Scienziato e lo Sciamano*, 136–37.   [4n51]
52. Ibid.   [4n52]
53. Ibid, 140–41.   [4n53]
54. Mackinder, "The Geographical Pivot of History," 433.   [4n54]
55. Dossena, *Lo Scienziato e lo Sciamano*, 141.   [4n55]
56. Mackinder, "The Geographical Pivot of History," 434.   [4n56]
57. Ibid.   [4n57]
58. However, in his 1919 schema, Mackinder will dilate the Heartland's strategic borders   [4n58]
with the inclusion of the water basins of the Black Sea and Baltic Sea and their surrounding
areas.
59. Spykman will call this is vast stripe of land the "Rimland."   [4n59]
60. Mackinder, "The Geographical Pivot of History," 436.   [4n60]
61. Ibid.   [4n61]
62. Ibid, 437.   [4n62]
63. Halford J. Mackinder, *Democratic Ideals and Realities : A Study in the Politics of*   [4n63]
Reconstruction (London: Constable and Company Ltd, 1919), 21–51 (the seaman's point view)
and 53–81 (the landsman's point of view).
64. Kaplan, *The Revenge of Geography*, 71–72.   [4n64]
65. Mackinder, *Democratic Ideals and Realities*, 24.   [4n65]
66. Kaplan, *The Revenge of Geography*, 71.   [4n66]
67. Mackinder, *Democratic Ideals and Realities*, 27.   [4n67]
68. Kaplan, *The revenge of geography*, 71.   [4n68]
69. Similarly, Xerxes's Persian army had tried to outflank the Greek sea power penetrating   [4n69]
through land from Thrace into the Hellenic peninsula with the coverage of the navy. Even
Alexander the Great had invaded through land the Persian Empire, confiding in his navy for
supplies and cover.
70. Mackinder, *Democratic Ideals and Realities*, 29.   [4n70]
71. Ibid, 31.   [4n71]
72. Ibid, 32.   [4n72]
73. The rule of the Mediterranean would be achieved sequentially by the Ottomans, the   [4n73]
Spaniards (after the battle of Lepanto, 1571), and the English.
74. Mackinder, *Democratic Ideals and Realities*, 38.   [4n74]

[4n75]   75. Ibid.
[4n76]   76. Ibid, 34–36.
[4n77]   77. Ibid, 41.
[4n78]   78. Dossena, *Lo Scienziato e lo Sciamano*, 137.
[4n79]   79. Mackinder, *Britain and the British Isles*, 344–46.
[4n80]   80. Dossena, *Lo Scienziato e lo Sciamano*, 137–38.
[4n81]   81. Ibid, 138.
[4n82]   82. Mackinder, *Democratic Ideals and Realities*, 49.
[4n83]   83. Ibid, 43.
[4n84]   84. Ibid, 45–46.
[4n85]   85. Ibid, 46.
[4n86]   86. We will use the term Pan-America to designate the combined lands of the three Americas, i.e. North, Central and South America and their Caribbean satellites.
[4n87]   87. Mackinder, *Democratic Ideals and Realities*, 46–47.
[4n88]   88. Ibid, 49–51.
[4n89]   89. Ibid, 51.
[4n90]   90. Ibid, 55.
[4n91]   91. Ibid, 54.
[4n92]   92. Ibid, 55.
[4n93]   93. Ibid.
[4n94]   94. Ibid.
[4n95]   95. Ibid, 55–56.
[4n96]   96. Ibid, 57–58.
[4n97]   97. Ibid, 58.
[4n98]   98. Ibid, 58–60.
[4n99]   99. Ibid, 59.
[4n100]   100. Ibid, 77–78.
[4n101]   101. Ibid, 78.
[4n102]   102. Ibid, 80.
[4n103]   103. Cf. Paolo Pizzolo, *Astuzia e Ragion Di Stato. Modelli di Politica Estera Europea Nell'Ottocento* (Rome: Gruppo Editoriale L'Espresso, 2016), 259–310.
[4n104]   104. Mackinder, *Democratic Ideals and Realities*, 95–96.
[4n105]   105. Ibid, 106.
[4n106]   106. Ibid, 81.
[4n107]   107. Scalea, *Halford John Mackinder*, 298.
[4n108]   108. Ibid, 276.
[4n109]   109. In considering the role of the League of Nations, Mackinder believed that "the test of the League will be in the Heartland of the Continent. Nature there offers all the prerequisites of ultimate dominance in the world; it must be for man by his foresight and by the taking of solid guarantees to prevent its attainment," see Mackinder, *Democratic Ideals and Realities*, 120.
[4n110]   110. Dossena, *Lo Scienziato e lo Sciamano*, 140.
[4n111]   111. Mackinder, *Democratic Ideals and Realities*, 111–12.
[4n112]   112. Ibid, 205.
[4n113]   113. Ibid, 120.
[4n114]   114. Mackinder, *The Geographical Pivot of History*, 436.
[4n115]   115. Scalea, *Halford John Mackinder*, 187–88.
[4n116]   116. This prospect was about to become reality after the negotiations for the entrance of the USSR in the Tripartite Pact and in the Molotov-Ribbentrop non-aggression agreement.
[4n117]   117. Dossena, *Lo Scienziato e lo Sciamano*, 140.
[4n118]   118. Ibid, 139.
[4n119]   119. See Fareed Zakaria, *The Post-American World* (New York: W.W. Norton, 2009).
[4n120]   120. Halford J. Mackinder, "The Round World and the Winning of the Peace," *Foreign Affairs* 21, no. 4 (1943): 595–96.
[4n121]   121. Ibid, 596.
[4n122]   122. Mackinder, "The Geographical Pivot of History," 436–37.
[4n123]   123. Mackinder, "The Round World and the Winning of the Peace," 598.

124. Ibid, 598–99.   [4n124]
125. Ibid, 599–600.   [4n125]
126. Dossena, *Lo Scienziato e lo Sciamano*, 434–35.   [4n126]
127. Mackinder, "The Round World and the Winning of the Peace," 601–2.   [4n127]
128. Ibid, 602.   [4n128]
129. Ibid.   [4n129]
130. Ibid, 605.   [4n130]
131. Karl Ernst Haushofer (27 August 1869–10 March 1946) was a German general, geogra- [4n131]
pher, and politician. In 1919, he left the army to dedicate himself completely to geopolitics,
assimilating the works of Kjellén, Ratzel, and Mackinder, and began to teach at Munich's
University, becoming director of the institute of geopolitics. He then founded the journal
Zeitschrift für Geopolitik ("Journal of Geopolitics") (1924), of which he would become chief
cooperator. Haushofer published a numerous series of essays on the relationship between
powers and territory, on the geopolitics of the Pacific Ocean, on the rise of imperial Japan, on
the parallelisms between German, Italian, and Japanese history, and on theoretical geopolitical
speculation. Among his main works are *Geopolitik des Pazifischen Ozeans* ("Geopolitics of the
Pacific Ocean") (1925), *Geopolitik der pan-ideen* ("Geopolitics of Pan-Ideas") (1931), *Weltpolitik von Heute* ("World Politics of Today") (1934), *Weltmeere und Weltmächte* ("Oceans
and World Powers") (1937), *Der Kontinentalblock: Mitteleuropa, Eurasien, Japan* ("The Continental Bloc: Central Europe, Eurasia, Japan") (1941), and *Japan Baut Sein Reich* ("Japan
Builds Its Empire") (1941).
132. Karl Haushofer, *Weltpolitik von Heute* (Berlin: "Zeitgeschichte" Verlag, 1934).   [4n132]
133. Kaplan, *The Revenge of Geography*, 84.   [4n133]
134. Karl Haushofer, *Geopolitik der Pan-Ideen* (Berlin: Zentral-Verlag, 1931).   [4n134]
135. Carlo Jean, *Geopolitica* (Bari: Ed. Laterza, 1995), 32–33.   [4n135]
136. William H. Parker, *Mackinder: Geography as an Aid to Statecraft* (Oxford: Clarendon [4n136]
Press, 1982), 148.
137. Ibid, 245.   [4n137]
138. Dossena, *Lo Scienziato e lo Sciamano*, 437.   [4n138]
139. Parker, *Mackinder*, 173.   [4n139]
140. Karl Haushofer, *Lo Sviluppo Dell'Idea Imperiale Nipponica* (Rome: Istituto Italiano per [4n140]
il Medio ed Estremo Oriente, 1942), 40.
141. Kaplan, *The Revenge of Geography*, 85.   [4n141]
142. Diodato, *Che Cos'è La Geopolitica*, 94.   [4n142]
143. Nicholas John Spykman (13 October 1893–1826 June 1943) was a Dutch-American [4n143]
political scientist and one of the founders of the classical realist school in American foreign
policy. He published several works on geopolitics and geo-strategy like *America's Strategy in
World Politics: The United States and the Balance of Power* (1942) and *The Geography of the
Peace* (1944).
144. Spykman, Nicholl, and Dunn, *The Geography of the Peace*, 43.   [4n144]
145. Ibid, 90.   [4n145]
146. bid, 91.   [4n146]
147. Ibid, 92. According to Spykman, similarly to what had happened with Athens through [4n147]
the control of the Greek Archipelago by dominating the Aegean Sea and with Rome through
the control of the Western world thanks to the rule of the Mediterranean basin, America
became a world power after taking control over its middle sea—the Caribbean—, which would
soon after allow the construction of the Panama Canal and the projection of sea power over
both the Atlantic and the Pacific Oceans.
148. Nicholas J. Spykman, *America's Strategy in World Politics: The United States and the* [4n148]
Balance of Power (New York: Harcourt, Brace, 1942), 89.
149. Ibid, 182.   [4n149]
150. Kaplan, *The Revenge of Geography*, 96.   [4n150]
151. Like in the cases of the Korean War, the Berlin crises, the Vietnam War, and the Afghan [4n151]
invasion.
152. Nicholas J. Spykman, "Geography and Foreign Policy, I," *American Political Science* [4n152]
Review 32, no. 1 (1938): 28.

[4n153]   153. Ibid, 30.
[4n154]   154. Ibid, 32.
[4n155]   155. Spykman, *America's Strategy in World Politics*, 466.
[4n156]   156. Diodato, *Che Cos'è La Geopolitica*, 72.
[4n157]   157. Ibid, 73–74.

Chapter Five

The Eurasianist Ideology

Theory, Mission, and Program

[5.0]   INTRODUCTION

[5.1]   The three following chapters will focus on Aleksandr Dugin's neo-Eurasia-
          nim, in the attempt to describe its main characteristics and implications.
          Dugin's neo-Eurasianist ideology is grounded on the two founding pillars of
          the affirmation of the "Fourth Political Theory" and the spread of a world-
          wide conservative revolution aimed at establishing a new multipolar world
          order based on civilizational big spaces. In this chapter, we will focus on the
          main features of Dugin's neo-Eurasianist thought and on the theoretical basis
          that depicts the Eurasianist vision of a new world order. In the first section
          we will describe the ideological foundations of neo-Eurasianism, in the sec-
          ond the core features of the so-called "Fourth Political Theory," in the third
          the ideological assumptions that characterize the so-called "Eurasian Mani-
          festo," and finally in the fourth the affirmation and rise of the Fourth Political
          Theory as a political doctrine.

[5.2]   THE IDEOLOGICAL FOUNDATIONS
                                   OF NEO-EURASIANISM

[5.3]   Eurasianism is essentially an ideology based on a constructivist analysis that
          bears a political and dogmatic scope. Reechoing somewhat Huntington's
          theoretical paradigm, the chief element upon which the Eurasianist philoso-
          phy is built is the concept of civilization. Eurasianists affirm as an axiom that
          different civilizations exist and that each possesses its own structure that
          describes its specific features, giving it meaning and coherence. In other

words, the idea that human societies represent a specific kind of semantic structure that is entirely exclusive and incomparable with any other is the basic principle of Eurasian philosophy in general.[1] The main criticism implied in this assumption refers to the Western-led globalization model that tends to homologate all nations into cosmopolitan individuals that lack specific civilizational or anthropological affiliation.

As seen, Eurasianism is a dogmatic doctrine that claims to represent a hermeneutic tool to unfold and interpret the world from a normative perspective. As an ideology, Eurasianism is inspired by a multifaceted corpus of norms and beliefs, since it simultaneously represents a worldview, a philosophy, a geopolitical project, an economic theory, a spiritual movement, and a core around which to consolidate a wide range of political forces.[2]   [5.4]

The Eurasian project has a worldwide, ecumenical scope since its principles are believed to bear a global potential.[3] Despite its alleged global scope, however, the Eurasianist ideology finds its cradle in Russia. The idea of the uniqueness of civilization was adopted by the Russian model since the Russian civilization gave birth to an original identity that bears features of both European and Asian—specifically Turanian—cultures, representing an organic synthesis that cannot be reduced to the mere sum of its Western and Eastern elements. The Eurasianist narrative interprets civilizations as organic wholes with their own semantics that reveal a specific identity and way to understand history, religion, politics, culture, and strategy—i.e. a specific *Weltanschauung*. The concept of unique civilizational backgrounds is considered as the valuable heritage of nations, which are believed to be worthy of protection and safeguard per se, i.e. for the simple fact of existing.   [5.5]

The hermeneutical vision of a plurality of civilizations puts Eurasianists in deep contrast with Westernists and post-liberals. Eurasianism radically rejects Western pretensions to universality and denies what it considers Western ethnocentrism, cultural imperialism, and civilizational standards. The entire Eurasianist ideology has been structured in the form of a political philosophy based on the multipolarity of civilizations, anti-imperialism, anti-modernism and on the Russian structure of the state.[4] Believing in the uniqueness of Russian society, Eurasianists seek to export this model elsewhere and to spread identitarian societies in a form that corresponds to the specificities of each nation, in accordance with their values and basic beliefs. This project implies the need to reject modernist "progress" and to consider social development as a natural cycle, and not in terms of a capitalist linear forced progression. For instance, Eurasianists tend to favor an agricultural economy to an industrial one; they replace materialism and consumerism with spirituality and ideocracy and deny democracy in favor of popular monarchism or social republicanism. They discard the concepts of individualism, superficial liberty, and modernization in favor of social responsibility, inner freedom, and the defense of traditionalist values.   [5.6]

[5.7]   As previously noticed, Eurasianism evolved into neo-Eurasianism in the early 1990s. Since the beginning, neo-Eurasianism was conceived as a Russian form of Third Way ideology affiliated with the philosophical family of the German Conservative Revolution. Neo-Eurasianism is a specifically Russian paradigm of an anti-modern philosophical and political tendency similar to traditionalism and the "Third Position."[5] While its rightist current identifies itself with traditional conservatism, its leftist current is represented by the ideology of National Bolshevism. In criticizing modernity and Eurocentrism, neo-Eurasianism is very close to the spirit of Alain de Benoist's "European New Right."

[5.8]   Significantly, neo-Eurasianist ideology enriched the earlier Eurasianist doctrine with geopolitical thinking. The opposition between the West and Eurasia is not conceived as merely ideological (liberalism against conservatism), but it bears the strategic meaning of struggle between thalassocracy (Atlanticism) and tellurocracy (Eurasianism).

[5.9]   Some of the main features of neo-Eurasianism include the close bond with traditionalism, a hermeneutical approach to international relations based on geopolitics, an ideological closeness to philosophers like Carl Schmitt and Martin Heidegger, the project of implementing a worldwide conservative revolution, and a civilizational *Weltanschauung* based on structural and cultural anthropology. The ultimate ideological goal that neo-Eurasianism promotes is to overcome the unipolar West-led world order and to replace it with a multipolar one based on civilizational big spaces. In this perspective, the Eurasianist doctrine is normatively anchored to the idea of an eternal struggle between the civilization of Land and the civilization of the Sea, dogmatically believing in the philosophical and strategic superiority of the former. This struggle should lead to the demise of the Atlanticist thalassocratic world rule and to the creation—in accordance with the advocates of continentalism, from Karl Haushofer to Jean Thiriart—of a pan-Eurasian empire stretching from Lisbon to Vladivostok. Thus, the Eurasianist project can be summarized as following: unification of Eurasia and construction of a peaceful multipolar world order.

[5.10]   As already noted, Aleksandr Dugin promoted the creation of the International Eurasian Movement, which, in his words, would endeavor an intensive dialogue between cultures, civilizations, faiths, states, social groups, and ethnicities of the Eurasian continent, from Tokyo to the Azores.[6] The main objective of this political movement would be to safeguard the distinctive nature of nations, cultures, faiths, languages, values, and philosophical systems, enforcing the dialogue between countries and peoples whose identities are put at stake by the homoginization of globalization. The movement considers identity as the richest heritage to preserve and upholds the idea that nations should encourage dialogue without losing their own uniqueness, insisting that the participants in the dialogue of cultures and civilizations should be sovereign and free.[7]

Dugin insists that the nations of Eurasia must be free and independent, and consequently condemns the powers of globalization that tend to dilute and overcome ethnic, cultural, and civilizational identities:

[5.11]

> "We are strongly against globalization as a form of ideological, economic, political, and value-based imperialism. No one has the right to impose one's own private "truth," value system, and sociopolitical model by force or ruse upon the great nations of the Eurasian continent.[. . .]. West and East, every confession, ethnicity and culture have their own truths. We have all the reason to share our truth with others, but we must never impose it by force."[8]

[5.12]

The International Eurasian Movement contrasts what Dugin calls the typically Western "Babylon blending" and considers it imperative to find a way to make globalization compatible with the preservation of each national character and identity, as well as to prevent the peoples of the Eurasian continent from turning into a global melting pot following the American and Western European model of society. What the movement claims, however, seems contradictory if we consider that many Eurasian societies—including Russia—are already a melting pot of ethnic and religious groups, though sharing a similar history.

[5.13]

Eurasianism can be considered a revisionist and revanchist philosophy. It is revisionist because it strives for a revision of the political and social paradigm of contemporary societies; at the same time, it is revanchist because it wishes to take revenge on modernism and post-liberalism for what it considers the current degenerate status quo of mankind that they have provoked.

[5.14]

It is interesting to note that the Eurasianist ideology is not anti-globalist *sensu stricto* but rather alter-globalist, since it offers an alternative form of globalization based on the principles of multipolarity. It does not exclude any nation or people from the adherence to its philosophy and wishes to create harmoniously a peaceful international environment. The Eurasianist doctrine opposes the creation of a world government based on liberal-democratic values as the one and only path for mankind and adheres to the principles of alter-globalization, which is a term that is synonymous with the acknowledgment of a multipolar world. By protecting the diversity of values structures, it represents a kind of "pluriversum" that provides living space for everyone, including the civilizations of Africa, both American continents, and the Pacific area that runs parallel to the Eurasian continent.[9]

[5.15]

Eurasianists recognize a dualism between the Old World—which literally indicates the sole European continent—and the New World—i.e. the American continent. Referring to the concept of Old World as the wider Eurasian territory, Eurasianism represents it as a multi-civilizational super-

[5.16]

space inhabited by different nations, ethnicities, cultures, and religions that are historically and geographically intertwined to each other by a dialectic destiny. On the other hand, it views the New World as an artificial and technical construction based upon man-made ideologies and as a civilization of radical liberalism where modernist European projects promoted by the Enlightenment have reached their fulfillment. This dualism between Old and New World would hence display the opposition of millenary cultures against modern man-made civilization, of organic society against artificial society, and of slow historical evolution against fast technological progress.

[5.17]   As enshrined in the movement's ideological foundations, neo-Eurasianism is built upon five fundamental pillars, which are the differentiation of civilizations and peoples, traditionalism, the rights of nations above individual human rights, ethnocentrism, and social fairness, human solidarity, and distributive justice. However, these five points contain unclear definitions and aspects. First, how can differentiation of civilizations and peoples be sustainable in today's interconnected world? Should all civilizations be an impenetrable closed environments? But how could this be compatible with international interconnections and flows of labor? Would rigid separation of peoples not interrupt dialogue and trade? Second, who interprets traditionalism? What kind of traditionalism is the movement referring to? Does traditionalism not differ from one country to another? Third, how could the rights of nations and ethno-centrism preserve ethnic minorities? How to deal with states that include different national ethnic groups? Most importantly, what defines an ethnic group? Is it its state, its history, its language, its race, its genetics or its religion? Finally, who decides what is social fairness and social justice? Would the interpretation of what is fair and unfair not be necessarily normative and subjective? It seems that beyond the ideological rhetoric, the Eurasianist project presents ambiguous features, nor does Dugin offer more detailed explanations in his works.

[5.18]   According to Eurasianism, the Atlanticist world order should be replaced with a multipolar system capable of defending and safeguarding human variety, but it is unclear whether multipolarity would ensure this task or merely replace the current hegemon with another or others. The Eurasian project would endorse the introduction of a new epoch of cultural renaissance and intellectual revival, in which wisdom and knowledge replace consumerism and materialism, but it is uncertain whether this would ameliorate mankind's conditions. Above all, the facticity of neo-Eurasianist goals seems unlikely and often problematic.

[5.19]   Despite the advocated rigid civilizational division, Eurasianisnts believe that the dialogue between different cultures and traditions would eventually guide the world towards a new golden age in which all nations share their heritage but preserve their uniqueness. Eurasianism believes in the need to

defend all living ethnic groups, cultural traditions and religious beliefs, upholding the principle of self-determination of peoples. [10]

As anticipated, although being semantically connected with the Eurasian   [5.20]
continent, the Eurasianist movement claims to bear a worldwide scope that
transcends all geographical borders:

> "The Eurasianists are not only the representatives of the peoples who live in   [5.21]
> the Eurasian continent. Being a Eurasianist is a conscious choice, which means
> combining the aspiration to preserve the traditional forms of life with the
> aspiration toward free and creative development, both social and personal. In
> this way, Eurasianists are all free creative personalities who acknowledge the
> values of tradition. Among them are also representatives of those regions
> which objectively form the bases of Atlanticism. Eurasianists and Atlanticists
> are opposed to each other in everything. They defend two different and mutu-
> ally exclusive images of the world and its future. It is the opposition between
> Eurasianists and Atlanticists which defines the historical outline of the twenty-
> first century." [11]

In philosophical terms, Eurasianists depict Atlanticism as characterized by an   [5.22]
ephemeral, temporary, and materialist vision of things, with no attention to
historical past. On the contrary, they claim to rely on a philosophy that
combines a deep trust in the past with an open attitude toward the future. [12]

In terms of spirituality, Eurasianism can almost be compared to a mystical   [5.23]
movement based on metaphysical and transcendent beliefs, which decidedly
opposes materialism and pragmatism, as well as atheism, relativism, and
skepticism. Eurasianists claim that spiritual development is the main priority
of people's life and cannot be replaced by economic or social benefits and
that traditional religions are all worthy of consideration and preservation:
every local religious belief or system of faith is perceived as the patrimony of
all mankind. However, Eurasianism affirms that only traditional religions
deserve care and concern, i.e. those religions that rest upon a solid and
ancient ritual; in this sense, schismatic groups, extremist religious associations, totalitarian sects, preachers of non-traditional religious doctrines, and
all other "modern" pseudo-faiths (e.g. Scientology) that promote the destruction of traditional religions are treated with enmity.

As for the national question, the Eurasianist ideology affirms that every   [5.24]
nation in the world, whether belonging to a great civilization or to smaller
ones, whether demographically numerous or exiguous, is an estimable element that deserves protection and safeguard. In this sense, the forced assimilation of peoples through external influences, the loss of a language or a
traditional way of life, the physical extinction of any ethnic group due to
systematic miscegenation is seen as an irreversible loss for all mankind and a
severe crime against humanity. Human civilization is enriched by the profu-
sion and variety of peoples, cultures, and traditions. In the Eurasianist mind-

set, the issue of interethnic mixture is accepted only when it responds to historical, extremely slow processes—like the stabilization throughout the centuries of the Russian ethnic phenotype through the fusion of the Slavic, Turkish-Mongol, and Finno-Ugric components—and not when it follows artificial patterns of assimilation at any cost like for the Western "melting pot." Eutasianism believes that nations are the result of a long historical organic process that contrasts with artificial interference and any attempt to give up their ethnic and cultural uniqueness.[13] This ethnocentric vision makes Dugin state that the rights of nations are no less significant than the human rights of individuals.[14] When rejecting miscegenation, however, Eurasianism reveals once again a highly ideologic and dogmatic sentiment, not supported or proven by significant forms of scientific evidence.

[5.25] The main strategic goal that the International Eurasian Movement attempts to realize consists in the coordination of all Eurasian powers into a united socio-political front—including the consolidation and integration of all anti- and alter-globalist movements, tendencies, political and social organizations, institutions, and funds—capable of contrasting unipolar globalization and the expansion of Atlanticism and willing to establish a multipolar world. This ambitious political project is extremely narrowminded, adopting a typical Manichean dialectical pattern of utopia (Eurasianist world) versus dystopia (Atlanticist world) that most ideologies follow.

[5.26] ## THE FOURTH POLITICAL THEORY

[5.27] The term "Fourth Political Theory" has been used by Dugin to introduce a new political doctrine that exceeds the three classical political theories of liberalism, communism, and fascism. The Fourth Political Theory appears as the last important shift in the philosophy of neo-Eurasianism, which occurred in 2007–2008 when Dugin arranged its basic principles:

[5.28] "That was the moment of the resolute and irreversible step from Eurasianism as a Russian version of the Third Position to the Fourth Position. This was a continuation of Eurasianist ideas—still consisting of anti-liberalism, anti-modernism, anti-Eurocentrism, the structuralist approach, and multipolarity—but instead of it being a creative synthesis of the anti-liberal (socialist) Right with the identitarian (non-dogmatic, or Sorelian for example) Left, it began to move in a direction taking it beyond all the varieties of political modernity. This is included transcending the Third Position, or rather the mixture of the far Left with far Right (National Bolshevism). The idea behind this was to create the normative for the future, completely removed from any modern political tendency—beyond liberalism, communism and fascism."[15]

[5.29] In other words, the Fourth Political Theory can be considered as the development and the metamorphosis of Eurasianism, in which the Eurasianist doctrine represents its basic paradigm and starting point. This new political theory is born from the rejection of the previous classical ones and appears as an attempt to overcome the political struggles of the last two centuries between liberals, nationalists, and socialists. Having acknowledged in his writings the limits of all previous political theories, Dugin introduces a new philosophical doctrine that attempts to go beyond all obsolete schemas linked to communism, fascism, and liberalism. [16]

The development of the Fourth Political Theory implies the reconsideration of the political history of the last centuries from completely new positions that stand beyond the framework of old ideologies. The Fourth Political Theory is conceived as a new doctrine that adapts to the structural features of the current global society and as a tool to decipher the paradigm of postmodernity. Its post-historical method is utilized for constructing an autonomous political view that may offer a new way to interpret global society and international events. Though less doctrinally rigid than the first three political theories, it presents itself as an invitation to political creativity characterized by a statement of intuitions and conjectures, an analysis of new philosophical-political conditions, and an attempt to reconsider the past. As a speculative project, the Fourth Political Theory embodies the evolution, or rather the fulfillment, of the closely related ideology of National Bolshevism. [5.30]

Having fought and destroyed fascism, rejected liberalism and denied communism, Dugin considers the Russian people as the natural promoters of the Fourth Political Theory, which could fill Russia's political-ideological vacuum inherited after 1991. Dugin argues that a return to the illiberal ideologies of communism and fascism would be unsuccessful since they have ultimately failed their objectives and proven to be inadequate to oppose liberalism; at the same time, embracing liberalism in its Western version would indicate the dissolution of Russian national and historical identity. The Russians would consequently have the moral task to develop and spread a political theory alternative to post-liberalism. [17] [5.31]

The need for introducing a fourth, new political theory is the consequence of the demise of the ideologies of the past century, which were liberalism—both in its leftist-contractarianist and rightist-capitalist acceptation—, socialism—including the various forms of Marxism, communism and social democracy—, and fascism—with its different variants, from German National Socialism to Francisco Franco's National Syndicalism, or Juan Perón's Justicialism. [5.32]

Liberalism was the first political theory of modernity, rising as a consequence of the Enlightenment. As we will consider in more depth in the following chapter, it turned out to be the most stable and successful ideology, ultimately prevailing over rival contenders. On the other hand, socialism appeared later than liberalism as a critical answer to the emergence of the bourgeois-capitalist system that had emerged in Europe with the Industrial [5.33]

Revolution, which appeared as the practical economic expression of the liberal ideology. Finally, the last political theory was fascism, which represented an evolution of the instances of nationalism and attempted to create an alternative collective and identitarian socio-politic model that would contrast both the individualist bourgeois-capitalist social structure and the cosmopolitan Marxist class struggle and dictatorship of the proletariat.

[5.34]   Each of the three original political theories possessed a subject around which the social system was founded. Indeed, defining a socio-historical subject is fundamental for the building of a political ideology.

[5.35]   The subject of communist ideology is class, since the Marxist society was meant to be constructed on the affirmation of one class—the proletariat—over all others. The Marxist vision of history is extremely pessimistic, for it represents a long-term struggle between the exploiter and exploited classes throughout the centuries. Following the Hegelian dialectical schema, Marxists affirmed that history is class struggle, politics its expression, and the proletariat a subject called to set itself free from the dominion of the bourgeoisie and to build a new society. Therefore, the individual as such bears little significance in a Marxist collectivist context, being conceived as a mere part of a class-based whole that acquires social meaning only during the process of rising class consciousness aimed at overthrowing the exploiting rulers.

[5.36]   On the other hand, the subject of fascism is either the nation or the state. For example, under Benito Mussolini's leadership the subject of Italian fascism was both the fatherland and the Italian people considered as an ontological whole, whereas in Adolf Hitler's National Socialist Germany the subject was the Aryan race in its struggle for survival against other "inferior" or rival human groups.

[5.37]   Finally, in liberalism the subject is represented by the individual unhooked from all types of collective identity and identitarian membership. The historical subject of liberalism is the individual conceived as an all-embracing rational unit, endowed with an autonomous will. For the liberal mindset, all forms of collective identity—ethnic, national, religious, social—avert the individual to develop self-awareness and self-realization. Liberalism encourages everyone to become an absolute entity, free of all social bonds and dependencies that may put at risk its freedom.

[5.38]   In the effort to describe what the historical subject of the Fourth Political Theory would be, Dugin affirms that it is neither the individual, nor the class, nor the state or race. Instead—although with a detectable uncertainty and insecurity—, he suggests five possibilities: 1) A combination of the individual, the class, the state, the nation and the race; 2) the Heideggerian principle of *Dasein* (i.e. "existence"; "to be there"),[18] which represents a complex, holistic model based on existential anthropology; 3) the principle of abstracting the individual from history and the consideration of history per se; 4) the idea of "imagination," as suggested by Gilbert Durand, [19] which structurally precedes individuals, collectivity, classes, cultures, races, and states; 5) geopolitics conceived as a philosophical and sociological hermeneutical criterion upon which the Fourth Political Theory could rest. [20]

With its premature disappearance in 1945, fascism cleared the field for the battle between the remaining first and second political theories. This struggle took the form of the Cold War and shaped the strategic geometry of the bipolar world that lasted until 1991. The demise of the Soviet Union and the dissolution of the Warsaw Pact and the COMECON caused the triumph of liberalism—which turned to be the only surviving political theory—and the global decline of communism. However, as we will see in the next chapter, the victory of liberalism coincided with the end of its classical acceptation and its evolution into post-liberalism.   [5.39]

It is in the context of post-liberalism, postmodernity, and unilineal globalism that Dugin's Fourth Political Theory emerges as a doctrinal instrument to contrast the status quo. Hence, the prerequisite for its appearance is dissent against post-liberalism as a universal practice, globalization, postmodernity, the idea of "end of history," the status quo, and the inertia of the processes of civilization at the dawn of the 21st century. [21] In other words, it is a theory that rises for the purpose of a global resistance to the current world order ruled by the laws of finance and economics and based on the annulment of the diversification of national and cultural identities. Dugin affirms that the Fourth Political Theory represents a crusade against four chief features of the current international system: postmodernity, the post-industrial society, liberal thought realized in practice, and the logistical and technological bases of globalization. [22] As a political doctrine, it expresses the amalgamation of a common anti-global, or rather alter-global, project stemming from the need to counter everything that has been discarded, toppled, and humiliated during the course of the construction of postmodernity. Since the terms Right and Left have lost significance in relation to post-liberalism, the new antinomy— and political cleavage—is now between the acquiescence to the globalist world order and the alter-globalist dissent.   [5.40]

The Fourth Political Theory does not only challenge liberalism, but also the second and third political theories of the past. However, in enunciating its principles, it considers it fruitful to rethink fascism and communism from new perspectives, avoiding their orthodoxy and selecting in their doctrinal corpus the concepts to discard and those to keep. If these two doctrines are to contribute somewhat to the formulation and affirmation of the Fourth Political Theory, Dugin suggests the necessity to cross-read them and thus to view Marxism through the lenses of the Right and fascism through the lenses of the Left. Their less dogmatic interpretation would find a synthesis in the political doctrine of National Bolshevism as theorized and developed, both in   [5.41]

Russia and Germany, by Nikolay Ustryalov, Eduard Limonov, and Ernst Niekisch.

[5.42]   The alternative to liberalism should be found in non-liberal versions of conservatism. In this sense, Dugin recalls the example of the philosophical heritage of Alain de Benoist, the pioneer of the European intellectual movement of the *Nouvelle Droite* that criticizes post-liberalism from right-wing positions,[23] and Immanuel Wallerstein's neo-Marxist critique of it as exposed in his work *After Liberalism*.[24]

[5.43]   The Fourth Political Theory is neither fascism, nor communism, nor liberalism, but rather the reinterpretation of the former two—which did not survive the course of history—and the negation of the latter—which is claimed to disappear in the future. It is represented as an effort to overcome the classical ideological and political paradigms and the beginning of an intellectual revolution that would replace the old clichés with a new ideocracy based on the principles of the understanding of Marxism from the lenses of the Right and of fascism from the lenses of the Left.

[5.44]   From each of the three past political theories, there are some elements that the Fourth Political Theory radically rejects, and some that wishes to include.

[5.45]   From fascism, it resolutely rejects its various forms of racism. It also denies all forms of xenophobia and aggressive chauvinism. A main axiom of Dugin's ideology is that the existence and conservation of differences between societies and civilizations does not imply any kind of superiority of one over another: the Fourth Political Theory discards all forms and varieties of racism and the normative hierarchization of societies based on ethnic, religious, social, technological, economic, or cultural backgrounds, since the differences between societies cannot ever imply the superiority of one over the other.[25]

[5.46]   The multipolar order envisioned by neo-Eurasianists would be founded on the mutual respect for all nations and races and on a constructive dialogue among the various civilizational big spaces. The differences in races would not imply qualitative judgements on their alleged superiority or inferiority, but only the acknowledgment of the significant differences that exist among human groups. Dugin himself believes that the cleavages between unipolarism/multipolarism and universalism/pluriversalism incarnate the Western Anglo-Saxon belief in the superiority of its civilizational model, unveiling a form of cultural racism and discrimination.[26] Instead of accepting the racist rhetoric based on the subdivision of humans in superior and inferior races or in developed and underdeveloped nations, the Fourth Political Theory focuses on upholding the idea of ethnos and ethnocentrism. In the wake of Gumilëv's ethnographic studies, an ethnos is described as a community of people that shares a common heritage, be it language, religion, customs, homeland, etc. An ethno*s* is considered the greatest value of the Fourth Political Theory and described as a cultural phenomenon; a community of language and religious belief, and as an organic entity written into an accommodating landscape.[27] Within this context, the ethnos is conceived as a potential candidate for being the historical subject upon which developing the Fourth Political Theory. Ethnicities are perceived as diversified subjects, each universal and unique, but without any hierarchical relationship among them. The unacceptable elements in the fascist theories were racism, xenophobia, and chauvinism, which reflected both moral failings and theoretical-anthropological inconsistent attitudes. According to the Fourth Political Theory, the difference between "ethnoses" cannot indicate superiority or inferiority, since ethnic differences should be accepted and affirmed without racist pretenses. No common system of measurement to compare and evaluate different ethnic groups exists and when societies try to judge others, they commit intellectual violence. However, this same violence is often committed by globalization, which implicitly discriminates other forms of society different from the Western.[28]

Once again, it is nonetheless ambiguous and unclear how Dugin tries to [5.47] subdivide each ethnos, since the variables of heritage, language, religion, customs, and homeland may be shared among different ethnic groups or same ethnic groups may share different types of them.

There are, however, some elements of fascism and communism perceived [5.48] as assimilable by the Fourth Political Theory. The elements that the Fourth Political Theory could include from the fascist ideology are the corporatist socio-economic system, the nationalist philosophical paradigm, the social participation, the protection of the working class, the traditional values of family, spirituality, and fatherland, the quest for military and geopolitical supremacy. Regarding Marxism, the principles that the Fourth Political Theory criticizes and rejects are historical materialism, class hatred, the idea of progress and elimination of the past, materialist reductionism, economic determinism, the dictatorship of the proletariat, the dialectic class struggle, the idea of class as the only historical subject, cosmopolitism, the abolition of the idea of state, materialism, and forced atheism. However, at the same time, some features of Marxism are appreciated and accepted, among which the criticism of liberalism and the bourgeois-capitalist socio-economic model, social solidarity, collective responsibility, socialist policies, a holistic approach to society, the creation of strong social bonds, the care for the humble classes, the idea of distributive and social justice, and the safeguard of the working class. To contribute to the formation of the Fourth Political Theory, Marxism should be purged of its modern, atheist, materialist, and cosmopolitan aspects, whilst preserving its advocacy of social solidarity, social justice, and collective responsibility.[29] As already noticed, the Fourth Political Theory wishes to reinterpret Marxism from the point of view of the Right, as exposed by Alain de Benoist in its classic book *Vu De Droite*.[30]

[5.49]   Dugin detects how Marxism has failed in implementing its utopian vision of society. For Marxists, men enjoyed an original state of paradise known as "primitive communism" that was gradually lost due to the initial division of labor and the stratification of the primitive society consequent to the introduction of private property and ownership of the land. This confrontation between the ruling exploitative economic class and the exploited submitted people evolved rapidly in the struggle between Labor and Capital. Whereas the Capital embodied by the bourgeois-liberal democracies represented alienation, exploitation, selfishness, and inhumanity, Labor signified the dream to redistribute the original common goods to all, therefore subtracting its acquisition (the "surplus value") from the hands of the evil capitalist minority that had stolen it. It was therefore necessary to unite the proletariat and lead it towards a struggle against their wicked masters in order to build a new society based on the principles of communism. Notwithstanding, this utopia turned out to be impracticable and the attempt to apply it to the real society resulted in the creation of a socio-political model based on tyranny, poverty, mass slaughters, corruption, and deceit. Moreover, one of Marxism's most noteworthy contradictions is the unfulfilled prediction about the kinds of societies that would embrace the socialist model. Instead of taking place in the greatly industrialized countries of Western Europe, which possessed a high level of manufacturing and a large proportion of urban proletariat, the socialist revolutions and societies took place in agrarian countries of Eastern Europe and parts of Asia that had a traditional, rural population. In other words, in those areas where Marxists had expected to win, capitalism prevailed: this entailed the dissolution of the proletariat into the middle class and its disappearance inside the consumerist society. [31]

[5.50]   Finally, in considering liberalism, the Fourth Political Theory treats it as its main ideological enemy, rejecting almost all its theoretical and practical aspects. As we will analyze in-depth in the next chapter, the aspects of liberalism and post-liberalism that neo-Eurasianists discard are mainly individualism, the substitution of politics with capitalist-financial economics, and the abolition of collective identitarian bonds. In liberalism, the only feature that can be spared is the idea of freedom, which is however interpreted as human freedom as opposed to individual freedom. In this sense, Dugin accepts the idea of freedom insofar as it relates to the freedom of safeguarding ethnicity, culture, and traditional societies.

[5.51]   The Fourth Political Theory is essentially an anti-modernist philosophy that criticizes the monotonic process of modernization based on the endless idea of progress. The monotonic process—typical of modern societies—is the idea of endless growth, accumulation, development, and incessant progress. [32] In mathematics, this process is linked to the idea of monotonic value and monotonic functions. A monotonic process proceeds unidirectionally without ever stopping. In biological terms, this process is incompatible with the survival of life and is totally absent from nature, which instead favors cyclical fluctuations and circular sustainable evolutions. [33]

The three classic political theories embrace the notion of monotonic process, all originating from the idea of growth, development, progress, evolution, and improvement of society. They all view the world and the historical process as a linear growth, although differing in the interpretation of this process. In this sense, they all accept the irreversibility of history and its progressive character and—accordingly—uphold the idea of modernization. [5.52]

In liberalism, the idea of endless development coincides with the evolution of technology and science, the spread of the free market, the attempt to abolish the differences between cultures and civilizations—often considered as obsolete, primitive, or obscurantist—, and to forge "modern," rational men. Liberal societies are founded on the struggle among individuals that strive to achieve a better socio-economic status and prestige through the accumulation of capital and are evidently inclined to construct a competitive society that—when unrestrained—follows the logic of social Darwinism. [5.53]

In Marxism, the idea of unidirectional progress coincides with the outbreak of the communist proletarian revolution, which would redistribute the accumulated wealth resulting from the development of alienating technologies. Even Marxism is influenced by Darwinism, as the total acceptance of evolutionary ideas and the trust in the power of scientific progress and technological improvement show. The idea of the proletarian revolution and the creation of a "new" society based on different paradigms unveils the natural Marxist aversion for all forms of conservatism and traditionalism. [5.54]

Likewise, fascism is an evolutionary movement that affirms itself through a "revolution" that wipes out the previous form of society and replaces it with a new model. Fascism believes in progress and evolution and is heavily influenced by the Nietzschean belief that men should be overcome in favor of super-men. Thus, in countries like Germany where fascism had a specific racialist component, the idea of perfecting men manifested in the need to shape a stronger and fitter racial stock—the *Herrenvolk*, i.e. the master race—that would dominate the "inferior" others. [5.55]

On the contrary, the Fourth Political Theory replaces the principles of growth, progress, and development with the values of life: "And, most important, instead of growth, progress, and development, there is *life*. After all, there has been no proof offered yet to show that life is linked to growth. This was the myth of the Nineteenth century. Life, in contrast, is connected to the eternal return. In the end, even Nietzsche incorporated his idea of will to power into the concept of eternal return." [34] [5.56]

Essentially, unlike the other three political theories, the Fourth rejects the monotonic process in all its forms, including the ideas of evolution, growth, modernization, progress, and development, and pivots instead on the idea of the preservation of life. Instead of relying on the ideology of development, it [5.57] puts its trust into the ideology of conservation, which finds its philosophical manifestation in conservatism: in this sense, the Fourth Political Theory represents a perfect example of a philosophy of conservatism.[35]

[5.58]   The idea of progress implies the irreversibility of time since it is both an orthogenetic and a monotonic process. The three original political theories are based on the idea that there cannot be any form of reversibility of time and that history is a unidirectional phenomenon: time is irreversible, progressive, and rectilinear. On the contrary, the Fourth Political Theory believes that time can be reversible, and that history is not a linear progression that follows a straight path. We can thus state that the Fourth Political Theory is essentially an unmodern theory.[36] Progress and modernization are perceived as real, but in a relative, not absolute sense. In other words, they are relative to and intimately connected with current historical, social, and political semantic "occasions," as in the occasionalist theory: "The Fourth Political Theory suggests an alternative version of political history based on systematized occasionalism."[37] The fact that history and civilizational progress can bear infinite shades of diversity, and not just one, leads to the acceptance of political pluralism and to different interpretations of historical evolution. Interestingly, whereas in the context of modernity turning back from some point of history to a previous one is impossible, for the Fourth Political Theory time can be reversible and thus history can represent itself again. Historical stages and epochs are considered just as mere pre-concepts and formalisms. The idea is rejected that some aspects of traditional societies like theological paradigms, antiquity, caste, and ancient customs are *ipso facto* canceled by the evolution of history or the progress of scientific-technological research. On the contrary, there are some aspects of traditional societies that are believed to bear unchangeable validity throughout the centuries and that no new trend in politics or philosophy can discard. However, the Fourth Political Theory does not wish to represent itself as an attempt to completely return to traditional society, but rather to reconsider and reinterpret some aspects of tradition that the modern world has arbitrarily erased from its sociological and cultural foundations.[38]

[5.59]   As seen, the Fourth Political Theory can be included in the various spectra of philosophical-political doctrines closely linked to conservatism. Conservatism represents the possibility to repudiate liberalism and the modernist logic of history. It is an ontological, philosophical, sociopolitical, religious, and cultural resistance to the paradigms of the modern post-liberal world, and the antidote to the regression of unlimited evolutionary and reformist progress.

[5.60]   The term conservatism, as we have seen in the first chapter, bears a wide semantic scope that includes many variants and definitions. The first variant of conservatism is represented by fundamental conservative traditionalism. Traditionalism indicates the aspiration to preserve untouched all aspects of traditional societies and to refuse to modify the old way of life of peoples. Traditionalist conservatism upholds monarchism, believes in the principles of caste, defends the model of an aristocratic society, and supports religiosity rejecting the separation between spiritual and temporal power, which should instead coincide or hinge on each other. Traditionalists often believe that all features of the contemporary world are bad, representing a wicked degeneration of traditional values. The main European exponents of traditionalist conservatism in the 20th century have been René Guénon, Julius Evola, Titus Burkhardt, and Leopold Ziegler. In their works, these authors described traditional society as a super-temporal ideal and the modern world as a product of degeneration, degradation, blending of castes, decomposition of hierarchy, and the shift of attention away from the spiritual to the material, from the eternal to the ephemeral.[39]

[5.61] The second form of conservatism can be described as contemporary fundamental conservatism. This form of conservatism is often associated with religious integralism. Some examples of it are the following: 1) the Islamic fundamentalist doctrine close to Sunni Wahhabism and Salafism, which wishes to establish the global Muslim caliphate; 2) ultra-orthodox and Zionist Jewish congregations; 3) fundamentalist protestant groups in the United States—e.g. the Amish; and anti-modernist Catholic or Orthodox associations or sects—e.g. the Lefebrvians or the Russian Old Believers (*starovery*). These integralist groups deny the fact that time is progress and consider progress a regress of humankind.

[5.62] A third kind of conservatism is the so-called liberal conservatism. It is "liberal" in the sense that it accepts the main trends realized in modernity, but at each stage of a given trend it attempts to slow down the speed of its progression. This current accepts modern individualism but refuses post-individualism, which it perceives as a corruption and degeneration of the former. Liberal conservatives agree with the general trends of modernity but disagree with their more avant-gardist manifestations. They uphold the ideas of freedom, independence of men, progress, and equality, but seek to foster them not through revolution but rather through evolution.

[5.63] The fourth manifestation of conservative currents is revolutionary conservatism. The main idea here is that conservatives must change the status quo through a global revolution, which is customary to call "Conservative Revolution." This constellation of ideologies and political philosophies considers in dialectical and conflictual terms the issue of the correlation between conservatism and modernity.[40] Some chief exponents of this current have been Arthur Moeller van der Bruck,[41] Martin Heidegger, Ernst and Friedrich Jünger, Carl Schmitt, Oswald Spengler,[42] Werner Sombart, Othmar Spann, Friedrich Hielscher, and Ernst Niekisch. The basic conservative revolutionary assumption is that the forces of freedom, democracy, and free market have led the world to a process of degeneration, which degraded modern human beings. The solution to this problem is to undertake a worldwide revolution headed by conservatives that would grant a human revival and the end of chaos. In this perspective, conservative revolutionaries claim that the contaminated contemporary world cannot be opposed merely looking back at the past since it is not enough to slow down time or to pretend to reestablish the old golden epochs, but rather through a drastic revolution that would eradicate nihilism and laxness. We have already seen in the first chapter how part of the literature on conservatism rejects the idea that conservatism can be revolutionary since it opposes all forms of revolutions.

[5.64] Finally, the last form is left-wing conservatism or social conservatism. The major exponent of this current is Georges Sorel.[43] Social conservatives are aware that the common enemy of both the Left and the Right is represented by the capitalist bourgeoisie. In Russia, social conservatism is strictly linked to Nikolay V. Ustryalov's National Bolshevism.

[5.65] The Fourth Political Theory can be included among the theories of conservatism, although it represents a hybrid form of it. It is hybrid because it includes features from all the above-mentioned forms of conservatism—i.e. traditionalism, fundamentalism, revolutionary conservatism, social conservatism—except for liberal conservatism. Neo-Eurasianists that embrace Dugin's vision are concern that rather than being an organic political philosophy the Fourth Political Theory is instead an episteme that shares many characteristics with conservative ideologies. Though fully embracing the idea of Conservative Revolution, it still rejects all progressivist forms of conservatism. Nonetheless, its alternative to modernity is taken from societies historically co-existing with Western civilization, but geographically and culturally different from it.[44]

[5.66] The Fourth Political Theory considers the concept of civilization as its main ideological vector through which the establishment of a world order based on multipolarity could be made possibile. In opposing globalism, its promoters are aware of the weaknesses of the contemporary anti-globalist movements and of their unsystematic and ambiguous ideological orderliness. Hence, they wish to fill this vacuum with an ideology founded on the safeguard of civilizations and on the multipolar world that would reunite under its flag all anti-globalist—or rather alter-globalist—forces.

[5.67] Another salient characteristic of the Fourth Political Theory is its intimate connection with identitarianism. Being essentially a non-modern and often counter-modern ideology, its anthropological analysis is based not on how people are today, but on how they used to be in the past. A firm claim is that without identity people are deprived of their own existence. Identity delivers a unique human character. Language, culture, mentality, traditions, and social rules would be the consequence of each specific national and ethnic identity. The kind of identity that the Fourth Political Theory has sympathy for is the so-called "deep identity." Deep identity is described as an organic, existential and basic identity that lies below diffused identity,[45] giving its content, meaning and structure. It is not viewed as a superstructure constructed above diffused identity—like extreme identity—but rather as an infrastructure beneath diffused identity, giving it reality, sense, and inner harmony. Deep identity represents the essence of the people, transcending the collectivity in its actual state. People's language, culture, tradition, gestures, and psychological features do not appear in the present, but come from the past and move toward the future through the present moment: the deep identity is the whole that plays out in both time and space and epitomizes people as existence.[46]

Every human society acts and thinks according to its belonging to an identitarian group: identity creates social bonds and kinship. Being concrete human beings means first of all to be German, French, Russian, American, Chinese, African. Thinking, acting, willing, creating, and fighting makes a person think, act, wish, create, and fight as a German, French, Russian, American, Chinese, African.[47] [5.68]

Viewing people as part of the multiplicity of the world, each representing a specific and incommensurable treasure, leads to the total rejection of the political, economic and ideological forces that wish to overcome national identities in favor of the global, diluted and mixed "melting pot." [5.69]

One of the goals of the Fourth Political Theory is to unite all traditionalist movements into a single political force capable of opposing Western post-liberalism, unilineal globalization, and American imperialism. In Dugin's words, "traditionalists and partisans of traditional principles and values should oppose the West and defend the Rest, if the Rest shows signs of the conservation of Tradition, whether in part or in its entirety."[48] These partisans of traditionalism are not be found only outside the Western context, but also—and especially—inside Europe and America among those groups or individuals that disapprove modernity and postmodernity and that uphold the spiritual traditions of the pre-modern West. Dugin advocates the creation of an anti-globalist and anti-imperialist "Traditionalist International" that would coalesce to face the common enemy, i.e. globalism and post-liberalism.[49] [5.70]

As previously noticed, the Fourth Political Theory should embrace some aspects of both Marxism and fascism, chiefly anti-capitalism, anti-liberalism, and anti-individualism. Essentially, the Fourth Political Theory appears as a rather original attempt to reread Marxism and fascism. It is conceived as socialism without materialism, atheism, and progressivism, and fascism without racism and chauvinism, with the addition of pre-modern ideological sources typical of traditionalism—e.g. hierarchy, theology, the allure for the "Middle Ages," etc. This unique mixture of revised socialism and fascism would coincide with the ideology of National Bolshevism,[50] of which the Fourth Political Party is an expression. National Bolshevism is a synthesis of the two conflictual ideologies of Marxism (thesis) and fascism (antithesis). [5.71]

Freeing socialism from its materialist, atheistic and modernist features, and rejecting the racist and ultranationalist aspects of the various forms of fascisms would lead to a completely new kind of political ideology known as Fourth Political Theory (or 4PT), the first being liberalism, the second communism; and the third fascism. The elaboration of the Fourth Political Theory starts from the point of intersection between different anti-liberal political theories of the past—namely communism and fascist theories—and arrives to National Bolshevism, which embodies socialism without materialism, atheism, progressivism, and modernism, and the modified Third Way theories.[51]

[5.72]   Being a transversal ideology, the Fourth Political Theory wishes to establish a pact of cooperation between ideological rivals in order to struggle against the perceived common enemy. This would imply the need to unite communists with fascists, Muslims with Christians, Muslims with Jews, Muslims with Hindus, etc. The multilateral pact of cooperation should put aside anti-communist feelings by fascists and anti-fascist prejudices by communists. It should also avoid any form of confrontation between the various religious groups, since inter-confessional wars and tensions are believed to be tools that the global elite would use to divide peoples.

[5.73]   The three core beliefs that the Fourth Political Theory recognizes as its ideological foundations are social justice, national sovereignty, and traditional values. Another principle it embraces is the necessity to create a new world order based on an all-encompassing multipolarity, whose scope would touch the geopolitical, cultural, axiological, and economic spheres.[52] In conclusion, the key word of the Fourth Political Theory is "multipolarity" in all senses—geopolitical, cultural, axiological, economic, and so on.[53]

[5.74]   THE EURASIAN MANIFESTO

[5.75]   The contemporary Eurasianist ideology is conceived by its promotors as more than a speculative theory. The corollary to its doctrine entails practical programs, strategies, and plans aimed at establishing its goals. The major duty that Dugin and other exponents of the Eurasianist intelligentsia strive to achieve is the creation of a transversal revolutionary coalition that would gather all alter-globalist forces belonging both to the left-winged and right-winged political spectrum in order to overwhelm the globalist New World Order. This gigantic enterprise is summarized in what Eurasianists call "The Manifesto of the Global Revolutionary Alliance," whose motto—reechoing the slogan of the Communist Manifesto of Marx and Engels—sounds "Dissatisfied all over the world, unite!." In the following paragraph, we will try to account the main features of the political-philosophical program of the Eurasian Manifesto.[54]

The basic assumption of the Manifesto is that the modern world has come to its existential end. The current historical cycle represents the final one since all processes that constitute the flow of history have come to a logical impasse. [5.76]

Likewise, the evolution of capitalism has led to the end of capitalism itself, since its development has reached its natural limit. The world economic system is doomed to collapse upon itself. The self-destruction of capitalism is due to the progressive increase of purely financial institutions—i.e. banks and stock structures—that are totally disconnected with real economy, from the balance of aggregated supply and demand, from the production and consumption ratio, and from sustainable development. Moreover, all the world's wealth is believed to be concentrated in the hands of a financial oligarchy, which would represent an impersonal, selfish, reckless, ultra-liberal elite strong enough to manipulate the global economy. [5.77]

At the same time, the overall demographic expansion would be leading the planet to an unsustainable exploitation of resources, augmentation of pollution, and destruction of natural habitats. [5.78]

The world would be also witnessing the end of society. Under the influence of Western liberal values, societies would suffer from atomization since people are no longer connected with each other by any form of social and communitarian bonds. The logic consequence of the end of society has been the end of the individual: human identities, which are increasingly fluid in terms of race, gender, and status are spread across virtual networks, assuming online personalities and turning into a game of confused elements,[55] and a risk exists that soon men may be replaced by the post-human, i.e. a mutant, cloned android or cyborg, with more virtual than real characteristics. [5.79]

The other aspect of the modern world, closely linked to the former, is the end of nations and peoples. Globalization attempts to interfere in the domestic affairs of sovereign states by systematically diluting peoples' ethnic differentiations and by destroying their national identities. [5.80]

Finally, the materialistic and consumerist logic of the free market and capitalism would be undermining human knowledge and separating men from all forms of spirituality and metaphysical religiosity. [5.81]

The Eurasianist Manifesto introduces a normative solution to counter what it considers the evilness of the modern world by establishing the main principles upon which a new, just world order ought to be founded: [5.82]

1. The introduction of an economic model that is alternative to the current system of speculative financial capitalism. Among the possible alternatives could be the models of real industrial capitalism, of Islamic economics, of socialist political economy, and of environmental projects. The use of new forms of sustainable energies and the guarantee of fair economic mechanisms should become the essential basis of [5.83]

the new system. Mostly, the new economic model should ensure the lack of discrepancy between finance and real economy and increase the welfare of the peoples rather than the enrichment of banks.

[5.84]   2. The distribution of natural resources based on a plan that is common and beneficial to all mankind. The delivery of global resources should reject the principles of egoistic and Darwinian competitive struggle for their control. Resources should be equally distributed to all mankind and every nation should benefit from their sustainable use. Accordingly, wars for grabbing resources should be completely suppressed, since no nation has the right to deprive others of global resources *manu militari*.

[5.85]   3. The preservation of social collective structures that safeguard the heritage of culture, knowledge, languages, custom, and beliefs of nations from one generation to another. Liberal individualism and the dissipation of human existence into atomized beings should be overcome by forms of social solidarity and collective identity. The protection of social structures that grant national cohesion—e.g. the family, productive work, public institutions, etc.—should come before the protection of single individuals.

[5.86]   4. The foundation of societies and states should be based on their historical and civilizational tradition. The diversity of peoples and nations should be preserved and treated as a treasure of mankind; consequently, its forced abolition through the creation of a global, rootless melting pot should be stopped and reversed. A normal society should be diverse, plural, and polycentric, featuring many open possibilities of dialogue and cultural interchange. However, dialogue among civilizations should be free, not forced. Each society should choose freely for itself its spiritual and material development. The domination of wealth and its pursuit should not supersede ethical, spiritual, and axiological principles: the ephemeral of materiality should be overwhelmed by the power of the soul.

[5.87]   5. The international order should be founded on national sovereignty, multipolarity, civilizational big zones, and non-interference in the affairs of other states.

[5.88]   The Manifesto also exposes the need for redistributing international power from a global oligarchy that is believed to detain it to other centers. This global oligarchic clique is accused of retaining power indirectly under the appearance of free markets, democracy and the façade of a diversity of global decision-making centers;[56] as an elite, it would advocate and promote Atlanticism and Western liberalism. According to Eurasianists, in a normal society, power should not be held by an anonymous political and financial elite but be delivered in a meritocratic sense to uncorrupt politicians and policymakers who pursue the good of their country and prepend national wellness to selfish greed. Meritocracy should be the golden rule for recruiting the political and economic figures that would guide states and societies.

A new world order should also be characterized by cultural pluralism. [5.89] The Manifesto specifies that dissimilarities amongst societies do not imply a qualitative hierarchy, with better or worse models, but represent the natural existence of diversity. Instead, believing that a cultural model is superior to others displays a racist and colonialist mentality, which Eurasianists categorically reject. The acceptance of cultural pluralism would imply the need for criticizing and opposing globalism, Western-centrism, and universalism. Societal norms are considered to be as numerous and varied as are societies, since the only universal norm would be the absence of a uniform standard for all and the freedom and right to choose.[57]

The Manifesto considers as imperative a global revolution against the [5.90] current world order. The revolution would acquire a global scope only if capable of gathering all the political and social forces that are dissatisfied with the existing status quo. The global revolution would also require concerted actions implemented through the formation of a global alliance. The members of the alliance could ideologically differ and even, to some degree, conflict with one another, but only a worldwide coalition is believed to bear enough strength to end the rule of the present global elite.[58]

Unlike the revolutions of the 19th or 20th centuries, which for various [5.91] reasons did not achieve universal scope, the revolution of the 21st century would be characterized by a planetary and all-encompassing dimension. All nations should revolt against the existing world order jointly, but in the name of different ideals and norms. The global oligarchy should be crushed in the name of the different purposes and horizons of nations. The revolution of the twenty-first century would be successful only if all nations would fight against the common enemy in the name of their different goals, but within its overall framework.[59]

In the pages of the Manifesto, Dugin describes in detail the goals that the [5.92] global revolution should achieve and which plan to follow. The revolution should aim radically overthrowing the global oligarchy and world's elite and at dismantling the world system associated with it. Its presence should be uprooted simultaneously in different parts of the world. The struggle for the obliteration of the global elite should be synchronized, though asymmetrically. The revolution would necessitate a strategy of asymmetric, hybrid warfare that would include the cyberspace and other unconventional strategic realms.[60]

In ideological terms, the bonding element that should hold together the [5.93] various factions and groups of this anti-systemic global alliance would be the common animosity towards liberalism. The main vector of global revolution would be the total war against liberalism.[61]

[5.94]   The forces of the global revolutionary alliance are asked to oppose the status quo through the creation of a worldwide anti-Americanist front. However, Eurasianist anti-Americanism does not mean enmity against America as a whole. The Eurasian struggle is not against America as a country, nor against the American people and masses, but affirms to be against Americanism as a principle and against the oligarchic elites and lobbies that would have subjugated and deceived the American people. Notwithstanding, Eurasianists who adhere to Dugin's Manifesto are aware that the war against Atlanticism is not just an eventuality, but rather a compelling necessity. They believe that the question is not whether to fight or not, but how to fight. The enemy—namely the global oligarchy—is considered difficult to vanquish since it would carry out its plans either with the direct use of American forces and NATO troops, or indirectly by organizing local conflicts or "colored revolutions" with the massive use of fifth columns. The response to the globalist aggressiveness would entail the use of asymmetrical strategies, including civil wars, insurgencies, and cyberwar. [62]

[5.95]   The zone of combat operations would include everyday aspects of behavior, lifestyle, fashion, work, and leisure to ideology, information flows, technology, networking, and virtual worlds. The maximum damage possible would be inflicted on the global oligarchy on all levels, including military, economic, cultural, and informational. [63]

[5.96]   The leader of the Eurasianist movement, with radicalism and fanatic enthusiasm, does not hide the need for fighting the struggle against the enemies of Eurasia by all possible means, including the eventuality of resorting to military might supervised by the world revolutionary counter-elite. [64]

[5.97]   Dugin is firmly convinced that the struggle against the global oligarchy is a typical example of just war. Eurasianists do not consider themselves warmongers, but they believe that a just war is surely better than an unjust peace. The just war that the Eurasian mission endorses is perceived by its promoters as a real moral crusade aimed at vanquishing the evilness of the world incarnated by the liberal globalist elite. [65]

[5.98]   According to the program of the Manifesto, the Global Revolutionary Alliance would be structured as a fully functioning political organization. At the top of the structure would be the subject that is at the core of the new world revolution, namely the worldwide counter-elite, to which Dugin probably believes to belong. The main task of this counter-elite would be the promotion of subversive and destabilizing revolutionary activities that would overthrow the power of the global oligarchy and its entourage. The structure of the Global Revolutionary Alliance is conceived as flexible and polycentric: it is envisioned not as a political party, movement, order, lodge, or sect, but rather as a complex network without a single center of authority or a fixed membership, since only a mobile and fluid organization is believed to provide the immunity against the inevitable planetary forces that would oppose it. The organization would not have a single territorial, national, and religious center, but would represent a delocalized entity, with veiled branches in all continents. The Alliance would operate everywhere, regardless of frontiers, races, and religions: in this sense, it is intended to represent—so to speak—the armed wing of the Eurasianist International. Moreover, the axis of its revolutionary strategy should be characterized by the absence of a fixed, general strategy and by the lack of a hierarchical headquarter.[66]

The structure of the Alliance would be asymmetric, including potentially states, social movements, political forces, groups of pressure, and single individuals who adhere to its principles.[67]   [5.99]

Finally, the membership of the Alliance would be open to all forces,   [5.100] either of the Right or the Left, who " ultra-liberalism, strategic Atlanticism, the domination of the oligarchic and cosmopolitan financial elites, individualistic anthropology, and the ideology of human rights, as well as typically Western racism in all spheres—economic, cultural, ethical, moral, biological and so on—and who are ready to cooperate with Eurasian forces in defending multipolarity, socio-economic pluralism, and a dialogue among civilizations."[68] At the same time, the foes of the Alliance would be represented by those on the Right who support Atlanticism and neoliberalism, white supremacists who are against the Third World and other ethnic groups, antisocialist and pro-liberal movements, NATO supporters, those of the Left who attack traditionalism and conservative values, and those who advocate Huntington's idea of the clash of civilizations.

In stark terms, Dugin affirms that the world is presently living under   [5.101] martial law and that the revolution he promotes finds its intrinsic morality in the righteousness of the struggle against global despotism. According to him, war and revolution appear as the only hope to liberate the world from the dictatorship of Western liberal oligarchies. The revolutionary powers that Dugin summons insist on a universal awakening, on total mobilization, and on the general awareness of the dangers that post-liberalism would embody for mankind.

THE RISE OF THE FOURTH POLITICAL THEORY   [5.102]

The book *The Fourth Political Theory* represents Dugin's starting point for   [5.103] the construction of his philosophical and political doctrine. Recently, the author issued a second book named *The rise of the Fourth Political Theory—* or *The Fourth Political Theory Vol. II*—that represents the continuation and evolution of the former. In this work, the key issues investigated are the following: the dialectics between democracy and conservatism, the concept of "Empire" in relation to the Eurasian idea, the anthropological and soci-

[5.104] The Fourth Political Theory's doctrinal core is once again a refusal of
modern democracy in favor of conservatism. Dugin argues that democracy
does not represent the best form of political organization and that the common belief that it incarnates a civilized practice that ensures political equality
of all individuals in society is false.[69] In its original manifestation, democracy was typical of primitive and "barbarian" political societies, in which the
decisions related to the fate of the tribe or folk were adopted collectively
amongst those who were entitled to vote—often the tribe's warriors and
freemen—gathering in a parliamentary assembly. Democracy is founded on
the principle of the collective form of decision making; however, in archaic
societies, the voter was not considered a separate individual but rather a
single part of the whole clan, which shared a common destiny: in this sense,
liberal individualism of modern democracies would be very different from
the original ethnic collective idea of democracy. In fact, democracy does not
recognize individual equality, since all ancient democratic societies separated those who were allowed to participate in the decision process from those
who were not. All types of ancient democracies were characterized by the
principle of the political inclusion of some and the exclusion of others. For
instance, in the political system of ancient German tribes—*Sippen*—only free
warriors and priests were admitted to the parliament—*Thing*—for voting,
whereas slaves of war, women, children, and foreigners were excluded. Similarly, the Greek *poleis* enabled only "citizens" of the *polis* to participate in
voting, and citizenship was enjoyed only by those who belonged to higher
classes, who possessed a certain level of material goods, and some moral
qualities; the poor people, slaves, women, and even noblemen from foreign
polities were denied the right to vote and considered "non-citizens"—*idiotes*
(ἰδιώτης). Moreover, philosophers like Aristotle believed that democracy
was easily subject to tyranny.

[5.105] The political evolution of Western civilization proceeded from a rejection
of archaic democracy in favor of aristocracy and monarchy: "Between the
ancient democracy of Athens and the modern European parliamentary republics, many centuries of Western history were marked by monarchic-aristo-
cratic political systems."[70] It was not until the Renaissance and the Enlightenment that European men decided to rediscover the democratic and republican forms of government, this time depriving them of sacred aspects typical
of archaic democracy. The final step was the birth of contemporary liberal
democracy, which in Dugin's words represents a secularized and caricatural
form of the archaic.[71]

ological analysis of Russian society, and the future of international relations
after the Russo-Georgian conflict of 2008 in the context of a growing multipolar global order. An interesting appendix on Dugin's appreciation of Martin Heidegger's philosophy concludes the book.

Opposed to the idea of democracy—which, unlike what is commonly [5.106]
believed, is in fact a rather primitive and unequal form of political order—is
the concept of conservatism. Conservatism does not represent the mere philosophy of the preservation of the past and of the rejection of innovation, but
a system of understanding and body of ideas—i.e. an episteme—with a peculiar notion of time and being. While progressists bear a diachronic approach
to history, separating time in the idea of past, present, and future, conservatives believe in the synchronic model based on the eternal constant. The
fundamental constants of society and humanity are considered by conservatism immutable and unmodifiable, and the idea of time does not follow a
progressive unidirectional path. Dugin's approach towards conservatism appeals to the Heideggerian philosophical model, which places Being before
Time: "The most important idea of conservatism is that it thinks not about
the past but about what has *been*, not about the present but about that which
is right now, not about that which will come, but about that which *will be*
realized [emphasis added]."[72] In other words, for the conservative mindset
Time is a function of Being, since the former is subordinate to the latter: what
concerns Being surpasses Time, is absolute, and does not depend on chronol-
ogy. Placing Being above Time, conservative philosophy acknowledges the
immutability of society and the everlasting validity of cultural norms.[73]

The final goal of conservatism is thus constituting the Being or Existence [5.107]
(the Hegelian and Heideggerian *Dasein*) in its a-temporal aspect, revealing
the essence of the present and obtaining the key to the ontological decipher-
ing of the past.

In defending eternity, conservatism likewise defends the idea of the eter- [5.108]
nal man. The human being is conceived as an invariable structure—as opposed to the theory of evolution—and is provided with unchanging traits and
inalienable identity. All efforts to modify the everlasting model of humanity
represent, for the conservative mentality, the willingness to alter the unchangeable natural laws.

Embodying essentially the philosophy of Eternity, conservatism very of- [5.109]
ten discovers a natural ally in religion and metaphysics. Like many theolo-
gies, most forms of conservatism share eschatological features that believe in
the idea of a final struggle between Good and Evil through which the world
must come to a redemption thanks to a *deus ex machina*.

Generally, conservatives are supporters of the imperial idea, since they [5.110]
conceive the Empire as the maximal society and the greatest possible scale of
government. Empires can combine different units into an integrated general
matrix while preserving themselves as such. The ideal Empire is the representation of Man himself, who is trichotomous, being the result of body,
spirit, and soul. The Empire's trichotomy is manifested as follows. The geographical soil, territorial space, and zone of influence represent the body,
which for conservatives takes the sacral semblance of the Motherland. The

folk personifies the soul, with his ethno-sociological distinctiveness and his unchangeable features, handed down generation after generation through a common blood that forged the Fatherland. Finally, religion symbolizes the spirit, since all conservative Empires form symbolically a bridge that connects the Earth with Heaven.

[5.111]   At the same time, conservatives believe in the value of warfare. War is considered to be just and lawful when waged for the truth, for love, for right, and for good. The conservative mind does not reject war per se but pays great attention to whether it may be a just war or not. War is conceived as a natural manifestation and condition: the utopian objective to abolish it is inevitably destined to fail, since a warlike attitude exists within all living beings for the purpose of their survival. Most conservatives accept the Hobbesian vision of the *bellum omnium contra omnes*, sharing the idea that peace represents a mere truce between conflicts. Otherwise stated, when men renounce fighting they will inexorably decay since the enemies that surround them will take advantage and subjugate them.

[5.112]   The conservative episteme stands on three chief disciplines. The first is theology, which is considered to represent the crown of education and the science of all sciences. The second is ethno-sociology, which defines the ethnological characteristics of a folk and understands its ontology and essence. The third is geopolitics, or the study of the relation of a state to a territorial space. Per Dugin, "theology, ethnosociology and geopolitics constitute the trichotomous structure of science in the conservative understanding. The teaching of other social and humanitarian sciences should line up around these three pivots, agree with them, and orient themselves around their force-lines."[74] It follows, for instance, that disciplines like economics and jurisprudence derive from philosophy, which may be considered in turn a branch of (ethno-) sociology and theology.

[5.113]   Another issue that Dugin investigates in *The Rise of the Fourth Political Theory* is Russian identity. The author claims that contemporary Russia can be investigated in two ways: either as a country or as an independent civilization. Although many consider Russia a European state, the moral, social, political, cultural, and psychological identity of the country differs greatly from that of European and American societies. Historically, from the Romanov monarchy onwards, the Westernization/modernization of Russia represented a forced and exogenous phenomenon. The main elements that made Russia differ from the West would have been the absence of capitalism, individualism, democracy, rationalism, personal responsibility, legal self-consciousness, and civil society. Likewise, some of Russia's distinguishing features like paternalism, collectivism, hierarchy, religiosity, a relation to the state and to society as family, the superiority of morality over rights, and ethical reasoning over rational behavior lack or are lacking evermore in Western societies. Therefore, it is disputable whether Russia may be considered a Western country, a sort of "other West" different from the rest, or something else than West. While Westernizers and pro-Atlanticists wish to consider it part of the West, Eurasianists, Slavophiles, and National-Bolsheviks claim that Russia represents an independent civilization and a distinctive cultural-historical type. More specifically, Russia should be considered as a distinct bloc with its own original values and interests, like Europe as a whole, the Islamic world, the Chinese civilization, and so on. Russian civilizational unity is manifestly linked to the Eurasian continent, so that Russia-Eurasia constitutes a kind of state-world of its own. As Dugin affirms, Russia is neither a part of the West nor a part of the East, but rather a civilization in itself and the preservation of its freedom, independence, and self-being comprises the vector of Russian history.[75]

Russian civilization represents the summation of Christian-Orthodox, Slavic, and Eurasian identities. Consequently, it denies the universality of the historical experience of European civilization, repudiating all its pretensions to be the leading track of human development. In this sense, Eurasianists believe that the West is a local and regional phenomenon, and its attempts to show itself as a universal standard for all mankind discloses a colonialist and racist pretension to absolute power over humanity. At the same time, Western modernization should not be imposed exogenously, but should be either adopted or rejected voluntarily by each nation. Contemporary Russia—like many other Eurasian, Asian, and African societies—is judged to be completely unfit to adopt the materialist, atheist, consumerist, and utilitarian attitude of the West, but inclined to safeguard historical identity, traditional society, religiosity, custom, folklore, and so on. [5.114]

Russia's declaration of civilizational independence does not imply a negation of modernity. On the contrary, Russia and other civilizations (China, Iran, etc.) should have the full right to establish their own peculiar political, social, legal, economic, cultural, and technological models to reach modernity. [5.115]

The acknowledgement of idiosyncratic civilizations would lead to the foundation of the multi-polar world, whose poles are much more than mere sections of the West, but rather separate and absolute entities, with their own understanding of history, their own specific historical time—be it cyclical or linear—, their own ontology, anthropology, sociology, political science, and so on. [5.116]

If Russia will recognize itself as a civilization—as most of its population does—, the logical conclusion would be a crusade against Western pretensions of universality and the establishment of a new social model for all mankind based on pluralism. [5.117]

This "international revolution" Dugin auspicates would bear enormous consequences in international relations. First, the strengthening of Russia's bond with those countries that contrast somewhat the West—e.g. China, Iran, [5.118]

Syria, Palestine, Venezuela, Bolivia, Nicaragua, North Korea, Belarus, Serbia. Second, the launch of a Russian strategy to split up the West, consolidating ties with Continental Europe—chiefly Germany, France, and Italy—and gradually leading it out of Atlanticist control. Third, the steady dissolution of the Western model of globalization and the establishment of the civilizational multi-polar order instead.

[5.119]   Another significant topic Dugin considers is Carl Schmitt's contribution to the foundation of the Fourth Political Theory thanks to his principles of "Empire" (*Reich*). Apart from *Land und Meer: Eine Weltgeschichtliche Betrachtung* ("Land and Sea: A World-Historical Meditation") (1942),[76] Schmitt's main work with a direct impact for neo-Eurasianism is *Völkerrechtliche Gro ß raumordnung mit Interventionsverbot f ü r Raumfremde M ä chte: Ein Beitrag zum Reichsbegriff im V ö lkerrecht* ("The *Grossraum* Order of International Law with a Ban on Intervention for Spatially Foreign Powers: A Contribution to the Concept of Reich in International Law") (1941).[77] What Schmitt wrote at the end of the 1930s with regard to Germany is believed to be perfectly applicable to contemporary Russia and other countries that bear an imperial destiny. His reflections on the genesis, nature, and scope of "Empire" transcend the German historical, political, and geographic context of both the Weimar Republic and the Hitlerite Third Reich. Schmitt's imperial paradigm lays the foundations of a superior political-juridical model of thinking that is considered to be forever valid and that may be transposed to Russia.

[5.120]   Carl Schmitt's theory of *Großraum* —i.e. "Large Space"—stems from the study of the American Monroe Doctrine of 1823, when the United States took on the responsibility for supporting the independence of the entire American continent from European interference and meddling. The Monroe Doctrine implied the fact that the United States enjoyed the role of becoming the leading country—albeit indirectly—of the Pan-American big space, with an imperial area of influence over the continent, which formally maintained its independence and sovereignty:

[5.121]   "The 'large space' [*Großraum*] proceeds from an anti-colonial strategy and proposes (purely theoretically) a voluntary alliance of all countries of the [American] continent, collectively striving to defend their independence. The initiative in the defense of this independence is to be proportionally placed on the stronger powers, from which follows the natural lead of the US. The lead position in securing the independence of the entire American 'large space' also signifies recognition of the US's leadership by other countries and the assignment to them of the fundamental burden in the goal of maintaining the freedom of the whole 'large space'. This in no way suggests that American countries become 'provinces' of the US or that they will lose their sovereignty even a little. But inasmuch as they can in practice secure sovereignty on a planetary scale (in the face of colonial European powers) only all together and with the

supremacy of the US, the significance of the US grows for all countries, for
union with them directly influences the real substance of the sovereignty of
each American country."[78]

From a geopolitical perspective, the meaning of the Monroe Doctrine consists in the need for guaranteeing the United States' independence and sovereignty by indirectly controlling the strategic neighboring areas, which thus
constitute zones of vital interest.   [5.122]

> "In contrast to Europe, where great states placed close to one another com-   [5.123]
> peted among themselves (England, France, Germany, Austria, Italy, Spain,
> Portugal, Holland, and so on), the US was the sole leader on the American
> continent and only external, European powers posed a threat. The other
> American countries were theoretically interested in the same things as the US
> (an independence from European colonialism), but were not real competitors
> for it; the extent of their sovereignty was much weaker. In Europe, the idea
> that the security of France depends on the political condition of England or
> Germany would be absurd, since both England and Germany possessed power
> comparable to France's [. . .]. The US found itself in a principally different
> situation, and its own safety depended directly on the political situation of
> other American countries, which, taken by themselves, could not defend their
> sovereignty and did not represent a real competitor for the US. All this is
> reflected in the 'Monroe Doctrine'."[79]

American foreign policy deeply relies on the "Monroe Doctrine," which   [5.124]
unfolds the key global strategies of the United States. Any country that does
not belong to the Americas that wishes to extend its dominion over them is
considered an enemy of the US, while all American republics are considered
friends through the slogan "America for Americans." Most importantly, the
sovereignty and security of the US are granted by an integrated strategic big
space that includes the entire American continent.

The Monroe Doctrine was further developed by the US Presidents Theo-   [5.125]
dore Roosevelt and Woodrow Wilson. Roosevelt contribution to its improvement—known as the Roosevelt Corollary (1904)—consisted in the notion
that, in accordance with the Monroe Doctrine, the United States was justified
in exercising "international police power" to put an end to chronic unrest or
wrongdoing in the Western Hemisphere. Thus, while the Monroe Doctrine
had sought to prevent European intervention, the Roosevelt Corollary was
used to justify US intervention throughout the Americas. In this regard, the
Roosevelt Corollary modified the sense of the Monroe Doctrine, which was
from now on used as a cover for colonial policies and imperial (indirect)
control inside the continent. The submission of all peoples of the Western
Hemisphere under the guide of the US was a subtle strategy that—unlike the
openly aggressive colonialist policy of European states—concealed its impe-

rialism under the guise of the spread of liberal-democratic values, hinging upon consent and allure.

[5.126]   Another shift in the doctrine occurred under Wilson's presidency and after the victorious participation of the US in World War One. Through the direct US participation in world issues for the consolidation and diffusion of democratic and liberal principles, the Monroe Doctrine passed well beyond American borders and turned into a universalistic theory that justified American disguised "democratic" imperialism. This drift became even more evident under the presidency of Franklin D. Roosevelt, who showed to be extremely intrusive in relation to European affairs, condemning with animosity what he considered—from a liberal perspective—"authoritarian" countries. The final evolution of the doctrine took place after the US victory in World War Two and the subsequent establishment of the bipolar order, when it ideologically turned into the NATO bloc.

[5.127]   According to Schmitt, the idea of *Großraum* bears a qualitative rather than quantitative meaning. If we divide the term, the concept of "large" indicates not just the physical-geographical aspect of a territory but rather the level of internal organization, mastery, and integration of a socio-cultural, civilizational, strategic, and political unit. At the same time, "space" refers not to an abstract category of physics, but rather to a concrete landscape that includes woods, fields, meadows, mountains, and river basins, in which nations dwell. Thus, *Großraum* represents a political organization on vast portions of land that forges an unbreakable bond between the population that dwells therein and the surrounding natural environment. People, soil, climate, landscape, and fauna and flora embody a "spiritual" eternal unit that forms a political-geographical specific ideal type. *Großraum*—be it in Europe, Asia, or Eurasia—is the spiritual and spatial zone that creates the "Empire" (*Das Reich*), which in turn represents both a metaphysical and physical political entity. Within the *Reich*, the folk forms a solid reality linked together by a common mindset, system of values, and *Weltanschauung* that develops through a common will the path of its civilization.

[5.128]   For Eurasianists, the idea of Empire coincides exactly with Schmitt's: Empire is a concrete part of the world space that embodies a civilizational unity. Whereas liberals and globalists believe that the subject of global universalism is the individual with his human rights, for the theory of "large space" the subject is the organic collective of the people (*Volk* in German, *narod* in Russian), with a historical and sacral meaning. The dichotomy between liberals and conservatives is reflected in the contrasting notions of multi-polar and unipolar world order: the former entails the existence of ethno-historical polities founded on several "empires" with large space bases, the latter a unipolar order founded on universalist-cosmopolitan values and a single world government.

Schmitt perceived Hitler's Third Reich as a "large space" with a broader   [5.129]
European meaning rather than only German. It was the expression of continental European civilization, the core of the tradition of the peoples of Europe, and the Defensor of the rights of Europeans. However, he strongly
opposed the racist and narrowly German or Aryan interpretation that most
Nazis gave to it and believed that all European *ethnoses* should have partici-
pated in a common imperial history with identical rights in the future. [80]

Similarly to Schmitt, the Eurasianist Savitsky used the term "place-devel-   [5.130]
opment" and "state-world" to indicate the idea of "large space." For Eurasianists, the Eurasian landmass represented a "large space" with a common
civilizational identity; many believed that the Eurasian Reich ended in Eastern Europe and that Western Europe began with Germany, whereas Schmitt
believed that Germany represented the core of Mitteleuropa (Central Europe)
while the West started beyond the river Rhine. The Eurasianist mindset considered the Soviet Union and its satellites as the best example of Schmitt's
"Reich," since—unlike the Bolsheviks, who based their theories on Marxism—Eurasianists interpreted the USSR as a historical, territorial, civilizational, and geopolitical organism, and not only as an ideological construction. [81]

Carl Schmitt's contributions to the construction of the Fourth Political   [5.131]
Theory are believed to be substantial, especially due to the following theorization by the German philosopher:

1. The "Large space" (*Der Großraum*).   [5.132]
2. The "Empire" (*Das Reich*).   [5.133]
3. The rights of peoples and nations.   [5.134]
4. Geopolitical sovereignty.   [5.135]
5. The geopolitical struggle between thalassocracies and tellurocracies   [5.136]
   (*Das Meer gegen das Land*).

Schmitt imagined a world order consisting of several "empires" and "large   [5.137]
spaces." This vision is shared by the Fourth Political Theory, which perceives it as the safest platform for the construction of a multi-polar, anti-
globalist, and national-conservative international community. In this sense,
neo-Eurasianism is conceived as the ideological tool for the foundation of
Schmitt's idea of "Empire" and of large spaces in the present and in the
future.

Eurasianists are aware that the creation of a Eurasian Empire represents   [5.138]
an ambitious political project and strive to understand what political shape
this empire should have. Dugin suggests that the Eurasian Empire should be
an empire without an emperor, believing that the imperial principle does not
necessarily entail the presence of a leading figure. The sole monarchical or
aristocratic power would not be a compulsory condition for the existence of

an empire. Many monarchical, despotic, tyrannical, or dictatorial governments throughout history had nothing in common with the notion of empire, and many empires had nothing in common with absolute power and authoritarianism. Therefore, Dugin's Eurasian Empire would be an empire without an emperor.[82]

[5.139]   Second, empires would have always incarnated the optimal tool for the making of civil society. In other words, the imperial rule would have always granted the evolution of the peoples and societies that reside within the Empire's borders. Empires would have been constituted to safeguard peace and to bolster prosperity. The creation of a peaceful, secure, ordered, and wealthy world was the basic principle, for instance, of the *Pax Romana* (*Pax Augusta*) and of the *Pax Britannica*. Empires would overcome the Hobbesian fear of natural chaos and enmity among people, discipline enormous portions of land through the creation of societies ruled by the law, unify diverse ethnic communities guaranteeing a dialogue amongst them whilst safeguarding their own traditional customs, foster technological, infrastructural and artistic development, and facilitate trade and exchanges. Since all people that live inside the imperial borders enjoy citizenship, without any discriminations or limitations, the Eurasian Empire would be the instrument for the creation of a peaceful, prosperous, and advanced society based on rights and duties.

[5.140]   Third, in institutional terms, empires are perceived as political-territorial polities that combine a strict strategic centralism[83] with the broad autonomy of the local intrastate entities,[84] often united into a federal system. It follows that the Eurasian Empire would merge centralization with wide-ranging forms of autonomy for its inner administrative and local entities.

[5.141]   Dugin believes that the creation of the Eurasian Empire would represent a concrete universal alternative—though not the only—[85] to the global American Empire. Although Russia would epitomize its fundamental core, its borders would comprise much of the Eurasian *Großraum*, including in the first place the post-Soviet space and the countries of the Commonwealth of Independent States. Moreover, it would represent an empire surrounded by numerous other empires that are expected to live peacefully together, respecting the principles of multi-polarity and mutual sovereignty. The only exception to this rule regards the American Empire, which—according to Dugin—does not uphold the project of a multi-polar world and thus deserves to be contrasted by an international united front.[86]

[5.142]   The first step for the creation of the Eurasian Empire would be the integration of the post-Soviet space. Although these countries differ greatly one from another in ethnic, religious, and cultural terms, they are believed to share a common Eurasian spirit and to constitute natural parts of the Eurasian *Großraum*. The integration of Central Asian countries like Kazakhstan—whose leader Nursultan Nazarbayev is a Eurasianist supporter—, Uzbekistan, Tajikistan, Turkmenistan and Kyrgyzstan would be much easier than others, because they are perceived as "quasi-failed states" orbiting either around Russia or NATO. The integration of South Caucasian countries, except for Armenia, would be much more problematic since Azerbaijan and expressly Georgia express skepticism or hostility towards Russian revisionism.[87] In Europe, the integration of Belarus would be very feasible, that of Moldova uncertain, but that of Ukraine and especially of the Baltic republics extremely difficult, if not impossible. However, Dugin believes that the Eurasian Empire could not exist without the inclusion of Ukraine and Georgia in Russia's area of influence. Like Zbigniew Brzezinski noticed, if the two countries were to become part of the American empire, the position of Atlanticism in Europe would be much stronger, and the Russian imperial project suffocated.[88] In 1870, the German Chancellor Otto von Bismarck had already understood that separating Ukraine from Russia would imply an important downsizing of Russian power and his words seem like the echo of the contemporary Atlanticist project to subtract Ukraine from Russian influence:

> "The power of Russia could be undermined only by separating Ukraine from it [. . .]. Ukraine should not only be torn away from Russia but also set against it. We should play off one part of the single nation against the other and watch one brother killing the other. In order to accomplish this, we need to find and cultivate traitors among the national élite and using them we have to change self-consciousness of one part of the great nation to such an extent that they would hate everything connected with Russia, they would hate their origin not even realizing this. All the rest is about timing."[89] [5.143]

The consolidation of Russian power in the former Soviet space would not insist on direct colonization in the old sense, but rather on a unanimous consensus of all countries involved in the process of Eurasian integration and on agreements between peoples and leaders that support the project. [5.144]

Finally, in terms of ideology, the Eurasian Empire would recognize Eurasianism as its official political philosophy and would indorse its mission and goals. Eurasianism as expression of the Fourth Poltical Theory would be the liaison capable of uniting all Eurasian peoples inside a common imperial statehood.[90] [5.145]

NOTES [5.146]

1. Dugin, *Eurasian Mission*, 9. [5n1]
2. Ibid, 68. [5n2]
3. Ibid, 69. [5n3]
4. Ibid, 10. [5n4]
5. Ibid, 11. [5n5]
6. Ibid, 38–39. [5n6]
7. Ibid, 39. [5n7]
8. Ibid. [5n8]

[5n9]   9. Ibid, 44.
[5n10]   10. Ibid, 59.
[5n11]   11. Ibid, 60.
[5n12]   12. Ibid, 67.
[5n13]   13. Ibid, 68.
[5n14]   14. Ibid.
[5n15]   15. Ibid, 12.
[5n16]   16. Aleksandr Dugin, *The Fourth Political Theory* (London: Arktos, 2012), 12.
[5n17]   17. Ibid, 14.
[5n18]   18. See Martin Heidegger, *Sein und Zeit* (Tübingen: Max Niemeyer Verlag, 1963).
[5n19]   19. See Gilbert Durand, *Les Structures Anthropologiques De L'Imaginaire* (Paris: Presses Universitaires de France, 1960).
[5n20]   20. Dugin, *The Fourth Political Theory*, 38–42.
[5n21]   21. Ibid, 19.
[5n22]   22. Ibid, 21.
[5n23]   23. See Alain de Benoist, *Nuova Destra, Nuova Europa* (Rome: Pagine, 2012); Alain de Benoist, *La Fine Della Sovranità. Come la Dittatura Del Denaro Toglie il Potere Ai Popoli* (Bologna: Arianna Editrice, 2014); Alain de Benoist, *Le Traité Transatlantique et Autres Menaces* (Paris: Éditions Pierre-Guillaume de Roux, 2015); Alain de Benoist, *Survivre à la Pensée Unique* (Lille: Éditions Krisis, 2015).
[5n24]   24. Immanuel Wallerstein, *After Liberalism* (New York: Free Press, 1995).
[5n25]   25. Dugin, *The Fourth Political Theory*, 46.
[5n26]   26. Ibid.
[5n27]   27. Ibid, 47.
[5n28]   28. Dugin, *Eurasian Mission*, 103.
[5n29]   29. Ibid.
[5n30]   30. Alain de Benoist, *Vu De Droite: Anthologie Critique Des Idées Contemporaines* (Paris: Copernic, 1977).
[5n31]   31. Dugin, *The Fourth Political Theory*, 49–50.
[5n32]   32. Ibid, 60.
[5n33]   33. Gregory Bateson, *Mind and Nature: A Necessary Unit* (New York: Dutton, 1979).
[5n34]   34. Dugin, *The Fourth Political Theory*, 65.
[5n35]   35. Ibid, 66.
[5n36]   36. Ibid, 68.
[5n37]   37. Ibid, 69.
[5n38]   38. Ibid, 70.
[5n39]   39. Ibid, 88.
[5n40]   40. Ibid, 94.
[5n41]   41. See Arthur Moller van der Bruck, *Das Dritte Reich* (Berlin: Ring-Verlag, 1923).
[5n42]   42. See Oswald Splengler, *Der Untergang des Abendlandes* (Munich: Beck, 1922).
[5n43]   43. See Georges Sorel, *Réflexions Sur La Violence* (Paris: Rivière, 1919).
[5n44]   44. Dugin, *The Fourth Political Theory*, 99.
[5n45]   45. Diffused identity is described as a "vague feeling of a common belonging to a certain whole that is proper to every member of a given society" (Dugin, *Eurasian Mission*, 116).
[5n46]   46. Dugin, *Eurasian Mission*, 117.
[5n47]   47. Ibid, 115–16.
[5n48]   48. Dugin, *The Fourth Political Theory*, 194.
[5n49]   49. Ibid.
[5n50]   50. Dugin considers National Bolshevism and Eurasianism as secondary variations of the Fourth Political Theory (Cf. Dugin, *The Fourth Political Theory*, 197).
[5n51]   51. Dugin, *The Fourth Political Theory*, 195.
[5n52]   52. Ibid, 197.
[5n53]   53. Dugin, *Eurasian Mission*, 105.
[5n54]   54. Cf. Ibid, 129–65.
[5n55]   55. Ibid, 130–31.
[5n56]   56. Ibid, 139.

57. Ibid, 140.   5n57

58. Ibid, 141.   5n58

59. Ibid, 142.   5n59

60. Ibid, 143–44.   5n60

61. Ibid, 144.   5n61

62. Ibid, 152.   5n62

63. Ibid, 153.   5n63

64. Ibid.   5n64

65. Ibid, 154.   5n65

66. Ibid, 155.   5n66

67. Ibid, 156.   5n67

68. Ibid, 166.   5n68

69. Aleksandr Dugin, *The Rise of the Fourth Political Theory* (London: Arktos, 2017), 1.   5n69

70. Ibid, 4.   5n70

71. Ibid, 6.   5n71

72. Ibid, 9.   5n72

73. Ibid, 10.   5n73

74. Ibid, 18–19.   5n74

75. Ibid, 50.   5n75

76. Carl Schmitt, *Land und Meer: Eine Weltgeschichtliche Betrachtung* (Leipzig: Reclam,   5n76
1942).

77. Carl Schmitt, *Volkerrechtliche Großraumordnung: mit Interventionsverbot für Raum-*   5n77
fremde Mächte: Ein Beitrag zum Reichsbegriff im Völkerrecht (Berlin: Duncker & Humblot,
1941).

78. Dugin, *The Rise of the Fourth Political Theory*, 73.   5n78

79. Ibid, 74.   5n79

80. Ibid, 81.   5n80

81. Ibid, 83–84.   5n81

82. The Atlanticist Empire, for instance, is not led by a single emperor, but rather by various   5n82
figures that include the President of the United States, the European Union's leadership, the
Secretary General of NATO, and so on.

83. Imperial centralism often entails a single vertical line of power, a centralized model of   5n83
administration, the presence of a general set of codified juridical norms, a single system of tax
collection, a unified system of communication, and a strategic deployment of armed forces.

84. Imperial intrastate autonomies include a broadly developed system of local self-govern-   5n84
ment, the co-existence of different local models of power—from tribal democracy to principalities, republics, and even kingdoms—, the acknowledgement of different ethnic-confessional
rights, and the presence of a representative assembly for all imperial subunits in the case of a
federation.

85. Other alternative forms of contemporary universal empires are at least two. The first is   5n85
the Islamic Empire—or Global Caliphate, which represents the paramount project of fundamentalist Islam, especially of its Sunni Salafi and Wahhabi variant. The Islamic Empire has
universal ambitions, and it openly challenges the global American imperial order. The main
features of the Global Caliphate include the establishment of a global Islamic government; a
wide autonomy for ethnic groups, which will either adopt Islam as their faith or pay a tithe; the
introduction of the standards of Islamic economics, which for instance rejects usury, and
compels to distribute an amount of money to the poor; and the Islamization of the entire world.

86. Dugin, *The Rise of the Fourth Political Theory*, 103.   5n86

87. The Russo-Georgian war of 2008, which ended with the unilateral proclamation of   5n87
independence by Ingushetia and South Ossetia, has significantly tarnished since then the relations between the two countries.

88. Zbigniew Brzezinski, *The Grand Chessboard: American Primacy and Its Geostrategic*   5n88
Imperatives (New York: Basic Books, 2016).

89. Georgy Kryuchkov, *Ukraina Pered Sud'bonosnym Vyborom* (Kharkiv: Folio, 2010).   5n89

90. Dugin, *The Rise of the Fourth Political Theory*, 111.   5n90

Chapter Six

The Antagonists of Eurasianism

Post-liberalism, Atlanticism, and Unipolar Globalism

[6.0]   INTRODUCTION

[6.1]   Neo-Eurasianism is an ideology that, like all dogmatic theoretical perspectives, represents itself as truthful and just. Like most ideologies, it promotes a set of values that contrast with other worldviews and theories. The theme of the creation and representation of an enemy is typical of most political doctrines. Without a rival to contrast, no ideologies could affirm themselves: ideas have been struggling against each other since the beginning of human thought. In this chapter, we will analyze who are the philosophical and practical actors that Eurasianism considers as antagonists and the main features of the contemporary world order that it seeks to overcome.

[6.2]   THE VICTORY OF LIBERALISM AND
              ITS GLOBAL SPREAD AS POST-LIBERALISM

[6.3]   Neo-Eurasianism argues that since the 1990s, after the demise of the Soviet Union, the American—or Western—form of liberalism has affirmed itself as the only still existing ideology. Liberalism managed to fight and eliminate the rival ideologies of conservatism, monarchism, traditionalism, fascism, socialism, and communism; it therefore affirmed itself as the only political alternative, replacing the traditional view of politics with the logic of the free market. According to Dugin, after overwhelming conservatism, fascism, and communism, triumphant liberalism mutated into an exportable lifestyle based on consumerism, individualism, and hedonism: paradoxically, the defeat of all other ideologies transformed liberalism in an anti-political ideocracy.[1]

Liberalism arose as early as the 18th century, in conjunction with the spread of the Enlightenment throughout Europe and in the newly born United States of America. Since its birth, this ideology, though less dogmatic and subtler than Marxism, would appear as a powerful theoretical tool to overthrow the previous pyramidal world order of the *Ancien Régime*, thus replacing conservatism, traditionalism, religiosity, and monarchism with individualism, rationalism, secularism, and republicanism.   [6.4]

Liberalism as a political theory may be considered the purest and most refined expression of Western civilization. Being both a political and economic philosophy, it embodies the most relevant driving force of the modern age. Its most salient principles are the understanding of the individual as the measure of all things, the belief in the sacred character of private property, the assertion of the equality of opportunity as the moral law of society, the belief in the contractual basis of sociopolitical institutions, the abolition of governmental, religious, and social authorities that claim to possess the real "truth," a skeptical approach towards irrational beliefs, the separation of powers, social systems of control over government institutions, the creation of a civil society without races, peoples, and religions in place of traditional governments, the dominance of market relations over other forms of politics, and the certainty that the Western civilizational model of development and progress represents the world's imperative order to be taken as standard and pattern.[2] The philosophy of liberalism is based on the basic axiom that "freedom equals liberty." In this sense, liberals accept the idea of being "free from" something. From a sociopolitical point of view, liberals interpret the idea of "being free" as a form of liberty from the government and its control over economics, politics. civil society, religion, class systems, moral attachments, and any collective identity whatsoever (e.g. ethnic, religious, national, cultural, etc.). However, unlike anarchism, which is based on common labor, abolition of private property, collectivization of the factors of production and their outputs, liberalism considers the market and private property as a pledge for the realization of the optimal socio-economic model based on the maximization of individual profit. In this perspective, liberals do not oppose the government or the state as far as it is bourgeois-democratic and it facilitates the development of the capitalist model, believing that it will disappear in the future in favor of world market and global civil society. As for society in general, liberals repudiate traditional social institutions and are keen to eliminate sexual differentiations, to support the free choice of practices like abortion or euthanasia, and to question the classic model of family.   [6.5]

Liberalism is a natural antagonist of both nationalism and Marxism. Historically, liberalism exploited nationalism to struggle against the institutions of the *Ancien Régime* like the imperial-feudal system, the Church, and the   [6.6] estates, considered as remnants of the medieval "dark ages." From the French Revolution onwards, the nationalistic feeling was used to foster the principles of the Enlightenment, to gain independence from foreign rule, and to create nation-states. Nonetheless, as soon as nationalism turned into chauvinism and fascism, with a collectivistic and identitarian view on economics and society, liberalism turned its back to it and began to consider it as an authoritarian and militaristic political doctrine set up against the principles of freedom. At the same time, liberalism opposed Marxism in all its forms. What the liberal mind could not accept of the Marxist doctrine was its anti-individualistic collectivist nature, its recognition of the unjust system of appropriation of surplus value by capitalist exploiters, its anti-bourgeois class criticism, its aspiration to call for a proletarian revolution and for the abolishment of free market and private property, and its social collectivization of property and factors of economic production. Ultimately, liberalism managed to defeat identitarian nationalism in 1945 and Marxism in 1991, thus turning into the world's hegemonic ideology.

[6.7]   Ideological liberalism affirms that all rival ideologies that proclaim the superiority of the community over the private domain and the individual—like communism or fascism—are "totalitarian": in this sense, totalitarianism is a word that only liberals use to depict a collectivist form of government.[3] However, the belief that the individual is the measure of all things and that bears the highest value is likewise, in a certain sense, a totalitarian idea. In other words, liberalism transposes individualism to a micro level in the sense that it considers the individual as a micro-totalitarian apparatus that is an end in itself and the only socially relevant subject. In considering liberalism, Dugin openly labels it "third totalitarianism" and considers it to be the most dangerous and absolute one, which does not accept a coexistence with any other form of ideology while at the same time disguising its very absolutistic nature.[4]

[6.8]   Dugin argues that a liberal, being essentially an individualist, when extroverted, has the capability of destroying his community and the social bonds that links him to it. Overcoming the old values of traditionalism, the liberal individual accomplished the victory of pure nothingness.[5]

[6.9]   The essence of the bourgeois-capitalist liberal ideology rests on the principles of technological development, individualism, the pursuit of freedom at any cost, materialism, economic reductionism, egoism, and a fetish for money: apparently, these features are the ultimate outcome of Western civilization.[6]

[6.10]   The history of Western Europe led its societies, especially through the colonial era, to the point in which individualism, rationalism, materialism, and economic reductionism gradually began to become dominant and opened the way to capitalistic abuse and to the formation of a bourgeois exploitative class.[7] Therefore, during the Modern Age and the Enlightenment, Europe became the cradle of a materialistic liberal civilization that imposed on other peoples of the world its colonialist and imperialist policies, which culminated with the practice of despicable institutions like legitimized slavery. The bourgeois-capitalistic exploitative system was installed in European colonies, along with the introduction of serfdom and submission. In this context, the United States of America were forged as a colonial state based on slavery, individualism and materialism that became the apex of this bourgeois Western civilization of the modern era.[8] Despite the formal abolition of slavery in the 19th century, after the victory in the two world wars, the United States became the core of all Western civilization and the pole around which the global capitalist system revolved. Moreover, after the collapse of the socialist bloc, the power of the US was no longer counterbalanced by the Soviet Union and turned into the unchallenged center of the global liberal bourgeois system.

Dugin affirms that the triumph of liberalism and its spread coincided with its own evolution into post-liberalism, transforming—paradoxically—into an individualist anti-political doctrine, with the replacement of *homo politicus* with *homo oeconomicus*. The beginning of the 21st century saw the advent—at least in Western countries—of the post-modern man living in a post-liberal environment. Humanity under post-liberalism, being automatically unhooked by any social and political forms of collective identity, would be naturally drawn towards universality, cosmopolitism, and globalism. The fact that the individual replaced as absolute subject the social groupage introduced the necessity to build a new international order no longer based on sovereign and national states but on world government and global governance. The corrosion of traditional "collective" polities has thus been the starting point for the birth and development of the phenomenon of globalism and globalization.   [6.11]

Postmodernity is therefore the expression of the ultimate spread and worldwide affirmation of post-liberalism. In a postmodern reality, the values of rationalism, scientism, and positivism are the only ones accepted, and their "irrational" pre-modern counterparts are implicitly denigrated and banned in a rather intolerant fashion. Dugin believes that the glorification of total freedom and the worship of the sole individual, unhooked from any kind of limits, including reason, morality, and social, ethnic and gender identity are salient features of postmodernism. This historical phase corresponds perfectly with the notion of "end of history" as exposed in 1992 by Francis Fukuyama, in which economics turns into a global capitalist market, politics is overwhelmed, and states and nations are dissolved in the melting pot of world globalization. In a deterministic fashion, post-industrial societies can now consider liberal economy the world's natural destiny. In other words, after destabilizing conservatism, fascism and communism, liberalism evolved into post-liberalism: this philosophical development coincided with the historical advent of the global market society.[9]   [6.12]

[6.13]   Postmodernity could rise and develop in Western Europe and especially in the United States, which represents the avant-garde of freedom and the locomotive of the transition to postmodernism. In this sense, the US-led unipolar world represents the pole of freedom, and the promoters of the multipolar order are considered as players who act against freedom just because they do not embrace or accept an American post-liberal global hegemony. Postmodernism indicates a specific civilizational term that is strictly linked to the theory of progress, which is based on the axioms that human development bears a progressive and unidirectional character, and that man represents a universal self-centered phenomenon. Paradoxically, Americanism embodies a totalitarian ideology in the sense that it does not accept any different vision of the world; the idea contained in liberalism is that there can be no alternatives to it. [10]

[6.14]   Post-liberal modernity affirmed itself by rejecting the values of tradition like religion, hierarchy, and family. The core of the new era of modernity coincided with the rebellion against sacredness, when man came to replace to God, philosophy and science replaced religion, and technology took place of the revelation. [11] The potential outcome of the hostility towards traditional religious values could result in the creation of a new global pseudo-religion based on syncretism, ecumenism, and the deification of the concepts of tolerance and human rights. Describing it in eschatological terms, Dugin asserts that postmodernity—which includes the notions of globalization, post-liberalism, and post-industrial society—represents the advent of the Apocalypse, that final stage of human degeneration described as "the Kingdom of the Antichrist" by the Christians, "Erev Rav" by the Jews, "Dajjal" by the Muslims, and "Kali Yuga" by the Hindus. [12] The supremacy of technology expresses the ever-increasing nihilism of postmodern societies, which in the name of materialism would have forgotten the essence of things and their true Being. Some of the main features of post-humanity in the post-modern context would thus be de-politicization, autonomization, microscopization, sub- and trans-humanization, and fragmentation. [13]

[6.15]   The Russian philosopher believes that the world state and the world government are gradually abolishing all nation-states. Instead of safeguarding the values of cultural diversity and civilizational variety, the globalists wish to homologate all nations, compelling them to submit to the dominant post-liberal ideology. The idea of unipolar globalization is considered deeply racist since it would take for granted that the history and values of Western—especially American—society are equivalent to universal laws. This abuse of self-styled civilizational development considers that the values of the West, i.e. democracy, free market, parliamentarism, capitalism, individualism, human rights, and unlimited technological progress, would bear a universal scope that is intrinsically and self-evidently valid. The attempt to impose the Western model on all would conceal the belief that the values of other nations and cultures are undeveloped, imperfect, and obsolete, therefore manifesting an alleged superiority and a form of cultural racism and discrimination. In other words, globalization would represent a globally deployed model of Western European, or, rather, Anglo-Saxon ethnocentrism, which implies a form of cultural discrimination. [14]

The phenomenon of globalization is strictly connected with the monotonic process of modernization, which implies a linear idea of progress. Liberals inherited an evolutionist and Darwinist approach to social development based on the struggle of the strong against the weak, the rivalry for resources, and social competition. According to liberals and social-Darwinists like Herbert Spencer, progress always coincides with the growth of economic power, since it continuously refines the struggle for survival of the animal species, the warfare methods of strong nations, and the castes within the framework of pre-capitalist states. [15] Therefore, a Darwinian form of natural antagonism is embedded in the liberal idea of progress, which is considered as the main trajectory of social development. [16]   [6.16]

The objectivist liberal approach, which reaches the limits of Max Weber's idea about the origin of capitalism in the Protestant ethic, admits that those that are rich are necessarily good whereas the poor represent evil: in this sense, objectivists like Ayn Rand have waged a war of the rich against the poor. [17]   [6.17]

THE SUBJECTIVIST INDIVIDUALISM OF MODERNIST MEN   [6.18]

The French Revolution of 1789 brought into existence the new revolutionary world and laid the grounds for the advent of liberal modernism, which finds today in Western democracies—specifically in the United States—its clear manifestation. The French Revolution, which followed the American Revolution of 1776, built a new European society based on different foundations. Instead of being founded on the medieval traditional institutions of Church and monarchy, Europe was now founded on democracy; instead of being founded on God it was now founded on men. The French Revolution did its best to pull down the throne and the altar. Before the Revolution, during the Middle Ages and the early Modern Age, Church and state were closely united. After the Revolution, the modern man, i.e. the revolutionary man, turned away from the traditional institutions and began worshipping the principles of the Enlightenment: he now believed in rationalism, humanism, liberty, equality, and fraternity.   [6.19]

Following the philosophical principles of liberalism, modern men replaced objective reality with subjectivism. This process led to individualism and to the destruction of social bonds and collective identity. The root of the   [6.20] modernist problem is the singular man replacing individually the collective traditional reality of the pre-modern world based on the communion between religion and monarchy. The modernist mind does not conceive tradition and is led by a sort of mania to reform and to change. What typically distinguishes the mind of a modernist is skepticism: modernists do not attack just one truth, but all truths, and thus their problem is not that they do not believe anything, but that they believe everything. In other words, the modernist mind is relativistic in the sense that every subjective reality can bear a portion of objective truth. Skepticism and relativism lead modern minds to believe that objective truth begins to change from one moment to another and from one person to another because truth and belief are subjective and cannot be real per se.

[6.21]   The modernist mind, which has been thoroughly influenced over the last two centuries by European philosophy—specifically by thinkers like Descartes and Kant—, follows, often unconsciously, a philosophical system that undermines all truths. Specifically, Immanuel Kant has influenced in a decisive way the liberal modernist way of thinking. Kant changed the relationship between the mind and reality, putting into effect the so-called "Copernican Revolution" in philosophy. In astronomical geography, the Copernican Revolution introduced by Copernicus, in questioning whether the Sun moves around the Earth or vice versa, had stated that it is the Earth that revolves around the Sun, thus undermining the previous Ptolemaic geocentric model. Kant followed Copernicus's model to investigate whether reality turns around the human mind or whether the mind turns around reality. In other words, Kant asked which goes around which: Is it reality or is it the singular human mind? Does the object tell objectively what it is or is it men telling subjectively what the object is according to their own opinion? Does the object turn around men's mind so that they can affirm it is whatever they want it to be, or is it men's mind that turns around the object so that, though seeing it from different perspectives, it can still affirm it is the same object? Common sense would answer that it is the human mind that turns around the object and submits to reality: reality tells the mind what an object is, and it is not the mind that tells reality what it is. However, surprisingly, Kant affirms the opposite. For the Prussian philosopher, it is not the mind that turns around reality (objectivism), but it is reality that turns around the single mind (subjectivism). In his philosophical thought, Kant built a system that enabled men's minds to escape from reality. This system allowed men to pretend that their minds are the master of reality. Per Kant, it is the mind that makes objects what they are, so that objects are no longer what they are per se: an object is not an object per se, but men decide what it is. Furthermore, the Kantian philosophical system that affirms that men's minds control reality is selective since it is used arbitrarily, when it is useful to deny a specific objective reality.[18] In other words, the principle of the mind controlling reality is used when men refuse to adopt an objective truth, but is not applied when adapting to daily objective realities like the need for eating, sleeping, working, etc. Therefore, this system may undermine all speculative principles that men wish to reject by affirming that reality depends on one's mind and not on objective truth.

The Kantian subjectivist system represents the theoretical foundation of modernism and liberalism. It is a system of liberty that liberates the mind from anything it wishes to be liberated from, because it unhooks minds from objective reality. Modernists believe that things are true as far as their mind assert they are so, not because they are true (or false) independently of their minds, which dominate things: subjectivity comes before objectivity and all reality is at the mercy of the modernists' own—often diverging—ideas. [6.22]

The Kantian system of liberalism adopted by modernists is based on two fundamental principles: the negative principle of phenomenalistic agnosticism and the positive principle of vital immanence. [6.23]

Phenomenalistic agnosticism is a doctrine that claims that phenomena are the only objects of knowledge or the only form of reality and that all things consist simply of the aggregate of their observable, sensory qualities. This principle states the lack of knowledge beyond the phenomenon. Per Kant, men can reach the appearances of an object with the senses, but their mind cannot know what is behind the senses. In other words, behind the appearances men do not know what things are, since it is the mind that fabricates what things are. Men see the appearance of things through their senses, but do not know the essence of a thing in itself, i.e. the noumenon or *Ding an sich*; their mind cannot know anything that goes beyond the appearance of things, i.e. the phenomenon. The mind follows the knowledge snatched by the senses, but focuses only on the appearances, where the sensory knowledge stops. Therefore, if the mind is unable to know the essence of an object, it is automatically cut off from the possibility of unfolding the essence of reality. The individual uses his mind to fabricate for itself its own knowledge: it exploits the appearance of things, then works out its own system of knowledge, and transposes its own system onto the appearances giving them an identity. Kant builds reality on appearances. The Kantian man, who is the present-day post-liberal, fabricates with his mind a reality based on the phenomena that his senses perceive. His knowledge originates from the inside, not from the outside. If a human being stares at a sunset, his visual sense gives him the appearance of a sunset, but his mind should make him understand that the phenomenon of the sun setting is an effect of a cause, not just a senseless and disconnected event of nature: if his mind cannot go beyond the appearance of the sunset, then it will not be able to understand the causal relation between objective reality and subjective perception of it, and it can no longer read behind the appearances. [6.24]

[6.25]   On the other hand, the positive principle of vital immanence is the psychological process of the human consciousness unfolding itself from within and giving its own interpretation of the world. In other words, vital immanence is what persists inside humans once they have wiped out through phenomenalistic agnosticism the possibility of knowing objective reality beyond the senses. Since the human mind cannot know anything that goes beyond the phenomenon, the heart, i.e. the individual emotions and feelings, will replace it in grasping reality: the emotions will feed from within the mind, taking its place. Thus, the truth of the liberal, modernist man originates from within: it is immanent and subjective. So being things, everyone possesses his own subjective truth and bears his own vision of reality: his heart and needs build the *Weltanschauung* he prefers most. Subjectivism, which is the superimposition of the subject over the object, is the core of post-liberalism and modernism. Subjectivism makes the object depend upon the subject, instead of making the subject depend upon the object. It follows that a mind governed from the inside is unable to pick reality and is destined to live in a world of appearances fabricated by its own.

[6.26]   Modernism coincides with the application of the philosophical system of subjectivism. Due to subjectivist individualism, liberal societies are often characterized by disconnection, atomization, alienation, and lack of collective identity and common sense.

[6.27]   THE UNIPOLAR AMERICANIST NEW WORLD ORDER

[6.28]   The advent of the New World Order (NWO) coincided with the demise of the Soviet Union and the end of the Cold War. The transition from a bipolar international order to a unipolar world led by the global hegemony of the United States represented the historical condition from which the idea of globalism and mondialism could arise. Dugin affirms that this newly forged world order ignored all other poles of power except that of the United States, its NATO partners, and its allies, and was built upon the principles of the universalization of free market economics, liberal democracy, and the ideology of human rights, with the idea of spreading—through coercive means when necessary—these values to all countries of the world.[19] The postulate for the implementation of the globalist project was the necessity to overcome the previous existing order of nation-states and national sovereignty, and to undermine the Westphalian system of international relations in favor of global governance. In this context, the ideological basis of Western liberal democracy, the market economy, and the strategic domination of the United States over the world became the only solution to all kinds of emerging challenges and was held to be a universal model that all humanity had to accept: if a country refused, the penalty to pay would be that of international marginalization and isolation or the accusation of being considered an "authoritarian" or "rogue" state.

Generally, regionalist and multipolar tendencies are perceived with hostility by the promoters of the NWO, who are aware that their global project has not yet been fully fulfilled: international actors that tend to resist against Americanism—be they emerging world powers or local political groups—show that the transition to the globalist world model is not yet accomplished. [6.29]

In *Eurasian Mission*, Dugin describes what he believes are the salient features of Americanism. First, the United States would be a country controlled by a financial oligarchy that personifies inequality, injustice, oppression, exploitation, alienation, neo-colonialism, and imperialism. In terms of economics, America would pivot on the dominance of the financial sector, which would have completely supplanted the value of industrial production and agriculture. America's financial system would apply to the entire world, since the US dollar is used as the primary global reserve currency: therefore, the world economy, being strictly hooked to the American financial system, would be US-centric and serve for the benefit of US interests regardless of whether this economy is efficient or not. Through its military, diplomatic, and economic dominance, the US would exploit resources from the rest of the world by setting, for instance, the global prices for a commodity from which it usually profits. This practice—perceived as aggressive—would produce a major imbalance in the world economic system, as well as an unsustainable exploitation of the planet's resources. As already considered, after 1991, liberal capitalism became the only widely accepted economic regime, outmatching the socialist model and the autarchic economic models of the so-called "third way." Financiarism, which would represent the final stage of capitalism, would prove today to be a dictatorship of markets over communities and peoples, and would follow the evolution of Marxist alienation: first alienation of the output of labor from the producers, then alienation of the surplus value, then the alienation of the productive sphere into the system of bank credit, finally the alienation of the entire real economy into virtual financial speculation. [6.30]

Second, Dugin affirms that American society is based on the disruption of social ties. The salient American social elements would be atomization and individualization. Built by immigrants from all over the world, American society based itself on the worship of individual identity.[20] Thanks to the lack of specific social and collective roots, individualism could reach its logical conclusion in the US. Moreover, since the very beginning of its political existence, America was a society based on a disjointed mixture of cultures, nations, and races according to the principle of the "melting pot": the result of this process was the absence of organic and stable ethnic ties. Spreading its influence throughout the world, the US would also promote this multicultural model to other countries, proclaiming the cosmopolitan princi- [6.31] ple as universally valid. This would imply the systematic de-sovereignization of nations and states and the violation of the norm of non-interference in domestic affairs of third countries.

[6.32]   Third, Dugin acknowledges that the mainstream global mass media express the representation of American interests and a continuation of American media and policies, in accordance with the global transnational elite. The American system of knowledge and information would be focused exclusively on pragmatic and materialistic interests and would be aimed at obtaining pecuniary and utilitarian benefits.

[6.33]   Finally, the American idea of progress would be based on the certainty of unlimited growth potential. The American idea of progress would entail the worldwide imposition at any costs of "democratization," "development" and "civilization," which would ultimately epitomize a form of global "liberal dictatorship" and—in Dugin's words—an "empire of absolute evil."[21]

[6.34]   The United States is considered to possess a sort of "messianic" manifest destiny that would be the result of liberal-democratic ideology combined with the radicalism of Protestant sects. As "New World," America would have overtaken all cultures of the "Old World," obliging them to adopt its universalistic model and to betray their own past.[22]

[6.35]   The affirmation of the Americanist model would imply the need to transform the entire world into a single political and economic system ruled by a globalist elite, thus giving fulfillment to the American motto "*E pluribus unum.*"[23]

[6.36]   Dugin affirms that the United States is currently undergoing a test of its global imperial rule. In this sense, he suggests three strategies that America should implement if it wishes to continue as the sole hegemonic international actor, despite the probable future rise of a multipolar order. The first, highly supported by neoconservatives, would be that of creating a full-fledged American imperial rule in which the US and its allies would represent the imperial core and the rest of the world a fragmented periphery subject to permanent unrest and destabilization. The second would be the creation of a "multipolar unipolarity" in which the US would cooperate with its allies (Canada, Europe, Australia, Japan, Israel, some Arab countries, etc.) in solving regional issues and putting pressure on antagonist states (Iran, North Korea, Venezuela, etc.), or preventing other powers from achieving regional hegemony (Russia, China, etc.). Finally, the third would be to promote the process of accelerated globalization with the creation of a world government that would undermine the sovereignty of all other nations in favor of the creation of a single global polity led by a globalist elite.[24]

[6.37]   The geopolitics of the unipolar world has replaced the Cold War bipolar system based on the contraposition between West and East with the model of "Center-Periphery": since 1991, the United States and the NATO countries of Western Europe represented the center of the world and all the others the

periphery. The symmetry of core-outskirts replaced the symmetry and balance of the two poles. The victors of the Cold War were now located at the
center, and around them in concentric circles rested all other countries scattered according to the level of their strategic, political, economic, and cultural proximity to the center.[25] The closest circle neighboring the American
center was in fact an extension of it, including Europe, the other NATO
countries, and Japan. This unipolar world would disguise an imperialistic
system of global rule in which the United States and NATO allies represented the leading core extending their domain over the remaining outskirts,
which included former countries of the so-called Second and Third World.

Still today, the American unipolar concentric empire would find its core   [6.38]
in the world's "rich North" and in the Atlanticist community, whereas the
rest of the world would be dismissed as the peripheral area of underdeveloped or developing countries that should move in the same direction of the
core countries of the West. In this context, although being tied to the core,
Europe would bear geopolitical interests that differ from those of the US.[26]

Eurasianists believe Europe possesses its own strategic interests that di-   [6.39]
verge substantively from American interests and from the needs of adopting
the project of Western globalization, especially in its attitude towards its
southern and eastern neighbors.

According to Dugin, there are several different levels that may describe   [6.40]
the US-centric global geopolitical arrangement that characterizes the current
unipolar world order. From a historical point of view, the United States is
aware of representing the logical conclusion and peak of Western civilization. Alleging that the Western civilization is implicitly superior to others,
Americans would have developed the belief to bear a special civilizational
mission and to contrast anyone eager to question it. Initially, this claim was
presented in terms of "Manifest Destiny," then in terms of the Monroe Doctrine and the Roosevelt Corollary, and later with Wilsonianism. In an imperialist schema, Americanism today would imply the spread and enforcement of
alleged universal human rights norms, promotion of democracy, technological development, and free market institutions. The American claim to possess
the best political and ideocratic paradigm would not be a new feature, but
would rather represent the continuation of a Western universalism that went
from the Roman Empire, Medieval Christianity, modernity in terms of the
Enlightenment and colonization up to the contemporary phenomena of post-
modernism and ultra-individualism.[27] In this sense, the terms Americanism
becomes a synonym for "universalism": all other cultures that oppose this
idea, especially when upholding the values of traditionalism and conservatism, would have no future at all unless they would adopt the "American"
model. Politically speaking, the American version of liberalism has spread
throughout the world, turning into the only possible political system: today,
the only form of government that the globalist establishment would accept

would be liberal democracy. This political system would hinge on the philosophical principles of a postmodern and post-individual vision of politics, that would coincide with post-humanism and, paradoxically, with anti-politics. According to some thinkers,[28] liberal democracy works as a self-generating virus that strengthens existing democratic societies and dissolves traditional societies; therefore, democracy could represent a weapon to create chaos and to govern the dissipating world cultures from the core, emulating and installing the democratic codex everywhere. Finally, from an ideological point of view, the spread and imposition of democracy would represent a violation of the principles of realism and balance of power in international relations.

[6.41]   The United States bears three different views of world system. The first coincides with globalism and mondialism, in the spirit of Fukuyama's earlier ideas on the "end of history" and the worldwide triumph of democracy and free market. This vision upholds the idea of de-sovereignization of existing nation-states and the need for the establishment of a global meta-state governance ruled by the principles of post-liberalism. The second believes that national governments should still be conserved and that the US should cooperate with its allies and oppose its enemies until globalism would finally become the world's standard in the future. Finally, the third vision, following the civilizational pattern given by Samuel Huntington, claims that civilizations are undeniable realities that—for the better or the worse—must interact with each other.[29]

[6.42]   Dugin interprets the struggle against liberalism as a crusade against the West—specifically against the US—since the ideology of liberalism would have followed the path of the West at the moment it rejected the principles of traditionalism and spirituality, introducing the ideas of modernism and rationalism. Countering liberalism would coincide with the need for supporting religious, civilizational, and ethnic identity. Although being only a civilization amongst many others, the Western one tends to believe in its intrinsic superiority and would attempt to overcome human history in favor of pure universalism. In this sense, the West would either lose its own identity turning into an automaton, or it would try to impose its alleged universal civilizational values on all other existing civilizations: whereas the first outcome would imply a struggle of automatons with humanity, the second would imply an unavoidable global liberation movement that would struggle against Western neo-imperialism.[30] If the "end of history" would coincide with universalism and globalization, then it would represent the abolition of the future; if globalization would represent the end of the state, then it would also represent the end of time and space.[31]

[6.43]   America would have built its own identity upon the denial of the "obsolete" European values of pre-modern age, considering them outdated by scientific development and positivistic rationalism. Having unhooked the relation between men and soil, America would acknowledge as its founding root only the modern individual as such. The absence of a link between the population and the soil represents a dramatic obstacle in the search for identity. The only roots the US would possess can be traced to modernity, lacking any pre-modern background whatsoever.[32] Dugin states that the American identity oscillates around the main vectors of liberalism, individualism, freedom, democracy, progress, process, development, welfare, efficiency, consumerism, materialism, and utilitarianism, but it does not necessarily require a linkage to the soil.

The current world order is unipolar, with the global West as its center and   [6.44]
the United States as its core. This unipolarity presents two different characteristics. From a geopolitical point of view, it would represent the strategic dominance of the planet by the American superpower, which would attempt to control the rest of the world through a battle of forces in such a manner as to be able to possess a global rule that follows its own national and imperialistic interests, depriving other nations and states of their real sovereignty in what may be considered as a form of "global dictatorship."[33] From an ideological point of view, unipolarity would be based on modernist and postmodernist values that are openly against traditionalism. In this sense, modernity and its ideological basis founded upon individualism, liberal democracy, capitalism, and consumerism would represent the future catastrophe of humanity, that the West would be dragging down into an abyss. Dugin summarizes this strong assertion by affirming that American values pretend to be "universal ones," overlooking the multiplicity of cultures and traditions still existing in the rest of the world.[34]

ATLANTICISM AND GLOBALISM   [6.45]

Neo-Eurasianism regards Altanticism and globalism as its main opponents.   [6.46]
In his writings, Dugin condemns both theories, considering them as a twofold personification of Western aggressiveness towards the rest of the world. But how do Eurasianists precisely interpret the terms?

The term Atlanticism denotes a geopolitical expression that encompasses   [6.47]
several concepts. Firstly, it describes the Western sector of world civilization, both from a historical and geographical point of view. Secondly, it specifically represents the member states of the North Atlantic Treaty Organization, the anti-Soviet military alliance created in 1949 and headed by the United States. Thirdly, from a cultural point of view, it includes the unified information network created by the Western media empires. Finally, from an economic and social point of view, it embodies the free market system, which coincides with the spread of liberal democracy and with the implementation of the process of globalization. Atlanticism would control the

global mass media and give support to a network of think tanks, agents of influence, political parties, NGOs, and religious bodies that would serve as instruments to establish, expand, and strengthen the unipolar world: all these tools are parts of what Eurasianists call the "Atlanticist International."[35]

[6.48]   The Atlanticists would aim at guaranteeing the entire world under the control of NATO and at imposing the social, economic, and cultural features of Western civilization upon it. The ultimate goal of Atlanticism would be to finish the construction of the New World Order, which would represent a global system that benefits an utter minority of the planet's population.[36] In a few words, for Eurasianists, the Atlanticist worldview would be based on "World Government" and the idea of "one global state."

[6.49]   Since the end of the Second World War, American and Western European foreign policy has centered around the transatlantic axis institutionalized through the birth of the North Atlantic Treaty Organization (NATO) in 1949. Through the creation of this military alliance, the United States decided to give military support to Western European allies in case of confrontation with the Soviet Union. At that time, Western Europe accepted America as its guardian and protector, even if this would mean a resizing of its strategic sovereignty. Many have considered the US initiative to aid Western Europe through the Marshall Plan as a strategy to assure military and economic submission of the Old Continent to Washington. Since then, the United States has constantly benefited from this military alliance to contain Russia, thus preventing the expansion and consolidation of a Eurasian continental land power. In fact, the fundamental purpose of American foreign policy for most of the 20th century has been to ensure that no single power would dominate the Eurasian landmass: three times during the last century, the US sent massive numbers of military forces overseas to defeat those who sought dominion of the Eurasian Heartland—during World War One, World War Two, and during the Cold War.[37] Once the Soviet Empire collapsed, the last severe contest for territorial dominion over the Eurasian landmass had been removed, and therefore the chief purpose of US foreign policy had been accomplished.

[6.50]   Since 1949, NATO evolved from a collective defense organization into Europe's main security institution, expanding well beyond the geographical area of the Atlantic Ocean, with a membership of 16 countries at the end of the Cold War to 29 by 2018, including many countries that had previously belonged to the Soviet sphere of influence and/or Warsaw Pact. The constant enlargement of the organization's members shifted NATO's borders extremely close to Russia and its sphere of influence, thus threatening the peace and stability of Eastern Europe. A hypothetical inclusion in NATO of countries like Ukraine or Georgia would mean a clear act of aggressiveness towards Russia: in this sense, Russia's interventions in Southern Ossetia, Abkhazia, and Crimea are easily comprehensible through the lens of national interest and national security.

Currently, the demise of the Soviet Union has probably made America's [6.51] role as European protector in the frame of NATO obsolete. Also, given the advanced stage of European integration—which could also include the military sphere in the future—the presence of US troops in the Old Continent seems to be more and more useless and costly (specifically for Americans). The task of transforming all Europe into a zone of peace falls now directly on Europe's shoulders, with the United States that could play at most a supporting role. Even the stabilization of Europe's periphery—from the Balkans in the south to Turkey, the Caucasus, and Ukraine in the East—implies a scenario in which Europe will have to increasingly engage without American support, but rather through a cooperation with Russia.[38]

Whereas Atlanticism would imply the strategic and military means [6.52] through which the West would try to impose its hegemony, the term globalism would entail the spread and affirmation of the Western socio-economic system based on the free market and the spread of democratization in the entire world. For Eurasianists, globalism and globalization would be strictly connected with the building of the New World Order, at the center of which would stand the political-financial oligarchy of the West. The natural victims of globalism would thus be sovereign states, national cultures, religious doctrines, economic and juridical traditions, alter-liberal-democratic political systems, and all diverging spiritual, intellectual, and civilizational manifestations on the planet. Eurasianists highlight that in its mainstream use the term globalism denotes simply "unipolar globalism," i.e. the imposition of the Western model upon the rest of the world.[39]

Globalism would represent a challenge to the nations and civilizations of [6.53] the Eurasian continent, as well as for the African and American ones. Being a Western phenomenon, it would negatively influence the East by annihilating peoples and cultures that bear values and norms that differ from Western ones. Globalization is considered as a Western and specifically Anglo-Saxon/American phenomenon that has reached its peak through the US domination of the unipolar world: in its pure essence, it would represent the worldwide imposition of the Atlantic paradigm.[40]

The affirmation of the pole of Atlanticism as the only pole would have [6.54] coincided with the end of geopolitical history, with the end of the conflict between Atlanticism (thalassocracy) and Eurasianism (tellurocracy), and with the advent of Fukuyama's "end of history": in one word, with the advent of the unipolar New World Order.[41]

Globalism is believed to be promoted by a global oligarchy that would [6.55] include political leaders of the United States, economic and financial tycoons, and agents of globalization who have built a planetary network in which resources are allocated to the supporters of globalization. This global elite and its agents would direct the flow of the information, control political, cultural, intellectual, and ideological lobbying, perform data collection, and infiltrate the structures of those states that have not yet been fully deprived of their sovereignty.[42]

[6.56]   Essentially, globalism would challenge the existence of sovereign nation-states, which altogether represent the core of the Westphalian system. This system, developed after 1648 at the end of the Thirty Years' War, has passed through several stages of its development, and somewhat continued to reflect objective reality until the end of the Second World War. It was born out of the rejection of the claims of medieval empires to universalism and "divine mission," and it corresponded with the bourgeois reforms in European societies. It was also based on the assumption that only a nation-state could possess the highest sovereignty, and that outside of it, there would be no other entity to possess the legal right to interfere in its internal policy, regardless of which goals and missions—religious, political, or otherwise—would guide it. From the middle of the 17th century to the middle of the 20th century, this principle predetermined European policy and, consequently, was transferred to other countries of the world with certain adjustments. The Westphalian system was at first pertinent only for European powers, and their colonies were considered merely as their continuation, not enjoying enough political and economic potential to claim the status of independent entities. Since the beginning of the 20th century, the same principle was extended to the former colonies during the process of decolonization. This Westphalian model assumes full juridical equivalence between all sovereign states. In this model, there are as many poles of foreign policy decisions in the world as there are sovereign states. Generally, this rule is still in force by inertia, and all international law is based on it. In practice, however, sovereign states are characterized by inequality and hierarchical subordination. During the two World Wars, the distribution of influence among the largest world powers led to a confrontation between separate blocs, where decisions were made in the country that was the most influential among its allies. After World War Two, owing to the defeat of Nazi Germany and the Axis Powers, the bipolar scheme of international relations—i.e. the Yalta bipolar system—developed into a global system. International law continued to recognize *de jure* the absolute sovereignty of any nation-state, but *de facto*, basic decisions concerning the fundamental issues of the world order and global policy were made only in two centers: Washington and Moscow. After the demise of the Soviet Union and the advent of the unipolar system under the hegemony of the United States, globalism could spread as the tool through which the transnational elites could establish their New World Order based on the abolition of nation-states and the creation of a global governance.

[6.57]   Today, Eurasianists believe that the process of globalism has not yet been totally accomplished; on the contrary, many clues would suggest that the future of international relations will assist in an overcoming of the Westphalian system based on nation-states, but this evolution would not be promoted by unipolar globalism but rather by a multipolar civilizational order.

WESTERNISM AND MODERNIZATION [6.58]

The modern world is essentially the result of Western civilization. In turn, [6.59] Western civilization is the expression of Western-European cultural evolution, which developed from one shore of the Atlantic Ocean to the other. From a historical perspective, Europe—or, better to say, Western Europe— became the place where the transition from traditional to modern society took place. Europe created a model of society unique among other civilizations and cultures, which is the result of Greek philosophy, Roman law, and the interpretation of Christian teaching—at first in the Catholic-Scholastic, and later in the Protestant spirit.[43]

Some key elements that Western Europe achieved through time which [6.60] differentiated it from other civilizations are the construction of secular and positivistic societies, the proclamation of the idea of social progress through the development of technology, the primacy of science and rationality, the introduction of the model of political democracy, the utter importance given to private property, free market, the rule of law, and individual rights, and the transition from an agrarian economy to a full-fledged industrial one. All these factors contributed in transforming Europe into the paradigm of modernity.

The term "West" can frankly be considered as a synonym of "Western [6.61] Europe." The chief contributions to Western civilization and modernity were given by the Western industrialized countries of Europe like England, the Netherlands, France, and Western Germany. On the other hand, Central Europe contributed little to shaping the Western civilizational paradigm, and Eastern Europe even less. From a cultural point of view, the terms "European" and "Western" refer specifically to the European West, where the transition from traditional society to modern society occurred. Furthermore, starting from the 17th century and especially after the Enlightenment (18th century), the term "West" acquired a civilizational sense becoming a synonym of "Modernity," "modernization," "progress," and social, industrial, economic and technological development.[44] In other words, the cultural evolution of Western Europe and its American projections forged a civilizational idea based on the concept of "modernization," which turned to be a synonym of "Westernization."

The imperialist and colonialist thrust that most Western European nations [6.62] experienced between the 17th and the 19th centuries led to the exportation of the ideas of modernization and progress outside Europe in the African,

Asian, and American colonies. While interacting with non-Western cultures, the Europeans grew the conviction that the path of development of Western civilization—especially the transition from traditional societies to modern ones—bore a universal scope and an intrinsic validity and represented the sole parameter for progress and emancipation. This belief, in turn, led to the idea that all countries and peoples of the world were obliged to adopt the Western civilizational archetype, lest they continue to stay in underdeveloped and retrograde conditions. The Western ideas of progress and modernization and the persuasion that the West is the mandatory model of the historical development of all peoples considerably contributed to justify and support both political colonization and cultural racism. All peoples who did not adapt to the Western mindset were considered by Westerners as barbaric, savage, backward, sub-normal, and so forth. Paradoxically, while spreading the ideas of democracy, equality and freedom, the Europeans related to "less developed" peoples outside Europe with rigid racist arrangements and harsh colonial rule. Furthermore, the sustainability of the European capitalist economy relied on the inhuman exploitation of aboriginal peoples, as in the case of Native Americans and African slaves.

[6.63]   In Dugin's view, yesterday as today, the West would bear a strong imperialist character, though atypical, which he renames "humanitarian imperialism." After officially rejecting the idea of Empire and its religious foundations—i.e. the Holy Roman Empire—, contemporary Europe preserved imperialism by relocating it to the level of values and narratives. Progress and technological development were hereafter thought of as a European mission through which implementing a planetary colonization strategy. [45]

[6.64]   As already seen, the process of planetary modernization began to unfold from the lands of Western Europe, from where it spread globally affecting the foundations of all traditional societies. The issue is that whereas in countries like England, France, Holland, and the United States, the process of modernization bore an endogenous character, since it developed within these societies, for countries and peoples outside Europe—and somewhat also inside Europe, in its Central, Southern, and Eastern regions—[46] it turned into a forced phenomenon insomuch as nations were forced into the process of modernization against their will becoming victims of colonization or else being reluctant to oppose European expansion. [47] In other words, modernization is an endogenous feature for Western Europe, but exogenous—i.e. imposed and brought in from without—for the rest of the world. The problem with exogenous modernization is that it did not emerge spontaneously from the internal needs and natural developments of traditional societies, but rather the result of coercion and oppression.

[6.65]   Generally, two categories of countries can be distinguished amongst those that had been exposed to exogenous modernization. The first category is that of countries that—despite their exposure to forced modernization—managed to preserve their political-economic independence, or else strove for it in anti-colonial wars. The second category includes all countries that by assimilating to modernization ended up losing their political-economic independence and thus turned into colonies or protectorates.

Although some scholars—chiefly Samuel Huntington—have argued that there can exist a "modernization without Westernization," the very concept of modernization is strictly linked to the idea of the West, thus it seems unlikely for a country and society to modernize in isolation from the West and without copying its values. However, some forms of exogenous modernization exist that are based on the presence of independent interests from those of the West and on the blend of national interests with the pragmatically imported Western values. Examples of what Dugin describes as "modernization plus partial Westernization"[48] include contemporary Russia, China, India, Brazil, Japan, some Islamic countries—e.g. Turkey—, and several countries of the Pacific region. The compromise between exogenous modernization on one side and the defense of one's own interests and traditional cultural-historical and civilizational forms on the other represents a major dilemma for non-Western countries.   [6.66]

At the end of World War Two, after that the Yalta Conference had reshaped the new international order, the concept of "West" acquired a more ideological and geopolitical meaning, representing the "free" liberal world vis-à-vis the "unfree" socialist bloc. The "West" embodied the totality of developed countries that embraced capitalism and liberal-democratic ideology. At the same time, the concept of "East" emerged to depict countries that adopted the Marxist ideology. Paradoxically, Marxism should be considered as a variant of Western-European political theories, since socialism and communism arose in the philosophical and social environment of the West. Still, Marxism spread and consolidated itself—despite Karl Marx's previsions—in Eastern-European, Eurasian, and Asian traditional and rural societies and not in industrialized Western-European countries; communist societies did not arise in England, Germany, or France, but rather in Russia, China, Vietnam, or North Korea. Communist parties won in societies where capitalism was in undeveloped condition and traditional society—mainly agrarian—prevailed economically and culturally. The history of capitalist societies displays that Marx's predictions of the inevitability of proletarian revolution in them have been contradicted by time. Marx claimed that the proletarian revolution could not occur in Russia or in other countries with a predominance of "the Asian means of production," but it was there where it did happen and not in societies with developed capitalism.[49]   [6.67]

A possible conclusion is therefore that in "Eastern" communist regimes, Marxism represented a model of exogenous modernization that combined Western values—which were adopted only partially—with local traditional beliefs.   [6.68]

[6.69]   In this perspective, the "East"—or "Second World"—included countries of exogenous modernization that managed to avail themselves of the socialist methods of modernization, borrowing the Western technological model but preserving an independence from capitalism. These countries have proved to be able to industrialize quickly and to preserve an ideological and geopolitical self-sufficiency, avoiding the direct and indirect colonization by the West.

[6.70]   On the contrary, the so-called "Third World" encompassed countries of exogenous modernization that could not manage to develop autonomously neither through capitalist nor through socialist means, and therefore were forced to rely on either the "West"—"First World"—or to the "East"—"Second World," becoming subordinate colonies to the one or the other, despite the declaration of nonalignment by some.

[6.71]   During the 1990s, with the end of the bipolar order, the concept of "West" once again underwent a new semantic transformation. It then symbolized the triumphant liberal-democratic system and free market based on the rules of capitalism, as well as the replacement of politics by economics and the worldwide acceptance or imposition of globalization. The "West" began to embody a globalist liberal-capitalist project according to which the only way to modernize was the adoption of its beliefs and practices by all the nations of the world.[50]

[6.72]   In this scenario, the "West" could consider itself the uncontested victor of history and ideologies. At the time of the "end of history," the concept of "West," world, and "globalization" almost overlapped. Indeed, globalization would embody the final stage of the Western project to spread universally its system of values. Believing in the intrinsic superiority of its civilization and in the universal validity of its norms—e.g. liberalism, human rights, rule of law, gender equality, secularization, democratization, etc.—the US-led trans-Atlantic society built up an absolute model. This model included the two distinct categories of the West and the rest. Whereas the former perceived itself as the fulfillment of liberal-democratic secular "messianism," the latter began to appear as an underdeveloped semi-Western periphery that necessitated to fully implement Western-oriented reforms in order to reach higher standards of modernity and civilization.

[6.73]   However, in the 1990s the concept of "modernization" varied significantly too. Once overcoming the inertial resistance of conservative structures and the competition from socialist alter-modernization, liberal-capitalist modernism reached its own determinate limits and ended the implementation of its program: at this point, as seen, the "West" as a concept turned into the idea of post-modernity. Post-modernity represents the condition of final exhaustion of the agenda of Westernization and modernization, since it displays the exasperation of the will to unfold modernity and progress at all costs, often beyond rationality and common sense. In other words, the faith in progress finished its business and ceded its place to playful temporality, deprived of an existential present.[51] Lacking collective identity, sense of religiosity, attachment to conservative values, respect for tradition and relying merely on consumerism, hedonism, and individualism, Dugin describes the final stage of Western modernization as the representation of the downfall into non-being.[52]

Even Francis Fukuyama accepted the idea that the post-modern West has significantly changed its image since the time of his proclamation of the "end of history,"[53] so that today a gap exists between completed modernity and incipient post-modernity, with clear consequences in the geopolitical sphere.   [6.74]

Moreover, it is possible to affirm that the West is not at all compact or united. This fact is evident when considering its two faces: The United States—which represents its most "advanced" part—on one hand and Europe on the other. Some authors have considered the former unit as the representation of a typical example of polity led by Hobbesian principles with an agenda oriented on security and power, while the latter an integrated union supported by Kantian pacifist ideas, particularly sensitive to issues like civil society, human rights, and tolerance.[54] It seems that the United States and Europe share common values but pursue different interests. This is particularly noticeable in the chief countries of continental Europe like Germany, France, Spain, and Italy, which generally believe that their geopolitical national interests do not automatically coincide with those of the trans-Atlantic partner. But this view is not accepted by all. Other Europeans—and Americans—believe that especially after the aftermath of Donald Trump's election, the United States and Europe still share common interests, but enjoy different values. Finally, there are those who believe—like Alain de Benoist—that the two parts of the West neither share common interests, nor common values. In addition, an even more significant cleavage exists within Europe itself, which bears at least three different identities. The first is the Euro-Atlanticist pole, which starkly highlights the unity of values and interests between itself and North America, and which includes primarily Great Britain and some Eastern European countries that somehow fear Russian revisionism like Poland, the Baltic republics, and Ukraine (when led by a filo-Western elite). The second includes countries of Continental Europe that—albeit linked to the United States through NATO—believe to share partially different identities, values, and interests than those of the US; these countries include France, Germany, Italy, and Spain. Finally, the last pole is represented by Eurasian Europe, and includes countries that are somewhat hostile towards the United States and consequently quite sympathetic towards Russia, among which Belarus, Moldova, and Serbia.   [6.75]

Western modernism consists of two parts: one is technical, the other social-cultural. The technical refers to scientific progress and high-tech development, while the social-cultural designates a specific model of society   [6.76] and man. The latter has implications in many spheres. Firstly, in the sphere of family relations, it initially rejects the church marriage, then marriage it-self—replacing it with domestic partnership—, it allows homosexual mar-riage, and ultimately it abolishes the rules of monogamy and unrestricted sexual behavior. Thus, a "modern" family in the Western sense of the word is a diversified nucleus unhooked from the traditional archetype, which is in-stead still widely present in non-Western environments like Asia, the Middle East, and Eastern Europe.

[6.77]   Secondly, in terms of religion, Western modernism secularizes all forms of transcendence belief, labeling metaphysical creeds as naïve and obsolete, being overcome by scientific positivism and rationalism. Dugin describes the historical and cultural evolution that he believes modern/Western men have experienced in their shift from religious to secular societies characterized by godlessness. [55]

[6.78]   Thirdly, moral modernization would lead to the destruction of traditional relations between people. This issue is strictly linked with the liberal idea of men as "absolute individuals," completely self-sufficient, and free from any social or cultural restraint. Dugin believes that in a "modernized" society, everyone bears a proper individuality, mindset, belief, and worldview, dis-missing the sense of collective identity typical of traditional forms of moral-ity, religious norms, the values of family, the idea of *narod* (people) and *ethnos*, and the spirit of community. [56]

[6.79]   In conclusion, modern men would be the result of the Nietzschean "death of God," who they killed with their own hands through free will.

[6.80]   NOTES

[6n1]   1. Dugin, *The Fourth Political Theory*, 11.
[6n2]   2. Ibid, 140–41.
[6n3]   3. Dugin, *Eurasian Mission*, 106.
[6n4]   4. Ibid, 108.
[6n5]   5. Ibid, 110–11.
[6n6]   6. Ibid, 133.
[6n7]   7. Ibid, 145.
[6n8]   8. Ibid.
[6n9]   9. Dugin, *The Fourth Political Theory*, 18–19.
[6n10]   10. Ibid, 85.
[6n11]   11. Ibid, 25.
[6n12]   12. Ibid, 27.
[6n13]   13. Ibid, 199.
[6n14]   14. Ibid, 45.
[6n15]   15. Ibid, 56.
[6n16]   16. Ibid, 57.
[6n17]   17. Ayn Rand, *Capitalism: The Unknown Ideal* (New York: New American Library, 1967).
[6n18]   18. For instance, atheists use the Kantian subjectivist principle to deny the objective reality of God's creation.
[6n19]   19. Dugin, *The Fourth Political Theory*, 71.

20. Dugin, *Eurasian Mission*, 147.
21. Ibid, 148.
22. Ibid, 46.
23. Dugin, *The Fourth Political Theory*, 148–49.
24. Ibid, 72–73.
25. Aleksandr Dugin, *Last War of the World-Island* (London: Arktos, 2015), 76.
26. Dugin, *Eurasian Mission*, 91–92.
27. Dugin, *The Fourth Political Theory*, 74.
28. Steven R. Mann, "Chaos Theory and Strategic Thought," *Parameters* (US Army War College Quarterly) 22 (1992).
29. Dugin, *The Fourth Political Theory*, 113–14.
30. Ibid, 163–64.
31. Ibid, 164–65.
32. Dugin, *Eurasian Mission*, 120.
33. Dugin, *The Fourth Political Theory*, 193.
34. Ibid, 194.
35. Dugin, *Eurasian Mission*, 72.
36. Ibid, 35.
37. Ivo Daalder, "The End of Atlanticism." *Survival* 45, no. 2 (2003): 149.
38. Ibid, 153.
39. Dugin, *Eurasian Mission*, 35.
40. Ibid, 42–43.
41. Ibid, 43.
42. Ibid, 135.
43. Dugin, *The Rise of the Fourth Political Theory*, 22.
44. Ibid, 23.
45. Ibid, 25–26.
46. In the European case, the ideas of progress and modernization spread from Western Europe to the rest of the continent either peacefully or after traumatic events like revolutions and wars. It is a historical fact that liberal or socialist ideas found it harder to penetrate the traditional and conservative environment of Central and Eastern Europe, at least until the aftermath of World War One.
47. Dugin, *The Rise of the Fourth Political Theory*, 27.
48. Ibid, 30.
49. Ibid, 32.
50. Ibid, 35.
51. Gilles Deleuze, *The Logic of Sense* (New York: Columbia University Press, 1993).
52. Dugin, *The Rise of the Fourth Political Theory*, 40.
53. Francis Fukuyama, *Our Post-Human Future: Consequences of the Biotechnology Revolution* (New York: Farrar Strauss & Giroux, 2002).
54. Robert Kagan, *Of Paradise and Power: America and Europe in the New World Order* (New York: Vintage Books, 2004).
55. Dugin, *The Rise of the Fourth Political Theory*, 187–88.
56. Ibid, 186.

[6n20]
[6n21]
[6n22]
[6n23]
[6n24]
[6n25]
[6n26]
[6n27]
[6n28]
[6n29]
[6n30]
[6n31]
[6n32]
[6n33]
[6n34]
[6n35]
[6n36]
[6n37]
[6n38]
[6n39]
[6n40]
[6n41]
[6n42]
[6n43]
[6n44]
[6n45]
[6n46]
[6n47]
[6n48]
[6n49]
[6n50]
[6n51]
[6n52]
[6n53]
[6n54]
[6n55]
[6n56]

Chapter Seven

The Eurasianist Vision of Global Order

The Quest for a Multipolar World

[7.0]   INTRODUCTION

[7.1]   In this chapter we will examine the Eurasianist project for the construction of a future multipolar global order. The Eurasian vision of multi-polarity entails several steps including the advent of a multipolar world order, the rediscovery of the Russian geopolitical mission, and the foundation of integrated geo-economic zones and big spaces founded on civilizational blocs. In international relations, the main goals of the International Eurasian Movement are the struggle for a multipolar world based on the cooperation of different peoples and civilizations for peace and mutual prosperity; a close partnership between European and Asiatic countries, with Russia playing the part of primary mediator; the integration of the post-Soviet space into a united Eurasian polity; the improvement of multilateral dialogue between traditional confessions and ethnic groups; the preservation of the cultural, religious, and ethnic identities of nations; the construction of a global enduring peace based on the principles of multipolarity, sovereignty, and identity; and the opposition towards unipolar and unidimensional globalism, terrorism, drug trafficking, ecological and demographic catastrophes.[1] According to Eurasianists, multipolarity would not imply a clash of civilizations, but the only instrument to grant a long-lasting world peace.

THE OVERCOMING OF THE UNIPOLAR ORDER [7.2]

From the point of view of international relations, neo-Eurasianism questions [7.3]
both the existing order of nation-states based on the principle of national
sovereignty and the American-led globalist project. Eurasianists claim that
the Westphalian system—which shaped the modern-day system of international relations basing it on the principles of sovereignty and territorial integrity—no longer corresponds to the current global balance of powers.[2] In fact,
the appearance of new actors of trans-national and sub-national nature would
imply the need for the creation of a new paradigm in international relations.
According to Eurasianists, one of the chief features that will characterize the
future of international relations will be the dichotomy between globalism and
regionalism. The question they raise is whether the upcoming world order
will fully implement the globalist project through the creation of a single
world government, whether it will maintain the current status quo of unfin-
ished globalism, or whether regionalist tendencies will eventually prevail and
form several geo-economic and geopolitical blocs.

The shape of the future global order will considerably depend on the [7.4]
United States' projection of international power. Nowadays, while other
international actors are rising, the US is experiencing a decrease of its global
imperial rule and must face many worrisome challenges. Recent studies suggest that the rise of new international actors is reshaping the nature of international relations. For instance, the book *Post-Western World*[3] introduces
some innovative arguments regarding the future of world politics from a
quite uncommon perspective for Western mainstream analyses. The chief
thesis of the research claims that the understanding of the creation of today's
international order is limited, since it depicts a post-Western world from a
closed-minded Western-centric standpoint. In this context, non-Western actors are barely perceived as constructive rule-makers and institution-builders,
because the West is widely conceived as the sole actor entitled to enhance the
norms by which the international system is disciplined. However, the author
suggests that the study of the future's world order needs to undertake the
inevitability of a bipolarization between the United States and China or even
of a multipolarization given by the rise of BRICS countries. The end of the
unipolar world—which represents a historical fact—implies a more overarching international analysis that overcomes the traditional Western-centric
perspective and a more balanced reading of the distribution of global power.
The chief aim of the work is to show on one hand that most observers—both
Western and anti-Western—tend to exaggerate the role the West has played
in the past and, on the other, to discuss on how to adapt to a multipolar world
order. Some of the key arguments that can be found in the book are the
following. First, a Western-centric worldview tends to underestimate the role
that non-Western actors have played in the past and play in contemporary

international politics, but also the constructive role they are likely to play in the future. The book argues that a post-Western order will not necessarily be more violent than today's global order.

[7.5]   Second, the economic rise of the rest, specifically China, will allow it to enhance its military capacity and to increase its international influence and soft power—since soft power is easy to generate from a large hard power base.

[7.6]   Third, emerging powers are crafting a parallel international order, with several institutions and international regimes that represent an alternative to Western-led ones.[4] The book argues that, rather than directly confronting existing institutions, rising powers—primarily China—are quietly building a parallel global order that will initially complement today's international institutions.

[7.7]   Finally, the creation of new parallel institutions is the main strategy that non-Western actors use to better project their power. This alternative order is already in the making, but its structures do not emerge because China and others bear new ideas on how to address global challenges, but rather they create them to project their power, emulating what the West has already done before. The book claims that, as part of a heading strategy, China-led emerging powers will continue to invest in existing institutions and embrace most elements of today's "liberal hierarchical order," but they will seek to obtain the "hegemonic principles" so far only enjoyed by the United States. The creation of several China-centric institutions will allow China to embrace its own type of competitive multilateralism, picking and choosing among flexible frameworks, in accordance with its national interests, thus slowly institutionalizing its own exceptionalism and enhancing its policies autonomously by becoming increasingly immune to Western threats of exclusion.

[7.8]   Moreover, the book *The Post-American World*[5] argues that the United States remains a political and military superpower, but in every other dimension—industrial, financial, educational, social, and cultural—the distribution of power is shifting away from American authority. With the rise of China, India and other emerging markets, with economic growth sweeping much of the planet, and the world becoming increasingly decentralized and interconnected, the world is moving into a post-American environment defined and directed from different geographical areas and by numerous actors.

[7.9]   The author claims that today the world is experiencing the third great tectonic power shift that occurred over the last five hundred years: the first was the rise of the West, which produced modernity through science and technology, commerce and capitalism, and the agricultural and industrial revolutions. The second was the rise of the United States in the 20th century after the two world wars. The third is what the author calls "the rise of the rest," with China and India becoming mighty powers in their neighborhoods and beyond, Russia reasserting its international role, and the European Union transforming into a commercial and economic giant.

Paradoxically, the "rise of the rest" is largely a result of American ideas [7.10] and actions. It was the United States that pushed countries to open their markets, democratize their politics, and embrace the idea of free trade and technological development. It was the American socio-economic model that helped emerging countries to adopt capitalism and to compete in the global economy, freeing up their currencies, and developing new industries.

The book *The End of American World Order* affirms that the rise of a [7.11] non-US-led global order is imminent.[6] It argues its thesis through three chief points. First, the United States' liberal hegemonic order is already over, the unipolar moment has come to an end, and America no longer finds itself in a hegemonic position. Second, the rising powers—primarily the BRICS—cannot alone provide global governance due to their lack of inner cohesion and coherence, and therefore they will have to cooperate with Western established powers. Finally, the emerging world order will be multipolar, with two or three major powers, but will also be characterized by complex interdependence.

Moreover, some claim that the future scenario will be that of a G-Zero [7.12] world in which no country will possess real leadership.[7] In other words, nobody will replace the United States in terms of leadership, but the US will no longer be the sole global leader. Nowadays, he affirms, the world is facing a transition—or an inter-regnum—and it is unclear where this process will bring.

On the other hand, the book *The Future of Power* introduces the idea that [7.13] the future of international relations will be played simultaneously on three levels—or chessboards:[8] the military, the economic, and the transnational. The European Union will bear the economic and transnational (diffused) power, China the military and economic one, and the US all three. The fact that the US can combine all levels of power makes it a so-called "smart power."

According to neo-con realists, until the international system will be led by [7.14] the US it will be sustainable, but if the US will decline, the system will automatically collapse.[9]

Besides, Dugin states that today, in order to contrast its resizing in the [7.15] international scenario, the United States could proceed in three different ways.[10] First, the United States could create an American Empire *stricto sensu*, with a highly integrated and technically developed central area, or imperial core—i.e, the Atlanticist region with North America and Western Europe—,[11] and a vast world periphery kept separated and fragmented in a condition of permanent unrest: this project would be largely endorsed by neoconservatives. Second, the United States could create a multilateral unipolarity where it would cooperate with other friendly powers and allies—

Canada, Europe, Australia, New Zealand, Japan, South Korea, Israel, Arab allies,[12] etc.—in resolving regional issues and putting pressure on so-called "rogue states"—Iran, Syria, Venezuela, Belarus, North Korea—, or averting other powers from attaining regional independence and hegemony—e.g. China and Russia. Third, the United States could promote an accelerated globalization that would lead to the abolition of nation-states and the creation of a world government ruled by the global elite. One of the most effective practices to destabilize and extinguish states would be, for instance, the funding of rebellious groups and uprisings to overthrow leaders perceived by the promoters of liberal democracy as authoritarian.[13]

[7.16]   Dugin believes that the United States often seems to be promoting all three strategies at the same time, as part of a multi-vector foreign policy. However, the American-centric world perspective, despite being the most significant and dominant global tendency, is not the only one possible. On the contrary, several alternative visions exist that depict world order from a non-American point of view.

[7.17]   The first group of alter-globalists includes nation-states that wish to maintain their independence and sovereignty and are not willing to devolve their power to a supranational exterior authority neither in the form of open American hegemony, nor in the Western-centric forms of world government or global governance, nor in the disordered dissolution of a chaotic international system characterized by failed states. This category includes countries like China, Russia, Iran, India, and several South American, African, and Islamic states. The position these countries share is to avert a loss of sovereignty and to resist the main trends of the global American-centric geopolitical arrangement, or adapt to it so that it would be possible to avoid the logical consequences of its success either through an imperialist or globalist strategy.[14] Albeit united in leaning against the wind of the loss of sovereignty, generally these countries lack concrete alternative visions of the future international order or, when they have some, they are unable or unwilling to combine them into a common strategy. In other words, what they share is the will to preserve the international status quo as enshrined in the United Nations' Charter and thus keep their own sovereignty and identity as nation-states in their present form, modernizing according to an internal developmental path. The category of nation-states that seek to preserve their sovereignty vis-à-vis US/Western hegemonic or globalist strategies can be divided in four subcategories:

[7.18]   1. Nation-states that try to adapt their societies to Western standards and to maintain friendly relations with the West and the United States, but that avoid direct and complete de-sovereignization. Some examples are India, Turkey, Brazil and somewhat Russia and Kazakhstan;

2. Nation-states that are willing to cooperate with the United States, but under the condition of non-interference and meddling in their domestic affairs. These nations include Saudi Arabia and Pakistan; [7.19]

3. Nation-states that, while collaborating with the United States, preserve strictly the uniqueness of their society by filtering those elements of Western culture that are compatible with their internal culture from those that are incompatible, and that try to gain more national independence and strength through the cooperation with the West. This restrained cooperative attitude is typical of China and Russia; [7.20]

4. Nation-states that oppose the US and the West directly, rejecting *in toto* Western values, culture, unipolarity, and hegemony. Among these countries are Iran, Venezuela, and North Korea. [7.21]

The second group consists of non-state actors or theories that oppose American hegemony and dominance due to ideological, religious, philosophical, or cultural reasons. These actors differ from one another and vary from state to state. Some are bearers of a religious belief that is incompatible with the secular doctrine of Americanization, Westernization, and globalization. In this sense, amongst the most significant are some Islamic integralist groups—mostly Sunni—which aspire to forge a universal Islamic state in the form of a Caliphate ruled by the sharia law. However, also integralist Christian and Jewish movements and sects tend to consider their faith as irreconcilable with Western modernism and secularism. Some others believe in the theory of transnational neo-socialism as represented by the South American Left and by Chavism, which merges the Marxist criticism to capitalism with nationalist emotivity and rhetoric. The supporters of Chavism and neo-socialism reject the principles of capitalism, imperialism, and neo-colonialism that they believe characterize the United States and the West. The imperialism of Western countries would represent what Lenin considered the highest stage of capitalism,[15] and the major cause of underdevelopment and dependence of poor countries. Others believe instead in the principle of racial superiority—like white supremacists and neo-Nazis—and therefore strongly reject the American and European cosmopolitan model of interracial mixing, multiculturalism, and loss of ethnic identity. These groups often believe in conspiracy theories like the one that suggests that the American world order, chiefly headed by the Jews or the freemasons, is aimed at extinguishing the white race. Finally, others—like the Eurasianists—uphold the theory of multipolarity, proposing an alternative model of world order based on the paradigm of unique civilizations, big spaces, and empires. The latter project presupposes the creation of different transnational political, strategic, and economic entities united regionally by a community of common geographic areas and shared religious or cultural values. These entities should consist of states integrated along regionalist lines and epitomize the poles of the multi- [7.22] polar world. Examples of it are the European Union and the Eurasian Economic Union; other possible entities could be an Islamic Union, a South American-Bolivarian Union, a Chinese Union, an Indian Union, and a Pan-Pacific Union are other possibilities. [16]

[7.23]   The multipolar world that Eurasianists envision is founded on civilizational "large spaces." In Dugin's lexicon, a "large space" signifies a common geopolitical, territorial, and cultural civilization. The "large space" differs from other existing national governments since it is built on the foundation of a common value system and historical kinship, merging a multitude of different governments tied together by a "community of fate." In the "large spaces," the integrating factor can vary; sometimes being religion; sometimes ethnicity, culture; socio-political tradition or geographic position. [17]

[7.24]   An example of such space is represented by the supra-national political and economic organization of the European Union, which is a prototype of "internal globalization" that includes in its boundaries countries and peoples that share a common culture, history, religion, and system of values. Dugin upholds the idea that the creation of a European Union demonstrates that the incarnation of the "large space" in practice, the transition from a government to a supra-governmental apparatus grounded on the foundation of civilizational commonality is possible, constructive and real. [18]

[7.25]   In his famous book *The Clash of Civilizations*, Samuel Huntington suggested the existence of nine different civilizations: Western, Chinese/Confucian, Buddhist, Japanese, Islamic, Indian, Orthodox, Latin American, and African. [19] This register appears quite reductive and sometimes too approximate. First, the idea that the Western civilization represents a unique bloc does not consider the fact that Europe possesses different identities—a Euro-Atlanticist, a continental, and a Eurasian—and that the interests and values of North America do not always coincide with European ones. Second, despite Huntington's correct claim that the Islamic civilization does not enjoy a leading country, [20] it is underestimated the inner cleavage between Sunni and Shia. The Orthodox civilization appears like a big lot that includes countries that should more properly belong to the Western civilization—e.g. Greece—and others that, albeit formerly Soviet, should belong to the Islamic one—e.g. Kazakhstan. Moreover, Huntington establishes strict borders between the zones of influence of Chinese and Japanese civilization in the Pacific region even though their civilizational identity remains open to a significant degree. Finally, the separation of Tibet from China seems more a political provocation against Beijing rather than a truly civilizational scheme.

[7.26]   Nevertheless, by affirming that the clash of civilizations would occur more likely within those countries that included or bordered two or more different civilizations, Huntington correctly predicted several international crises like the secessionist wars in former Yugoslavia, the secession of South Sudan, the conflict in Ukraine, and so on.

The main difference between Huntington's civilizational idea and the   [7.27]
Eurasianist one is that for Eurasianists the existence of civilizational blocs
would avoid clashes between nations rather than encourage them and that a
multipolar world would ensure peace in an easier way than a unipolar Western-led one. In other words, Eurasianists believe that civilizations would not
declare war one another when enjoying self-government and full sovereignty. Dugin summarizes his view on the multi-polar ideal in the following
terms:

> "We shall have a model with the availability of 'regional universalism' [like   [7.28]
> the European Union] in concrete 'large spaces', which will give to enormous
> zones and significant segments of humanity an unavoidable social dynamic,
> characteristic of globalization and openness, but without those shortcomings
> that globalization has taken on a global scale."[21]

Dugin believes that today the Western world is divided into two components: [7.29]
the first is the Atlanticist, formed by the United States and the United Kingdom and based on the Anglo-Saxon culture, which could not be integrated in
the Eurasian project; the other is the continental-European component,
formed by France, Germany, Italy, and Spain and based on the Roman-
Germanic tradition, which could be potentially integrated.

RUSSIA'S GEOPOLITICAL MISSION   [7.30]
IN A HISTORICAL PERSPECTIVE

Russian geopolitics can be better understood through a deep study of Russian   [7.31]
society, history, and geography. Geographical determinism is perhaps the
main key to comprehend the guidelines of Russia's foreign policy and of its
power projection. A comprehensive understanding of Russia's geopolitical
mission cannot be separated from the examination of the geographical structure of the Russian territories—both contemporary and historical. Classical
geopolitics, both Anglo-Saxon (Mackinder, Mahan) and continental-European (Haushofer, Schmitt) offered fundamental incentives for the edification
of Russian geopolitics. Russia has assimilated the notions of classical geopolitical theorists applying them to its own reality and shaping them to its own
history and culture: it can be stated that Russia's geopolitical perception
depends on the position of the Russian observer and interpreter of classical
geopolitical theories.[22] The Russian geopolitician views himself not as a
neutral observer, but as a witness embedded in a specific historical and
spatial context. This "geopolitical apperception" consists in the ability to
recognize the entirety of geopolitical factors consciously, with a clear understanding of both one's subjective position and the regularities of the perceived structures.[23] The geopolitician is an advocate of his national interest

and an analyst of geo-strategic *constants* that historically characterize his society.

[7.32]   Geopolitics interprets the world through the fundamental cleavage between thalassocratic power and tellurocratic power. As already said, Sir Halford Mackinder called these two expressions of global rule respectively "the seaman's point of view" and "the landsman's point of view."[24] In this division, Russia embodies the perfect example of tellurocratic power. Classical geopolitics considers the territory of the former Russian Empire and Soviet Union the land-based (telluric) core of the entire Eurasian continent, which Mackinder initially called "the geographical pivot of history" and later "the Heartland." This Eurasian core territory is a typical geopolitical concept whose intrinsic geographic and strategic relevance transcends the nation that controls it—be it Russia, Germany, or the ancient Mongol Empire of Genghis Khan. It bears a "spatial meaning"—or *"Raumsinn"* in Friedrich Ratzel's terminology—[25] , which can become the heritage of the society located in this vast territory. Russia's eastward expansion towards Siberia and Central Asia between the 16th–19th centuries had meant the shift of the Eurasian Heartland under Russian control. This led to the identification of Russian society with the civilization of Land, or tellurocracy: Russian geopolitics is by definition the geopolitics of the Heartland and of land-based power.[26]

[7.33]   The long historical development that characterized medieval and modern Russia, which lasted centuries, brought the country at each stage closer and closer to becoming an expression of tellurocratic power. Previously, the Eastern-Slavic peoples and Kievan Rus' represented the outskirts of the Orthodox, Eastern Christian civilization in the sphere of influence of the Byzantine Empire. However, two major events transformed Russian identity, shifting its pole from Eastern Europe to Eurasia: the Mongol invasion and the fall of Byzantium. After the invasion of the Mongols, Rus' was included in the Eurasian geopolitical construct of the land-based, nomadic empire of Genghis Khan and of its western heirs of the Golden Horde. Then, the Ottoman conquest of Constantinople in 1453 and the weakening of the Golden Horde transformed the Muscovite Czardom into the heir of two traditions: the political and religious Byzantine one, with the myth of Moscow as "the Third Rome" and as the continuer of the Roman imperial and Orthodox-Christian civilization, and the Eurasianist imperial one, which passed to the Russian princes—and later to the czars—from the Mongolic khaganates. From then on, all the chief geopolitical force-lines of Russian foreign policy had only one aim: the integration of the Heartland and the strengthening of its influence in Northeastern Eurasia, until the shores of the Pacific Ocean. The spatial enlargement of Russian control over Eurasian territory expanded gradually, until Russia occupied the entire Heartland and the areas adjoining it.[27] In pursuing its geopolitical mission of Eurasian unification, Russia found an obstacle in the aggressive adversary of Western Europe—or, more precisely, the Anglo-Saxon world—, incarnated from the 18th century by Great Britain and later, in the 20th, by the rising power of the United States, which was in process of realizing its role as "civilization of the Sea," or thalassocracy. Eurasianists believe that this duel characterized by direct or indirect warfare for the control of the World-Island (Eurasia) between Russia and England—and later the US—, which lasted two centuries and would somewhat still be taking place, which some called "the great war of continents"[28] or simply "Great Game,"[29] unfolds the geopolitical logic and key reading of world history.

Today, the Russian Federation is the natural heir to the preceding historical and political forms that took shape around the territory of the Northern Eurasian landmass, from Kievan Rus', through the Golden Horde, the Muscovite Czardom, the Russian Empire, and to the Soviet Union: in this sense, the Russian Federation represents a geopolitical continuity with its historical past. The large territorial extensions and the imperial, centralized form of government made Russia a civilization of the continental type, similarly to Prussia/Germany, Austria-Hungary, Persia, or China. Continental civilizations often share some fundamental features, among which the ideas of conservatism, traditionalism, collective identity, idealism, faithfulness, spirituality, honor, loyalty, discipline, and militarism. On the other hand, islander societies would be generally characterized by liberalism, rationalism, progressivism, trade, individualism, and more democratic forms of government. [7.34]

Geopolitically, the fact that Russia constitutes the Heartland makes its sovereignty a global issue, since its major international rivals are aware of the Heartland's relevance for ruling the World-Island, as Mackinder had originally highlighted. Therefore, despite its political-economic arrangement—imperial, communist, or democratic—, Russia would be doomed to clash with the civilization of the Sea, represented today by the United States and its European (NATO) and Asian (Japan, Australia, South Korea, etc.) allies and the unipolar American-centric world order: [7.35]

> "Geopolitical dualism has nothing in common with the ideological or economic peculiarities of this or that country. A global geopolitical conflict unfolded between the Russian Empire and the British monarchy, between the socialist camp and the capitalist camp. Today, during the age of the democratic republican arrangement, the same conflict is unfolding between democratic Russia and the bloc of the democratic countries of NATO treading upon it. *Geopolitical regularities lie deeper than political-ideological contradictions or similarities.*"[30]   [7.36]

Moreover, in geopolitical terms, in the same way that the United States is more than just North America, but rather a big space with areas of influence in the Pacific and Atlantic Oceans and in the entire Western Hemisphere, Russia is something more than just the Russian Federation in its current [7.37] administrative borders, since the Eurasian civilization, established around the Heartland, is much broader than contemporary Russia. Consequently, Russia's global geopolitical strategy consists of completely integrating Eurasia around its Heartland core.

[7.38]   In the 20th century, the tellurocratic nature of Russia was confirmed by the October Bolshevik Revolution of 1917. This fact became clear with the shift of the capital city from Saint Petersburg—a maritime city—to Moscow—a continental one. Geopolitically, whereas the czar Nicholas II, the liberal-democrats, the bourgeois parties, and the Socialist Revolutionaries where in favor of the Entente, and therefore indorsed thalassocracy, the Bolsheviks pursued a policy of cooperation with the Central Powers, especially with Germany, and thus expressed to be in favor of tellurocracy. The Bolshevik propensity for land-based power materialized with the friendly orientation towards Germany—which culminated with the conclusion of the Brest-Litovsk Treaty—,[31] with the rejection of the bourgeois capitalistic order based on trade and the free market—which distinguishes thalassocracy—, and with the hostility towards the thalassocratic Triple Entente. Later, during the Civil War, Bolsheviks controlled inner-continental zones (the Heartland), whilst the Whites—supported by Western sea powers and Japan—kept under control Russia's periphery and coastal zones. This showed clearly enough that the fight between the Reds and the Whites meant more than an ideological struggle, but it rather embodied the contraposition between land-based geopolitical power and coastal-projected power.

[7.39]   It was within the context of the Russian Civil War that Sir Halford Mackinder—at the time British High Commissioner for Southern Russia in support of the Whites—developed the idea of *cordon sanitaire*—or 'quarantine line'—, which would be one of the main pillars of the international order created after the Treaty of Versailles, separating Germany from Russia through the creation of buffer states in Eastern Europe so to avoid a pan-Eurasian union and a future war between the two countries:

[7.40]   "In the era of the Civil War, we see a phenomenon that is highly symbolic and important for geopolitics. In 1919, the founding father of geopolitics, Halford Mackinder, was appointed British High Commissioner for southern Russia and was sent through Eastern Europe to support the anti-Bolshevist forces led by General Denikin. This mission allowed Mackinder to give his recommendations about geopolitics in Eastern Europe to the British government, which laid the foundations for his book, *Democratic Ideals and Reality*. Mackinder called on Great Britain to strengthen its support for the White armies in the south of Russia and to involve the anti-Bolshevist and anti-Russian regimes of Poland, Bulgaria, and Romania for this purpose. In his negotiations with Denikin, they were in agreement about the separation from Russia of the southern and western regions and the South Caucasus, for the creation of a pro-English buffer state. Mackinder's analysis of the state of affairs in Russia during the Civil

War was absolutely unequivocal: he saw in the Bolsheviks the forces of the Heartland, destined either to bear a Communist ideological form or to cede the initiative to Germany. England could allow neither. So Mackinder offered to support the Whites however he could and to dismember Russia. It is important to note what countries he tried to establish under the purview of a nominally integral (for that period) government: Belarus, Ukraine, Yugorussia (under the primary influence of pro-British Poland), Dagestan (including the entire North Caucasus), Armenia, Azerbaijan, and Georgia. These countries were to be a *cordon sanitaire* between continental Russia and its neighboring regions, Germany in the west, and Turkey and Iran in the south."[32]

At the same time, Major General Aleksey Yefimovich Vandam (Edrikhin), one of the heralds of Russian Eurasian continental geopolitics, became the Russian counterpart of Mackinder's geopolitical visions, promoting a rigid anti-English and pro-tellurocratic position.[33] [7.41]

During the entire course of the Civil War, all military actions took place according to the scheme of the "Red core" (Heartland) against the "White periphery" along the borders of the sea. It is quite clear that this gruesome struggle represented a mortal combat for holding the Heartland, and, in perspective, for controlling the World-Island. [7.42]

At that time, thalassocracy and tellurocracy were struggling against each other in two Eurasian neighboring theaters of war: in the north, in core Russia, were the Bolsheviks, fighting against the Whites and the Western interventionists; in the south, in Anatolia, were the Kemalists, carrying out their continental geopolitics against Greece and its thalassic allies. Both telluric powers came out as winners of the combat. [7.43]

The end of World War One and the Treaty of Versailles produced a new balance of power. After demolishing German continental power and isolating Bolshevik Russia, the geopolitics of the Versailles peace resulted in the triumph of thalassocracy. The postwar arrangement focused on the global interests of sea powers, principally the British Empire, which was recognized as the only lawful proprietor of the world's oceans. At this point, the main duty—as Mackinder pointed out—was to avert the rise of Bolshevist Russia and revanchist Germany and to foreclose any future strategic alliance between them. The mean to avoid a Russo-German entente was to create—as seen—a *cordon sanitaire* out of existing or newly established Eastern European states oriented towards Britain and France that would separate, for better or for worse, Germany from Russia. [7.44]

The other then-emerging thalassocratic power to gain an enormous success from victory was the United States. President Woodrow Wilson upheld Mahan's idea of American global oceanic power. The Wilson Doctrine auspicated the end of American isolationism and non-interference in European affairs, as well as an active policy on a planetary scale under the leadership of sea-based (Anglo-Saxon) civilization. From this moment, the gradual shift of [7.45] the center of gravity from Great Britain to the US began. The birth of an Anglo-Saxon American-British axis systematized geopolitical Atlanticism. Altanticism was formalized by institutions like the Council on Foreign Relations (CFR), which became one of the most important landmarks in the formation of American foreign policy on a global scale in the thalassocratic spirit.

[7.46]   Notwithstanding, on the side of the vanquished, the German geopolitical school—whose main exponent, as seen, was Karl Haushofer—began to analyze the aftermath of the Treaty of Versailles in the spirit of Mackinder's method, but from the German point of view. In the 1920s and 1930s, Haushofer considered the solutions that could lead Germany to a future rebirth and to overcome the shameful conditions of the Versailles *Diktat*. From a geopolitical perspective, a promising resolution was the creation of the "continental bloc," which represented an alliance of land-based, continental, tellurocratic states—i.e. Germany and Russia—with the addition of Japan, an emerging thalassocratic power with a growing continental bridgehead in the Far East (Korea, Manchuria, etc.). Haushofer and the other German geopoliticians of the Munich School made use of Mackinder's theories for the sake of defeated Germany, auspicating what Mackinder wished to avoid: the unification of Central Europe (Greater Germany) with Eurasia (Greater Russia). The *Kontinentalblock* project—which eventually failed after Hitler's decision to invade the Soviet Union—appeared like a large-scale response to the strategy of the Atlanticists and geopoliticians of the thalassocratic creed, first and foremost Mahan and Mackinder.[34]

[7.47]   In 1922, after winning the Civil War, Bolshevik Russia formalized itself in the Union of Soviet Socialist Republics (USSR): since then, the Russian borders expanded step-by-step in Eastern Europe, the Caucasus, and Central Asia, reuniting most of the lands of the former Russian Empire and gathering them around the Heartland, which maintained the form of geopolitical core.

[7.48]   Finally, under Stalin's rule, Soviet Russia became a full-fledged tellurocracy, appearing like a new version of the great Turanic Eurasian empire of Genghis Khan, the core of land-based civilization.[35] In Carl Schmitt's terms, the consolidation of the USSR and the rise of the Anglo-Saxon thalassocracies was the manifestation of the most important and perhaps culminating phase of the "great war of continents," the struggle between the land-based Behemoth and the sea-based Leviathan. Stalin's Soviet Union sustained and developed the geopolitical progressions of a land-based civilization on a formerly unparalleled scale, forming anew the state of the Great Turan; this time, the great Eurasian pancontinental spirit was hidden under the guise of the theory of socialism. As already noticed, this process was exemplified by the transfer of the Soviet capital from Saint Petersburg/Leningrad to Moscow. Also, the Third International—*Komintern* in abbreviated form—

(1919–1943) represented the geopolitical tool for the propagation of land-based telluric Russian influence all over the world.

In the 1930s, with the gradual revision of the Versailles status quo, the world was ruled by a new balance of power that presented four poles. The first pole was the Eurasian great-continental USSR that ruled the Heartland, the core of the global continental force. The second was the thalassocratic alliance of Great Britain, France, and the US, which included those allied countries of Eastern Europe that belonged to the *cordon sanitaire* (e.g. Poland) and to the Little Entente (Czechoslovakia, Romania, Yugoslavia). The third was the Central European tellurocratic Nazi Germany and its future allies (Fascist Italy and signatory countries of the Tripartite Pact). Finally, the fourth pole was Japan, aligned with Germany, in search for land-bases in China and East Asia. [7.49]

This quadripolar world could develop into three possible scenarios. First, in the realization of the continental bloc following Haushofer's model. In this case, the Axis and the USSR, which would join the Tripartite Pact, would form a pan-Eurasian empire that would project power from the Atlantic Ocean to the Pacific Ocean. Consequently, the thalassic powers of Great Britain and the US would be isolated in the outer periphery of the world. The Molotov-Ribbentrop Pact (August 1939) was a step toward such an alliance. [7.50]

Second, the Axis would align with Western powers against the USSR. This circumstance would most likely create the conditions for a Soviet defeat and a partition of Russia-Eurasia amongst the victors. The Munich Agreement (September 1938), which represented the apex of the appeasement policy towards Hitler, was a step in this direction. [7.51]

Finally, the third scenario would be that of an alliance of the Western powers with the USSR against the Axis. Eventually, Hitler's aggression against Poland and the Japanese attack against the US at Pearl Harbor would make Western powers opt for the strategic alliance with the Soviet "enemy": [7.52]

> "Thus, the representatives of three geopolitical powers and three ideologies clashed against each other in the Second World War. The Heartland was represented by Soviet Russia, Stalin, and socialism (Marxism). The sea power, in the coalition of England, the USA and France, was united under a liberal bourgeois-democratic ideology. The continental power of Europe (Central Europe) was represented by the Axis countries (the Third Reich, Fascist Italy and their satellites) and by the ideology of the "Third Way" (National Socialism, Fascism, and Japanese samurai traditionalism)."[36] [7.53]

After World War Two, the world's geopolitical map shifted from a tripolar to a bipolar one. The bipolar world created after the Yalta Conference saw the final assertion of American-English thalassocracy—ideologically exemplified by liberal-democracy—on one side and of Soviet tellurocracy—ideologically exemplified by socialism—on the other. In geopolitical terms, a [7.54] planetary balance occurred between the global thalassocratic and capitalist West and the global tellurocratic and communist East.

[7.55]   Many geopolitical analysts investigated the postwar balance of power and the structure of borders between the Western and Eastern worlds, among whom Jean Thiriart, founder of the movement "*Jeune Europe*." The Belgian political scientist noticed that the structural borders between the Western and Eastern blocs, passing through the divided European space was remarkably advantageous for the United States and to the same degree disadvantageous for the Soviet Union.[37] The advantages of the US were given by several favorable circumstances, among which its safe position secured by the oceans, and the disadvantages of the USSR by elements like the difficulty to protect land-based borders not connected to natural obstacles. The disadvantages for the USSR were due to the fact that the security and defense of land-based borders is extremely difficult, expensive, and resource-consuming, especially in the case when the border is not connected by natural obstacles such as mountains and river basins and when both sides of the border are not ethnically, culturally, and religiously homogeneous: "The border between the countries of the Warsaw Pact, a continuation of the USSR and a continental tellurocracy, was such a border. By contrast, the USA was safely secured by the oceans that surround its borders, which do not demand large resources or expenses to defend and permit focus on other strategic problems."[38]

[7.56]   Given these circumstances, in the early 1950s, the Soviet government elaborated plans for the "Finlandization" of Europe, through the creation of governments in Eastern and Central Europe that would be neutral toward the USSR and NATO—but the creation of the Warsaw Pact alliance in contraposition to NATO made this plan fail.

[7.57]   At the end of the 1960s, Thiriart proposed his famous Eurasian project with the creation of a Euro-Soviet empire "from Vladivostok to Dublin" and the expansion of the Warsaw bloc to the shores of the Atlantic.[39]

[7.58]   From a geopolitical point of view, the Cold War represented nothing more, on one hand, than the US-NATO attempt to enclose the Rimland, encircling the Heartland, and, on the other, the USSR attempt to break this encirclement and project its power onto the Rimland and the warm seas. The Cold War officially began in 1947, when the American diplomat George F. Kennan openly called for the containment of the USSR. The containment strategy suggested by Kennan and supported by President Truman was aimed at the asphyxiation of the Soviet Union by enclosing the coastal zones of Eurasia; by contrast, the Soviets responded to this strategy trying to break the US-NATO control over the World-Island's coastal zone of the Rimland. Dugin affirms that Kennan, following the ideas of Mackinder, Spykman, and Strausz-Hupé, elaborated a model of a configuration of global zones controlled by the US, that would lead America to the domination of Eurasia. This strategy was based on the asphyxiation of the USSR in the inner-continental space of Eurasia and the restriction and blockade of Soviet influence worldwide. The main strategy consisted in enclosing the coastal zone (Rimland) within itself, under the control of the US, from Western Europe through the Middle East and Central Asia to the Far East, India, Indochina and Japan. The USSR reacted to this strategy trying to break the control of the US and NATO over the coastal zone (Rimland). Evidence of this reaction occurred during the confrontation between the US and the USSR at the time of Vietnam, the Korean War, and the Chinese Revolution. Moreover, the USSR also supported socialist tendencies in the Islamic world, in particular "Arab socialism"—like Nasser's Egypt and the Ba'athist regimes of Iraq and Syria— and gave support to pro-Soviet Communist parties in Western Europe. Therefore, per Dugin, the great war of the civilization of the Sea and the civilization of Land was also carried to the continents of Africa and Latin America, specifically in Angola, Ethiopia, Somalia, and Mozambique (Afrocommunism) and, in Latin America, in Cuba and in the powerful communist movements in Chile, Argentina, Peru, and Venezuela.[40]

This chief global strategy of the bipolar world would not lead—luckily— to an open generalized conflict between the two superpowers also due to nuclear deterrence and the so-called equilibrium of terror.[41]   [7.59]

During the Cold War, land power reached its historical maximum thanks   [7.60]
to Soviet superpower represented by the USSR and the aligned countries of the Warsaw Pact; Eurasia became a world empire, spreading the networks of its influence on a global scale, from Latin America to East Asia. The world was therefore divided into two rival political blocs—the civilization of Land against the civilization of Sea—and a non-aligned neutral one.[42]

The bipolar world conceived at the Yalta Conference[43] and fixed at the   [7.61]
Potsdam Conference[44] became the basic model of international relations from the 1950s until the demise of the Soviet Union in 1991.

The first Soviet leader to rule the newly founded and consolidated Eur-   [7.62]
asian empire—from Berlin to the Pacific Ocean—was Stalin. Under his guidance, a steady Eurasian geopolitical policy was deliberately implemented. Pro-Soviet tendencies throughout the world were encouraged and supported.

Later, under Khrushchëv, the Cuban crisis[45] broke out as a consequence   [7.63]
of Fidel Castro's communist revolution and political takeover. The geopolitical meaning of the Cuban Revolution was a symmetrical response to American and NATO Atlanticism in Eurasia.[46]

Therefore, from a geopolitical perspective, the Cuban Missile Crisis rep-   [7.64]
resented the apex of the great war of continents. Anyhow, its aftermath resulted in both superpowers following the path of détente for fear of total nuclear obliteration.

At the same time, the Vietnam War too represented a characteristic strug-   [7.65]
gle between thalassocracy (USA) and tellurocracy (USSR) for control over the Rimland, the coastal zone of the World Island. Whereas the Americans

tried to detract Indochina from continental rule, pro-Soviet forces strove to free the peninsula from capitalist-thalassic rule. The aftermath of the war represented a clear victory for tellurocracy and the Soviet bloc.

[7.66]   Moreover, the Soviet occupation of Afghanistan may also be interpreted in geopolitical terms as a confrontation of thalassocracy and tellurocracy struggling for the influence over the Rimland. Though landlocked, Afghanistan adjoined closely the regions of the USSR in Turkestan and it was therefore a key actor for the entire US containment strategy against the USSR. The key role of Afghanistan as the strategic junction of Asia and buffer zone between thalassocracy and tellurocracy was already clear between the 19th and 20th centuries in the context of the "Great Game" between Russia and Great Britain. Indeed, Afghanistan bore a deep strategic significance both for imperial Russia and for the USSR. [47]

[7.67]   When Gorbachëv took office, the telluric soul of the Soviet empire started to crumble. The Soviet decision to withdraw from Afghanistan in 1989 was a clear indication of the weakening of the USSR's strategy oriented towards Eurasianism. Gorbachëv's *perestroika* bore a deep geopolitical meaning. Instead of considering Russia's historical path as Eurasian great-continental Heartland and as the core of the civilization of Land, the liberal reforms turned the Soviet Union into a pro-Western country. In other words, due to Gorbachëv, Atlanticism replaced Eurasianism and liberalism substituted traditionalism; thus, the destruction of the Heartland occurred from within. [48]

[7.68]   Gorbachëv's liberal reforms led to the quick collapse of the USSR. This epochal event implied the end of the bipolar "Yalta World" and the birth of the unipolar new world order, characterized by the undisputed hegemony of thalassocracy, represented politically by liberal-democracy and economically by free market. The West strengthened its capitalist and liberal ideology and began to expand in Eastern Europe replacing the ideological vacuum that was formed. Thus, countries that belonged to the former Warsaw Pact and even some former Soviet republics (e.g. Estonia, Lithuania, and Latvia) joined NATO. [49]

[7.69]   The demise of the Soviet Union coincided with the worldwide affirmation of globalism. From now on, the world would have been globalized and liberal. Consequently, the collapse of the socialist bloc put an end to the Soviet era of Russia's telluric geopolitics. The 1990s would be years of Russian international marginalization, in which the country had to face the risk of political fragmentation—as the Chechen Wars showed—and of social turmoil.

[7.70]   In conclusion, from a geopolitical and historical perspective, Russia is to be considered mainly as a land power. Being landlocked or semi-landlocked, land powers perceive themselves as unsafe and insecure, mainly because they do not have direct or permanent access to the sea, and thus to international trade. Russia was a semi-landlocked country until the 18th century. In the Russian case, being semi-landlocked means being seasonally landlocked because of the Arctic Ocean's freezing during wintertime, which entails the consequent suspension of trade towards Europe and East Asia. This geographical condition, as well as the need to protect the frontiers, gave birth to Russian territorial expansionism. The imperatives of Russian historical foreign policy were two: on one hand, the defense of the steppes from the continuous raids of the nomadic horse-riding Turkic-Mongolian tribes,[50] and, on the other, the quest for warm water ports for carrying on commerce during wintertime.[51]

One of Russia's key strategic asset is represented by the control of Ukraine—whose relevance is exposed by the name it bears, which means "borderland." The reason for Ukrainian past and present territorial crises relies on the fact that this cramped flatland lays exactly in-between the Eurasian Heartland and the European Rimland. Losing Ukraine, Russia would still be a relevant superpower, but at the cost of being a predominantly Asian one. Ukraine plays a strategic role for the relationships between the European Union and the Russian Federation: it is throughout the Ukrainian flatland that superpowers like the US, the EU, and Russia currently confront each other. In the context of the present Ukrainian crisis, as suggested by Brzezinski,[52] Poland could play a pivotal role, for better or for worse.
[7.71]

Another fundamental asset is the maintenance of the unity of Russian territory, which implies, for instance, the need to preserve and defend the sparsely populated and incredibly rich in resources Siberian vastness, as well as the restless and diversified Ciscaucasia. Historically, the Russian expansion into Siberia implied the birth of a coercive and centralized kind of government. The building of railways helped to adjoin the vast Siberian widths, though suggesting a sense of insecurity typical of Russian historical mentality. In Siberia, rivers play a relevant role: the Yenisei River divides Western from Eastern Siberia and the Lena River Eastern Siberia from the Russian Far East; similarly, the Ussuri River forms the natural border between the Russian Far East and Chinese Manchuria. The annexation of Siberia obliged Russia to participate in the Pacific geopolitical contest, competing with actors like Japan, China and, later, the United States. When the Soviet Union replaced imperial Russia, the Bolsheviks had to face the evidence that a land power always suffers the threat of an attack on its outskirts: the gruesome years of the civil war and of foreign interventionism (1918–1923) reestablished the difficulty of defending the Russian borders. Bolshevik imperialist realism was able enough to retransform Moscow as Russian capital in place of Saint Petersburg/Petrograd, a core region that could provide easier control over Eurasia. Later, the United States perceived the birth of the great Soviet empire onto the ashes of the shattered German Third Reich as the occurrence of Mackinder's prophecies on the control of the World-Island. Indeed, after World War Two, the Eurasian Rimland—including the Greater
[7.72]

Middle East, Western Europe and Southeastern Asia—would feel jeopardized both by the spread of Soviet land power and by the pressure of American sea—and air—power. After the USSR's demise and the outburst of newly discovered nationalistic feelings amongst the variegated former Soviet subjects, vulnerability was again Russia's keyword, deriving mainly from the unbalanced ratio between Russian demographic rates and the geographic extensions of the country.

[7.73]   Today, things in Eurasia are rapidly evolving. Despite Russian political and geopolitical awakening, it seems that China is gaining faster and faster a hegemonic role on the Eurasian continent. So being things, should Russia focus its attention on the Eurasian Heartland or on its fringes (the European peninsula and the Pacific Rim)? What would Russia need to lure back the non-Russian people of the former Soviet Union? Unfortunately, Russia still needs to face its everlasting weakness: that of being, in fact, borderless. [53]

[7.74]   According to Eurasianism, in the upcoming years, Russia should give absolute priority to geopolitics and base its political choices on it. Rearticulating the Marxian thought, geopolitics should be Russia's base (or substructure), whereas the economic issues, the domestic policy, and the social questions the superstructure. The ultimate Russian geopolitical mission—as seen in previous chapters—would be to create the global Eurasian alternative to the Atlanticist model of the "New World Order."

[7.75]   The Eurasianist project could only be accomplished by preserving Russia's nuclear and strategic potential, as well as by conserving the Russian veto power in the UN Security Council. In the future multipolar world, the nuclear potential of NATO and Russia (and its military allies) should remain in substantial equilibrium; the threat of using strategic weapons against NATO countries could be used by Russia to contain the possible neo-imperialist and neo-colonialist tendencies of Atlanticism.

[7.76]   Russia should conclude military pacts to guarantee the consistency of the Eurasian bloc on the most strategically important borders. In this sense, a Russian-Iranian military alliance is viewed by Eurasianists as very useful to assure Russia access to the southern seas and to place armaments in southern Eurasia in order to defend itself, Central Asia, and Iran. Other advantageous military pacts could be signed with Iraq, Syria, and Lybia in order to increase the Eurasian presence and might in the Mediterranean region. In Eastern Europe, Russia's Eurasianist strategy could be carried out through military pacts with Serbia and Macedonia and through the neutralization of—or alliance with—the NATO countries of Bulgaria, Greece, Romania, and Montenegro. Likewise, Russia could conclude military pacts with China and India. The ultimate Eurasianist geopolitical strategy of Russia is based on the idea of dividing NATO countries and transforming Europe and the Pacific area in strategically neutral zones. Notwithstanding, the European Union and Rus-

sia-Eurasia should be benevolent partners in the future and friendly stabiliz-
ers of the Eurasian continent if they both wish a peaceful coexistence.

According to Dugin, there are four categories of countries that are—or [7.77]
could become—Russia's natural partners:

1. Powerful regional formations (countries or groups of countries), [7.78]
   whose relations with Russia are complementary. This entails that these
   countries have something vital for Russia, while Russia has something
   indispensable for them. Some countries that belong to this category of
   symmetrical complementarity are the European Union, Japan, Iran,
   India, and Turkey. For instance, Russia could provide natural resources—chiefly natural gas, oil, and coal—, weaponry, and strategic
   equipment to these countries, and receive in turn economic and technological aid from the EU and Japan, political partnership from Iran
   and India, and strategic friendship from Turkey;
2. Geopolitical formations allured by multipolarity, but not symmetrical- [7.79]
   ly complementary with Russia, among which China, Pakistan, and
   most Arab countries. Russia could be a mediator between these countries and their rivals: for instance, it could help countries like Egypt,
   Saudi Arabia, and Pakistan to overcome their rivalry towards Iran,
   help Pakistan to overcome its rivalry with India, and help Pakistan and
   China to overcome their rivalries with India;
3. Developing countries in Africa, Latin America and Asia that do not [7.80]
   yet possess a true geopolitical might. Russia could support their development and transform some into regional poles of the future multipolar world;
4. The United States of America once it would resolutely opt for isola- [7.81]
   tionism and for the upholding of the Monroe Doctrine. Russia would
   acknowledge the geopolitical interests of the US in the American continent if the US would abandon its interventionist practice and renounce to its Atlanticist neo-imperialist doctrine. If this would occur,
   America could become a major Russian-Eurasian partner, working
   together for the maintenance of international peace and for the augmentation of global economic development and prosperity.

THE STRUCTURE OF THE MULTIPOLAR WORLD: [7.82]
GEO-ECONOMIC ZONES AND GREAT SPACES

As seen, the Eurasianist ideology asserts on one hand the need to establish [7.83]
conservative and identitarian societies within nations and, on the other, to
announce the advent of the multipolar world in international relations. Being
a borderless ideology, Eurasianism does not refer only to the geographical

boundaries of the Eurasian continent, but it is rather a global-scale strategy that believes in the need to overcome both globalism and the idea of nation-states. In this sense, it proposes a scenario that entails neither a unipolar world order nor a universal world government, but several global zones—or poles—representing a multipolar version of globalization.[54] According to the Eurasianist vision of the future world, traditional states will cease to exist and will be replaced by integrated civilizational structures ("Great Spaces") united into "geo-economic belts" ("geo-economic zones").[55] The International Eurasian Movement aims at consolidating and integrating the Great Spaces inside the four geo-economic belts. It also believes that a multipolar world will rise only after a political-economic consolidation of all Great Spaces, which today are represented by one or more nation-states.[56] For Euasianists, the first goal is to abolish nation-states and to constitute civilizational macro-agglomerations. The transition from the nation-state model to the Great Space model should proceed on different levels (economic, geopolitical, strategic, political, cultural, and linguistic) following a multidimensional integration pattern.

[7.84]   Eurasianists believe that nation-states are an obsolete form of political organization that has characterized five centuries of history (from the 15th to the 20th). Instead of outdated nation-states, the peoples of the world should unite in political formations that combine the strategic unification of the great continental spaces with a complex, multi-dimensional system of national, cultural, religious, economic, and anthropologic autonomies. The models of integration that future political formations should take into consideration are both the ancient multinational empires of the past—e.g. the Macedonian Empire, the Roman Empire, the Carolingian Holy Roman Empire, the Austro-Hungarian Empire—and contemporary political structures like the European Union or the Commonwealth of Independent States. Per Dugin, contemporary nation-states should choose one of the three following options: self-liquidation and integration into a single planetary space under Americanist domination through Atlanticism and globalism; opposition to globalization while attempting to conserve their formal sovereignty; integration into supra-state formations of geographic-regional nature—i.e. Great Spaces—based on historical, civilizational, and strategic commonalities: the latter option represents the Eurasianist plan for the future multipolar world.[57] Believing in the necessity to overcome the idea of the nation-state in favor of imperial macro-areas, Eurasianists support the creation of supra-national formations at a pan-regional level that would reflect the historical, cultural, and civilizational features of their peoples. The idea of Great Spaces would represent an alternative to two worldviews: the globalist model based on world government and the traditional, Westphalian model of sovereign nation-states.

Multipolar globalization may be considered as a form of alter-globaliza-   [7.85]
tion. Eurasianism rejects the hermeneutic model based on the dichotomy
between a global Center and its Outskirts. On the contrary, it claims the
existence of several autonomous living spaces that constitute a "pluriversum." The world order that Eurasianists envision is represented by a coalition
of states organized into continental federations or "democratic empires" with
a large degree of domestic self-government. Each of these areas should be
multipolar in all senses, i.e. ethnically, culturally, religiously, and administra-
tively. [58]

The consolidation of a multipolar world would find its starting point in   [7.86]
the integration of the Eurasian continent. The Eurasian integration would
also largely depend on the European one. Today, the alliance of the US and
Western Europe represents the Atlantic vector of European development.
However, the European integration under the aegis of the major continental
countries—Germany and France—, which is the distinguishing feature of the
European Union, represents the core of European Eurasianism. Charles de
Gaulle conceived Europe as stretching from the Atlantic Ocean to the Urals;
Thiriart even unto Vladivostok. In a Eurasianist perspective, the integration
of Europe should include the vast territory of the Russian Federation. In this
context, Eurasianism would uphold an ambitious project for the strategic,
geopolitical, and economic integration of the northern region of the Eurasian
continent—cradle of European history and matrix of European peoples. Despite the huge differences, specifically the ones related to national identity
and to the forms of economic system, the Eurasian project of integration
recalls somewhat the Pan-Europeanist project of the International Pan-European Union advocated by Count Richard Coudenhove-Kalergi, [59] with the
addition of Russia of course.

Russia would represent the natural bridge that adjoins the Eurasian peo-   [7.87]
ples of Western Eurasia (Europeans) with the peoples of Central and Eastern
Eurasia (Turkic peoples, Mongolian, and Caucasian). In this perspective,
Eurasianists suggest the integration of continental Europe and Russia in a
Eurasian dimension in both the symbolic and geographical senses, in terms
of the identification of Eurasianism with continentalism.

Dugin unfolds the division of the world in civilizational zones and big   [7.88]
spaces as follows. The integration of the northern strip of the Eurasian continent represents the horizontal vector of integration. The horizontal vector of
integration is followed by a vertical vector represented by four geographical
belts, also called meridian zones, which partition the world from north to
south. These zones are large geo-economic agglomerations that include different civilizations inside. According to Dugin, the four geographical
zones—or belts—are the following: [60]

[7.89]   1. Atlantic meridian zone, with both American continents forming one
             common space oriented toward and controlled by the United States
             within the framework of the Monroe Doctrine;

[7.90]   2. Euro-African meridian zone, with the European Union as its center;

[7.91]   3. Russian-Central Asian meridian zone;

[7.92]   4. Pacific meridian zone.

[7.93]   Each meridian zone is meant to counterbalance the others, and the latter three
together are meant to counterbalance the first. In the future, these belts would
represent the nucleus of the multipolar world, which would include at least
four poles.[61] The existence of four geo-economic zones cooperating with
each other would make the risk of world wars and general conflicts less
likely.

[7.94]   In Dugin's Eurasianist project, the meridian zones consist of several
Great Spaces, or "democratic empires"; each Great Space possesses a certain
degree of independence and freedom in relation to the others but is still
strategically integrated into a corresponding meridian zone. The Great
Spaces are conceived as more than geo-economic agglomerations, like the
meridian zones, but would correspond to the boundaries of civilizations and
comprise several nation-states or unions of states. According to Dugin's
schema, each geo-economic meridian zone includes the following Great
Spaces:[62]

[7.95]   1. The Euro-African zone includes Europe, the Arab Great Space, and
             Trans-Saharan Africa;

[7.96]   2. The Russian-Central Asian zone includes the Russian-Eurasian Space,
             the Islamic Continental Space, and the Great Space of Hindustan;

[7.97]   3. The Pacific zone includes the Chinese Great Space, the Japanese Great
             Space, and the Indo-Chinese-Australasian "New Pacific" Space;

[7.98]   4. The American zone includes the North American Space, Central
             American Space, and South American Space.

[7.99]   The geopolitical zonal maps that Dugin presents in his book *Eurasian Mission*[63] describe in detail the Eurasianist subdivision of the world in meridian
zones and civilizational large spaces. The analysis of the map depicting the
Great Spaces displays some significant data. The North American Space
includes the United States of America, Canada, the United Kingdom, and
Ireland. It is unclear whether Australia and New Zealand would belong to the
North American Space or to the Pacific one. Due to their Anglo-Saxon
cultural affiliation, it is likely to suppose that they would fit better in the
former. In this respect, Dugin affirms that the Pacific meridian zone is determined by a condominium of two Great Spaces, China and Japan, and also
includes Indonesia, Malaysia, the Philippines, and Australia, "the latter of

which some researchers connect to the American meridian zone,"[64] without, however, quoting them. Undoubtedly, the hegemon country of the North American Space is represented by the United States. The Central American Space comprises all countries of Central America, both in the continent (Mexico, Guatemala, Nicaragua, Panama, etc.) and in the Caribbean Basin (Cuba, Haiti, Jamaica, etc.). We may suggest with enough confidence that the leading country of the area would be Mexico. The South American Space includes all South American countries, from Venezuela to Argentina. It is difficult to claim which country would play a hegemonic role, since at least four of them (Brazil, Argentina, Venezuela, and Colombia) enjoy a notable strategic position. However, though not a Spanish-speaking country like all the rest, Brazil may have the potential—demographically, economically, and geographically—to become the South American hegemon. The integration of the American zone would require a broader civilizational independence of the Central and Southern American Spaces from the Northern Space. Three should be the main tenets regarding the integration of the American zone: 1) the limitation of North American strategic, political and economic interests to the boundaries of the American meridian zone, in support of North American isolationism and expansionism as limited by the Monroe Doctrine; 2) maximum autonomy and sovereignty for democratic, ecological, and na-tional-cultural movements; 3) the integration of Latin American countries into Central and South American Great Spaces in order to strengthen their cultural autonomy and to break their dependency from North America.[65] In this context, the United States should reject interventionism and world hege-monic plans and accept its role as pan-regional superpower within the bor-ders of the American meridian zone alone.

The Pacific zone is one of the most variegated areas that Dugin suggests. [7.100] First, the Chinese Great Space represents a Greater China, with the inclusion of Taiwan and the acknowledgment of Tibet, Xinjiang (East Turkestan), Inner Mongolia, and Manchuria as integral parts of the Chinese state. Sec-ondly, the Japanese Great Space is significantly homogenous, being formed by the Japanese archipelago. The Japanese Space is conceived as indepen-dent from all forms of dominion by North America: geopolitically, political-ly, and militarily. Interestingly, the two Koreas are neither located within the Chinese Space nor the Japanese: it is fair to believe that Dugin imagines that both China and Japan should equally share an influence over the Korean Peninsula. Nothing is said, however, about the overlapping interests of China and Japan over the disputed Senkaku/Diaoyiu islands.[66] Finally, the so-called "New Pacific Large Space" includes all countries of mainland Southeast Asia (the Indochinese Peninsula), Malaysia, the Indonesian archipelago, the Phi-lippines, and Papuasia. In demographic terms, Indonesia may become the hegemonic country of the area, but other candidates may be Thailand, Viet-nam, and Myanmar. Australasia may well be integrated in the Pacific Space, if emancipated from its colonialist Anglo-Saxon heritage.[67] Interestingly, the Chinese island of Hainan is included in the latter Great Space rather than in the Chinese one.

[7.101]   The Euro-African zone is also represented as a diversified area, encompassing many different civilizations, cultures, and races. The European Great Space embodies a clear example of a Greater Europe of the continentalist tradition. This area comprises all EU member states (except for Ireland) and other European countries like Norway, Iceland, Switzerland, Bosnia-Herzegovina, Montenegro, Albania, and Macedonia; Greenland, which is still a Danish possession, would belong to this area too. As previously mentioned, Great Britain and Ireland are considered part of the North American Space rather than the European Space. Three considerations seem to be dutiful: first, Romania and Bulgaria—albeit EU members—are separated from the European Great Space and included in the Russian-Eurasian one; at the same time, Western Ukraine is included in the European Space, but separated from its central and eastern regions, which are included, as we will see, in the Russian-Eurasian Space; second, Serbia, which is a pro-Russian country with a remarkable Eurasianist mindset, is excluded from the Russian-Eurasian Space and located within the European one; third, notwithstanding Russian strategic interests, the Baltic states are left inside the European Space. At present, the European Union's integration process is the best model that other Great Spaces should emulate. The EU exemplifies a superpower that rejected the notion of nation-state in favor of an economic—and perhaps, in the future, also political—union with a common market and with a common currency for several member states. However, the Eurasianist view of European integration suggests the implementation of two fundamental projects for the pan-European Space: 1) the European Union should not be characterized by bureaucratic interests, speculative financialism and oligarchic lobbyism, but rather represent and preserve the identity of European folks and rediscover their traditions; 2) the EU should be completely independent from North American control and Trans-Atlantic partnership, which requires the cessation of the NATO alliance in favor of a European autochthone system of collective defense.[68] The European Space is conceived as the leading political formation of the Euro-African zone.

[7.102]   The Arab-Islamic Great Space is formed by the following areas: North Africa (Maghreb), Egypt, the Arabian Peninsula, the Horn of Africa, part of the Sahel, and a small part of the Mashrek (Israel/Palestine and Jordan). This area—with the significant exception of Israel and Ethiopia—is characterized by the civilizational imprint given by Islam—especially the Sunni version. The potential hegemons of the area could either be Egypt or Saudi Arabia. The integration of this area into one geopolitical structure should be accompanied by the establishment of peaceful economic and political relations with Europe and Trans-Saharan Africa. Sunni Islam would be used as the integrating vector for the area. Generally, Eurasianism rejects Islamic radical movements that tend to universality, typical of Sunni extremism—especially related to the Wahhabi and Salafist tradition—; accordingly, it opposes jihadi movements like Al-Qaeda or ISIS, Middle Eastern countries like Saudi Arabia, and political movements like the Muslim Brotherhood—believed, by the way, to be supported by Atlanticism. Dugin claims that the opposition between the West and Islam does not represent a true fact, believing that radical Sunni Islam would be a power built up and constantly nurtured by the United States and directed against Eurasia, against a potential Eurasian alliance, against Russia, Iran, China, India, and Europe. Firstly, the expansion of Islamic extremism inside Arab countries and into non-Arab Islamic countries (Turkey, Iran, Turkestan, Caucasus, Indonesia, etc.) is perceived as the main destabilizing factor of the Muslim world and the main opposition to the peaceful integration of its Great Spaces. On the contrary, Eurasianism considers as natural allies in the Islamic world Sufi Muslims and Shi'ites: Sufism and Shi'a are believed to be the two forms of Islam compatible and companionable with Eurasianism. Secondly, another factor of constant instability for the region is considered to be the presence of Israel, which would represent an Atlanticist agent in the region. Regarding Israel, Eurasianism supports the right to the existence of a Jewish state but recommends that the termination of the Arab-Israeli conflict should rest upon a joint Israeli-Palestinian participation in the construction of a shared homeland in the framework of a two-state solution—albeit integrated into the corresponding Great Space.

On the other hand, the Trans-Saharan Large Space comprises all African [7.103] countries that lay below the Sahara Desert, with the exception, as seen, of the countries that belong to the Horn of Africa, but with the inclusion of the island of Madagascar. The integration of this area suffers from the fact that almost every African border is inherited from the colonial age and is careless of the historical, ethnic, cultural, and economic conditions of the African peoples. The fragmentation and artificiality of African states would be the cause of many of its ethnic problems and of neo- or crypto-colonialism. The solution Eurasianists propose is to abolish the artificial borders of African states and to deeply integrate Black Africa into a single Great Space that would incarnate a new representation of the idea of Negroland or Nigritia.[69]

Finally, the Russian-Central Asian Big Space is formed by exceptionally [7.104] heterogonous Eurasian and Asian countries. The Russian-Eurasian Large Space resembles somewhat the Soviet Union's geographical extension, albeit with remarkable exceptions. It includes the Russian Federation—which is conceived as the hegemonic power of the area—, Belarus, Moldova, Kazakhstan, Uzbekistan, Kyrgyzstan, Turkmenistan, Tajikistan, and Mongolia. Oddly, though being former Soviet countries and members (or former members) of the Commonwealth of Independent States, the Transcaucasian countries of

Armenia, Georgia, and Azerbaijan are not included in the area.[70] As previously noticed, central and eastern Ukraine, as well as Romania and Bulgaria are included in the area. The Islamic Continental Large Space is formed by Eurasian and Asian Muslim countries. It includes Turkey with Eastern Thrace (i.e. European Turkey), the major countries of the Mashrek (Syria, Lebanon, and Iraq), Iran, Afghanistan, Pakistan, and Transcaucasian countries (although Georgia and Armenia are, of course, Christian nations). Some Asian countries of the Commonwealth of Independent States, specifically Tajikistan and Turkmenistan, intersect with this zone. Clearly, the hegemonic role of this area is contended by Turkey on one side and Iran on the other. Cyprus appears to reside in between the Islamic Continental Large Space and the European Large Space. The last great space is that of Hindustan, which includes India, Sri Lanka, and Nepal.

[7.105]   Dugin's major attention refers to the integration of the Russian-Central Asian zone. If the boundaries of India and China almost reach the limits of their Great Space, this is not the case of the Russian Federation, the countries of the CIS, and continental Muslim countries (Iran, Pakistan, Afghanistan, and possibly Turkey, Iraq, and Syria). Therefore, the integration of the Russian-Eurasian Space and of the Islamic Continental Space is considered to be one of the chief aims of the International Eurasian Movement.

[7.106]   Furthermore, Dugin believes that the integration of the Russian-Central Asian meridian zone depends on the consolidation of strategic axes among the chief actors of the pan-region. The first he considers is the Moscow-Teheran axis. He claims that the whole process of integration relies on the successful establishment of a strategic middle- and long-term partnership between Russia and Iran. Both Russia and Iran are considered self-sufficient powers capable of creating their own organizational model for the region, making the development of this zone irreversible and autonomous, with no foreign interferences. The creation of the Moscow-Teheran axis would allow Russia to gain access to warm-water ports in the Persian Gulf and in the Indian Ocean, projecting more easily its power both in the Middle East and in the Indian subcontinent. This axis would also be pivotal for the reorganization of Central Asia and for the reaffirmation of areas of interest in the Asian countries of the CIS, in Afghanistan, and in Pakistan. In Dugin's words, "close cooperation [of Russia] with Iran presumes the transformation of the Afghani-Pakistani area into a free Islamic confederation that is loyal both to Moscow and Teheran."[71]

[7.107]   The second precondition is represented by the creation of the Moscow-New Delhi axis. This alliance would be crucial for the ordinate integration of the Eurasian continent and for the development of a collective Eurasian security apparatus. Russia would help India to decrease its tensions with Pakistan over Kashmir. The Great Space of Hindustan would form a federation aware of the diversity of Indian society and protective towards all ethnic and religious minorities (Sikhs, Jains, Zoroastrians, Christians, Muslims, etc.).

The third crucial element would be the creation of the Moscow-Ankara axis. Turkey is perceived as the main Russian regional partner in the integration process of Central Asia. Together with Russia, Turkey is a country that perceives the importance of Eurasianism for its regional goals and interests. Like Putin's Russia, Erdoğan's Turkey acknowledges its civilizational differences with the European Union and the West, fears a further loss of sovereignty, and considers with skepticism the pushes of globalism. Undoubtedly, one of the major difficulties to overcome in integrating the area would be the rivalry between Turkey and Iran. However, the consolidation of a Moscow-Teheran-Ankara axis is considered pivotal for the future affairs of the Middle East and Central Asia. [7.108]

In Dugin's scheme, due to its fragmented ethnic and cultural mosaic, the most problematic area for Eurasian integration is represented by the Caucasus. As already seen, Transcaucasia is included in the Islamic Continental Space, whereas—obviously—Ciscaucasia is considered part of the Russian-Eurasian Space. Dugin suggests as follows the solution to the issue of Caucasian integration: "The Eurasian solution to this problem [the integration of Caucasus] lies not in the creation of ethnic-based states or in assigning one people strictly to one state, but in the development of a flexible federation on the basis of ethnic and cultural entities within the common strategic context of the [Russian-Cental Asian] meridian zone."[72] Therefore, Dugin recommends the creation of a system of three half-axes: the first half-axis would between Moscow and the Caucasian centers (Moscow-Baku, Moscow-Yerevan, Moscow-Tbilisi, Moscow-Makhachkala, Moscow-Grozny, Moscow-Vladikavkaz, Moscow-Tskhinvali, Moscow-Sukhumi, etc.); the second half-axis would be between the aforementioned Caucasian regions and Turkey (Ankara-Baku, Ankara-Tbilisi, Ankara-Yerevan, etc.); the third half-axis would be between Iran and the Caucasian centers (Teheran-Baku, Teheran-Tbilisi, Teheran-Yerevan, etc.). As a matter of fact, the creation of the "three half-axes" system would allow a peaceful Russo-Turkish-Iranian condominium in the Caucasian region, in which the interests and influences of the Russian, Ottoman, and Persian empires had overlapped for centuries. [7.109]

As for Central Asia, the vector of its integration would be the solidification of a united strategic and economic bloc with the Russian Federation within the framework of the Eurasian Economic Union, which Dugin considers the successor to the CIS.[73] One of the chief strategic functions of Central Asia is represented by its role as bridge to securely connect Russia with the countries of continental Islam (Iran, Afghanistan, and Pakistan). [7.110]

The Russian re-integration of post-Soviet territories, both in Europe and Asia, is one of the main goals of Dugin's Eurasianist doctrine and necessary precondition for the realization of the Russian-Eurasian Large Space; Eura- [7.111] sianism would represent the philosophy of the integration of the post-Soviet territory on a democratic, non-violent, and voluntary basis without the domination of any single religious or ethnic group.[74] The integration of the post-Soviet territory would concern three distinct areas: Central Asia, the Caucasus, and Eastern Europe. First, the integration of Central Asia seems to be a simpler task in relation to some countries, but more difficult in relation to others: Astana, Dushanbe, Bishkek, Tashkent, and Ashgabat bear different views on Eurasian integration. The most active regional country favorable to integration is Kazakhstan, since President Nursultan Nazarbayev affirmed to be a steadfast supporter of Eurasianism.[75] Tajikistan and Kyrgyzstan also support the process of integration, though to a lesser extent than Kazakhstan. Uzbekistan and Turkmenistan are the least favorable to integration.

[7.112]   Second, in relation to the Caucasus, Armenia represents the main Transcaucasian country eager to bolster Eurasian integration. Yerevan considers the Russian Federation an important supporter and mediator to manage relations with its Muslim neighbors. It is well known that Armenian relations with its Turkic neighbors of Turkey and Azerbaijan are complex. In this sense, Russia could play a fundamental role as intermediary to overcome the reciprocal Turkic-Armenian prejudices. On the other hand, Baku remains neutral towards Eurasian integration, but this situation would change drastically with the continued movement of Ankara towards Eurasianism, which would have immediate consequences for Azerbaijan.[76] As for Georgia, Dugin believes that this country is the core problem for the integration of Caucasus since the mosaic character of the Georgian state has been the cause of various problems during the construction of a new national state that is strongly rejected by its ethnic minorities in Abkhazia, South Ossetia, Adjara, and because the Georgian state does not have any strong partners in the region and is therefore forced to seek a partnership with the US and NATO to counterbalance Russian influence.[77] The solution to the problem is identified by Dugin in the Orthodox culture of Georgia, with its Eurasian features and traditions, and in its historical connection with Russia.

[7.113]   Finally, regarding Eastern Europe, the two countries that would be involved in the Eurasian integration project are Belarus and Ukraine. Now, Belarus is much less problematic than Ukraine: the intention to integrate is much more evident and a Moscow-Minsk axis is already a concrete reality. Obviously, the largest issue here would concern the Ukrainian integration. In considering the various areas of the country, Crimea would already be integrated into the Eurasian project because of its annexation to Russia in 2014; likewise, the Donbass region, with the pro-Russian self-declared Donetsk and Luhansk People's Republics, would likely be joining the Russian-led Eurasianist project. The rest of Ukraine would represent the real difficulty to overcome, but, in Dugin's scheme, its belonging to the Russian-Eurasian Large Space appears an irrevocable condition.

Dugin claims that gaining the support of Kazakhstan and Ukraine would [7.114] suffice to succeed in creating the Eurasian Large space. He believes that a Moscow-Astana-Kiev triangle would represent a flawless frame to guarantee the Eurasian integration and affirms that Russia and Ukraine have much in common in cultural, linguistic, religious, and ethnic terms and that Russophobia and separation from Russia have been promoted in Ukraine since the beginning of its recent sovereignty.[78]

The Eurasianist vision of the future world upholds the principle of multi- [7.115] polarity and asserts the necessity of maintaining peaceful relations among all poles; unlike the Atlanticist globalist vision, the Eurasianist one claims that only the recognition of a multipolar, diversified world order would grant peace and equality among all peoples.[79]

The idea of identitarian and multipolar Great Spaces would be opposed [7.116] by the forces of globalism. Dugin claims that what globalism would fear above all are geopolitical blocs. It would also prefer that nationalist tendencies would develop only on a reduced and advantageous scale. The only form of nationalism that represents a real danger for it would be the imperial one, which personifies a union based on religion, race, and traditional culture that creates a unitary geopolitical bloc.[80]

In relation to the United Nations, Eurasianism affirms that this interna- [7.117] tional organization should be transformed in a truly representative structure of multipolarity.[81] This may presuppose a profound reform of its organs: on one hand, the General Assembly should gain more decisional power and be subdivided into agglomerations of nations that represent their common Great Space; on the other, the Security Council should reflect the distribution of power of the multipolar world, with the further inclusion as permanent members with veto power of some other key international actors.

THE EURASIANIST VISION OF THE POLITY: DIVISION OF [7.118] POWERS, "AUTONOMIES," FEDERALISM, "*DEMOTIA,*" ECONOMY, RELIGION, AND NATIONHOOD

In this last section we will consider how Eurasianists intend to organize— [7.119] from a domestic sociopolitical view—the Great Spaces they advocate.

At the local level, the government would be controlled through the so- [7.120] called "system of the Autonomies," which are conceived as local societies of different kinds and numerically flexible, from those with millions of people to small communities of few people. Autonomy, which in Greek means "self-government," represents a natural form of organization of a group of people, united by a characterizing mark (be it national, religious, ethnic, etc.). "Autonomy" is opposed to "sovereignty": in the case of sovereignty, the right of territorial free organization has priority; in the case of autonomy, on the other hand, there is a distinction between the arrangement of the collective life of populations and states and the territorial organization.

[7.121]   A distinctive feature of the "autonomy" would be the greatest freedom guaranteed in the domestic fields that do not concern the strategic interest of broader political formations—like those with continental dimensions. In the "autonomies," the government is regarded as unconstrained in its actions and deregulated by any higher authority. The people that belong to an "autonomy" would have the right to freely choose the political form of their "autonomy," in tune with their traditional and cultural characteristics. This principle entails that some "autonomies" may be democracies, some aristocracies, and some monarchies. Specifically, some "autonomies" would resemble a democratic representative polity, some an aristocratic republic, some a theocratic regime, some an absolute monarchy, some an autocratic political entity, and so on. The people would be entitled to decide what form their "autonomy" should have according to their historical and civilizational ideal type. The "autonomies" would have authority over the following political areas: 1) civil and administrative issues; 2) the social sphere; 3) education and medical services; 4) all spheres of economic activity.[82] In other words, all local and domestic issues would fall under the sphere of competence of the "autonomies," except for the strategic issues and problems concerning the security and the territorial integrity of the Great Spaces.

[7.122]   The Eurasianist vision of domestic affairs centered on the idea of the "autonomies" is based on the principle of the so-called "*demotia*," which represents a form of "organic democracy" and "direct democracy" as theorized, for instance, by Rousseau. The idea of *demotia* is that the people participate directly in choosing what kind of political system they wish to adopt. Implicitly, this means that if the majority of the people that represent a collectivity would wish to establish a monarchy, or a theocracy, or, for that matter, a democracy, it would be fully entitled to do so. In Dugin's words, the thesis of *demotia* would represent the continuation of the political theories of "organic democracy" as developed by Jean-Jacques Rousseau, Carl Schmitt, Julien Freund, Alain de Benoist, and Arthur Moeller van den Bruck. The Eurasianist concept of "*demotia*" is defined as the "participation of the people in its own destiny."[83]

[7.123]   The legitimation of power in Eurasianist societies would be founded on three principles: the idea of *demotia*, the primacy of ideocracy, and the development of the doctrine of the "ontology of power" founded on the Orthodox conception of power as "*katechon*,"[84] which is a biblical concept that has subsequently developed into a notion of political philosophy.

[7.124]   On the other hand, the issues related to strategic security and all activities that concern topics that go beyond the frame of a single continental space—e.g. inter-zonal macroeconomic issues, diplomacy, economic partnership, environmental issues, and so on—would be attributed to a "single strategic center" for each Great Space. These single strategic centers would deal with all those instances when control is delegated to the strategic regional governments of the Great Spaces and are conceived as rigidly hierarchical structures that combine elements of the military, the judiciary, and the administrative-bureaucratic branches. In broad terms, the strategic center would be endorsed to elaborate the geopolitical planning and the general strategies of the Great Space.

The balance and competences between the two levels of government—i.e. the strategic and local levels—are imagined as clearly and strictly delimited.[85] The autonomies would be characterized by self-rule in domestic affairs: issues of strategy, foreign relations, and strategic planning would fall outside the autonomy's competence and jurisdiction. However, the "autonomies" could still be empowered to have rule over the issues that currently, in federal systems, are entrusted to the federal authority and regulated by federal legislation—e.g. civil and administrative law, the judicial system, the management of the autonomy's economy, and so on. [7.125]

In turn, the single Great Spaces could be structured into federal political agglomerations, taking the form of huge federations. In this sense, a special political assembly would be created representing all the federated autonomies.[86] The congressmen representing the "autonomies," if not specified diversely in the constitution of a single "autonomy," would be selected through organic democracy, i.e. directly by the citizens of the "autonomy." [7.126]

The "autonomies" would have full sovereignty only on their territorial boundary and would not be allowed to alienate any other territory belonging to other "autonomies." The ownership of the land would belong to the entire people who constitute the "autonomy."[87] [7.127]

In relation to "autonomies" and megalopolises, Dugin advocates that all big cities with demographic surplus should be depopulated in favor of the countryside.[88] Being essentially an anti-bourgeois and rural movement, Eurasianism encourages bucolic forms of life in harmony with nature rather than what it considers grey experiences in urbanized, alienating contexts. [7.128]

In the model of Eurasian federalism, the strategic unity would be accompanied by ethnic plurality: in this sense, the juridical emphasis would be placed more on the concept of the "right of peoples" rather than on that of individual human rights. [7.129]

The armed forces of Eurasia and the power of public officials would represent the strategic backbone of the Eurasian civilization. The social role of the military should thus be increased, with the restoration of prestige and public respect. [7.130]

In terms of demographic policies, the peoples of Eurasia should be morally, economically, and psychologically encouraged to augment their offspring: proliferation is meant to be the Eurasian social model. [7.131]

[7.132]   In the field of education, the Eurasian policymakers should reinforce the moral and scientific education of youth, in the spirit of fidelity to historical roots, social solidarity, and appreciation of one's own identity.

[7.133]   Moreover, Eurasianists also bear a proper vision of the economy. For them, all economic systems should stem from the historical and cultural features of a people and of its society. They affirm to be skeptical regarding the idea whether a decisive truth may or not exist in the field of economics, be it liberalist, mercantilist, or socialist, believing in a "third way" economic model that combines the market approach with the notion of the regulated economy on the basis of supra-economic considerations and principles.[89]

[7.134]   Eurasianism encourages the coexistence of a variety and plurality of economic systems and upholds the idea that some economic sectors should be under strict control while others should develop freely. There are six chief tenets that characterize the Eurasianist vision of the economy: 1) the subordination of the economy to higher civilizational spiritual values; 2) the principle of macro-economic integration and the division of labor on the scale of the Great Spaces, which are also conceived as customs unions; 3) the creation of a single financial, logistic, energetic, and informational system within the Great Spaces; 4) the establishment of separate economic borders between neighboring Great Spaces and—more broadly—between geo-economic meridian zones, which would not at all imply, anyhow, the elimination of economic exchanges amongst different Great Spaces; 5) a strategic control and planning by the center of the branches that form the basis of the economy, along with maximal freedom of economic activity at the level of medium- and small-scale businesses; 6) the organic combination of the forms of the market structure with the social, national, and cultural traditions of the regions and peoples of the Great Spaces.[90]

[7.135]   The Eurasian general approach towards economy is based on two tenets: state regulation in strategic sectors (military production, industrial policies, budgetary policy, public expenditure, monetary policy, commercial policy, and so on) and maximum liberty for medium and small enterprises.

[7.136]   In terms of monetary policy, Eurasianism contrasts the idea of a single currency pretending to the role of being the universal reserve currency. The regional vision of the multipolar world supposes the existence of different currencies for each geo-economic and geopolitical agglomeration. This means that each meridian zone would have its general currency, that within meridian zones each Great Space would have its own currency, and that in turn within Great Spaces all "autonomies" would have their own currency. The currency of the geo-economic meridian zones would consist of money and paper values, it would be the legal tender within the specific zone, and it would represent the tool of financial relations among the strategic centers of the Great Spaces. At the same time, the currency of a Great Space would also consist of money and paper values, it would be the legal tender within a

given Great Space, and a tool for financial relations among the "autonomies."
Finally, the currency at the level of the "autonomies" would represent different forms of equivalent exchange. Accordingly, each geopolitical pole—
zones, Great Spaces, and "autonomies"—should organize its proper financial
system of credit institutions at a regional level (central bank of a meridian
zone, central bank of a Great Space, and central bank of an "autonomy").

Regarding finance, in the Eurasianist vision the financial sphere is con-   [7.137]
ceived as an instrument of real production and exchange, directed towards
the qualitative side of economic development. In this sense, Eurasianism
accepts finance to the extent that it maintains a solid bond with real economy.
At the same time, it rejects financialism when conceived as the economic
system of capitalist societies based on the subordination of the real sector of
the economy to virtual financial operations—e.g. stock markets, financial
paper markets, portfolio investments, operations with international liabilities,
futures transactions, speculative forecasting of financial trends, and so on.
Above all, Eurasianism discards financialist monetary policies that separate
the monetary sphere—i.e. world reserve currencies and electronic money—
from production.

Also, for what concerns religion, Eurasianists bear a comprehensive atti-   [7.138]
tude. Unlike the ephemeral and materialistic principles that would distinguish the Atlanticist thought, Eurasianism believes that spiritual development is life's main priority and cannot be replaced by economic or social
benefits. Thus, every local religious tradition or system of faith is considered
the heritage of all mankind and worthy of protection. In organizational terms,
the representatives of traditional religions should be supported by the single
strategic centers of the Great Spaces. Eurasianism does not claim that one
religion or faith is the only carrier of truth but accepts as true that all traditional cults—most of which have risen in Eurasia—bear a spiritual merit and
value. At the same time, it discredits schismatic groups, extremist religious
associations, totalitarian sects, preachers of non-traditional religious doctrines and teachings, and any other forces that are against traditional religions.[91] Eurasianists consider "traditional" those sects and religions that possess historical legitimation and widespread worship, e.g. Christianity, Islam,
Judaism, Zoroastrianism, Bahá'í Faith, Buddhism, Hinduism, Jainism, Sikh-
ism, Taoism, Confucianism, Shintoism, Shamanism, Animism, Tengrism,
some forms of Paganism, and so on.

Finally, regarding nationhood, Eurasianists, as seen, insist on the need for   [7.139]
defending and safeguarding all ethnic and cultural groups of the world. In the
Eurasianist view, all nations should develop freely and sovereignly within
their "autonomy," inside its Great Space. All "autonomies," despite their
different form of government, should be established on the principle of self-
determination of nations and ethnic groups.

[7.140]   In conclusion, in the Eurasianist society the equilibrium between public and private spheres would be based on the following scheme: all fields that are related to the strategic sphere—i.e. the military and industrial apparatuses, security, diplomacy, macroeconomics, economic growth, natural monopolies, demography, education, and so on—would be state-controlled; on the other hand, small and medium economic production, the field of services, free time, the entertainment industry, and private life would be entrusted to personal and private initiative.

[7.141]   NOTES

[7n1]   1. Dugin, *Eurasian Mission*, 89–90.
[7n2]   2. The modern international system was conventionally established with the Peace of Westphalia (1648), which put an end to the Thirty Years' War (1618–1648) and recognized a society of territorially sovereign and politically independent states. It also admitted the legitimacy of all forms of government and recognized the notion of religious tolerance. In particular, this new international society was based on three fundamental principles: 1) *Rex in regno suo imperator est*, which meant that the sovereigns were not subject to any superior political authority (e.g. the Holy Roman Emperor or the Pope) and thus all kings were independent and equal; 2) *Cuius regio eius religio*, according to which the territorial sovereign decided the religion to worship within its borders (which represented the first example of "domestic jurisdiction," i.e. the principle of non-interference in a state's domestic affairs); 3) Balance of power, based on a system of European alliances aimed at avoiding the emergence of a continental hegemon. The Westphalian system replaced the medieval idea of universal Christian religious authority (*Res Publica Christiana*) with secular relations between sovereign and independent states, and somewhat introduced the principle of nationalism.
[7n3]   3. Oliver Stuenkel, *Post-Western World: How Emerging Powers are Remaking Global Order* (Cambridge and Malden: Polity, 2016).
[7n4]   4. The author divides the parallel institutions and international regimes into several sectors: finance, trade and investment, security, diplomacy, and infrastructure. The finance sector includes the Asian Infrastructure Investment Bank (AIIB), the BRICS-led New Development Bank (NDB), the BRICS Contingency Reserve Agreement (CRA), the global infrastructure to internationalize the yuan, China International payment system (CIPS), China Union Pay, the Shanghai Global Financial Center (GFC), the Universal Credit Rating Group, the Chiang Mai Initiative Multilateral (CMIM), the ASEAN+3, and the ASEAN+3 Macroeconomic Research Office (AMRO). The trade and investment sector contemplates the Regional Comprehensive Economic Partnership (RCEP) and the Free Trade Area of the Asia Pacific (FTAAP). The security sector takes account of the Conference on Interaction and Confidence Building Measures in Asia (CICA), the Shanghai Cooperation Organization (SCO), and the BRICS national security advisors (NSA) meeting. The diplomacy sector embraces the BRICS Leaders Summits, the BRICS and IBSA working groups, and the Boao Forum for Asia (BFA). Finally, the infrastructure sector consists of the projects of the Silk Road Fund/One Belt-One Road (OBOR), the Nicaragua Canal, and the Trans-Amazonian Railway.
[7n5]   5. Zakaria, *The Post-American World*.
[7n6]   6. Amitav Acharya, *The End of the American World Order* (Cambridge: Polity, 2014).
[7n7]   7. Ian Bremmer, *Every Nation for Itself: Winners and Losers in a G-Zero World* (New York: Portfolio/Penguin, 2012).
[7n8]   8. Joseph S. Nye, *The Future of Power* (New York: PublicAffairs, 2011).
[7n9]   9. See Robert Kagan, *The World America Made* (New York: Vintage Books, 2013).
[7n10]   10. Dugin, *The Fourth Political Theory*, 72–73.

11. This region has its central core in the basin of the Atlantic Ocean and its two opposite shores. Cf. Mackinder's article *The Round World and the Winning of the Peace* where the British geopolitician calls this area "Midland Ocean." [7n11]
12. Chiefly, Saudi Arabia and Jordan. [7n12]
13. Examples of unrests backed by the United States' government or privately-owned foundations (e.g. the Soros Foundation) would be the Color Revolutions that took place in the nations of the former Soviet Union and the Balkans during the early 2000s, and later those that took place in the Middle East under the name of Arab Springs. [7n13]
14. Dugin, *The Fourth Political Theory*, 79. [7n14]
15. Vladimir I. Lenin, *Imperializm kak Vysshaya Stadiya Kapitalizma* (Petrograd: Zhizn' i Znaniye, 1917). [7n15]
16. Dugin, *The Fourth Political Theory*, 81–82. [7n16]
17. Ibid, 117. [7n17]
18. Ibid. [7n18]
19. Samuel P. Huntington, *The Clash of Civilizations and the Remaking of World Order* (New York: Simon & Schuster, 1997). [7n19]
20. The potential leaders of the Muslim world may be Turkey—which is populous but non-Arabic—, Saudi Arabia—which is scarcely populated but represents the core of Arabic civilization—, Egypt—which is highly populated—, Iran—which nonetheless follows Shi'a Islam—, and Indonesia—which is the most populous Islamic country, but it is neither Arabic nor close to the Middle East. [7n20]
21. Dugin, *The Fourth Political Theory*, 119–20. [7n21]
22. Aleksandr Dugin, *Geopolitics* (Moscow: Academic Project, 2011). [7n22]
23. Dugin, *Last War of the World-Island*, 3. [7n23]
24. See Mackinder, *Democratic Ideals and Realities*. [7n24]
25. Friedrich Ratzel, *Die Erde und das Leben. Eine Vergleichende Erdkunde* (Leipzig: Bibliographisches Institut, 1901). [7n25]
26. Aleksandr Dugin, *Osnovy Geopolitiki* (Moscow: Arctogaia, 1996). [7n26]
27. George Vernadsky, *A History of Russia* (New Haven: Yale University Press, 1969). [7n27]
28. Mikhail Leont'yev, *Bol'shaya Igra: Britanskaya Imperiya protiv Rossii i SSSR* (St. Petersburg: Astrel', 2008). [7n28]
29. Peter Hopkirk, *The Great Game: On Secret Service in High Asia* (London: John Murray, 2006). [7n29]
30. Dugin, *Last War of the World-Island*, 10. [7n30]
31. The Treaty of Brest-Litovsk was a peace treaty signed on the 3rd of March 1918 between Russia's new Bolshevik government and the Central Powers (Germany, Austria-Hungary, Bulgaria, and the Ottoman Empire), which ended Russia's participation in World War One. The treaty was signed after two months of negotiations. According to it, Bolshevik Russia defaulted on all of Imperial Russia's commitments to the Triple Entente alliance. In the treaty, Bolshevik Russia ceded the Baltic States to Germany, which were meant to become German vassal states. Russia also ceded its province of Kars in the South Caucasus to the Ottoman Empire and recognized the independence of Ukraine. Russia formally renounced all territorial claims in Finland (which it had already acknowledged), Baltic States (Estonia, Latvia and Lithuania), Belarus, and Ukraine. The territory of the Kingdom of Poland was not mentioned in the treaty, since Russian Poland had been a personal possession of the czar, not part of the Russian Empire. [7n31]
32. Dugin, *Last War of the World-Island*, 23. [7n32]
33. Ibid, 24. [7n33]
34. Ibid, 30. [7n34]
35. After World War Two, the Soviet Union would appear even more as a replica of Genghis Khan's Eurasian empire, with the inclusion of the countries of the Warsaw Pact in its sphere of influence. [7n35]
36. Dugin, *Last War of the World-Island*, 38. [7n36]
37. Jean Thiriart, *Un Empire de Quatre Cents Millions D'Hommes, l'Europe* (Nantes: Avatar Editions, 2007). [7n37]
38. Dugin, *Last War of the World-Island*, 42–43. [7n38]

[7n39]   39. This project was developed by Thiriart in *Euro-Soviet Empire*; however, this book was never completed and never published.

[7n40]   40. Dugin, *Last War of the World-Island*, 44–45.

[7n41]   41. The equilibrium of terror was also known as "mutual assured destruction" (MAD) and was based on the theory of deterrence. The core of this theory was founded on the idea that the threat of using strong weapons against the enemy would prevent the enemy's use of those same weapons.

[7n42]   42. Dugin, *Last War of the World-Island*, 46.

[7n43]   43. The Yalta Conference was held from the 4th to the 11th of February 1945. During the summit, the heads of government of the United States, the United Kingdom and the Soviet Union discussed German and European post-war reorganization.

[7n44]   44. The Potsdam Conference represented the last summit—after those that had took place at Teheran and Yalta—between the three great allied powers of World War Two and was held from the 17th of July to the 2nd of August 1945. During the meeting, the victorious powers of World War Two (the United States of America, the Soviet Union, and the United Kingdom) discussed and reached agreements on how to manage the immediate post-war period. The goals of the conference included the establishment of post-war order, peace treaty issues, and countering the effects of the war.

[7n45]   45. The Cuban missile crisis (15th–28th of October 1962), also known as the "October crisis" or "Caribbean crisis," was a confrontation between the United States and the Soviet Union on the deployment of Soviet ballistic missiles in Cuba in response to those that the US had deployed in Italy and Turkey. The incident, which occurred during the presidency of John Fitzgerald Kennedy, was considered one of the most critical moments of the Cold War, and an event that could lead the world closer to a nuclear war. In reaction to the unsuccessful Bay of Pigs Invasion in 1961 and the presence of American ballistic missiles in Italy and Turkey, Soviet leader Nikita Khrushchev decided to accept Cuba's request to place nuclear missiles on the island in order to discourage a possible future invasion. The agreement was reached during a secret meeting between Khrushchev and Fidel Castro in July 1962 and the construction of the missile launch facilities was launched a little later. The White House denounced the presence of dangerous Soviet missiles not far from Florida's coast. The United States set up a military bloc to prevent further Soviet missiles from reaching Cuba, announcing that they would not allow further deliveries of offensive weapons to Cuba and demanding that the missiles already on the island would be dismantled and returned to the Soviet Union. After a long period of close negotiations, an agreement was reached between US President John F. Kennedy and Russian President Nikita Khrushchev. The Soviets announced that, after a UN verification, they would have dismantled their offensive weapons in Cuba and would have returned them to the Soviet Union, asking in return for a public US declaration that would affirm the US intention to never try to invade Cuba again. When the Soviets withdrew all missiles from Cuba, the US formally removed the naval blockade (21st of November 1962). The negotiations between the United States and the Soviet Union highlighted the need for rapid, clear and continuous consultations between Washington and Moscow. Later, some further agreements gradually reduced tensions between the United States and the Soviet Union.

[7n46]   46. Dugin, *Last War of the World-Island*, 47–48.

[7n47]   47. Andrei E. Snesarev, *Afghanistan: Preparing for the Bolshevik Incursion into Afghanistan and Attack on India, 1919–1920* (Solihull: Helion & Co., 2014).

[7n48]   48. Dugin, *Last War of the World-Island*, 59.

[7n49]   49. The Warsaw Pact system of collective-defense—founded in 1955 by Nikita Khrushchev—included the Soviet Union, Hungary, Romania, Bulgaria, Czechoslovakia, Poland, East Germany (since 1956), and Albania (which de facto left the alliance in 1961 and formally in 1968). On the other hand, since 1990, the NATO alliance saw a progressive expansion eastward with the inclusion of East Germany (1990), Poland, the Czech Republic, and Hungary (1999), Romania, Bulgaria, Slovakia, Slovenia, Lithuania, Latvia, and Estonia (2004), Croatia and Albania (2009), and Montenegro (2017).

[7n50]   50. The incessant struggle between Cossacks and Tatars exemplifies the matter.

[7n51]   51. Kaplan, *The Revenge of Geography*, 159–60.

[7n52]   52. Brzezinski, *The Grand Chessboard*, 46.

53. Kaplan, *The Revenge of Geography*, 180.   [7n53]
54. Dugin, *Eurasian Mission*, 42.   [7n54]
55. Ibid, 60.   [7n55]
56. Ibid, 73.   [7n56]
57. Ibid, 61.   [7n57]
58. Ibid, 43–44.   [7n58]
59. Richard N. Coudenhove-Kalergi, *Pan-Europa* (Vienna-Leipzig: Paneuropa Verlag,   [7n59]
1923).
60. Dugin, *Eurasian Mission*, 47.   [7n60]
61. Ibid.   [7n61]
62. Ibid, 48.   [7n62]
63. Ibid, 57–58.   [7n63]
64. Ibid, 48.   [7n64]
65. Ibid, 75.   [7n65]
66. Seokwoo Lee, *Territorial disputes among Japan, China and Taiwan concerning the*   [7n66]
Senkaku Islands (Durham, UK: International Boundaries Research Unit, Department of Geography, University of Durham, 2002).
67. Dugin, *Eurasian Mission*, 78.   [7n67]
68. Today, the European Union seems to be closer in realizing an organic and structured   [7n68]
indigenous system of collective defence. This inclination is expressed in the introduction of the Permanent Structured Cooperation (PESCO), which represents the structural integration pursued by 25 of the 28 national armed forces of the EU. PESCO is based on Article 42.6 and Protocol 10 of the Treaty on European Union and incorporated in the Union's Common Security and Defence Policy (CSDP). PESCO was enabled by the Treaty of Lisbon in 2009 and initiated in 2017, with the initial integration being a number of projects planned to launch in 2018. Together with the Coordinated Annual Review on Defence (CARD), the European Defence Fund and the Military Planning and Conduct Capability (MPCC) it forms a new comprehensive defence package for the European Union. PESCO is similar to enhanced cooperation in other policy areas, in the sense that integration does not require that all EU member states participate. In light of a changing security environment, the EU Global Strategy for Foreign and Security Policy (EUGS) started a process of closer cooperation in security and defense. Member States agreed to step up the European Union's work in this area and acknowledged that enhanced coordination, increased investment in defense and cooperation in developing defense capabilities are key requirements to achieve it. This is the main aim of PESCO, as outlined in the Treaty of the EU, Articles 42 (6) and 46, as well as Protocol 10. Through PESCO, Member States increase their effectiveness in addressing security challenges and advancing towards further integrating and strengthening defense cooperation within the EU framework.
69. "Negroland" or "Nigritia" was an archaic term in European mapping, describing the   [7n69]
partly undiscovered Sub-Saharan African regions inhabited by black people. A synonym could be "Black Africa."
70. Dugin contradicts himself here by claiming that the Russian-Eurasian Large Space in-   [7n70]
cludes all the countries of the CIS that are also part of the Eurasian Economic Union (cf. Dugin, *Eurasian Mission*, 48). This would imply that also Armenia would belong to this large space, though he places it in the Islamic Continental Large Space along with Georgia and Azerbaijan.
71. Dugin, *Eurasian Mission*, 49.   [7n71]
72. Ibid, 50.   [7n72]
73. Ibid, 51.   [7n73]
74. Ibid.   [7n74]
75. Aleksandr Dugin, *Yevraziyskaya Missiya Nursultana Nazarbayeva* (Moscow: ROF   [7n75]
"Yevraziya," 2004).
76. Dugin, *Eurasian Mission*, 52.   [7n76]
77. Ibid, 52–53.   [7n77]
78. Ibid, 53.   [7n78]
79. Ibid, 60–61.   [7n79]
80. Dugin, *Continente Russia*, 72.   [7n80]

[7n81]   81. Aleksandr Dugin, *Eurasian Mission. Program Materials of the International Eurasian Movement* (Moscow: ROF "Yevrazia," 2005), 46.

[7n82]   82. Dugin, *Eurasian Mission*, 63.

[7n83]   83. Ibid, 33.

[7n84]   84. In Greek, τὸ κατέχον signifies "that which withholds," or ὁ κατέχων "the one who withholds."

[7n85]   85. Dugin, *Eurasian Mission*, 64.

[7n86]   86. Ibid, 84.

[7n87]   87. It is unclear whether Dugin would preserve or abolish the principle of private property within the suggested Great Spaces' autonomies. Probably, he acknowledges the maintenance and safeguard of private property since his successive statement about the necessity to guarantee maximal economic freedom for medium- and small-scale businesses would imply the existence of a socio-economic system based on private property.

[7n88]   88. Dugin, *Eurasian Mission*, 85.

[7n89]   89. Ibid, 65.

[7n90]   90. Ibid.

[7n91]   91. Ibid, 67.

Conclusion

[D01.0]   The main goal of this research was to investigate what kind of ideology Eurasianism is and what are its chief purposes and objectives. Specifically, it explored Aleksandr Dugin's neo-Eurasianist ideology and analyzed geopolitical theories that pivot on the strategic relevance of the Eurasian continent. The questions raised have been whether the Eurasianist ideology—and specifically Dugin's neo-Eurasianism—could represent a theoretical contribution to the description of the advent of a multipolar international order, whether geopolitical theories could still offer a valid tool for interpreting international relations and global power, and whether Eurasia could be considered a strategic continent for global hegemony.

[D01.1]   It is a widespread idea that the unipolar order that emerged from the demise of the Soviet Union has entered a period of significant crisis during the first years of the 21st century. We may consider the years between 1989 (fall of the Berlin Wall) and 2001 (fall of the Twin Towers of the World Trade Center) as the years of American unipolarism. After the year 2001, the world quickly began to shift towards multipolarity, and is still shifting towards it. Some clues that have indicated this change have been the following. In 2001, the first meeting of the World Social Forum (WSF) was held in Brazil to promote alternative answers to global economic problems in opposition to the "capitalist" rival World Economic Forum (WEF) of Davos, Switzerland. In the same year, as seen, the Shanghai Cooperation Organization—a mutual security, political, and economic organism—was founded, with its headquarters in Beijing, which some have considered as a counterpart of American-led NATO.

[D01.2]   The year 2003 saw an internal contrast between western nations as to whether to participate in the Iraq War or not, with Germany and France opposing the US-UK initiative.

Later, the year 2008 was a turning point for the advent of multipolarism. [D01.3]
The crucial events of the year had been the bankruptcy of Lehman Brothers
and the consequent outbreak of the financial crisis in the US and Europe, the
G-20 inaugural leaders' summit, the Russian war against Georgia, and the
Chinese Summer Olympics—whose opening ceremony had been boycotted
by European leaders.

In 2009, other events contributed to shaping the beginning of a new era: [D01.4]
the inaugural BRIC summit—that took place in Yekaterinburg, Russia—,
China becoming the first trade partner in Africa—undermining the US—,
and the new military tensions between China and the US in the South China
Sea.

In 2013, the initiatives of the Silk Road Economic Belt (SREB) and of the [D01.5]
21st-century Maritime Silk Road (MSR)—also known jointly as the One Belt
and One Road Initiative (OBOR)—were unveiled by President Xi Jinping.
Similarly, between 2013 and 2016 the Asian Infrastructure Investment Bank
was established, with its headquarters in Beijing. Between 2014 and 2015,
the New Development Bank (NDB), formerly referred to as the BRICS Development Bank—which is a multilateral development bank advocated by
the BRICS countries—was established in Shanghai.

In 2014, Russia annexed the Crimean Peninsula and supported the separ- [D01.6]
atist regions in Donbass, preventing Ukraine from shifting towards the West
(EU and NATO).

In September 2015, the Russian military intervention in the Syrian Civil [D01.7]
War began, which is leading today towards President Bashar al-Assad's final
victory.

The Russian interventions in Georgia and Ukraine had ultimately stopped [D01.8]
NATO's eastward expansion and the one in Syria has consolidated Russia's
presence in the Middle East alongside with that of the US. Finally, in 2015
the Russian-led Eurasian Economic Union was founded.

In this context, neo-Eurasianism embraces the idea that the world is [D01.9]
undergoing a phase of important changes that display the likelihood of the
advent of civilizational poles and areas of interest that could replace unipolar
globalization. Neo-Eurasianism embodies a typical example of alter-globalist
theory that does not reject totally the idea of globalism, but only its unilateral
Western interpretation. The globalization as conceived by the United States
and its allies is criticized because of its claim to bear universal values that are
allegedly believed to be qualitatively superior to others. Instead, Eurasianism
claims that the existence of different cultures and civilizations should be
regarded as a value and heritage to preserve and safeguard, despite their
dissimilarities with the Western one. Any attempt to erase, minimize or reject
civilizations that the West—implicitly or explicitly—may consider inferior
would manifest a biased example of cultural racism. Eurasianists believe that
different political systems, economic models, religious beliefs, historical

paths, and ethnic peculiarities should be accepted and valorized, rather than contrasted or marginalized. Through these lenses, we can affirm that Eurasianism could represent a useful doctrinal support for granting the freedom and survival of all human societies and for building an international system founded on sovereignty, self-determination, and equality. However, the type of world order and society that Eurasianism seeks to establish presents many problematic issues that have been considered throughout the book. Eurasianism bases its international system on a normative and constructivist scheme that often appears as unhooked from reality. As an ideology, it contains dogmatic truths that are accepted by its supporters in a rather irrational and fanatic way, lacking a grip on reality. The Eurasianist paradigm based on a strange mix between traditionalism and geopolitics bears a questionable legitimation and validity. Still, it is true that Eurasianism highlighted what could be considered a fact, namely the shift towards an international system that presents rising powers that could question the unipolarity of the West. The general international trend seems to shift towards multipolar regional blocs. If we think of the proliferation and success of intergovernmental economic and political organizations—chiefly the European Union, but also the Eurasian Economic Union—, it is perhaps more likely that in the long-term the world will be divided into economic blocs rather than nation-states. This process seems to be to some extent inevitable since the economic interdependence and the increase of movement of labour, capital, and people that characterizes modern states could easily lead to the creation of great political-economic zones. Therefore, we can affirm that—despite its questionable normative narrative—, Eurasianism represents a theoretical contribution to the description of the advent of a multipolar international order.

[D01.10]   As seen throughout this work, one of Eurasianism's hermeneutic and epistemological pillars is given by geopolitics. Geopolitics has been often criticized—especially by liberals and Marxists—for representing a deterministic theory based on power politics and an excessive adhesion to geographic reality. Can we still affirm today that geopolitical theories offer a valid tool for the analysis of international relations? On one side, it is true that technological evolution—both in military and civil domains—has somewhat overcome geography and its limits given by space. If we think of cyberspace and the so-called Internet of Things (IoT), we can positively assert that the geographical space's meaningfulness has decreased. Also, in military affairs, the evolution of technology and cyber systems of warfare appears to have resized the importance of the geographical factor. Critics highlight the fact that the advances in technology and the rise of airpower, space power, and nuclear power constitute a drastic downsizing of the geographic factor in international relations. Moreover, globalization—with the spread of free market, economic interdependence, financialism, and the proliferation of supranational organizations—has clearly reshaped the nature of human geography.

However, on the other hand, how can analysts completely wipe out the [D01.11]
geographical dimension from international studies? Geography—both physical and political—represents the spatial reality in which we all dwell. Without a landscape to inhabit, human beings could live no longer. The quest for
land and the dominion over it has been a primordial need for human survival.
It is difficult to negate the fact that most wars throughout history have been
fought for the control of territories or economic resources residing therein.
Today, territorial integrity is still considered one of the chief principles of
international law. Therefore, we believe that technology, economic globalization, and cybernetic evolution in warfare have partly modified, but not
erased, the strategic relevance of geographic space, which appears as an
everlasting physical reality.

Having said that, we should now address a further question: Can Eurasia [D01.12]
as a continent be considered truly strategic from a geopolitical point of view?
As seen, the promoters of Eurasian strategic primacy have been several geopolitical authors including Halford Mackinder, Nicholas Spykman, and Karl
Haushofer. These analysts have conjectured Eurasian supremacy through
theories and schemas that one can either accept or reject.

As we have previously noticed, while Mackinder pointed to a struggle of [D01.13]
Heartland-dominated land power against sea power, locating the Heartland-
based land power in the better position, Spykman believed that the Rimland
was the key to global hegemony, as the maritime-oriented Rimland was
fundamental to contact with the outer world.

Beyond geopolitical theories, we believe that there are some empirical [D01.14]
indicators that show that world powers have perceived Eurasia as fundamental for hegemony throughout the centuries. In fact, there is much evidence
that most modern wars—significantly, the two World Wars—have been
fought primarily in the Eurasian continent for the control of the Rimland, the
Heartland, or both. The creation of NATO and the conclusion of various
security agreements in East Asia such as those with South Korea and Japan
indicated the will of the United States to contain Soviet Heartland-based
power and to avoid its expansion in the Rimland; at the same time, the
creation of the Soviet-led Treaty of Friendship, Cooperation, and Mutual
Assistance (the Warsaw Pact) and the Soviet initiatives in Indochina, East
Asia, Central Asia (e.g. the invasion of Afghanistan in 1979), Middle East,
and Europe epitomize the USSR's attempt to penetrate the Rimland, to join it
with the Heartland, and to break the US-NATO encirclement. Furthermore,
the logic of the contraposition between sea powers and land powers has been
fully displayed in the context of the Eurasian continent. The modern history
of Eurasia has been characterized by a continuous attempt by land powers
(Napoleonic France, Czarist and Soviet Russia, Wilhelmine and Hitlerite
Germany) to seize and unify the continent and by the consequent effort by
sea powers (the British Empire, the United States) to avert its unification and

to keep it divided. Especially during the Cold War, the US-NATO containment against the USSR followed the logic of preserving Eurasia from being unified. Still today, the cleavage between NATO countries and some former Soviet states within Greater Europe seems to recall Spykman's schema as exposed in the Rimland theory. We believe that these empirical facts—as well as many others conflictual episodes in Eastern Asia, the Middle East, and Northern Africa—show clearly enough the strategic relevance of the Eurasian landmass and its intrinsic value from a geopolitical perspective: therefore, we claim that Eurasia as a geo-strategic principle bears a significant and unceasing meaning.

[D01.15]   As previously analyzed, Eurasianism upholds the idea that worldwide conservative revolutions—similar, for instance, to the Iranian Revolution of 1979—could contribute to establishing alternative societies to liberal ones based on more traditional values. It is questionable whether this normative belief could be substantially true or not. Indeed, we must admit that some aspects of post-liberal societies—chiefly extreme individualism, unrestrained capitalism, completely deregulated markets, the reject of traditional values like hierarchy, family, religion and nation, the uncontrolled exploitation of natural resources, and the abolition of identitarianism—can be regarded with skepticism and criticism. However, liberalism is also characterized by positive principles such as the ideas of free speech and thought, private property, rule of law, human rights, division of political power, and equality of opportunities for all citizens. Thus, we view negatively the total disregard of liberal principles that Eurasianism promotes.

[D01.16]   As seen, Eurasianism presents itself as a conservative ideology. We can affirm that conservatism presents pros and cons. The positive aspects may include the fact that it tends to establish societies based on righteous beliefs, like for instance the care and respect for elder people, a higher propensity towards collective forms of socio-political participation, a reverence for political institutions (the military and police forces, the political leaders, the bureaucratic administration, and so on), a respect for religious associations, and a major veneration towards one's own state, nation, and civilization. However, the negative aspects are also conspicuous: generally, traditional and conservative societies tend to be more intolerant, narrow-minded, and backward; often, they also lack political pluralism, democratic institutions, and the safeguard of human rights, and rely overwhelmingly on military power and nationalist rhetoric. In this regard, we believe that the worldwide spread of traditional societies should be partially discouraged since the outcome could result in unstable and insecure international relations based on fanatism and unreasonableness. What could be accepted, instead, as a basis for future societies is the renovation of liberal-democratic values, depriving them of their most extreme, unilateral, and ultra-progressive narratives.

Bibliography

[D02.0] Acharya, Amitav. *The End of the American World Order*. Cambridge: Polity, 2014.
[D02.1] Adorno, Theodor W., Else F. Brunswik, Daniel J. Levinson, and Robert N. Sanford. *The Authoritarian Personality*. New York: Harper, 1950.
[D02.2] Akhiezer, Aleksandr S., and Viktor V. Il'in. *Rossiiskaya Gosudarstvennost': Istoki, Traditsii, Perspektivy*. Moscow: Moskovskii gosudartvennyi universitet, 1997.
[D02.3] Art, Robert J. "A Defensible Defense: America's Grand Strategy after the Cold War." *International Security* 15, no. 4 (1991): 5–53. doi:10.2307/2539010.
[D02.4] Ball, Terence, Richard Dagger, and Daniel I. O'Neill. *Political Ideologies and the Democratic Ideal*. New York: Routledge, 2019.
[D02.5] Barabanov, Oleg N. "Global'noye Upravleniye i Global'noye Sotrudnichestvok." In *Globalizatsiya: Chelovecheskoye Izmereniye*, edited by Anatoly V. Torkunov, Andrey Yu. Melville, and Mikhail M. Narinsky, 44–52. Moscow: MGIMO, Rosspen, 2002.
[D02.6] Barabanov, Oleg N. "Suverennyye Gosudarstva i Global'noye Upravleniye." in *"Privatizatsiya" Mirovoi Politiki: Lokal'nyye Deystviya – Global'nyye Rezul'taty*, edited by Marina M. Lebedeva, 89–91. Moscow: MGIMO, 2008.
[D02.7] Bassin, Mark, and Konstantin E. Aksenov. "Mackinder and the Heartland Theory in Post-Soviet Geopolitical Discourse." *Geopolitics* 11, no. 1 (2006): 99–118.
[D02.8] Bateson, Gregory. *Mind and Nature: A Necessary Unit*. New York: Dutton, 1979.
[D02.9] Benoist, Alain de. *La Fine Della Sovranità. Come la Dittatura Del Denaro Toglie il Potere Ai Popoli*. Bologna: Arianna Editrice, 2014.
[D02.10] Benoist, Alain de. *Le Traité Transatlantique et Autres Menaces*. Paris: Éditions Pierre-Guillaume de Roux, 2015.
[D02.11] Benoist, Alain de. *Nuova Destra, Nuova Europa*. Rome: Pagine, 2012.
[D02.12] Benoist, Alain de. *Survivre à la Pensée Unique*. Lille: Éditions Krisis, 2015.
[D02.13] Benoist, Alain de. *Vu De Droite: Anthologie Critique Des Idées Contemporaines*. Paris: Copernic, 1977.
[D02.14] Bluhm, Harald. *Karl Marx, Friedrich Engels: Die Deutsche Ideologie*. Berlin: Akademie Verl., 2010.
[D02.15] Bogaturov, Aleksei D. "Amerika i Rossiya: Ot Izbiratel'nogo Partnerstva k Izbiratel'nomu Soprotivleniyu." *Mezhdunarodnaya Zhizn'* 6 (1998): 8–17.
[D02.16] Bogaturov, Aleksei D. "Pluralisticheskaya Odnopolyarnost' i Interesy Rossiyi." *Svobodnaya Mysl'* 2 (1996): 25–36.
[D02.17] Bogaturov, Aleksei D. "Sovremennyi Mezhdunarodnyi Poryadok." *Mezhdunarodnyye Protsessy* 1 (June 2007): 6–23.
[D02.18] Bremmer, Ian. *Every Nation for Itself: Winners and Losers in a G-Zero World*. New York: Portfolio/Penguin, 2012.

Brzezinski, Zbigniew. *The Grand Chessboard: American Primacy and Its Geostrategic Imperatives*. New York: Basic Books, 2016.   [D02.19]

Buzan, Barry, Charles A. Jones, and Richard Little. *The Logic of Anarchy: Neorealism to Structural Realism*. New York: Columbia University Press, 1993.   [D02.20]

Cohen, Saul B. *Geography and Politics in a World Divided*. New York: Oxford University Press, 1975.   [D02.21]

Cohen, Saul B. *Geopolitics: The Geography of International Relations*. Lanham, MD: Rowman & Littlefield, 2015.   [D02.22]

Corbett, Patrick. *Ideologies*. London: Hutchinson, 1963.   [D02.23]

Coudenhove-Kalergi, Richard N. *Pan-Europa*. Vienna-Leipzig: Paneuropa Verlag, 1923.   [D02.24]

Daalder, Ivo. "The End of Atlanticism." *Survival* 45, no. 2 (2003): 147–66.   [D02.25]

Deleuze, Gilles. *The Logic of Sense*. New York: Columbia University Press, 1993.   [D02.26]

Destutt De Tracy, Antoine Louis Claude. *Mémoire Sur La Faculté De Penser. De La Métaphysique De Kant Et Autres Textes*. Paris: Fayard, 1993.   [D02.27]

Destutt De Tracy, Antoine Louis Claude. *Projet D'éléments D'idéologie*. Paris: L'Harmattan, 2005.   [D02.28]

Diodato, Emidio. *Che Cos'è La Geopolitica*. Rome: Carocci, 2011.   [D02.29]

Dossena, Paolo A., and Giorgio Galli. *Lo Scienziato e Lo Sciamano: Mackinder, Hitler e L'Isola Del Mondo*. Turin: Lindau, 2011.   [D02.30]

Dugin, Aleksandr. *Continente Russia*. Parma: All'Insegna del Veltro, 1991.   [D02.31]

Dugin, Aleksandr. *Eurasia: La Rivoluzione Conservatrice in Russia*. Rome: Nuove Idee, 2004.   [D02.32]

Dugin, Aleksandr. *Eurasian Mission. Program Materials of the International Eurasian Movement*. Moscow: ROF "Yevrazia," 2005.   [D02.33]

Dugin, Aleksandr. *Eurasian Mission: An Introduction to Neo-Eurasianism*. London: Arktos, 2014.   [D02.34]

Dugin, Aleksandr. *Geopolitics*. Moscow: Academic Project, 2011.   [D02.35]

Dugin, Aleksandr. *Last War of the World-Island*. London: Arktos, 2015.   [D02.36]

Dugin, Aleksandr. *Osnovi Geopolitike. Geopolitička Budućnost Rusije*. Zrenjanin: Ekopres, 2004.   [D02.37]

Dugin, Aleksandr. *Osnovy Geopolitiki*. Moscow: Arctogaia, 1996.   [D02.38]

Dugin, Aleksandr. *The Fourth Political Theory*. London: Arktos, 2012.   [D02.39]

Dugin, Aleksandr. *The Rise of the Fourth Political Theory*. London: Arktos, 2017.   [D02.40]

Dugin, Aleksandr. *Yevraziyskaya Missiya Nursultana Nazarbayeva*. Moscow: ROF "Yevraziya," 2004.   [D02.41]

Durand, Gilbert. *Les Structures Anthropologiques De L'Imaginaire*. Paris: Presses Universitaires de France, 1960.   [D02.42]

Fettweis, Christopher J. "On Heartlands and Chessboards: Classical Geopolitics, Then and Now." *Orbis* 59, no. 2 (2015): 233–248.   [D02.43]

Freeden, Michael. "Ideology and Political Theory." *Journal of Political Ideologies* 11, no. 1 (2006): 3–22. doi:10.1080/13569310500395834.   [D02.44]

Freeden, Michael. *Ideologies and Political Theory: A Conceptual Approach*. Oxford: Clarendon Press, 2008.   [D02.45]

Fukuyama, Francis. *Our Post-Human Future: Consequences of the Biotechnology Revolution*. New York: Farrar Strauss & Giroux, 2002.   [D02.46]

Fukuyama, Francis. *The End of History and the Last Man*. New York: Free Press, 1992.   [D02.47]

Gerring, John. "Ideology: A Definitional Analysis." *Political Research Quarterly* 50, no. 4 (1997): 957–94. doi:10.2307/448995.   [D02.48]

Gray, Colin S. "The Continued Primacy of Geography." *Orbis* 40, no. 2 (1996): 247–59. doi:10.1016/s0030-4387(96)90063-0.   [D02.49]

Gumilëv, Lev N. "Pis'mo v Redaktsiyu 'Voprosov Filosofii'." *Voprosy Filosofii* 5 (1989).   [D02.50]

Gumilëv, Lev N. "Zametki Poslednego Yevraziitsa." In *Ritmy Yevrazii: Epokhi i Tsivilizatsii*. Moscow: Progress, 1993.   [D02.51]

Gumilëv, Lev N. and Vladimir Iu. Yermolaev. "Gore ot Illiuzii." In *Osnovy Yevraziistva*, edited by Aleksandr Dugin. Moscow: Arktogaya Tsentr, 2002.   [D02.52]

Gumilëv, Lev N. *Chërnaya Legenda: Druz'ya i Nedrugi Velikoy Stepi*. Moscow: Progress, 1994.   [D02.53]

[D02.54]   Gumilëv, Lev N. *Etnogenez i Biosfera Zemli*. Leningrad: Gidrometeoizdat, 1990.
[D02.55]   Gumilëv, Lev N. *Ot Rusi do Rossii*. Saint Petersburg: Iuna, 1992.
[D02.56]   Hamilton, Malcolm B. "The Elements of the Concept of Ideology." *Political Studies* 35, no. 1 (1987): 18–38. doi:10.1111/j.1467-9248.1987.tb00186.x.
[D02.57]   Haushofer, K. *Lo Sviluppo Dell'Idea Imperiale Nipponica*. Rome: Istituto Italiano per il Medio ed Estremo Oriente, 1942.
[D02.58]   Haushofer, K. *Weltpolitik von Heute*. Berlin: "Zeitgeschichte" Verlag, 1934.
[D02.59]   Haushofer, Karl. *Geopolitik der Pan-Ideen*. Berlin: Zentral-Verlag, 1931.
[D02.60]   Haushofer, Karl. *Il Giappone Costruisce il Suo Impero*. Parma: All'Insegna del Veltro, 1999.
[D02.61]   Hayek, Friedrich. "Why I Am Not a Conservative." In *The Essence of Hayek*, edited by Nishiyama, Chiaki, Leube, Kurt R., and Campbell, Glenn W. Stanford: Hoover Institution Press, 1984.
[D02.62]   Heidegger, Martin. *Sein und Zeit*. Tübingen: Max Niemeyer Verlag, 1963.
[D02.63]   Hopkirk, Peter. *The Great Game: On Secret Service in High Asia*. London: John Murray, 2006.
[D02.64]   Huntington, Samuel P. "Conservatism as an Ideology." *American Political Science Review* 51, no. 2 (1957): 454–73. doi:10.2307/1952202.
[D02.65]   Huntington, Samuel P. *The Clash of Civilizations and the Remaking of World Order*. New York: Simon & Schuster, 1997.
[D02.66]   Jaspers, Karl. *Die Geistige Situation Der Zeit*. Berlin: De Gruyter, 1933.
[D02.67]   Jean, Carlo. *Geopolitica*. Bari: Ed. Laterza, 1995.
[D02.68]   Kaehne, Axel. *Political and Social Thought in Post-communist Russia*. London: Routledge, 2009.
[D02.69]   Kagan, Robert. *Of Paradise and Power: America and Europe in the New World Order*. New York: Vintage Books, 2004.
[D02.70]   Kagan, Robert. *The World America Made*. New York: Vintage Books, 2013.
[D02.71]   Kaplan, Robert D. *The Revenge of Geography: What the Map Tells Us about Coming Conflicts and the Battle against Fate*. New York: Random House Trade Paperbacks, 2013.
[D02.72]   Kearns, Gerard. *Geopolitics and Empire: The Legacy of Halford Mackinder*. Oxford: Oxford University Press, 2011.
[D02.73]   Khara-Davan, Ėrenzhen. "O Kochevnom Byte." In *Tridtsatye Gody*. Paris, 1931.
[D02.74]   Khara-Davan, Ėrenzhen. *Čingis-kan kak Polkovodec i Ego Nasledne*. Belgrade: Feniks, 1929.
[D02.75]   Kirby, Andrew. "Pseudo-random Thoughts on Space, Scale and Ideology in Political Geography." *Political Geography Quarterly* 4, no. 1 (1985): 5–18. doi:10.1016/0260-9827(85)90024-2.
[D02.76]   Kozyrev, Andrei V. *Preobrazheniye*. Moscow: Mezhdunarodnyye Otsosheniya, 1995.
[D02.77]   Kremenyuk, Victor. "Rossiya Vne Mirovogo Soobschestva," *Mezhdunarodnyye Protsessy* 4, no. 3 (June 2007).
[D02.78]   Kryuchkov, Georgy. *Ukraina Pered Sud'bonosnym Vyborom*. Kharkiv: Folio, 2010.
[D02.79]   Kulagin, Vladimir M. "Mir v XXI veke: Mnogopolyusnyi Balans Sil ili Global'nyi Pax Democratica?" In *Vneshnyaya Politika i Bezopasnost' Sovremennoi Rossiyi, 1991–2002*, edited by Tatyana A. Shakleyina, 145–61. Moscow: Rosspen, 2002.
[D02.80]   Kulagin, Vladimir M. "Netlennost' Avtoritarnosti?." *Mezhdunarodnyye Protsessy* 6, no. 1 (January-April 2008).
[D02.81]   Laclau, Ernesto. "The Death and Resurrection of the Theory of Ideology." *Mln* 112, no. 3 (1997): 297–321. doi:10.1353/mln.1997.0038.
[D02.82]   Lacoste, Yves. *Géopolitique: La Longue Histoire D'Aujourdhui*. Paris: Larousse, 2006.
[D02.83]   Laruelle, Marlène. *Russian Eurasianism: An Ideology of Empire*. Washington, DC: Woodrow Wilson Center Press, 2008.
[D02.84]   Lebedeva, Marina M. "Politicheskaya Sistema Mira: Proyavleniya 'Vnesistemnosti'." In *"Privatizatsiya" Mirovoi Politiki: Lokal'nyye Deystviya – Global'nyye Rezul'taty*, edited by Marina M. Lebedeva 53–66. Moscow: MGIMO, 2008.
[D02.85]   Lee, Seokwoo. *Territorial disputes among Japan, China and Taiwan concerning the Senkaku Islands*. Durham, UK: International Boundaries Research Unit, Department of Geography, University of Durham, 2002.
[D02.86]   Lenin, Vladimir I. *Imperializm kak Vysshaya Stadiya Kapitalizma*. Petrograd: Zhizn' i Znaniye, 1917.

Leont'yev, Mikhail. *Bol'shaya Igra: Britanskaya Imperiya protiv Rossii i SSSR*. St. Petersburg: [D02.87] Astrel', 2008.

Loewenstein, Karl. "The role of ideologies in political change." *International Social Science* [D02.88] *Bulletin* 5, no. 1 (1953): 51–74.

Luttwak, Edward N. "From Geopolitics to Geo-Economics: Logic of Conflict, Grammar of [D02.89] Commerce." *The National Interest*, no. 20 (1990): 17–23.

Mackinder, Halford J. "On the Scope and Methods of Geography." *Proceedings of the Royal* [D02.90] *Geographical Society and Monthly Record of Geography* 9, no. 3 (1887): 141–174. doi:10.2307/1801248.

Mackinder, Halford J. "The Geographical Pivot of History." *The Geographical Journal* 23, no. [D02.91] 4 (1904): 421–37. doi:10.2307/1775498.

Mackinder, Halford J. "The Round World and the Winning of the Peace." *Foreign Affairs* 21, [D02.92] no. 4 (1943): 595–605.

Mackinder, Halford J. *Britain and the British Isles*. London: Heinemann, 1902. [D02.93]

Mackinder, Halford J. *Democratic Ideals and Realities: A Study in the Politics of Reconstruc-* [D02.94] *tion*. London: Constable and Company Ltd, 1919.

Mann, Steven R. "Chaos Theory and Strategic Thought," *Parameters* (US Army War College [D02.95] Quarterly) 22 (1992): 54–68.

Mannheim, Karl, and Gernot Kaube. *Ideologie Und Utopie*. Frankfurt Am Main: Klostermann, [D02.96] 2015.

Martill, Benjamin. "International Ideologies: Paradigms of Ideological Analysis and World [D02.97] Politics." Journal of Political Ideologies 22, no. 3 (2017): 236–55. doi:10.1080/ 13569317.2017.1345139.

Mcclosky, Herbert. "Consensus and Ideology in American Politics." *American Political Sci-* [D02.98] *ence Review* 58, no. 2 (1964): 361–82. doi:10.2307/1952868.

Moller van der Bruck, Arthur. *Das Dritte Reich*. Berlin: Ring-Verlag, 1923. [D02.99]

Mullins, Willard A. "Sartori's Concept of Ideology: A Dissent and an Alternative." In *Public* [D02.100] *Opinion and Political Attitudes*, edited by Wilcox, Allen R. New York: Wiley, 1974.

Nartov, Nikolai A. *Geopolitika*. Moscow: UNITI, 1999. [D02.101]

Nye, Joseph S. *The Future of Power*. New York: PublicAffairs, 2011. [D02.102]

Oakeshott, Michael. *Rationalism in Politics and Other Essays*. Carmel, IN: Liberty Fund, 1991. [D02.103]

Owens, Mackubin T. "In Defense of Classical Geopolitics." *Orbis* 59, no. 4 (2015): 463–78. [D02.104]

Panarin, Aleksandr S. "Predely Faustovskoy Kul'tury i Puti Rossiyskoy Tsivilizatsii." In *Ros-* [D02.105] *siya i Vostok*, edited by Aleksandr S. Panarin and Boris S. Yerasov (1994).

Panarin, Aleksandr S. "Slavyano-Tyurkskoye Yedinstvo: Konstruktsiya Rossiyskoy Gosudarst-* [D02.106] vennosti." *Rossiya i Musul'manskiy Mir* 1 (1996).

Panarin, Aleksandr S. *Global'noye Politicheskoye Prognozirovaniye*. Moscow: Algoritm, [D02.107] 2002.

Panarin, Aleksandr S. *Iskusheniye Globalizmom*. Moscow: Algoritm, 2000. [D02.108]

Panarin, Aleksandr S. *Pravoslavnaya Tsivilizatsiya v Global'nom Mire*. Moscow: Algoritm, [D02.109] 2002.

Panarin, Aleksandr S. *Rossiya v Tsivilizatsionnnom Protsesse. Mezhdu Atlantizmom i Yevraziist-* [D02.110] *vom*. Moscow: Institut Filosofii RAN, 1995.

Panarin, Aleksandr. S. *Rossiya v Tsiklakh Mirovoy Istorii*. Moscow: Izdatelstvo Moskovskogo [D02.111] Universiteta, 1999.

Pareto, Vilfredo, and Georges Henri Bousquet. *Les Systèmes Socialistes*. Paris: Giard, 1926. [D02.112]

Pareto, Vilfredo. *Trattato Di Sociologia Generale*. Torino: Unione Tipografico-Editrice Tori- [D02.113] nese, 1988.

Parker, Geoffrey. *Geopolitics: Past, Present and Future*. London: Pinter, 1998. [D02.114]

Pavlovski, Gleb. "Rossiya Vsye Yeschye Ischet Svoyi Rol' v Mire." *Nezavisimaya Gazeta* [D02.115] (May 2004).

Pivovarov, Yuri, and Andrei Fursov. "'The Russian System:' An Attempt to Understand Rus- [D02.116] sian History." *Social Sciences* 33, no. 4 (2002): 141–55.

Pizzolo, Paolo. *Astuzia e Ragion Di Stato. Modelli di Politica Estera Europea Nell'Ottocento*. [D02.117] Rome: Gruppo Editoriale L'Espresso, 2016.

Popper, Karl. *The Open Society and Its Enemies*. London: Routledge, 1966. [D02.118]

[D02.119] Primakov, Yevgeny M. "Mezhdunarodniye Otnosheniya Nakanune XXI Veka: Problemy, Perspektivy," *Mezhdunarodnaya Zhizn'* 10 (1996): 3–14.

[D02.120] Primakov, Yevgeny M. "Rossiya v Mirovoi Politike," *Mezhdunarodnaya Zhizn'* 5 (1998): 3–9.

[D02.121] Rand, Ayn. *Capitalism: The Unknown Ideal*. New York: New American Library, 1967.

[D02.122] Rathbun, Brian. "Politics and Paradigm Preferences: The Implicit Ideology of International Relations Scholars." *International Studies Quarterly* 56, no. 3 (2012): 607–22. doi:10.1111/j.1468-2478.2012.00749.x.

[D02.123] Ratzel, Friedrich. *Die Erde und das Leben. Eine Vergleichende Erdkunde*. Leipzig: Bibliographisches Institut, 1901.

[D02.124] Sargent, Lyman T. *Contemporary Political Ideologies: A Comparative Analysis*. Belmont, CA: Wadsworth, 2009.

[D02.125] Sartori, Giovanni. "Politics, Ideology, and Belief Systems." *American Political Science Review* 63, no. 2 (1969): 398–411. doi:10.2307/1954696.

[D02.126] Savitsky, Pëtr N. *Šestina Sveta: Rusko jako Zemepisní a Historickí Celek*. Prague: Melantrich, 1933.

[D02.127] Scalea, Daniele. *Halford John Mackinder: Dalla Geografia Alla Geopolitica*. Rome: Fuoco Ed., 2013.

[D02.128] Schmitt, Carl. *Land und Meer: Eine Weltgeschichtliche Betrachtung*. Leipzig: Reclam, 1942.

[D02.129] Schmitt, Carl. *Volkerrechtliche Großraumordnung: mit Interventionsverbot für Raumfremde Mächte: Ein Beitrag zum Reichsbegriff im Völkerrecht*. Berlin: Duncker & Humblot, 1941.

[D02.130] Schwarzmantel, John J. *Ideology and Politics*. Los Angeles: SAGE, 2008.

[D02.131] Seliger, Martin. *Ideology and Politics*. London: Allen & Unwin, 1976.

[D02.132] Semënov, Yuri N. *Die Eroberung Sibiriens*. Berlin: Ullstein, 1937.

[D02.133] Shevtsova, Lilia F. "Presentation." In *Rossiya i Zapad*. Foundation "Liberl'naya missiya," 2003.

[D02.134] Snesarev, Andrei E. *Afghanistan: Preparing for the Bolshevik Incursion into Afghanistan and Attack on India, 1919–1920*. Solihull: Helion & Co., 2014.

[D02.135] Sorel, Georges. *Réflexions Sur La Violence*. Paris: Rivière, 1919.

[D02.136] Splengler, Oswald. *Der Untergang des Abendlandes*. Munich: Beck, 1922.

[D02.137] Spykman, Nicholas J. "Geography and Foreign Policy, I," *American Political Science Review* 32, no. 1 (1938): 28–50.

[D02.138] Spykman, Nicholas J. *America's Strategy in World Politics: The United States and the Balance of Power*. New York: Harcourt, Brace, 1942.

[D02.139] Spykman, Nicholas J., Helen R. Nicholl, and Frederick S. Dunn. *The Geography of the Peace*. New York: Harcourt, Brace and Co., 1944.

[D02.140] Steger, Manfred B. *Globalisms: The Great Ideological Struggle of the Twenty-first Century*. Lanham, MD: Rowman & Littlefield, 2009.

[D02.141] Steger, Manfred B., and Erin K. Wilson. "Anti-Globalization or Alter-Globalization? Mapping the Political Ideology of the Global Justice Movement." *International Studies Quarterly* 56, no. 3 (2012): 439–54. doi:10.1111/j.1468-2478.2012.00740.x.

[D02.142] Stuenkel, Oliver. *Post-Western World: How Emerging Powers are Remaking Global Order*. Cambridge and Malden: Polity, 2016.

[D02.143] Thiriart, Jean. *Un Empire de Quatre Cents Millions D'Hommes, l'Europe*. Nantes: Avatar Editions, 2007.

[D02.144] Trenin, Dmitry V. *The End of Eurasia: Russia on the Border between Geopolitics and Globalization*. Washington: Carnegie Endowment for International Peace, 2003.

[D02.145] Trubetskoy, N. S., "Naslediye Chingiskhana. Vzglyad na Russkuyu Istoriyu ne s Zapada, a s Vostoka." In *Istoriya, Kul'tura, Yazik*. Moscow: Progress, 1995.

[D02.146] Trubetskoy, Nikolai S. "O Turasnkom Elemente v Russkoi Kul'ture." In *Rossiya mezhdu Yevropoi i Aziei: Yevrasiyskiy Soblazn*. Moscow: Nauka, 1993.

[D02.147] Trubetskoy, Nikolai S. "Religiy Indiy i Khristianstvo." In *Na Putiakh: Utverzhdenie Yevraziitsev*. Berlin, 1922.

[D02.148] Trubetskoy, Nikolai S. "Vavilonskaya Bashnia i Smeshenie Yazikov," *Yevrasiyskiy Vremennik* 3 (1923).

[D02.149] Trubetskoy, Nikolai S. "Verkhi i Nizy Russkoi Kul'tury." In *K Probleme Russkogo Samopoznaniya*. Paris: Yevraziyskoye Knigoizdatel'stvo, 1927.

Tsygankov, Andrei P., and Tsygankov, Pavel A. "National ideology and IR Theory: Three [D02.150] Incarnations of the 'Russian Idea'." *European Journal of International Relations* 16, no. 4 (2010): 663–86.

Vernadsky, George V. *Opyt Istorii Yevrazii*. Berlin: Izdaniye Yevraziytsev, 1934. [D02.151]

Vernadsky, George. *A History of Russia*. New Haven: Yale University Press, 1969. [D02.152]

Voss, Jason. "The Value of Geopolitical Analysis." *CFA Institute Magazine* 25, no. 3 (2014). [D02.153]

Wallerstein, Immanuel. *After Liberalism*. New York: Free Press, 1995. [D02.154]

Wallerstein, Immanuel. *The Capitalist World-economy*. Cambridge: Cambridge University [D02.155] Press, 1979.

William H. Parker, William H. *Mackinder: Geography as an Aid to Statecraft*. Oxford: Claren- [D02.156] don Press, 1982.

Zakaria, F. *The Post-American World*. New York: W.W. Norton, 2009. [D02.157]

Žižek, Slavoj. *Mapping Ideology*. London: Verso, 1994. [D02.158]

Zyuganov, Gennady A. *Geografiya Pobedy*. Moscow: Mir, 1997. [D02.159]

Zyuganov, Gennady A. *Globalizatsiya i Sud'ba Chelovechestva*. Moscow: Molodaya Gvar- [D02.160] diya, 2002.

Appendix

Further Reading

[D03.0] Dugin, Aleksandr. *Ethnos and Society*. London: Arktos, 2018.

[D03.1] Dugin, Aleksandr. *Osnovy Geopolitiki: Geopoliticheskoe Budushchee*. Moscow: Arktogeya, 1999.

[D03.2] Billington, James H. *Russia in Search of Itself*. Washington, DC: Woodrow Wilson Center Press, 2004.

[D03.3] Fenenko, Aleksey V., ed. *Kontseptsii i Opredeleniya Demokratii. Antologiya*. Moscow: URSS, 2006.

[D03.4] Gaidar, Yegor. *The State and Evolution: Russia's Search for a Free Market*. Seattle, WA: University of Washington Press, 2003.

[D03.5] McDaniel, Tim. *The Agony of the Russian Idea*. Princeton, NJ: Princeton University Press, 1998.

[D03.6] Laruelle, Marlène, *Le Nouveau Nationalisme Russe: Des Repères Pour Comprendre*. Paris: L'Œuvre éditions, 2010.

[D03.7] Parker, Geoffrey. *Western Geopolitical Thought in the Twentieth Century*. London: Routledge, 1985.

[D03.8] Waltz, Kenneth T. *Theory of International Politics*. Reading, MA: Addison-Wesley Pub. Co., 1979.

[D03.9] Modelski, George. *Long Cycles in World Politics*. Basingstoke: Macmillan, 1987.

[D03.10] Morgenthau, Hans. *Politics Among Nations : The Struggle for Power and Peace*. New York: Knopf, 1967.

[D03.11] Laruelle, Marlène, ed. *Eurasianism and the European Far Right: Reshaping the Europe–Russia Relationship*. Lanham, MD: Lexington Books, 2017.

Acknowledgements

[D04.0]   First, I would like to thank Prof. Raffaele Marchetti, who constantly advised me on how to structure the research.

[D04.1]   I am especially grateful to Prof. Andrea Carteny and Prof. Emidio Diodato for suggesting me how to improve some aspects and chapters of the book.

[D04.2]   Additionally, I would like to thank Prof. Roberta Mulas, Prof. Silvia Menegazzi and Prof. Marco Mayer for their help, advice, and support.

[D04.3]   I would like to express my gratitude to the staff of the Political Science Department for all their support.

[D04.4]   I would also like to recognize and thank my fellow peers, with whom I am lucky enough to share friendships: Rolf Nijmeijer, Jochem Rietveld, Akif Cem Özkardeş, Ludovic Bonduel, Manfredi Valeriani, Luca Carrieri, Irene Landini, Tiziano Zgaga, Margherita Galassini, Kevin Kalomeni, Matteo Bocchialini, Giulia Melideo, Heidi Koolmeister, Jan Kermer, Laurence Marquis, Mattia Zunino, Muhammad Salman, Irfan Mohammed, and Felix Okwa Agbo. Each one of them offered me some thought-provoking advice and delighted me with smart and helpful conversations.

[D04.5]   I am also grateful to my colleagues and friends, Dr. Megan Foster, for proofreading the final manuscript and to Olga Kalinina for helping me with the translation of sources in Russian.

[D04.6]   Additionally, I would like to thank my darling Lauren Brooks for all the love and support she gives me every day.

[D04.7]   Finally, I would like to thank my mother for always believing in me.

About the Author

[J01.0] **Paolo Pizzolo** is a Research Fellow in International Relations at the University LUISS Guido Carlo of Rome. He graduated in Political Science and International Relations and holds a Ph.D. in Political Science, Political Theory and Political History.

Lightning Source UK Ltd.
Milton Keynes UK
UKHW012224310120
357982UK00001B/26